Also by Elaine Showalter

Hystories

Hysterical Epidemics and Mass Media

Hysteria Beyond Freud
(with Sander Gilman, Helen King, Roy Porter, and George Rousseau)

Sister's Choice
Traditions and Change in American Women's Writing

Sexual Anarchy
Gender and Creativity in the Fin de Siècle

The Female Malady
Women, Madness, and Culture

A Literature of Their Own
British Women Novelists from Brontë to Lessing

Inventing Herself

CLAIMING A FEMINIST
INTELLECTUAL HERITAGE

Elaine Showalter

A LISA DREW BOOK

SCRIBNER

New York   London   Toronto   Sydney   Singapore

SCRIBNER
1230 Avenue of the Americas
New York, NY 10020

SCRIBNER and design are trademarks of Macmillan Library
Reference USA, Inc., used under license by
Simon & Schuster, the publisher of this work.

DESIGNED BY ERICH HOBBING

Set in Granjon

Mauifactured in the United States of America

1   3   5   7   9   10   8   6   4   2

Library of Congress Cataloging-in-Publication Data
Showalter, Elaine
Inventing herself : claiming a femisnist intellectual heritage / Elaine Showalter.
p. cm.
"A Lisa Drew book."
Includes bibliographical references and index.
1. Feminists—History. 2. Women intellectuals—History. I. Title.
HQ1154.S527 2000
305.42'09—dc21   00-041007

ISBN 0-684-82263-6

For Wendy Martin

ACKNOWLEDGMENTS

Many thanks to the Princeton University Council for Research in the Humanities for funding my travel for this book. In London, my research assistant Stuart Michael Burrows helped me track down the details for women in the nineteenth century, and a brilliant and multitalented Princeton undergraduate, Anne Griffin, assisted with work at the British Library, Fawcett Library, London Library, and Wellcome Institute for the History of Medicine, along with everything else from picking up frozen mocha latte at Starbucks to surfing the Net.

I first shared my ideas on feminist icons in a women's studies seminar at Princeton in spring 1996. Thanks to a wonderful group of students: Stephanie Blackburn, Carolyn Bradner, Melissa Buttles, Julie Cho, Kristin Cornuelle, Lauren Freeman, Julie Hinckley, Lea Johnston, Jenny Korn, Eden Miller, Joy Radice, and Anadelia Romo.

Although this book concentrates on women in the United States, Britain, and France, I owe much to those scholars in other countries whose responses and whose work have helped me think about the feminist icon in modern history: in Copenhagen, Tania Orum, Elisabeth Moller Jensen, Beth Juncker, Karin Lutzen, and Ebba Witt-Brattstrom; in Helsinki, Mar Jonsson; in Jerusalem, Shuli Barzali; and in Stockholm, Danuta Fjellestad and Eleanor Hergronje.

In New York, Elaine Markson and Lisa Drew; and in London, Mary Clemmey, Tanya Stobbs, and Ursula Doyle have been patient, encouraging, enthusiastic, and unflappable as this book slowly took shape. And, as always, I couldn't have done it without my husband and co-adventurer, English Showalter.

CONTENTS

Inventing Herself

ONE

Adventures in Womanhood

At the end of the summer of '97, the death of a famous English-woman shocked the world. Still young, the mother of two children, she died despite all the efforts of emergency medicine at exactly the moment when she seemed most poignantly close to achieving in her life the combination of autonomy, meaningful work, and intimacy she had long been seeking. To many women, she was a feminist role model, whose struggle to confront her contradictions was as illuminating as her effort to be independent. To others, she was dangerous and unstable, a hysteric given to unpopular causes, unhappy love affairs, nervous illnesses, even attempts at suicide. But however they viewed her life, women found it meaningful as a model of their own identities and potentialities. To confront her legacy was also a way of confronting and reinventing ourselves.

The woman was Mary Wollstonecraft, author of *A Vindication of the Rights of Woman,* who died September 10, 1797, at the age of thirty-eight, after giving birth to the daughter who would become Mary Shelley. Wollstonecraft's tempestuous life and tragic death is intensely modern and iconic because it represents a seemingly timeless division in the feminist psyche, the split between the need for independence and the need for love. Moreover, from Mary Wollstonecraft on, the great feminist icons were anything but saints. They too stumbled, loved the wrong men, took terrible risks, made bad decisions, behaved foolishly, made people angry, alienated their friends, felt despair. In September

1997, as I watched the television reports on the death of Diana, Princess of Wales, I realized that Diana Spencer, like Mary Wollstonecraft, had become a role model for her time. She too had evolved an ideal of the fullest, most meaningful life she might dare to live as a woman in her historical circumstances, and then courageously tried to live it. Those who mourned her, particularly the women who cried at her funeral, brought bouquets to her grave, and bought books about her life, were confronting their own lives through her legacy.

From Mary Wollstonecraft to Diana Spencer, a small group of women have become feminist icons, symbols of aspiration who have exercised both spiritual and psychological power over women for the last two centuries. Absent from the standard compendia, conferences, coffee-table books, and CD-ROMs of notables and legends, these women have nonetheless constituted a subterranean, subconscious tradition as they have been rediscovered and reinvented by successive generations of rebellious, intellectual, and adventurous daughters.

I intend the term *icon* in its classical sense of "revered symbol." But the term has been debased in popular culture to mean a commercialized visual image or nonverbal sound endlessly repeated, packaged, parodied, marketed, and plugged. Nowadays, *icon* is a word usually linked with "celebrity" or superstardom. At worst, writes fashion journalist Holly Brubach, the icon is a "human sound bite, an individual reduced to a name, a face, and an idea."[1]

At best, the icon is someone worshiped from afar, as Wayne Koestenbaum explains in regard to Jacqueline Kennedy Onassis: "We called Jackie an icon because she glowed, because she seemed ceaseless, because she resided in a worshiped, aura-filled niche. We called Jackie an icon because her image was frequently and influentially reproduced, and because, even when she was alive, she seemed more mythic than real. We called Jackie an icon because her story provided a foundation for our own stories, and because her face and the sometimes glamorous, sometimes tragic turns her life took were lodged in our systems of thought and reference, as if she were a concept, a numeral, a virtue, or a universal tendency, like rainfall or drought."[2]

But the feminist icon is different. Before Princess Diana, they have not been primarily famous for their images; we don't really know how Wollstonecraft or Margaret Fuller looked. Unlike the contemporary icons of the mass media, their faces and stories have not been used to sell products or lifestyles. Their styles have not been fetishized as accessories or collector's items. Although they may have been beautiful and dashing, they are not imitated by drag queens or turned into paper dolls.

Instead, they are known for the daring and range of their demand for a full life. While women in every era have been instructed or advised to follow rules of conduct, seduction, and success, those who have become feminist icons and heroines were rule-breakers who followed their own paths, who were determined to experience love, achievement, and fame, and who wanted their lives to matter. We do not ask them for perfection. Rather, their fallibility and humanity make them real to us, and even their tragedies are instructive and inspiring for women today who are still trying to combine independence, adventure, and love.

Over the centuries, we find that women have turned to mythology and religion for clues to the feminist epic life, reaching back to the Amazons, Diana of Ephesus, Cassandra, Penelope, Minerva, or Isis. They have sometimes sought in history a Feminist Messiah, a saint or savior who can redeem the lives of other women by sacrificing her own. George Eliot wrote about the yearning for the epic life in her greatest novel, *Middlemarch* (1871), in which she traced the development of an ardent young Englishwoman, Dorothea Brooke, a "later-born" Saint Theresa, whose "spiritual grandeur" meets "no coherent social faith and order." For Dorothea, noble aims conflict with "the common yearning of womanhood" for love and maternity.

But while some women were thwarted by these desires, others made them part of the experiment. In 1917, the American anthropologist Ruth Benedict wrote of how she "longed to speak out about the intense inspiration that comes to me from the lives of strong women. They have made of their lives a great adventure."³ Benedict planned to write a book called "Adventures in Womanhood," which would pay thoughtful tribute to the feminist icons who had inspired her. She wrote, but never published, the chapter on Mary Wollstonecraft, calling her the mother of us all. "The story of Mary Wollstonecraft," Benedict writes, "is that most precious of human documents: the story of a life that achieved an idea. . . . For her, life had no axioms; its geometry was all experimental. She was forever testing, probing; forever dominated by an utter unwillingness to accept the pretense, the convention, in place of the reality . . . a passionately intellectual attitude toward living was her essential tool."

Like the feminist icons who lived after her, Wollstonecraft was ahead of her time, as incomprehensible to the eighteenth century as "the fourth dimension to a class in fractions." She shocked her contemporaries with her ideas about women's rights to full humanity, and she brought all her powers of reason and persuasion to the elaboration of those ideas. Yet of all these contributions, Benedict writes, "her own life is the commentary incomparably the most arresting and the most significant." Indeed, "the knowledge she won, the price she paid, her books may hint to us, but it is her life through which we understand. It is there that we can measure that passionate attitude toward living out of which all the restlessness of modern womanhood has grown. It is her life story that makes her our contemporary."⁴

Life stories retain their power when theories fade. In many twilight conversations during the past few years, over coffee or over white wine, I have mentioned to men that I am writing a book about women with a passionate attitude toward living, and they have nodded and smiled and said, "Oh, yes, Madame Curie." But this is not a book about Madame Curie. Nor will you find Eleanor Roosevelt in these pages, or Jane Addams, Harriet Tubman, Susan B. Anthony, Amelia Earhart, Helen Keller, Rachel Carson, Mother Teresa, Margaret Thatcher, or many other highly intelligent, pathbreaking, or gifted women who are frequently prescribed to us as role models. To be sure, there are great women, notable women, admirable women in history who have preached the doctrine of female self-realization and practiced self-denial. But as the very unsaintly Victoria Woodhull said during her daring campaign for the presidency of the United States in 1872, "To preach the doctrine you must live the life."

My choices among those who both preached and lived their freedom reflect my own situation as a literary critic and sixties feminist activist who has lived in England, France, and the United States. These choices, ranging from Wollstonecraft in the 1790s to Eleanor Marx, Olive Schreiner, and Charlotte Perkins Gilman in the 1890s, and Hillary Clinton, Princess Diana, and Oprah Winfrey in the 1990s, may not suit everyone, but they cover a spectrum from the intellectual to the celebrity that I believe reflects both cultural change and the span of identification that goes far beyond the academic and political. Obviously my definition of feminism is broad and inclusive and refers to those who would not accept limits to a woman's life on the basis of sex. Many intellectual women who lived adventurously had no interest whatsoever in the organized women's movement of their day, while many women whose lives exemplified feminist goals never thought of themselves as intellectual pioneers. I am most interested in the risk-takers and adventurers.

Moreover, I have put some of my own history into this book, in places where it intersects with the history of feminism in our time. And as I've studied the lives of my heroines, of course I've also asked whether these patterns describe and help explain phases in my own life. I never met a feminist when I was growing up. I never even met a "career girl," as she would have been called in the forties and fifties. None of the women in my huge extended family—aunts, cousins, cousins once or twice removed—had a job outside her home. But the Boston suburbs were an ideal place for a bookish girl; when I had read everything in the house, I took the nickel streetcar ride, first to the Brookline Public Library at Coolidge Corner, and later to the secondhand bookstores of Cambridge and Scollay Square. I met my women of adventure first in books, and I have tried to write about my heroines of the past as if they were my friends and contemporaries, and to write about my friends and contemporaries as if they were historical figures whose milieu I am trying to reconstruct.

I have not discovered any tidy patterns or plots in the lives of feminist rule-breakers, but I have noticed some common and recurring themes. Above all, these were women who defined themselves, however painfully, as autonomous. In her 1892 address "The Solitude of Self," the American suffrage leader Elizabeth Cady Stanton insisted that "in discussing the rights of woman, we are to consider, first, what belongs to her as an individual, in a world of her own, the arbiter of her own destiny, an imaginary Robinson Crusoe with her woman, Friday, on a solitary island. Her rights under such circumstances are to use all her faculties for her own safety and happiness." Like men, women ultimately "must make the voyage of life alone."

Women who became feminist icons and leaders tended to define themselves in opposition to their mothers. "If you look for the provenance of the feminist writer," notes Lorna Sage, "mother is the key. The women who really nailed patriarchy weren't on the whole the ones with authoritarian fathers, but the ones with troubled, contradictory mothers: you aim your feminism less at men than at the picture of the woman you don't want to be, the enemy within."[5] Yet they also formed strong and sometimes romantic friendships with other girls and sustained these intimate friendships with women throughout their lives. In their relationships with men, they consciously sought male doubles, or twins, with whom they could form an intellectual, political, or professional partnership. Sometimes these partnerships were unequal. Toril Moi sees in Simone de Beauvoir's career the classic dilemma "of the intellectual woman's relationship to love." Because "thinking women have worried about their capacity to inspire love," Moi writes, they are vulnerable to forming intense "erotico-theoretical transference relations" with their male mentors, who they hope will appreciate both their minds and their bodies.[6] The strongest of the women moved beyond this dependence.

In *Writing a Woman's Life* (1988), Carolyn G. Heilbrun sees the crucial element in the adventure of women as coming to terms with power. "What has been forbidden to women," she declares, "is ... the open admission of the desire for power and control over one's life (which inevitably means accepting some degree of power and control over other lives)." Many women, even feminists, abjure and deny the necessity of power. They "would prefer (or think they would prefer) a world without evident power or control." Heilbrun hypothesizes that some gifted women unconsciously and indirectly take power over their lives by committing an "outrageous act," a social or sexual sin that frees them from the constraints of conventional society and its expectations—defying parents, rejecting religion, leaving a marriage.

She also points to the significance of the age of fifty for women's lives. "It is perhaps only in old age, certainly past fifty, that women can stop being female impersonators, can grasp the opportunity to reverse their most cherished principles of 'femininity.'"[7] For Simone de Beauvoir, the age of fifty was the moment to write her memoirs: "I took that child and that adolescent girl, both so long given up for lost in the depths of the unrecalled past, and endowed them with my adult awareness. I gave them a new existence—in black and white, on sheets of paper."[8]

Reclaiming our feminist icons is a necessary step in our collective memoir. As we come to the end of a century in which women have made enormous gains, we still lack a sense of the feminist past. Other groups have celebrated their heroic figures, but women have no national holidays, no days of celebration for the births or deaths of our great heroines. Whether they lived in the eighteenth, nineteenth, or twentieth centuries, all of these women lived before their time, trying to work, think, love, mother, even die, in ways that were in advance of what their societies approved and allowed. On the brink of a new millennium, we need to know about the patterns in our own intellectual tradition, to engage and to debate with the choices made by women whose restless, adventurous, and iconic lives make them our heroines, our sisters, our contemporaries.

TWO

Amazonian Beginnings

Mary Wollstonecraft

Anyone writing about the epic feminist intellectual has to begin with Mary Wollstonecraft (1759–97). Before Wollstonecraft, to be sure, there were learned women, bluestockings, and maybe even feminists, but none as honest, courageous, or determined to live according to her theories of freedom. No other woman of her time crowded such a range of experience into thirty-eight years or came so thrillingly, poignantly close to succeeding in all her dreams. After a series of unhappy love affairs, and the birth of an illegitimate child, Wollstonecraft had almost miraculously found a partner, the philosopher William Godwin, who loved and supported her for being the emancipated woman she was. Having survived two suicide attempts, she died just as she had begun to realize in her own life the happiness and satisfaction she imagined in her fiction, giving birth to the daughter who would become Mary Shelley, the author of *Frankenstein*. Wollstonecraft's great manifesto, *A Vindication of the Rights of Woman* (1792), anticipates virtually every idea of modern feminism. But Wollstonecraft is important not just because of the *Vindication,* but also because of her Promethean reaching for the largest dimensions of womanhood. As her contemporary Mary Anne Radcliffe wrote in her book *The Female Advocate,* "All women possess not the Amazonian spirit of a Wollstonecraft."[1]

What is "the Amazonian spirit"? To Radcliffe, it meant unwomanly self-assertion, only excused by "unremitted oppression." To Wollstonecraft, it also consisted of the determination to survive alone, to be financially independent, to succeed as a single parent, to live as an individual. At one point, in the depths of depression, Wollstonecraft called herself "a particle broken off from the grand mass of mankind." But for Wollstonecraft, the Amazonian spirit never meant living alone or without love, rejecting marriage, or avoiding motherhood. Even at her lowest moments, "some involuntary sympathetic emotion, like the attraction of adhesion, made me feel that I was still a part of a mighty whole, from which I could not sever myself."[2] However tough and even harsh her writing sounded to her contemporaries—and she horrified conservatives, who called her a "hyena in petticoats"—Wollstonecraft desired emotional and sexual liberation for women as well as political rights. That liberation could not be achieved by isolation, but connectedness also brought her rejection and pain.

Indeed, "Wollstonecraft is important," writes Margaret Walters, "because of her passionate and lifelong struggle in confronting her own inconsistencies. Her inevitable confusions and failures—and her efforts to articulate them—are as illuminating as her achievements." She "spent much of her life trying to reconcile love and motherhood—the difficult life of the emotions—with being an intellectual. . . . She is an extraordinarily open and suggestive writer who speaks directly to us today."[3] From the beginning of her life to its tragic end, Wollstonecraft was paradigmatic, a woman who uncannily anticipated and pioneered virtually all of the contradictions between theory and practice that would challenge the women who came after her, down to our own time.

"A VERY GOOD HATER"

Nothing in the Wollstonecrafts' family background gives a hint of the extraordinary person she would become. Mary was born on

April 27, 1759, in Spitalfields, in London, one of six children of a choleric father and a submissive mother. Neither parent favored her among their children, and her mother insisted on imposing various restraints and disciplines on her as a child; but even as a little girl she began to demonstrate the strength of character and independence that would characterize her life. She did not like dolls and preferred to play outdoors with her brothers. She was the one who intervened when her father beat his dogs, or his wife. According to Godwin's memoir of her, Mary was "a very good hater."[4]

She was also a good manager and a forceful organizer, the sort of person who takes control of other people's lives while they offer feeble, passive resistance. Her family needed such a person; her father's various business plans failed, they moved frequently, and after her mother's death in 1780, Mary took charge of her father's support through a variety of jobs as companion, governess, and teacher. She also educated her younger brothers and sisters and even helped one sister run away from an unhappy marriage. In short, as Godwin wrote in his memoir, Mary's intelligence "surmounted every obstacle; and by degrees, from a person little considered in the family, she became in sort its director and umpire."[5]

She also played this role with her women friends and, in doing so, tried out and developed an emotional style of romantic fantasy, jealousy, and possessiveness that would persist and plague her in her relationships with men. In letters written to another fifteen-year-old, Jane Arden, she says: "If I did not love you, I would not write so;—I have a heart that scorns disguises, and a countenance which will not dissemble: I have formed romantic notions of friendship. . . . I must have the first place or none." Walters says sagely that this melodramatic self-definition "is the way most of us grow up, although we may lack Wollstonecraft's naive but impressive openness about the process. . . . She is even on the verge of a real insight about the way we all slip into patterns that may trap us for life."[6]

In Mary's relationships with her sisters, in her passionate

friendship with another young woman, Fanny Blood, who also died in childbirth, and in her early love affairs with men, her demands and decisions in their behalf seem also like an acting out of her own psychological scripts, rebellion, and ego. In 1782, when she was the driving force in her sister Eliza's separation from an abusive husband, Walters notes that "she thoroughly enjoys her role as . . . savior and protector, and seems proud that the world will condemn her as a 'shameful incendiary.' "[7] Of course, Eliza would never forgive Mary for her interference; and Mary would never understand why Fanny Blood was often so resistant to her urgent advice about where to live and what to do.

Mary's dominant personality invariably created a resistance she could not understand. During the years from 1782 to 1792, Godwin writes, Wollstonecraft "may be said to have been, in a great degree, the victim of a desire to promote the benefit of others. She did not foresee the severe disappointment with which such an exclusive purpose of this sort is pregnant; she was inexperienced enough to lay a stress upon the consequent gratitude of those she benefited; and she did not sufficiently consider that, in proportion as we involve ourselves in the interests and society of others, we acquire a more exquisite sense of their defects, and are tormented with their untractableness and folly."[8] So the recipients of her benefaction were never sufficiently appreciative, or adaptable, and in calling her management urges "kindness," Mary disguised from herself how much power she needed to have.

In her twenties, she tried out many roles in an effort to find a use for her restless intelligence, and an outlet for her stifled sexuality and passion. Moreover, she did not realize how sharp and intimidating she could be with her friends: "She was occasionally severe and imperious in her resentments and, when she strongly disapproved, was apt to express her censure in terms that gave a very humiliating sensation to the person against whom it was directed."[9] She started up a school in Newington Green with her sisters, but ended it because she could not endure living with them; "cohabitation," explains Godwin, "is a point of delicate experiment, and is, in the majority of instances, pregnant with ill-humor and unhappiness."[10] She poured much of this discontent and her energy into writing about teaching, and into a romantic novel, *Mary, a Fiction* (1788).

Margaret Walters is both critical about this period in Wollstonecraft's life and insightful about how unavoidable it must have been: "The letters Wollstonecraft wrote all through her difficult twenties show her trying out a remarkable variety of roles. Without stint, without fear of absurdity, she throws herself into a bewildering succession of parts—romantic heroine, protective parent, poor invalid, teacher, businesswoman, and finally, writer. . . . She is contradictory and absurd, self-pitying, self-dramatizing. But I think her preoccupation with *herself* makes her so compelling, so curiously modern. In a society where a woman was not really expected to have a self, except insofar as she was daughter, wife, mother, what choice did Wollstonecraft have but to playact, experiment, try to invent herself?"[11]

A PHILOSOPHESS IN THE CITY

And then, in 1787, at the invitation of Joseph Johnson, a radical London bookseller with whom she had been corresponding, and who had agreed to publish her novel, she moved to London, to write for his journal, *The Analytical Review,* and to become part of an intellectual and artistic circle that included the painter Henry Fuseli, the chemist Joseph Priestley, the writer Tom Paine, and the poet William Blake. The move marked a major change in her career, for Johnson was not only "without a doubt the best friend" Wollstonecraft ever had, but also her ideal publisher, flexible with deadlines, encouraging, patient, and loyal.[12] As a young woman professional living alone in the city, Wollstonecraft saw herself as "the first of a new genus."[13]

She moved to rooms on Store Street, where, writes Claire Tomalin, "the first faint whiff of the North London bohemian intelligentsia seems to rise in the air at about this time, to thicken, and remain hanging over the place ever after."[14] Adjacent to the

British Museum and the University of London, Store Street today is lined with small shops and cafés where young women academics and researchers meet over cappuccino. Like them, now, Wollstonecraft wore long black stockings and cultivated carelessness about her appearance. She despised fashion, Tomalin writes, "with the confidence of the deliberately dowdy intellectual woman."[15] How such a woman should look and dress, as well as how she should think and feel, was as much an enigma then as it is today. In the earliest surviving portrait of Wollstonecraft, painted around 1791, she is dressing for success, "sober and serious, the professional woman, with conventionally powdered and curled hair."[16]

She was a self-described "spinster on the wing," affectionate and maternal, but cut off by her uniqueness from the love she sought and trapped in the emotional impasse of the exceptional woman who believes she can love only an even more exceptional man. According to one recent biographer, "the greater her achievements as an emancipated woman, the more exacting were her standards and the fewer the men who came up to them; and fewer still, those who were willing to try. By creating an unfamiliar image of what a woman should be, she had effectively isolated herself from the opportunity to put her theories into practice."[17]

Moreover, for all her romantic fire, she was sexually inexperienced, ignorant of even the folk remedies for birth control, and hampered by conventional ideas about female chastity and the sinfulness of sexuality. All in all, between repressed sexuality and loneliness, she was an easy target for a Don Juan, and she became infatuated with the painter Henry Fuseli. He was fifty (writing when she herself was in her thirties, Claire Tomalin sternly calls this "an age when fires are not always entirely extinct"[18]), a dandy who knew eight languages, drew pornographic pictures as well as scenes from Shakespeare and Milton, and had just married for the first time. Mary was smitten; Fuseli was the male mentor, the genius, of her fantasies. But, although Tomalin speculates that he must have told Mary a lot about sex and enjoyed shocking her, they were never lovers. In the summer of 1792, she actually went to visit Fuseli's wife, Sophia, with a proposal that she join their household permanently as a "spiritual partner."[19] That ended the matter quickly; Sophia threw her out of the house, and Fuseli kept his distance and his silence.

But out of this embarrassing and unsuitable infatuation came two major results for her: the rapid composition and publication of *A Vindication of the Rights of Woman* (1792), and her decision to go to Paris at the end of that year.

VINDICATING WOMEN

The *Vindication* was grounded in the political and philosophical turmoil surrounding the American and the French Revolutions and applied the idea of human rights and democratic reform to the situation of women. It is the "feminist declaration of independence."[20] Following up on her earlier *Vindication of the Rights of Man* (1790), Wollstonecraft argued that women were first of all human beings, God's creations, entitled to the same education and the same political freedom as men; and that society as a whole would be improved when women became the equals of their brothers, husbands, and sons—when they were self-sufficient in every way. She insisted that love and passion were fleeting emotions, in contrast to the fundamentals of reason and independence.

But Wollstonecraft was a passionate writer, who composed the *Vindication* in six weeks, and the haste shows in its disorganization. Godwin was the first to admit that it was "eminently deficient in method and arrangement." The book begins with three chapters on the fundamental principles of women's rights; then criticizes the representation of women in the works of leading eighteenth-century writers, especially Jean-Jacques Rousseau; explains women's limitations in terms of their social constraints; and presents arguments about education, family life, sexual mores, and the care of children. But it is much more personal, idiosyncratic, and digressive than this outline makes it sound. Wollstonecraft qualifies, backtracks, fulminates, exclaims, narrates, and philosophizes. She relates every detail of oppression or error to an overall indignation with the diminished lives that middle-class women—her main subjects—are allowed to lead. The effect is not that of a treatise but of a dramatic monologue. One leading scholar, Miriam Brody, writes that Wollstonecraft's argument has "a freshness and immediacy of attitude as if the author herself had only now entered the contemporary debate on women's rights," which "speaks as much to the problems of women at the turn of the twenty-first century" as it did to the women at the turn of the nineteenth century. [21]

The *Vindication* seemed peculiar and incoherent to its contemporary readers in part because it was the first effort at a new hybrid genre of feminist manifesto, an attempt to combine patriarchal and matriarchal rhetoric. Two centuries later, feminist literary critics analyzed these feminist polemics, or womanifestos, as texts that embody a struggle between reason and emotion. In Wollstonecraft's case, the feelings and desires she was working so hard to repress surfaced in her writing, "accounting," one critic comments, "for its apparent disorganization, digressiveness, sporadic examples, apostrophes, and outbursts. . . . The resulting earthquake is the prose tempest of the *Vindication*."[22]

Wollstonecraft opposes "flowery diction" but takes many of her images of women from gardening and flowers. Women in the eighteenth century, she writes, are like "flowers which are planted in too rich a soil, strength and usefulness are sacrificed to beauty." This "barren blooming" is the product of a "false system of education" that encourages girls to "inspire love when they ought to cherish a nobler ambition, and by their abilities and virtues exact respect." In order to appear like "the sweet flowers that smile in the walk of man," women waste their intellectual energy on the art of pleasing, concern for their clothes, romantic daydreams, artifice, and manipulation. A first-time reader of the *Vindication* will be surprised at how critical it is of women's timidity, laziness, lack of discipline, "infantine airs," petty vanity. And Wollstonecraft does not mince words or try not to offend her readers. Her basic argument is that "if woman be allowed to have an immortal soul, she must have, as the employment of life, an understanding to improve. And when . . . she is incited by present gratification to forget her grand destination, nature is counteracted, or she was born only to procreate and rot."[23]

In the Enlightenment spirit, Wollstonecraft recommends education as the cure, but takes the extra step of advocating coeducation for boys and girls. Serious intellectual training, she insists, would benefit both sexes and be good for marriage and maternity. But it would also protect women from dependency, invisibility, and insignificance. "How many women thus waste life away the prey of discontent," she exclaims, "who might have practiced as physicians, regulated a farm, managed a shop, and stood erect, supported by their own industry, instead of hanging their heads surcharged with the dew of sensibility?"[24]

The legend has it that Wollstonecraft's fiery feminism made her an outcast, but the truth is that the *Vindication* was well-received, translated into a number of languages, and generally acclaimed for its common sense. Its success owed a great deal to its sexual conservatism, denunciations of sex and free love, and endorsement of marriage and motherhood. But the author was discovering how hard it was to follow her own precepts about rationality and self-respect. At a time when she should have been consolidating her success by writing a second book, she was unable to write much at all. Instead, she brooded about Fuseli and languished, "surcharged with the dew of sensibility."

THE REVOLUTION WITHIN

Like many women born after her, Wollstonecraft decided that travel would be a good remedy for unrequited love. On November 12, 1792, she set out to see the French Revolution, with a breezy farewell to her friend William Roscoe: "I have determined to set out for Paris in the course of a fortnight or three weeks and I shall not now halt at Dover, I promise you; for I shall go alone—neck or nothing is the word." She was undeterred by rumors of the Terror and the guillotine: "Meantime let me beg you not to mix with the shallow herd who throw an odium on immutable principles, because some of the mere instruments of the Revolution were too sharp.—Children of any growth will do mischief when they meddle with edged tools."

Richard Holmes, the great English biographer and historian, has studied the experience of the English Romantics during the French Revolution, and he says that Wollstonecraft's voice "was like that moment in a Shakespearean play when, after the muffled scene-setting of the minor characters, the hero abruptly enters from an unexpected angle in the wings, speaking with the sudden clarity and assurance that a major actor brings to his part."[25] But Mary Wollstonecraft's entrance was even more dramatic and paradigmatic in terms of her own life; the Revolution transformed her as a woman. Holmes writes: "I found her to be exemplary in a more profound, indeed spiritual way than I had supposed when I first set out looking for a simple witness to events. The Revolution was, in a sense, internalized in her own biography: from the clever rational feminist to the suffering and loving woman writer with a deep understanding of her fellow-beings, she had passed through a revolution of sensibility."[26]

She had planned to stay in Paris for six weeks, but instead she stayed for two years. During those years, her naive political views were checked and sobered by an encounter with the bloody horror of real revolutionary violence. Moreover, she transformed intellectual theory into existential practice when she fell in love, had her first sexual experience and awakening, gave birth to an illegitimate daughter, and suffered the agony of being betrayed and abandoned. The revolution became psychological for her, and Holmes says that her metamorphosis "transformed my conception of the inner nature of the revolutionary experience."[27]

Wollstonecraft's ideological defense of violence was soon undermined by emotions of horror, compassion, anger, and fear.

She saw the king on his way to trial and that night was haunted. "I wish I had even the cat with me!" she writes to Johnson. "I want to see something alive; death in so many frightful shapes has taken hold of my fancy."[28] Her feminist friends among the Girondists—Olympe de Gouges, Madame Roland—were executed, and the women's movement within the Revolution was crushed.

Nonetheless, in spring 1793, when most of the English were fleeing Paris, Mary stayed. She had fallen in love with Gilbert Imlay, an American radical, patriot, and businessman who was trying to make a deal with the French government about land speculation in Kentucky. They quickly became lovers—Godwin writes that with him "she entered into that species of connection for which her heart panted, and which had the effect of diffusing an immediate tranquillity over her manners." Indeed, he goes on, she was visibly transformed by sexual gratification and the sense of being loved: "She was like a serpent upon a rock, that casts its slough, and appears again with the brilliancy, the sleekness, and the elastic activity of its happiest age. She was playful, full of confidence, kindness, and sympathy. Her eyes assumed new luster, and her cheeks new color and smoothness."[29]

They set up a household together at Neuilly, and the months there were the happiest of her life. In October, when the Revolutionary Committee ordered the arrest of all British citizens and began to round them up, Imlay took her to the American embassy, registered her as his wife, and obtained papers of American citizenship for her. By this time, she knew that she was pregnant.

But the idyll did not last long. Imlay had started to make frequent business trips, and she followed him to Le Havre. He was often away. In April she writes, "I could not sleep—I turned to your side of the bed, and tried to make the most of the comfort of the pillow."[30] Her discursive language of the mind had become an urgent language of the body.

But they were together when their daughter, Fanny Imlay, was born May 14, 1794. It was an easy birth, and Mary felt that in some way it vindicated her philosophical beliefs about liberated women. She boasted to a friend, "Nothing could be more natural nor easy than my labor—still it is not smooth work—I dwell on these circumstances not only as I hope it will give you pleasure; but to prove that this struggle of nature is rendered much more cruel by the ignorance and affectation of women. My midwife has been twenty years in this employment, and she tells me, she never knew a woman so well. . . . I feel great pleasure at being a mother."[31] Mary breast-fed Fanny without difficulty: "My little Girl begins to suck so MANFULLY that her father reckons saucily on her writing the second part of the R. . . . s of Woman."[32]

But her relationship with Imlay began to deteriorate; she and Fanny moved to London, while he stayed in Paris, promised to join her, broke his promises, and slowly but inexorably distanced himself. Godwin describes the period as one of deep despair, humiliation, and shock for her. "The agonies of such a separation, or rather desertion . . . were vastly increased by the lingering method in which it was effected, and the ambiguity that, for a long time, hung upon it." Throughout 1795, she sent him beseeching, desperate letters and tried to persuade herself that he would come back. "But," Godwin records, "the hopes she nourished were speedily blasted."

All of her brave, ignorant words in the *Vindication* about the stoic indifference of an intelligent and educated woman must have returned to mock her. Then she had written that romantic love is "a dying flame, which nature doomed to expire when the object became familiar, when friendship and forbearance take place of a more ardent affection. This is the natural death of love."[33] Then she had imagined the mother who has lost her husband as calm, virtuous, resigned, easily sublimating sexual desire into maternal devotion. Then she had disdained women's "sexual privileges" and defended the high ideals of chastity. Then she had belittled women who try desperate measures to win back straying lovers. Now, when she discovered in April 1795 that Imlay was unfaithful, she took an overdose of laudanum.

THE COMMERCIAL TRAVELER

The suicide attempt may have been a last-ditch call for Imlay's help and affection. He was alarmed and concerned enough to step in with another plan, a sort of half-promise of reconciliation if she would help him with some business affairs. The plan was this: Imlay's shipping business had run into problems, and he asked her to go as his agent to settle matters with his partner, Elias Backman, who was in Gothenburg. He made her his legal representative with power of attorney in Scandinavia and entrusted her with the mission of tracing a stolen treasure ship that had been pirated away by its Norwegian captain from Imlay's fleet. She was to go, accompanied by her baby and maid, on a lengthy undercover mission to Scandinavia to "discover the fate of the treasure ship, the attitude of all parties concerned, and to reach if possible some financial agreement, probably on an 'out of court' basis."[34] Imlay held out hints that he would join her in Norway; they would once more be together.

It was risky, even bizarre; but Mary jumped at the chance. Testing herself against the most extreme conditions of solitude, hardship, loneliness, and depression, she also wrote a series of letters to Imlay describing the trip that show how much she projected her own turbulent emotions onto the landscape, and how, despite herself, she responded to the challenge, novelty, and adventure of the trip. We are now accustomed to travel books by women in strange countries, under difficult circumstances; but Wollstonecraft's remains one of the most amazing. Renting boats, finding huts to spend the night, eating strange foods, making her way in wild and unknown country, "beyond the pale of Western culture," with her baby and her maid, Marguerite, she was almost fearless.[35] And against all the odds, she succeeded in her mission.

In many respects, the three-and-a-half-month journey through Sweden, Denmark, and Norway restored her self-confidence and self-esteem. On one of her first stops, she reported proudly,

her host "told me bluntly that I . . . asked him men's questions."[36] Reading her letters, with their flood of judgments and
brisk opinions on everything from the cooking, the coffee, the
gardens, and the heating to personal hygiene, sexual customs,
and government is like hearing from a bossy but entertaining
friend. In Sweden she was shocked by the poor treatment of servants, especially women, who had to do the laundry by hand in
icy water; in Norway she deplored the absence of a university.
She remarked on the tastelessness of a mansion in Gothenburg,
with a stone staircase in a wooden house, and statues outside of
Venuses and Apollos "condemned to lie buried in snow three
parts of the year."[37] She found Swedish women sluggish and fat;
Norwegian women lazy, playful, but extremely blond; Danish
women weak, indulgent mothers who spoiled their children.
She got sick of eating herring. She hoped but failed to see a bear.

At the same time, the letters show how much time she had for
introspection, and how she began to understand herself much
better than ever before. In particular, she began to understand and
accept her need for companionship, a city, the modern conven-
iences of the 1790s. She also became comfortable with herself as a
mother and could trust her impulses with Fanny. She even began
to plan a book on infant care. And in thinking about her daughter's future, and the situation of other women, she came more
fully to terms with the intractability of emotions and allowed herself to acknowledge their legitimacy and power. Instead of recant-
ing any of her views on sexual honesty and women's rights, she
explored them at a deeper and more genuine level.

Imlay's letters to her do not survive. But he did not show up at
any of the places he had vaguely appointed for their rendezvous,
and she returned to London in October to discover that he was living with a new mistress, an actress from a strolling theater company. This time she was determined to die. In an episode that
became famous and paradigmatic for women novelists, such as
George Eliot in the nineteenth century and Virginia Woolf in the
twentieth, Mary rowed out by herself on the Thames in a rain-
storm in the middle of the night, waited until her clothes were

drenched, and jumped off Putney Bridge. Miraculously, she was rescued and revived. And even then the relationship with Imlay dragged on for months, while she deceived herself that somehow they would be reunited. She was unable to deliver an ultimatum and make the final break until March 1796. She set up house with Fanny in Somers Town in London, near what is now St. Pancras Station and the British Library. Still calling herself Mrs. Imlay, she renewed her acquaintance with London friends.

During the winter, however, she had revised her letters from Scandinavia, editing out any reference to Imlay, and Johnson had published them. The book was a triumph, popular with readers and critics, translated into German, Dutch, Swedish, and Portuguese, and much admired in Romantic and artistic circles in England. William Godwin read it and decided that "if ever there was a book calculated to make a man in love with its author, this appears to me to be the book. She speaks of her sorrows, in a way that fills us with melancholy, and dissolves us in tenderness, at the same time that she displays a genius which commands all our admiration."[38] When Mary, characteristically, took matters into her own hands by making an unchaperoned call on Godwin, as a neighbor, in April, they developed a friendship that, he said, melted into love.

AN EXEMPLARY UNION

Mary Wollstonecraft's love affair and marriage to William Godwin was not only an astonishing happy ending for her, but an exemplary union of the Philosopher and the Feminist that set a psychological and political style for radical generations for centuries to come. Godwin, the respected philosopher of reason, the anarchist author of *Political Justice* and novelist of ideas, was a bachelor of nearly forty, awkward with both women and children, still emotionally dependent on his old mother. He had ideological beliefs against marriage. He was not the romantic demon lover of her dreams. Wollstonecraft was not beautiful; she had a child already; when he had met her at a dinner party some years earlier, he had found her overbearing and opinionated.

Now they became lovers. They continued to live apart, and to meet in the evenings, but when she became pregnant in March 1797, they married at Old St. Pancras Church like any other conventional couple. When the news of the wedding became public, some of their circle made malicious jokes, but overall, Richard Holmes explains, "Godwin and Wollstonecraft were seen to bring together, through their books, their complementary views, their experiment in living, two most powerful strands in the tradition of progressive reform. They were seen as transitional figures, pointing towards a freer life, and a more just society, and the new 'empire of feeling.'"[39]

But Claire Tomalin thinks that "it was only in Godwin's violently emotional retrospect that their wooing and marriage took on the coloring of high romance," and that the marriage was a compromise and an admission of defeat for her: "It is tempting to say that Mary's love for Godwin was more mature and in some way worthier than her love for Imlay; the theory satisfies a natural wish to see her life arrive at a happy climax after so much frustration. But there is really not much evidence for this in letters, and at least one of her friends considered that her 'real' love had gone to Imlay and that Godwin was no more than a consolation prize of a most superior kind."[40]

They continued to live separate lives, with separate dwellings, and both seemed to flourish in this odd arrangement, writing to each other and meeting in the evenings. Toward the end of her pregnancy, they began to call each other Mama and Papa. Commenting on her portrait at this time, Miranda Seymour describes her as "warm-faced and seductive."[41] She was preparing Fanny for the birth of a baby brother and expecting another easy delivery.

On August 30, Mrs. Blenkinsop, the midwife, told Wollstonecraft that everything was going well. "Mrs. Blenkinsop tells me that I am in the most natural state, and can promise me a safe delivery," she wrote to Godwin, who had gone to his own apartment to work as usual. "But that I must have a little patience."

Why a midwife? Godwin says that Mary did not want a male physician; she was "influenced by ideas of decorum." But midwives were also experienced professionals. In London, they were required to have two years' training under a physician, and Mrs. Blenkinsop had trained at the Westminster Lying-In Hospital. The baby, Mary, was born at 11:20 P.M., apparently without complications. But at 2 A.M. the midwife told Godwin that the placenta had not been removed, and that she wanted to call in a "male practitioner." Godwin immediately went for Dr. Louis Poignard, chief surgeon and man-midwife of Westminster Hospital, who came to the house and extracted the placenta in pieces, with his hand and without anesthetic. Wollstonecraft's condition immediately became serious; she fainted and hemorrhaged. But over the next few days she seemed to rally, and Godwin was not too alarmed. On Sunday, September 3, he went out to pay a visit, and when he returned, she was having chills and shivering fits. From that point on, there was little hope that she would recover, although her doctors—several more had been called in—tried various remedies, including bringing in puppies to draw off her milk.

On the morning of September 10, at twenty minutes to eight, as Godwin recorded in his journal, she died, of what was called puerperal fever and was actually septicemia caused by the effort to extract the placenta. Only two years before, there had been a breakthrough in obstetrics and antisepsis. A Scottish physician, Alexander Gordon, "had published his findings that the women who died of puerperal fever had been attended by a practitioner or nurse who had been in previous contact with a woman suffering from the disease. His discovery went unheeded. In the mid-nineteenth century a Viennese physician, Ignaz Philip Semmelweiss, insisted that all medical practitioners and students in the Vienna Lying-In Hospital should wash their hands in chlorinated lime before entering a labor ward. His advice, too, went largely unheeded elsewhere. It was not until well into the twentieth century that puerperal fever was successfully controlled."[42]

That Wollstonecraft should have died in giving birth to this daughter seems the cruelest, most compelling part of her life for many women readers. Childbirth, despite medical advances, is a confrontation with mortality for women as war is for men. Even now when technology makes warfare a matter of computerized targets and modern medicine makes childbirth painless and safe, that fundamental sense of existential risk remains. For Mary Wollstonecraft, death came as a cruel reversal of fortune at a moment when she seemed to have resolved the conflict between her principles and her heart.

Four months after Mary's death, Godwin published his memoir, a remarkable and candid account of their lives and beliefs that created a scandal about her sex life and his tactlessness. Robert Southey accused Godwin of "a want of all feeling in stripping his dead wife naked."[43] His revelations of her love affairs, her suicide attempts, and her passions alienated other women and frightened feminists of her time and after, who kept their distance from Wollstonecraft as a precursor.

Moreover, having discovered the satisfactions of marriage, and unable to care for two children on his own, Godwin remarried four years after her death. Fanny and Mary did not get on with their stepmother, and Godwin was prone to favoring his own child. In 1816, Fanny Imlay killed herself with laudanum. Mary Godwin ran off with Shelley and wrote *Frankenstein*.

THE AFTERLIFE

The historian Joan Scott says that "the history of Wollstonecraft as a feminist . . . is the history of the uses made of her by subsequent generations."[44] There were many different Mary Wollstonecrafts conjured up by the women of the nineteenth century. George Eliot described Wollstonecraft as a ponderous intellectual and viewed the *Vindication* as "eminently serious, severely moral, and withal rather heavy."[45] In the United States, the women's suffrage leader Elizabeth Cady Stanton summoned up Wollstonecraft's messianic spirit in defense of the free-love radical Victoria Woodhull: "We have enough women sacrificed to this sentimental hypocritical prating about purity. . . . We have crucified the Mary Wollstonecrafts. . . . If Victoria Woodhull must be crucified, let men drive the spikes and plait the crown of thorns."[46]

But in many respects, Wollstonecraft was overlooked by the decorous Victorians. As Margaret Tims argues, "She seems almost to leap straight from the eighteenth century into the twentieth, where she would perhaps have felt more at home."[47] By the beginning of this century, as I will be showing in the pages to follow, Wollstonecraft returned as an enigmatic but inspiring figure. Indeed, historian Alice Wexler writes, "By the early twentieth century a number of rebellious women were finding that life a major statement of female potentiality. Despite, or perhaps because of, her complex and ambivalent legacy, the attempt to assess that legacy was for some women, at least, a way of clarifying their own identities and options."[48] Her Amazonian spirit could not be stilled.

THREE

Radiant Sovereign Self

Margaret Fuller

In January 1820, New England lawyer Timothy Fuller wrote to his wife: "I have been reading a part of Mary Wollstonecraft's 'Rights of Women' & am so well pleased with it that if I find nothing more exceptional than what I have yet seen, I will purchase it for you. It will tend to give us some very sensible & just views of education."[1] Ironically, he was worried that they had neglected his ten-year-old daughter's household and domestic training. That daughter, Margaret Fuller, born May 23, 1810, in Cambridge, Massachusetts, would become the American Wollstonecraft, "the best-known American feminist intellectual of her day," and "antebellum America's foremost female activist of the mind."[2]

In her own great feminist manifesto, *Woman in the Nineteenth Century* (1845), Fuller looked back at Wollstonecraft's legacy with compassion and indignation: "Mary Wolstonecraft [*sic*] . . . was a woman whose existence better proved the need of some new interpretation of woman's rights, than any thing she wrote. Such beings as these, rich in genius, of most tender sympathies, capable of high virtue and a chastened harmony, ought not to find themselves, by birth, in a place so narrow, that, in breaking bonds, they become outlaws."[3] Fuller was deeply moved by the loyalty and perception of Godwin's memoir. "This man had courage to love and honor this woman in the face of the world's sentence, and of all that was repulsive in her own past history. He believed he saw of what soul she was, and that the impulses she had struggled to act out were noble, though the opinions to which they had led might not be thoroughly weighed. He loved her, and he defended her for the meaning and tendency of her inner life. . . . He acted as he wrote, as a brother."[4]

Margaret Fuller hoped for the same good fortune in love, as she also hoped to equal Wollstonecraft's genius. In many respects, the conflicts she faced as an American woman living in the midst of New England Transcendentalism were similar to those of Wollstonecraft among the Romantic poets and philosophic Dissenters. But Fuller struggled even more with her culture's hostility to intellectual women, with its fetishism of feminine beauty, with its sexual puritanism and horror of female sexuality, and with its insistence that intellectual work had to come packaged in traditional rigid forms.

From childhood, Fuller's experiences "made her feel torn between terms that her society considered mutually exclusive: female and intellectual."[5] As a woman, she was mocked for not conforming to standards of feminine beauty; as a thinker, she was patronized for deviating from the solemnity of the sermon or the essay.

The self-division that Mary Wollstonecraft represented as the conflict between principle and the heart, Fuller imagined as a split between her masculine and feminine sides. She perceived her New England family as sharply divided between the sexes. As the critic Jeffrey Steele writes, "Inhabiting the worlds of both mother and father, but totally at home in neither, she was in the perfect position to understand the strengths and limitations of both masculinity and femininity in the nineteenth century."[6] She wrote about her own psyche in an exalted imagery of gender duality we never encounter in Wollstonecraft: "My history presents much superficial, temporary tragedy. The Woman in me kneels and weeps in tender rapture; the Man in me rushes forth but only to be baffled. Yet the time will come when, from the union of this tragic king and queen, shall be born a radiant sovereign self."[7]

Fuller's ideal of the "radiant sovereign self" was not an Amazon warrior-woman, but a mystical union of the heroic, active masculine principle—the King—and the emotional, spiritual feminine principle—the Queen—which would create fulfillment and power. The great temptation for the intellectual woman of Fuller's era, whose environment was more religious than political, was to become the Feminist Messiah, the exceptional female savior who would change women's lives, but who would also be superior to them. Fuller indeed wrote that she felt "chosen among women" and sometimes saw herself as immune from the ordinary sexual needs and emotional yearnings of her sisters. Fuller's Transcendentalist contemporaries also shared the vision of this savior; Hawthorne, for example, wrote in *The Scarlet Letter* of the "destined prophetess" whose coming would reveal "a new truth" between men and women, an "angel and apostle" who would be "lofty, pure, and beautiful" as well as wise. Fuller gradually came to understand that she could not live up to this ideal of chaste self-sacrifice, and to seek out her happiness on her own terms.

Fuller was educated by her father, who came from a family in which the men too were limited by strict gender codes. As she recalled in a memoir, "As a boy, my father was taught to think only of preparing himself for Harvard University, and when there of preparing himself for the profession of Law."[8] He taught his daughter in the same way, although she could never hope to follow her brothers to Harvard. But "he hoped to make me the heir of all he knew, and of as much more as the income of his profession enabled him to give me means of acquiring." Thus he crammed her with learning and had her studying Latin at the age of six. In addition, she did her lessons with her father late at night when he had finished work and often went to bed late, worried that she had done badly.

Later, Fuller believed that the stress of this precocious intellectual training, and her immersion in Virgil and Dante, had overstrained her nerves and caused her to have nightmares and episodes of sleepwalking: "In childhood I was a somnambu-list—I was very subject to attacks of delirium—I perceive I had what are now called spectral illusions—For a long time I dreaded excessively going to bed for as soon as I was left alone—huge shapes—usually faces—advanced from the corners of the room and pressed upon me growing larger and larger until they seemed about to crush me—Then I would scream and sit up in bed to get out of the way."[9] She dreamed that she was "wading in a sea of blood—I caught at twigs and rocks to save myself: they all streamed blood on me."[10] When she cried out in her sleep, her father scolded her, and "sharply bid her 'leave off thinking of such nonsense, or she would be crazy.' "[11]

Mary Wollstonecraft, throughout all of her crises, never mentions anxieties about the way she looks. But for Fuller, appearance, beauty, fashion were all problems. Although she had been a pretty blond child, when she turned twelve, Fuller's complexion was affected by what she calls "a determination of the blood to the head." Blotches? Acne? Whatever the cause, her father attributed it "to my overheating myself, my mother to an unfortunate cold—both were much mortified to see the fineness of my complexion destroyed—My own vanity was for a time severely wounded, but I made up my mind to be bright and ugly. My father could not be so easily reconciled but was always scolding me for getting my forehead so red when excited."[12] Like the red mark on the cheek of Hawthorne's heroine in "The Birthmark," the redness on Fuller's forehead seemed to be an eruption of her intelligence and her femaleness, a blemish her father blamed her for as if she could control it. Perceptions and accounts of Fuller's looks vary wildly throughout her life. No man ever called her beautiful, but many found her attractive, vivacious, and graceful, especially in social contexts when she felt confident, while women recalled her at parties as plain and dowdy, "eyes half shut, hair curled all over head . . . dressed in badly cut, low-necked pink silk . . . and danced quadrilles very badly."[13]

Fuller found an escape from her father's world of books behind the gate of her mother's garden, where she discovered another kind of world that was sensual, emotional, aesthetic. "I loved to gaze on the roses, the violets, the lilies, the pinks; . . . I looked at them on every side, I kissed them, I pressed them to my bosom with passionate emotions, such as I have never dared express to any human being."[14] As a child and young woman, Fuller also directed her most passionate emotions toward other women and was demonstrative with them in a way that Wollstonecraft, who reserved a section of the *Vindication* to complain about the indecency of schoolgirl intimacies, would have deplored. Fuller developed a crush on Ellen Kilshaw, a pretty young Englishwoman visiting in the neighborhood, who played the harp, sympathized with the child, and otherwise embodied all that was attractive and angelic. When Kilshaw returned to England, Fuller fell into such a visible depression that her parents decided to send her away to school.

In her adolescent friendship with Anna Barker, Fuller was even more romantic and possessive. Later she wrote in her journal, "It is so true that a woman may be in love with a woman, and a man with a man. . . . It is regulated by the same law as that of love between persons of different sexes, only it is purely intellectual and spiritual, unprofaned by any mixture of lower instincts."[15] Fuller's comments, writes her biographer Charles Capper, "definitely have a bisexual flavor that seems rather different from what one usually finds in either the sentimental female friendship literature or Anglo-American Romantic writings." He believes that although she was basically heterosexual, her "latent bisexual feelings . . . were not a mere literary affectation, but a deeply ingrained part of her emotional makeup . . . [that] often led to tense relations and sometimes serious social crises."[16]

In 1835, Timothy Fuller died, and his family discovered that this meticulous man had not left a will. Margaret's uncles became the executors, and for years she fretted against their financial control. Moreover, her brothers seemed unable to sort out their own lives and careers, and Margaret had to give up her own wishes for travel to become the family's managing force and chief financial support. She considered becoming a novelist when she read George Sand, but rejected the idea as too feminine: "I have always thought . . . that I would keep all that behind the curtain, that I would not write, like a woman, of love and hope and disappointment, but like a man, of the world of intellect and action." She was annoyed by Sand's autobiographical *Lettres d'un Voyageur:* "What do I see? An unfortunate, wailing her loneliness, wailing her mistakes, writing for money! She has genius and a manly grasp of mind & woman's heart, but not a manly heart. Will there never be a being to combine a man's mind and woman's heart, & who yet finds life too rich to weep over? Never!"[17] Instead of writing fiction, she supported herself as a teacher and journalist, working for the eccentric Bronson Alcott (Louisa May's father) at his progressive Boston school, teaching languages, and translating Goethe's essays.

During these years, she was sociable and made many new friends, including the Emersons and the Hawthornes; but as she approached the age of thirty and remained single while her friends paired off, Fuller was forced to think about whether she would ever marry and have children. She pondered Goethe's comments—"How can a woman of genius love & marry? A man of genius will not love her—he wants repose. She may find some object sufficient to excite her ideal for the time, but love perishes as soon as it finds it has grasped the shadow for the substance. . . . Such a woman cannot long remain wed, again she is single, again must seek & strive."[18] Typically, she attributed her single state to her hybrid nature—"a man's ambition with a woman's heart—'tis an accursed lot."[19]

But unlike the usual stereotype of the desperate unmarried woman, Fuller hid her feelings and saw her situation as evidence of and the price for her special messianic destiny. "From a very early age I have felt that I was not born to the common womanly lot," she wrote to a friend. "I knew I should never find a being who could keep the key of my character; that there would be none on whom I could always lean, from whom I could always learn; that I should be a pilgrim and sojourner on earth." Intuitively, she explained, she had sensed "this destiny of the thinker, and (shall I dare say it?) of the poetic priestess. . . . Accordingly, I did not look on any of the persons, brought into relation with me, with common womanly eyes."[20]

Her claim was partly rationalization and bravado, a sublimation of frustrated sexuality and longing into myth. But Fuller's mythic persona, as the priestess, thinker, and uncommon woman, also gave her justification to be different and to make her own rules. Following the philosophical counsel of her friend Emerson, she was prepared to be self-reliant, to develop her own gifts. Accordingly, she took up two new projects: editing a new Transcendental literary journal, *The Dial,* and experimenting with a form of teaching ahead of its time in both content and form.

THE CONVERSATIONS

In November 1839, Fuller began a series of seminars or adult education classes for women that satisfied both her need to make money and her calling to inspire and lead. Twenty-five women came to the first morning meeting in Boston, some from as far away as Providence. Emerson thought that Fuller made "a disagreeable first impression on most persons . . . the effect of her manners, which expressed an overweening sense of power and slight esteem of others."[21] But Fuller made a most agreeable impression on these women, the effect of her beautiful clothes, her wonderful laugh, and her eloquent, resourceful speech. At the beginning, when she talked, the rest fell silent. But like a serious professional teacher, Fuller was mainly concerned with helping her students to think and speak for themselves. As one participant, Elizabeth Palmer Peabody, recalled, "Miss Fuller guarded against the notion that she was to teach any thing. She merely meant to be the nucleus of conversation."[22]

Sometimes Fuller started a discussion by asking for definitions; sometimes they began by analyzing assigned readings. She set a tone of informality and humor. "She is so funny—she makes me laugh half the time," wrote one of the women in the class. Although she could be formidable and withering, in the Conversations, as her classes were called, she was tactful and encouraging. At the same time, she demanded the highest standards of rational argument from her students, insisting that young women must learn to "systematize thought and give a precision and clearness in which our sex are so deficient, chiefly, I think, because they have so few inducements to test and classify what they receive." She asked tough, interesting questions. She had members of the group bring in short essays on the reading to share with everyone. In her letters to Emerson, she often sounds like an impatient young college professor—"I could not make these ladies talk about Beauty. They would not ascend to principles but kept clinging to details"—but she persevered.

The first series of Conversations was about Greek mythology, and it gave Fuller a chance to offer to her students role models of strong women. She "sought out material that would provide examples of strong women and women's friendships, in both pagan and Christian history; in allegory and in folktale, she found for her purpose virgin goddesses and nuns and laywomen who had dedicated themselves to holy or ascetic lives; they had enjoyed power and high respect and represented qualities no longer accorded to women."[23] A second series focused on the fine arts. For a while, Fuller experimented with an evening session of Conversations including men, but predictably the men dominated the discussion, the women were unhappy, and the experiment was not repeated.

In the following years, subjects for the seminars included education, ethics, culture, and woman—subjects related to the participants' lives in a way that made them a kind of women's studies program before their time. Early on, Fuller also encountered the kind of demands for political inclusiveness on issues of race that would become familiar to pioneers of women's studies in the next century. Maria Weston Chapman, the head of the Boston Female Anti-Slavery Association, asked Fuller in 1840 to include a discussion of abolition. But Fuller answered that her own interests led her in a different path, and that despite her support for abolition, she had different priorities in the seminar.

Reading the notes of the Conversations kept by Elizabeth Palmer Peabody, we can get a sense of Fuller's humor and values. Rather than preaching to her students about women's rights, she joked about the way most writers on gender "seemed to regard men as animals & women as plants . . . that men were made to get a living—to eat & drink—and women to be ornaments of society." Repeatedly she asked the women to think about the distinctions in society between the masculine and the feminine, but suggested that "the man & the woman had each every faculty & element of mind—but that they were combined in different proportions." Most important, Fuller maintained, whatever the social norms about masculinity and femininity, it was a mistake to stifle one's own abilities in order to conform. "Whatever faculty we felt to be moving within us, that we should consider it a principle of our perfection, & cultivate it accordingly."

She also touched from time to time on issues that were more personal. Asked whether women of genius suffered more than others, she replied staunchly that "thought & feeling brought exquisite pleasures—pleasures worth infinite sacrifices—but they inevitably brought sufferings," and while "she did not love *pain* . . . those who had not suffered had not *lived as yet*." And on the topic of marriage and single life, Fuller insisted that although it was true that one might find love late in life, women should not put off living with the hope of being married someday. "There came a time however when every one *must give up*."[24]

Was Fuller giving up hopes of marriage herself? The early 1840s were certainly a period of emotional crisis. Her two closest friends, Samuel Ward and Anna Barker, declared their love for each other and married. Fuller was half in love with both of them, and their wedding precipitated a depression in which she resigned herself to being unlovable. She had erotic dreams of being visited and comforted by Anna, which she rationalized away as loneliness. Fuller's self-awareness did not extend to sexuality.

She was invited to join the utopian commune at Brook Farm,

and refused, but did sell them one of her cows, helping Nathaniel Hawthorne to see her as a bossy, comic figure. To his future wife, Sophia, he wrote on April 13, 1841: "I went to see our cows foddered yesterday afternoon. We have eight of our own; and the number is increased by a transcendental heifer, belonging to Mrs. Margaret Fuller. She is very fractious, I believe, and apt to kick over the milk-pail. Thou knowest best whether in these traits of character, she resembles her mistress." Soon he was noting, "Beloved, Miss Fuller's cow hooks the other cows and has made herself ruler of the herd, and behaves in a very tyrannical manner."[25]

At the same time, Fuller's friendship with Emerson and his wife, Lidian, became tense and uncomfortable. Emerson was an intellectual soul mate, to be sure. He wrote in March 1843 that Fuller "rose before me at times into heroical & godlike regions, and I could remember no superior women, but thought of Ceres, Minerva, Proserpine, and the august ideal forms of the Fore-world." She gave the "most entertaining conversation in America," and she was a brilliant reader and critic with whom he could share his work in progress and his deepest philosophical thoughts.[26] But Fuller, although she could not admit it to herself, wanted more and, in the name of a Romantic friendship, upped the ante in their relationship through intimate letters, visits, long talks about the meaning of marriage, and late-night meetings. There were blowups when Lidian expressed her jealousy, but also harsh moments when Emerson made as clear as a Transcendentalist could that he could not deliver what Fuller wanted.

In 1843, Fuller spent the summer traveling west, an eye-opening experience of encounters with women of different races and classes, which she described in her book *Summer on the Lakes* (1844). Throughout 1844 as well, she extended her experience beyond New England intellectuals, especially by visiting women prisoners at Sing Sing. Her journalism and literary work were going well, but her life was at an impasse. In her journal in August 1844, she wrote poignantly, "With the intellect I always have—always shall—overcome, but that is not the half of the work. The life, the life, O my God! shall the life never be sweet?"[27]

A JOURNALIST IN THE CITY

At last, in December 1844, at the invitation of publisher Horace Greeley, she moved to New York to write for his *New-York Tribune*. At the age of thirty-four, she was finally on her own, a single working woman in the city. Like Wollstonecraft with Joseph Johnson, she had also found her ideal publisher, and over the next few years she would write 250 articles for Greeley, on subjects ranging from literary criticism to political observation and social commentary. She covered concerts, literature, art exhibits, and lectures as well and established herself as a literary presence.

Living in New York, Fuller also had a romantic affair with a man very different from her friends in Cambridge and Boston. James Nathan was a German businessman, probably the first Jew she had ever met. He was handsome, blue-eyed, dashing, experienced; he had come to New York as an immigrant and made his own way; he played the guitar and loved poetry. On their first date, he emphasized the exotic by taking her to see a panoramic model of Jerusalem. Fuller was swept away. By April 1845, she was writing a review for the *Tribune* titled "Modern Jews." In 1845 and 1846, she wrote Nathan more than fifty embarrassingly revealing letters, pretentious, high-minded, and romantic. She sent him flowers; she gave him poems.

When Fuller asked him about rumors that he was living with an English mistress, Nathan told her a preposterous story, a real *bobbe myseh,* that she was his "ward," an "injured" maiden he was trying to rescue and rehabilitate. She responded with tender and gullible sympathy, even offering to help with the rehabilitation effort: "You are noble. I have decided to abide by you."[28] Nathan must have realized how smitten she had become. Before too long, he left New York, explaining that he felt an urge to travel to the Holy Land, but would write to her and come back.

He left her his Newfoundland dog, Josie, to care for until his return. His letters became infrequent and evasive, but Fuller kept on writing and making emotional demands. "You said in the letter from Florence that you told me you 'would not be able to keep up a real correspondence with me while absent'—But, on the contrary, while you were here you used to be telling me that you could not write because people interrupted you at the office, or because you had a person with you at home who you did not wish to see you writing the letter. I often felt as if you sacrificed both writing to me and seeing me to trifles and wished it had been otherwise for I thought the greater was sacrificed to the lesser, even according to your own view of our relation."[29] Meanwhile she was stuck without a lover and with a dog.

WOMAN IN THE NINETEENTH CENTURY

What made this charade even more humiliating and contradictory was that Fuller was also writing *Woman in the Nineteenth Century,* a feminist manifesto as idiosyncratic, important, and controversial as Wollstonecraft's *Vindication.* She even sent Nathan a copy of it. An expansion of an essay she had written for *The Dial,* it applies Transcendental principles of full human development to women's intellectual and moral growth. At the heart of the book is Fuller's autobiographical portrait of the feminine intellectual she calls "Miranda," a female genius educated by her father but isolated from other women. She also invokes the figure of Cassandra as the other side of the woman of genius, the side of inspiration, prophetic insight, and passionate sensibility. Modern Cassandras, she argues, are "very commonly unhappy at present," because their intellectual style does not fit the prevailing masculine style. Yet both rational Mirandas and intuitive Cassandras represent women's intellectual nature, Fuller concludes, and to develop this nature completely, they should attempt to free themselves from male educational domination.

Cassandra had long been one of the mythical personae of the

feminist intellectual. Florence Nightingale often called herself "poor Cassandra" in her journals and letters to describe her own sense of intellectual frustration and futility. Just as Cassandra, having rejected the love of Apollo, was doomed to utter true prophecies without being believed, Nightingale believed that she herself, having rejected marriage and motherhood for career, had doomed herself to madness and isolation. In her autobiographical essay "Cassandra," written in the 1840s, Nightingale's heroine dies "withered, paralyzed, extinguished" at the age of thirty, asking why women have "passion, intellect, and moral activity," and yet are condemned to lead social lives in which "no one of the three can be exercised." Like Fuller, Nightingale thought that Woman "has an immense provision of wings, which seem as if they would bear her over earth and heaven; but when she tries to use them, she is petrified into stone, her feet are grown into the earth, chained to the bronze pedestal."

Woman in the Nineteenth Century is incoherent and rambling—Orestes Brownson thought it could be read either forward or backward—but it is studded with anecdotes and insights that show Fuller at her best. She insists throughout that distinctions of sex are arbitrary and limiting: "There is no wholly masculine man, no purely feminine woman." She argues that little girls should be raised without sexual stereotypes or restrictions: "In families that I know, some little girls like to saw wood, others to use carpenters' tools. Where these tastes are indulged, cheerfulness and good humor are promoted. Where they are forbidden, because 'such things are not proper for girls,' they grow sullen and mischievous." And she predicts the coming of the Feminist Messiah: "And will not she soon appear? The woman who shall vindicate their birthright for all women; who shall teach them what to claim, and how to use what they obtain?"

In an essay on Wollstonecraft and Fuller written in 1855, George Eliot praised *Woman in the Nineteenth Century* as a book that "has the enthusiasm of a noble and sympathetic nature, with the operation and breadth and large allowance of a vigorous and cultivated understanding. There is no exaggeration of

woman's moral excellence or intellectual capabilities; no injudi-
cious insistence on her fitness for this or that function hitherto
engrossed by men; but a calm plea for the removal of unjust laws
and artificial restrictions, so that the possibilities of her nature
may have room for full development."[30] Fuller seemed to have
gone beyond Wollstonecraft in her ability to integrate reason
and emotion.

LIVING AND ACTING

But Fuller's chosen role of messiah, or feminist vindicator of
women, came with much unhappiness, repression, and self-
sacrifice. In 1846, she decided to go to Europe in pursuit of
Nathan, with the excuse of writing as a travel correspondent for
the *New-York Tribune.* It was her first trip abroad, taken as a
remedy for unrequited love. Nonetheless, as she wrote her way
through Scotland and England, she began to find an environment more supportive and enhancing than any she had experienced ever before. In London she realized, "It was no false
instinct that said I might here find an atmosphere needed to
develop me in ways I need."[31] Working in Europe she could
shape a life for herself beyond the sexual prudery of feminist
America and the sexual prejudice of intellectual Boston.

When she arrived in Edinburgh, she received a letter from
Nathan explaining that he was about to be married and would
not be able to meet her. She allowed herself to feel some healthy
anger at his caddish behavior: "I care not. I am resolved to take
such disappointments more lightly than I have."[32] But it was not
the end of their relationship; he refused to return her letters, and
their exchanges became more and more hostile.

Nonetheless, Fuller threw herself into travel, sight-seeing
energetically (she got stuck one night on top of Ben Lomond),
going to the theater, making new friends, and deepening her
political understanding. In London and in Paris, she met the literary celebrities of the day, including Thomas Carlyle and

George Sand. Most important, she met political revolutionaries and exiles—in London, Giuseppe Mazzini, the leader of the revolutionary movement Young Italy, and in Paris, Adam Mickiewicz, the Polish nationalist, messianic poet, and mystic. Mazzini fueled her interest in Italian politics and won her to the cause; Mickiewicz appealed to her philosophical and religious side, and she attended some meetings of his Circle of God.

Mickiewicz was no puritan; he had a child with his mistress, and he believed in the power of the sexual drives as part of human force. He responded to Fuller's own messianic urges, but counseled her to reject the ascetic, celibate ideal of self-abnegation that she believed intrinsic to it. To Emerson, Fuller wrote that in Mickiewicz she had found "the man I had wished to see, with the intellect and passions in due proportion for a full and healthy human being, with a soul constantly inspiring."[33] Moreover, this guru was seriously interested in her as well. In language that was direct and explicit, he urged her to reconsider her belief in chastity, and to consider her sexual and sensual life as part of her feminism. "For you the first step in your deliverance and of the deliverance of your sex (of a certain class) is to know, whether you are permitted to remain a virgin."[34]

Her friendship with Mickiewicz was in its way as revolutionary as her political conversion by Mazzini. As her "spiritual adviser," a man she respected and admired was acting, in a sense, as her therapist. He was telling her that in repressing her erotic energies she was denying her full power, and thus limiting her usefulness as a leader of women. In a series of wonderful letters, Mickiewicz pursued this theme with eloquence: "You should not confine your life to books and reveries. You have pleaded the liberty of woman in a masculine and frank style. Live and act, as you write." He insisted that full self-development, of woman as well as man, involved a degree of expression, and that to seek happiness was not selfish. "You have persuaded yourself that all you need to is to express your ideas and feelings in books. You existed like a ghost. . . . Do not forget that even in your private life *as a woman* you have rights to maintain. . . . Literature is not the whole life."[35]

The message was truly liberating. In Rome, in 1847, for the first time in her life, Fuller began to live for herself, to arrange her life on her own terms rather than putting everyone else first. She made friends with the extensive Roman community of American expatriate artists and writers. Through Mazzini, she made contact with activists in the movement for Italian unification and for her American readers helped publicize its importance and its relation to other European revolutionary movements. She borrowed money from her family and friends to stay on in Rome. Above all, she entered into a love affair with an impoverished Italian nobleman, Giovanni Ossoli. Although he was casually educated, Catholic, and, at twenty-six, ten years younger than Fuller, he was affectionate and devoted. Fuller kept the relationship a secret. By the winter of 1848 she knew that she was pregnant.

The Italian uprising against Austrian rule had intensified, and Mickiewicz came to Rome to organize Polish exiles in support of the Italian battle for national sovereignty. He was reassuring to Fuller and told her that it was "very natural, very common" to be pregnant.[36] Not so common, however, for an unmarried New England intellectual living on her own in the midst of a war. As the American poet Amy Clampitt writes in "Margaret Fuller, 1847":

> *What would Carlyle, what would straitlaced*
> *Horace Greeley, what would fastidious*
> *Nathaniel Hawthorne, what would all Concord,*
> *all New England, and her own mother*
> *say now? An actuality more fraught*
> *than any nightmare: terrors of the sea,*
> *of childbirth, the massive, slow,*
> *unending heave of human trouble.*

On September 7, 1848, in the village of Rieti, Fuller gave birth to a baby boy, Angelino. Ossoli was there for the birth, but had to return to Rome, where he was in the Civic Guard. Fuller and Ossoli would claim that they had been married, but no one knows for sure, and the odds are against it, although the London Library, which traditionally shelves the works of women under their husbands' names, chivalrously gives her the benefit of the doubt. He would have needed a papal dispensation to marry a Protestant. Meanwhile, Fuller had to leave the baby with his nurse while she returned to Rome to cover the revolution for the *Tribune*.

The baby flourished but the short-lived Roman Republic would collapse. Fuller—now calling herself Marchesa Ossoli—and Ossoli spent some time in Florence, but it became clear to her that they had no real future as a family in Italy, and she decided to break the news to her family and friends and return to the United States.

The reaction of the American and British expatriate community to the radical feminist Margaret Fuller's appearance with a young Italian "husband" and a baby was not entirely kind; there was much scandalous gossip and conjecture. But her mother was overjoyed, and to her Fuller confided her feelings about the tenderness of Ossoli, especially her determination that since he was so much younger, he would be given his freedom if he should someday fall in love with someone else. They booked passage for New York on the *Elizabeth*. After a stormy trip, when they were four hundred yards from the shore of Fire Island, the ship encountered a terrible storm. On July 19, 1850, the *Elizabeth* was wrecked, and Margaret Fuller perished, with Ossoli and their two-year-old son. The bodies were never recovered. She was only forty years old.

THE AFTERLIFE

The shock to the survivors hearing the news was like that of Americans hearing about the death of John Kennedy Jr. in a plane crash in July 1999. Horace Greeley sent his star reporter to cover the story. Henry Thoreau traveled to the beach to hunt for remains—he found only a button that may have been on

Ossoli's coat. There was no public funeral. In 1853, the family put up a monument in Mount Auburn Cemetery in Cambridge.

Fuller's death took place only a few months before the first national Women's Rights Convention, held in Worcester, Massachusetts, in October 1850. Delegates observed a minute of silence, and the president, Paulina Wright Davis, recalled that "we were left to mourn her guiding hand—her royal presence."[37] Her Transcendentalist friends, Emerson, William Henry Channing, and James Freeman Clarke, set out at once to edit her papers as a memoir, and it became an unexpected best-seller. Reading it in 1852, George Eliot wrote to a friend of her pleasure that Fuller had at least found some fulfillment: "It is a help to read such a life as Margaret Fuller's. How inexpressibly touching that passage from her journal—'I shall always reign through the intellect, but the life! the life! O my God! shall that never be sweet?' I am thankful, as if for myself, that it was sweet at last."[38] Gradually, Fuller's American feminist contemporaries came to acknowledge her centrality. Caroline Dall urged *Woman in the Nineteenth Century* "on every female reader" as "the deepest thought and clearest utterance of [America's] noblest woman."[39] Elizabeth Oakes Smith saw in Fuller inspiration for women to "labor with new life"; and reading the memoir, Ednah Dow Cheney felt that "I see myself in it, as I always did in her."[40]

But in 1852, Hawthorne's third novel, *The Blithedale Romance,* painted a spiteful and malicious portrait of Fuller as the flamboyant, sensual feminist writer Zenobia, a presiding figure at Blithedale, a commune much like Brook Farm. Although Hawthorne insisted in his preface that the characters in the novel were "imaginary personages," and that Zenobia was a general type of the "high-spirited Woman, bruising herself against the narrow limitations of her sex," from the moment of its publication readers stubbornly identified Zenobia with Fuller.

We first encounter Zenobia through the eyes of the novel's narrator, Miles Coverdale: "She was dressed as simply as possible, in an American print (I think the dry-goods people call it so), but with a silken kerchief, between which and her gown there was one glimpse of a white shoulder. . . . Her hair—which was dark, glossy, and of a singular abundance—was put up rather soberly and primly, without curls, or other ornament, except a single flower. It was an exotic, of rare beauty, and as fresh as if the hothouse gardener had just clipt it from the stem. That flower has struck deep into my memory. I can both see it and smell it, at this moment. So brilliant, so rare, so costly as it must have been, and yet enduring only for a day, it was more indicative of the pride and pomp, which had a luxuriant growth in Zenobia's character, than if a great diamond had sparkled among her hair."[41]

Coverdale goes on to record his fascination with and disapproval of Zenobia. "Her poor little stories and tracts never did half justice to her intellect; it was only the lack of a fitter avenue that drove her to seek development in literature. She was made (among a thousand other things she might have been) for a stump-oratress. I recognized no severe culture in Zenobia; her mind was full of weeds. It startled me, sometimes . . . to observe the hardihood of her philosophy; she made no scruple of oversetting all human institutions, and scattering them as with a breeze from her fan. A female reformer, in her attacks upon society, has an instinctive sense of where the life lies, and is inclined to aim directly at that spot. Especially, the relation between the sexes is naturally among the earliest to attract her notice."[42]

Coverdale's view of Zenobia's feminism is steadily satiric. Despite her brave words about women ("Thus far, no woman in the world has ever once spoken out her whole heart and her whole mind. The mistrust and disapproval of the vast bulk of society threatens us, as with two gigantic hands at our throats!"), he believes that she is really a slave to romantic conventions and destroyed by her need for love. When she is rejected by the man she loves and drowns herself, Coverdale even finds her suicide arty: "Zenobia, I have often thought, was not quite simple in her death. She had seen pictures, I suppose, of drowned persons, in lithe and graceful attitudes. And she deemed it well and decorous to die as so many village-maidens have, wronged in their first-love, and seeking peace in the bosom of the old, familiar stream. . . . But in Zenobia's case, there was some tint of the Arcadian affectation that had been visible enough in all our lives, for a few months past."[43] Coming so close to the reality of the shipwreck, Hawthorne's cruel words gave rise to rumors that Fuller may indeed have chosen to drown herself rather than face social disapproval.

In the 1880s, Hawthorne's son Julian revived the controversy by publishing a passage from his father's notebooks that reported scurrilous gossip about Ossoli and included his own dismissive and sarcastic view of Fuller. Ossoli, Hawthorne had heard from an acquaintance in Rome, was "half an idiot" who could barely read or write. Fuller's attraction to him showed the "strong and coarse" side of her nature; despite her pretensions, she was a victim of her sexuality, who "proved herself a very woman, after all, and fell as the weakest of her sisters might."[44]

But to women, Fuller was one who had found her radiant sovereign self. In 1880, Lucinda Chandler founded the first Margaret Fuller Society in Boston, which celebrated Fuller's birthday with music and a lecture titled "The Lessons of Margaret Fuller's Life." By 1900, Lillie Devereux Blake had proposed a pavilion and a plaque memorializing Fuller at Fire Island, which was dedicated in July 1901. Unfortunately the wooden pavilion soon washed out to sea, and the bronze plaque has disappeared.[45] There is still no national holiday in her honor, no school or college or institute in her name.

In *The Feminization of American Culture,* Ann Douglas made Fuller the center of nineteenth-century intellectual women's culture. "Fuller was and is so disquieting," Douglas wrote in 1977, "because she does not lend herself to the fantasy life, to the essentially fictional identity, associated with women. Her image can be attacked or ignored, but it is not malleable. Fuller was finally not even metaphorically a heroine of fiction. . . . She openly demanded everything from anyone who knew or would know her; an ultimate effort was the simple price of admission to the sanctum. . . . She saw herself as a complex, rich, and perhaps hopeless problem whose confrontation might precipitate and tax her friends' finest resources. She could not be absorbed; she had to be dealt with. . . . In a culture which was beginning to identify femininity with male relaxation, Fuller found few takers."[46]

But in the decades since the 1970s, Fuller has found many takers. In a review of Robert Hudspeth's great edition of Fuller's letters in 1983, Bell Gale Chevigny marked the end of an era of feminist bonding over the Fuller archives: "More than once, Fuller scholars who had been strangers and even rivals to one another an hour earlier feasted, lunchless, on the scraps of her writing, straining to read a word through the crayoned cancellations of one of her censorious editors, or comparing notes to date a letter or identify a person described. Piecing together the clues, we became collaborators. But in a stroke, Hudspeth's volumes make obsolete these rare-book-room romances and close down whole agencies of amateur detectives."[47] Fuller has moved beyond the rare-book-room romances and finally found her place in literary history, becoming the "radiant sovereign self" who beckons to adventurous women across the ages.

FOUR

The New Women

The Feminine Predicament

In May 1886, Olive Schreiner told her best friend, Havelock Ellis, that she was going to write a preface to Mary Wollstonecraft's *Vindication of the Rights of Woman,* "if they will let me say just what I want to say." Introducing the *Vindication* to Victorian readers was an exciting prospect because Wollstonecraft was one of the women, along with George Sand, Margaret Fuller, and Madame Roland, whom Schreiner most admired. "What I have to say of Mary Wollstonecraft is not to excuse her and not even to *justify* her," she confided to Karl Pearson, a socialist academic she admired, "but to show that her greatness lay in this, her view with regard to marriage; and her action with regard to it. That she is the greatest of all English women because she saw a hundred years ago with regard to sex and sex relationships what a few see today, and what the world will see in three hundred years' time."[1]

But somehow the project did not go as well as Schreiner had expected. "I only glanced through the *Rights of Woman* before, never read it," she explained. "But the great point of interest to me is her life; I mean to treat her as a woman. . . ."[2] Over the next several months, she had frequent writing blocks and begged Pearson to collaborate with her: "I would copy it out to save you time if only you would take the responsibility. The relation of

Mary to Godwin gives one such a splendid opportunity for treating of the ideal form of marriage."[3] Two years later, she was still struggling with the book and putting all of her ideas about the sexes into it. She asked her editor, Ernest Rhys, to wait patiently: "It will take me still two months of night and day work at least to bring Mary Wollstonecraft to an end. It has cost me already about four times as much labour as *African Farm* did, but in one sense immeasurably more because I have gathered into it the result of my whole life's work. . . . Of course I am in all agony of giving birth to it, and perhaps it will not seem so valuable to me when it is done, but now it seems to me that if ever I bring it to an end I shall be willing to die feeling my work is finished!"[4]

In 1889, when she left England to return to South Africa, Schreiner tacitly abandoned the project. After her death, her husband, Samuel Cronwright-Schreiner, gave the unfinished manuscript to the Albany Museum at Grahamstown in South Africa. According to her biographers Ruth First and Ann Scott, it "does not really end, and interestingly, it is not really an evaluation of Wollstonecraft at all."[5] In the introduction, Schreiner used Wollstonecraft as a jumping-off point for her own ideas about women and culture. Although the *Vindication* "appeared to have had little influence," Wollstonecraft was "one of ourselves," for she had seen that "change in women's position revolutionized society, and that the movement was not of class against class but of sex towards sex."[6]

Why was she unable to finish? Schreiner explained that the project was too big, that she had too many ideas and could not condense them into the requisite shape. But obviously writing about Wollstonecraft brought Schreiner uncomfortably close to the contradictions and inconsistencies in her own career, and her inability to end the essay was symptomatic of the unfinished, incomplete strands of her own life. When Ruth First and Ann Scott collaborated on their biography of Schreiner a century later, they too cited the example not only of Wollstonecraft, but of Claire Tomalin's 1974 biography, which had highlighted these issues. As the historian E. P. Thompson had emphasized in his review of Tomalin's book, Wollstonecraft was emblematic of the feminist intellectual because she could not simply rationalize away her identity as a woman. "Wollstonecraft was reminded by every fact of nature and of society that she was a woman. She was *not* a mind which has no sex, but a human being exceptionally exposed within a feminine predicament."[7] And exactly this feminine predicament—reconciling her vocation and her needs, her theory and her desires—defined Schreiner's life.

WOMEN AND THE NEW LIFE

The intellectual milieu of London in the 1880s was one of excitement and optimism, much like the London of the 1780s when Wollstonecraft arrived to work as a journalist. The 1880s were the great decade of socialist organization, not only in political parties and trade unions but also in a spiritualized form of socialist revival concerned with individual transformation, and with parallels to religious conversion. Schreiner's calendar was crammed with meetings of the Progressive Association, the Fellowship of the New Life, and the Men and Women's Club. Her circle encompassed sex radicals such as James Hinton, sexologists such as Ellis and Edward Carpenter, scientists and socialists, philosophers and novelists. Ellis and Carpenter were "preoccupied with sexual pleasure, with how to live communally, how to live equally without fear of authority, how to love one another in a loveless world, how to create beauty democratically in the midst of ugliness and competition."[8]

Just as Wollstonecraft's circle thrilled to the news of revolution abroad, Schreiner's friends were thrilled by the work of Ibsen and the sexual revolution it presaged. In 1884, Schreiner wrote to Havelock Ellis, "Have you read a little play called *Nora?* by Ibsen. . . . It is a most wonderful little work." But she also felt that something was missing in the play: "In the ideal condition for which we look men and women will walk close, hand in hand, but now the fight has oftenest to be fought out alone by both. I think men suffer as much as women from the falseness of the relations. Helmer's life lost as much as Nora's did through the fact that they never lived really together."[9]

For intellectual women of the 1880s, *A Doll's House* was not about the New Woman walking out on the Old Man, but rather a revolutionary call for the redefinition of marriage. From the beginning of the play, where the Helmers have what most would see as a happy marriage, with its three children, servants, and nannies, to the shattering end, Ibsen forced his audience to rethink the meaning of marriage as a relationship between equals. Could the most wonderful thing happen? Nora asks as she leaves. Could they both change so that their life together would be a marriage?[10]

In Britain at least, women intellectuals were no longer isolated and solitary, like Wollstonecraft and Fuller, but part of a community of activists and thinkers. By the 1890s, the terms *New Woman* and *feminist* had come into use for the first time. According to the critic Margaret Gullette, "The nineties were preeminently, despite the persistence of other, flashier labels, a decade of change for women. Perhaps, considering the energies expended in that decade, the incredible expansion of a discourse about women *by women,* the revolutionary changes in fiction that occurred, and the long-term effects of that expansion, the nineties might be regarded as another symbolic starting point of the wider modern movement whose spread is still in the process of becoming worldwide and all-inclusive." In the 1890s, "feminism, which had been the province of intellectuals and activists . . . suddenly became a body of opinions about what women felt and suffered and wanted—opinions to which every woman could personally and emotionally contribute, whatever her age or class or marital status."[11]

When the aspiring young journalist Evelyn Sharp arrived in London in January 1894 to try her hand at a literary career, she felt exhilaration and a sense of opportunity. As she later wrote in her autobiography, "It was very heaven to be young when I came to London in the nineties. I arrived on the crest of the wave that was sweeping away the Victorian tradition . . . no hesitations or personal limitations could destroy the sense of escape I enjoyed."[12] Moreover, 1894 was the Year of the New Woman's Novel, the absolute high-water mark of women's fiction for the entire decade, and a year in which Shaw felt that "we are on the verge of something like a struggle between the sexes for the domination of the London theater," a struggle that women were winning.[13] In 1894, *The Idler* published a special issue on the "advanced woman," which predicted that "the next century will see a new man likewise."[14]

These new men were an eagerly awaited commodity, for New Women wanted true marriages, partnerships in which men and women shared responsibility, their fates inextricably bound together by love rather than law. Schreiner maintained that "the one and only ideal is the perfect mental and physical life-long union of one man with one woman. That is the only thing which for highly developed intellectual natures can consolidate marriage. All short of this is more or less a failure, and no legal marriage can make a relationship other than impure in which there isn't this union. How we should arrange that this great pure form of marriage may be oftenest and most perfectly reached seems to me to be a great problem."[15] Socialists believed that egalitarian marriage would evolve naturally once women were not economically dependent on men. In his treatise *The Origin of the Family, Private Property, and the State* (1884), Friedrich Engels had maintained that "the supremacy of the man in marriage is the simple consequence of his economic supremacy, and with the abolition of the latter will disappear of itself."

Moreover, Engels argued—and many radical thinkers of the 1880s agreed—monogamy was the most evolved and civilized form of human sexuality. Men married to their equals would "tend infinitely more to [become] really monogamous," and mutual affection alone would be the basis of the marital bond. When that disappeared, both partners would readily consent to a separation. Thus the "indissolubility of marriage" would become less and less important or necessary.

At the end of the century, feminist intellectuals turned to Dar-winian evolutionary theory as well as politics and art for their ideas about gender. Because Darwinian theory was so complex and ambiguous, feminists and socialist radicals could appropri-ate evolution for their own purposes. While some imperialists interpreted Darwinian theory to mean that the Anglo-Saxon male was the peak of evolutionary development, feminists emphasized the ongoing process of change, with women as the heralds of the future.[16]

Darwinian thinkers such as Schreiner also believed that human sexuality was evolving toward perfection, in which women's desire would be the equal of men's, and sex, separate from repro-duction, would reach its full aesthetic and emotional splendor. When the lives of men and women were equal, wrote Schreiner in *Woman and Labor,* then the "love of the sexes," at first "a dull, slow-creeping worm," then "a torpid, earthy chrysalis," would become at last "the full-winged insect, glorious in the sunshine of the future." Once sex had truly evolved, prostitution would dis-appear; women would not be economically compelled to sell their bodies, and men would not be driven to pay for sexually responsive partners.

This idealistic, logical view of human relationships was also hopelessly naive and, for women at the end of the century espe-cially, led to both tragicomic and tragic scenarios. The system Engels envisioned turned out to be a form of serial monogamy, with the erosion of legal and sexual restraints protecting women. Some progressive women courageously risked social ostracism by rejecting legal marriage as a vestige of women's ancient enslave-ment, and placing their faith in men's natural monogamous instincts, affections, and honor. In both literature and life, this gamble on the "free union" turned out to be a big mistake, espe-cially if children were involved. For women, real-life choices were very different. Karl Pearson wrote about the joys of the free egalitarian union, but rejected Olive Schreiner and married a conventional feminine homebody. George Gissing champi-oned the free union in *The Odd Women,* but was completely turned off by feminist intellectuals such as Camilla Collett or Louise Michel and married semi-illiterate prostitutes with a drinking problem. One of the best-sellers of the period, Grant Allen's *The Woman Who Did* (1895), warned women of the melodramatic catastrophes in store for them if they tried to reform the marriage laws. Real-life stories outdid fiction in terms of unhappy endings. The free union was a lot freer for some people than for others, and never free for women.

British feminist utopias of the fin de siècle also rewrote men's socialist utopias to include sexual rearrangements. In *Gloriana, or the Revolution of 1900,* Gloriana, whose feminist mother has raised her through childhood and adolescence disguised as the male Hector L'Estrange, gets elected to Parliament, where she is finally unmasked as a woman. Although Gloriana is defeated in her campaign for prime minister, her political vision prevails, and the novel ends with a glimpse of feminist London in the year 1999: "a scene of peaceful villages and well-tilled fields, a scene of busy towns and happy working people, a scene of peace and prosperity, comfort and contentment, which only a righteous government could produce and maintain."

But Ruth First and Ann Scott argue that the popularity of these utopian fantasies shows a kind of retreat from the solutions of public life. "In this new world the divisions between men and women are overcome by recourse to idealization and retreat—this to a 'far-away' place, perhaps uninhabited, perhaps a colony of 'new' men and women."[17] These cheerful visions were far from the reality. Instead, New Women came to see themselves as a tragic generation, compelled to sacrifice love or motherhood or both in the interests of women's future freedom and the full evolution of the sexes.

OLIVE SCHREINER

Olive Schreiner (1855–1920) was the chief spokeswoman of this generation. She was a South African who achieved literary success as a novelist, theorist, and political pamphleteer despite poverty, isolation, lack of education, and a narrow Calvinist upbringing by stern missionary parents in the Cape Colony. By the age of ten, when she began to menstruate, and to think of herself as already a woman, she had rejected her parents' orthodox Christianity and had begun to search for her own answers, reading Emerson, Darwin, Herbert Spencer, and John Stuart Mill. Schreiner's crisis of faith was not unusual for Victorian thinkers, but it was extraordinary that she came to it so young, in such a closed society—the only South African cleric who attempted a critical scholarly analysis of the Bible was excommunicated—and without access to the sort of alternative secular culture that helped English intellectuals to find moral meaning outside of religion. She was always an autodidact.

Schreiner's feminism was also solitary. She was never comfortable with organizations and always felt herself to be different from other women, in their dependence and timidity. Yet she missed having a community of women whose support could sustain her in the face of other sacrifices and hardships. She needed to take an active role in politics, but could not identify with any political party. These internal conflicts, among others, produced a series of psychosomatic disorders and writing blocks, and occasionally took her to the brink of suicidal despair. Her novel *The Story of an African Farm* (1883) was a great success, and her feminist manifesto, *Woman and Labor* (1911), influenced many of her contemporaries. But in many respects, Schreiner's complete intellectual legacy is contained in her letters, which have been fully available only since 1988. In the letters she freely explores and analyzes both the intellectual, scientific, and political controversies of the day, and the contradictions in her own psyche. "Our first duty is to develop ourselves," she wrote a woman friend in 1889. "Then you are ready for any kind of work that comes. The woman who does is doing more to do away with prostitution and the inequalities between man and woman and to make possible a nobler race of human being, than by all the talking and vituperation possible.

It is not against man we have to fight but against *ourselves* within ourselves."[18]

She had originally aspired to become a doctor. "I used to dissect ostriches' and sheep's hearts and livers, and almost the first book I ever bought myself was an elementary physiology," she told Ellis. "It seems to me that a doctor's is the most perfect of all lives, it satisfies the craving to know and also the craving to serve."[19] Women could attend medical school under certain severely limited conditions; they had to pass a rigorous entrance examination in Latin, algebra, geometry, physics, and chemistry. Nurse's training was much simpler, and after years of drudgery as a teacher and governess, Schreiner finally saved enough money to leave South Africa and applied for nurse's training at the Royal Infirmary in Edinburgh. But she became ill and lasted only three days. Two subsequent attempts to enter medical training also failed. "I am very strong and well now," she decided, "but have made up my mind that scribbling will be my only work in life."[20]

Schreiner had been scribbling for a long time. When she was only twenty, and supporting herself as a governess, she had begun a novel provisionally called *Mirage: A Series of Abortions.* In the summer of 1879, she sent the bulky, untidy manuscript, now titled *Lyndall* or *The Story of a South African Farm,* to her closest friend, Mary Brown, who had left South Africa to live with her husband in Lancashire. Brown later recalled that when she unwrapped the manuscript, it smelled like the pungent smoke of farm wood fires, and the pages were blotted and stained with candle grease.

For the next few years, as the novel made the rounds of publishers in Edinburgh and London, Schreiner made intensive revisions. "I have begun to revise *Lyndall,*" she noted in her journal. "Must leave out much, feel a little heart-sore. No one will ever like the book, but I have had the comfort." Finally, *The Story of an African Farm* was accepted by George Meredith at Chapman and Hall. The publisher, Frederic Chapman, was concerned that the heroine, Lyndall, bears a child out of wedlock and asked Schreiner to write in a secret marriage; but she refused indignantly, telling him to "leave the book alone, or I would take it *elsewhere*. He climbed down at once, and said it was only out of consideration for me; I was young, and people would think I was not respectable if I wrote such a book, but of course if I insisted on saying she was not married to him it must be so."[21]

Published in two volumes in 1883, under the pseudonym Ralph Iron, the novel was a surprise success. From its very first sentence—"The full African moon poured down its light from the blue sky into the wide, lonely plain"—*The Story of an African Farm* burst upon the decorous London literary world of 1883 with a note as brilliant and strange as the dazzling blue light of the South African moon. Instead of painting lush English gardens, Schreiner portrayed the dry and alien landscape of the Karoo; instead of depicting civilized ladies and gentlemen discussing courtship over tea, she told the story of passionate dreamers arguing about the oppression of women and children, the meaning of life, the battle of good and evil, and the existence of God. Readers expecting the structured plot of a typical three-volume Victorian novel were startled by the oddity of *African Farm,* with its poetic, allegorical, or didactic passages, and its defiance of narrative and sexual conventions. Tracing the development of three children, the rebellious Lyndall, the good-hearted and unimaginative Em, and the questing and persecuted Waldo, growing up on the farm of the Boer Tant' Sannie, the novel seemed first to be a realistic description of colonial experience; but its real affinities were with works of myth and symbolism that treated the universal longings of the human spirit.

After the publication of *African Farm,* Schreiner was lionized in London, but she was bitterly disappointed to discover that the men who sought her company and friendship as an intellectual did not really love or desire her as a partner. Who were these men? First, there was Havelock Ellis, then a pale medical student who wrote her an admiring letter about the novel and quickly became her "other self," a man with whom she shared scientific interests and to whom she confided her sexual secrets and her messianic yearnings. They saw each other and wrote to each other often, sometimes three times a day. They even shared a house on a holiday in Derbyshire, when Olive, "apparently unconscious of all else," suddenly emerged naked from her room to discuss a scientific matter with Ellis.[22] For his part, Ellis masturbated to obtain live sperm he could show her under a microscope.

But these daring gestures went no further. Ellis thought and wrote about sex all the time, but rarely practiced it. As the relationship continued, without any sexual contact, Schreiner developed more and more debilitating symptoms of psychosomatic illness, with Ellis acting as her physician. In his autobiography, Ellis explained that Schreiner was the sexually demanding person of the two, with "a powerfully and physically passionate temperament," but that he "was not fitted to play the part in such a relationship."[23] He seems to have been impotent with Schreiner (or anyone else—his primary sexual outlet at this time was nocturnal emission), and later she said that she always suspected something morbid and abnormal about him sexually.

The second "New Man" in Schreiner's life was the Nordically handsome Karl Pearson, a barrister and mathematician who was also such a committed socialist that he had changed the spelling of his name in honor of Marx. In July 1885, he convened a group of advanced, freethinking men and intellectual New Women to form a Men and Women's Club, which met once a month for four years to read papers about the relation between the sexes. Pearson wanted to call the club the Mary Wollstonecraft, but Schreiner thought that impulse was precisely the problem. For Pearson and the other male members, the sex question was simply the Woman Question. The female members were curious about male sexuality, men's emotions, masculine conflicts; but the club's discussion remained steadily fixed on women, especially on prostitution.

As the two most intense intellectuals of the group, Schreiner and Pearson were drawn together, and in her letters to him, she expounded some of her most original and perceptive ideas about social change. "Three things seem to me to have taken the place of the old powers that moved society," she wrote to Pearson in October 1886. "Science has taken the place of Theology, the press has taken the place of the ruler (to a large and always growing larger extent) and fiction has taken the place which painting and drama occupied in other ages. . . . These are the three *living* powers of our age, whose rule is only beginning."[24]

But Pearson was unable to transcend his own cultural assumptions in such a visionary way. He established the club's agenda of detached, scientific discourse, a style that the women found inhibiting. Moreover, and much worse, Schreiner fell in love with him, and he did not feel any sexual desire for her. Another woman in the club gave her secret away, and their friendship disintegrated in a series of awkward and painful letters, wherein Schreiner tied herself in knots trying to deny that she had ever felt anything but intellectual comradeship toward him.

In the embarrassing aftermath of the affair, Schreiner left England and made her way back to South Africa, halted along the way by more and more debilitating attacks of asthma, migraine, stomach trouble, back pain, and depression. "As a woman who suffered chronically and excruciatingly from asthma," one critic notes, "Schreiner was something of a specialist in suffocation."[25] But also, as a woman who suffered chronically from suffocation, Schreiner was something of a specialist on asthma. Her writing slowed to a halt; at this point her Wollstonecraft project, understandably, was put aside. For many years she wrote only very short pieces, which she called "dreams" or "allegories," about women's suffering and sacrifice in the interests of future free generations. In one short story, "The Buddhist Priest's Wife" (1891), she unburdened herself of the story of her unrequited love for Pearson, who had meanwhile married another woman in the club. The nameless heroine of the story arranges a final meeting with the man she secretly loves on the eve of her departure from England; they discuss the difficult situation of the advanced woman, and he jokes about how she should marry a Buddhist priest. Of course, Buddhist priests do not marry. But he does not realize until too late what her real feelings for him are.

When Schreiner returned to South Africa in 1889, she was regarded as a celebrity, although a strange, eccentric, and prickly one. Schreiner was trying to live on the frontiers of socialist, feminist, and anticolonialist struggle, and she felt isolated and despairing. To Edward Carpenter she wrote in 1892, "Edward, you don't know how bad things are in this land; we flog our niggers to death, and wealth as the only *possible* end and aim in life is more recognized here than in any country in the world. . . . There are money-making whites, and down-trodden blacks, and nothing between. And things will have to be so much worse here before they can get better; in Europe we have almost got to the bottom already and the tide is going to turn."[26]

By the summer of 1893, she had met Samuel Cronwright, a handsome young ostrich farmer, aged thirty, from the Karoo. "The wish to marry comes towards the man of *action,* the philistine, with me," she confided to Edward Carpenter.[27] Cronwright was no intellectual, but that may have seemed like a relief. He loved her, and he wanted to have a child. "That's one great bond between. No other man I've known has the same feeling about having children."[28] She also confided in Carpenter about Cron's sexual attractiveness, sure that he would sympathize. "When he came to see me he came very properly dressed, high collar, white shirt, tie, a very handsome young man. As we sat talking in the sun before my door, he suddenly unbuttoned his collar and threw it off without a word. In a few moments off went his necktie; then he took off his coat! then in his waistcoat he rolled up his shirtsleeves!"[29] She insisted that he roll up his shirtsleeves for a photograph.

But despite Cron's muscular forearms, she was unsure about marriage. In fall 1893, Schreiner had a number of gynecological operations, for a "twisted" womb. But by February, the doctors were reassuring her that she would be able to have a child; her health seemed good. They married quietly at the end of the month, and he took her name—"This has touched me more than anything he had done for me."[30] She was pregnant by September.

"Have you a good book giving the way a woman should treat herself while she is pregnant?" she wrote to her friend Mary Sauer. "If you have will you lend it me?"[31] Tragically, however, their daughter died, somewhat mysteriously, only a few hours after her birth on April 30, 1895. The labor was supervised by a doctor, and the baby was delivered with instruments under chloroform, weighing nine pounds, nine ounces. During the night, the baby was taken to the nurse's room so that Olive could rest, and in the morning it was discovered dead. She never recovered psychologically from the loss, and there are suggestions in her letters that she suspected, but could not discuss, the possibility of medical carelessness. Subsequently she had numerous miscarriages, perhaps as many as seven. In the absence of children, and because of their diverging political and professional interests, she and Cronwright drifted apart. Although she always maintained that they had the ideal marriage, in reality they lived separately for most of it and, toward the end of her life, quarreled bitterly.

Schreiner's political circumstances in South Africa were also troubled. She defended the Boers against the British, but despite her good intentions never clearly confronted the racial issues of South African nationalism, so that her support of the Boers could be taken as support for white rule. In terms of the franchise, she advocated political representation in principle for black and white, woman and man; but when it came to detailed proposals, she wanted to see adult franchise "with a high educational test" that would "tell heavily against the natives."[32]

The most important book of Schreiner's last years was *Woman and Labor* (1911), a summing-up of her ideas about the importance of women's access to every kind of work, and the centrality of maternity in binding women of all races and times together. In it, Schreiner demanded "labor and the training which fits us for labor" for all women and argued that the sharing of all labor by men and women would lead to "camaraderie and the existence of common, impersonal interests and like habits of thought and life." At the end of the book, like a feminist Moses, she looked into the future in which men and women would share all their responsibilities and joys: "To those of us who, at the beginning of a new century, stand with shaded eyes, gazing into the future, striving to descry the outlines of the shadowy figures which loom before us in the distance, nothing seems of so gracious a promise as the outline we seem to discern of a condition of human life in which a closer union than the world has yet seen shall exist between the man and the woman."

But Schreiner did not live to see these changes take place. After World War I, she traveled back to London for a visit, and Cronwright, who had not seen her for six years, joined her there. He was shocked by her appearance and barely recognized her: "She had aged greatly. Her bright hair was grey; her glorious eyes were almost closed and but little remained in the woman of that bursting elemental force which was so arresting and dominating in her tremendous personality. Her bright, vivid colour had gone; she looked small and dark and Jewish; her vibrating voice was so gentle."[33] A few weeks later, Olive Schreiner returned alone to South Africa, where she died quietly in December 1920.

ELEANOR MARX: DAUGHTER OF THE REVOLUTION

Olive Schreiner and the brilliant, vivacious Eleanor Marx (1855–98) had met and become close friends sometime in 1882. Eleanor was the youngest of three daughters of Karl Marx, and she carried on her father's mission as a political worker for socialism and an editor and translator of Marx's letters and writings. The three sisters—the sons had died in childhood—grew up in a peculiar atmosphere of revolutionary fervor and bourgeois respectability. Although he was frequently in debt and on the brink of bankruptcy, Marx managed, through various legacies and the generosity of his friend and comrade Engels, to maintain a conventional Victorian family life for his daughters, with music lessons and balls. Their facade of respectability was indeed so thick that Eleanor Marx's biographer Yvonne Kapp felt the need to defend the Marxes against politically correct British leftists a century later: "To be sure . . . it strikes one as grotesque that a man of such powerful intellect, a woman of such proper spirit as Karl Marx and his wife should have . . . persisted in employing two domestic servants and encouraged their almost full-grown daughters to draw and sing and thump upon the piano with indifferent talent while the household fell about their ears." But, Kapp lamely explains, at the time the gulf between the professional and the proletarian way of life was "vast and unbridgeable."[34]

Eleanor, called Tussy in the family, both enjoyed feminine home life and became the surrogate son as well, the intellectual and political heir in a family of girls. (After Marx's death, she would learn that she had a half brother, Freddy Demuth, who had been passed off as the housemaid's son and hinted to be the son of the long-suffering Engels.) As a little girl, Eleanor was imaginative and verbal, with a great love "for talking and telling stories. This," her mother believed, "she got from the Grimm Brothers, with whom she does not part day or night."[35]

In addition to the fairy tales that shaped her consciousness of romantic love and lifelong fidelity, Eleanor loved listening to her father read from Homer, Cervantes, and especially Shakespeare. He treated her as a serious person, and she grew up full of intellectual self-confidence. When she was moved by a church service, he set her straight on the merits of atheism. She listened to political discussions at the dinner table and, at the age of ten, wrote frequent letters to Abraham Lincoln advising him on the conduct of the Civil War. Her education was patchy—Kapp calls it "twittercrumbs of learning"[36]—but she traveled often to Manchester and to Paris, and in her teens served as her father's secretary.

After the collapse of the Paris Commune in 1871, various refugees and émigrés came to stay with the Marxes, and one of them, Hippolyte Lissagaray, a Basque French journalist, courted Eleanor. Indeed, as Ruth Brandon points out in her exuberant study of the New Women, although Marx did not want his daughters to marry penniless revolutionaries and spend their lives in debt and drudgery, penniless revolutionaries were exactly the sort of young men the Marx girls were most likely to meet.[37] Both of Eleanor's older sisters had married such men, but in her case, her parents were horrified: Lissagaray was thirty-four to her seventeen, penniless, beyond the pale. They forbade her to see him; she developed a range of hysterical ailments including anorexia nervosa, and Marx had to take her to the spa at Karlsbad to recuperate. Afterward, they withdrew their objection to an engagement, and it dragged on for years as Lissagaray wrote his history of the Commune, and Eleanor translated it into English. She finally broke off the engagement in 1882, when she was twenty-seven.

But out of the frying pan, into the fire. One of the reasons she broke the engagement was that she had met another man, Edward Aveling, probably the most disliked militant atheist, socialist radical, and Don Juan in London. At this time, according to Beatrice Potter's disapproving description, Eleanor was the epitome of the bohemian young woman, "comely, dressed in a slovenly picturesque way with curly black hair flying about in all directions. Fine eyes full of life and sympathy, otherwise ugly features and expression, and complexion showing signs of an unhealthy excited life, kept up with stimulants and tempered by narcotics."[38]

Aveling was pale, thin-lipped, with slicked-down, dark hair. Shaw thought he looked like a lizard, and Olive Schreiner disliked him almost on sight: "I have fear and horror of him when I am near. Every time I see him this shrinking grows stronger."[39] Later, the depth of his socialist commitment would be rudely called a "sudden conversion"; "he never touched Socialism in any way or knew anything about it until in 1882 he took to reading in the British Museum, and unfortunately fell into the company of some of the Bohemian socialists, male and female, who flourish there."[40] He had a reputation as a scrounger who did not pay his debts.

The couple went on holiday in Derbyshire with Schreiner and Havelock Ellis, who thought Aveling was all right, if somewhat odd and careless, and who perceived in Eleanor's "potent . . . axillary fragrance" the full force of her sexuality and personality.[41] But Aveling had been the lover of Annie Besant, had a wife living somewhere in London, and exuded a potent, if snaky, sexual fragrance of his own. One friend said about him, "Strange to say, in spite of an exterior that almost recalled Quasimodo, he always exercised a remarkable fascination for women."[42] Eleanor confided to a friend that "it was Edward who brought out the feminine in me. I was irresistibly drawn to him."[43]

Karl Marx died in 1883, and in the summer of 1884, Eleanor began to live openly with Aveling. To her sister Laura she wrote: "I am very fond of Edward Aveling—and he says he is fond of me—so we are going to 'set up' together. . . . I need not say that this resolution has been no easy one for me to arrive at."[44] To her friend Dolly Radford, Eleanor added: "You know he is married, & I cannot be his wife *legally,* but it will be a *true* marriage to me—just as much as if a dozen registrar's [*sic*] had officiated . . . and if love, a perfect sympathy in taste and work and a striving for the same ends can make people happy, we shall be so."[45] They set up housekeeping in a flat in Fitzroy Street, and Eleanor continued to defend her decision as politically appropriate. She wrote to the young socialist John Lincoln Mahon, "We have both felt that we were justified in setting aside all the false and really immoral bourgeois conventionalities, and I am happy to say we have received—the only thing we care about—the approbation of our friends and fellow-socialists."[46]

Like her peer group, Eleanor approached the question of marriage and setting up a household as both an issue of political principle and a complex social performance. Some of her fellow socialists held that a proper socialist home should not have servants, but Eleanor had grown up with them. On their return from the country, they moved to rooms on Great Russell Street, and Eleanor suddenly found herself the maid-of-all-work. Needless to say, the setting aside of immoral bourgeois conventionalities did not mean that Aveling would do his share of the housework. "Edward is the very devil for untidiness," she lamented to her sister.[47] Although she hated housework, Eleanor wound up doing it anyway. "How I wish people didn't live in houses and didn't cook, and bake, and wash, and clean! I fear I shall never, despite all efforts, develop into a decent 'Hausfrau,' " she wrote in April 1885. Later she discovered the joys of enamel paint and painted everything in the house: "If the climate only permitted, I should enamel myself."[48] Unlike Charlotte Perkins Gilman and other American feminist radicals, she did not rethink the organization of housekeeping.

In April 1885, Aveling developed an inflammation in the kidneys, had to give up his various classes and jobs, and went off to Ventnor for a rest, while she supported them both. By June, even Eleanor was wondering whether she had made a terrible choice. To Olive Schreiner she poured out her fears and resentments:

"I am so tired, Olive. The *constant* strain of appearing the same when nothing is the same, the constant effort not to break down, sometimes becomes intolerable. How natures like Edward's . . . are to be envied, who in an hour completely forget everything. If you had seen him, for example, going about today like a happy child with never a sorrow or sin in his life, you would have marvelled. Yet apart even from all the other troubles, we have mere money troubles enough to worry an ordinary man or woman into the grave. I often don't know where to turn or what to do. It is almost impossible for me now to get work that is even decently paid for, and Edward gets little enough. And while I feel utterly desperate he is perfectly unconcerned!"[49]

But in public, Edward and Eleanor, who was calling herself Madame Marx-Aveling, set themselves up as the model of a modern Marxist marriage. The Men and Women's Club was uncertain about whether Eleanor should be invited to join them, but she settled the matter by refusing, partly to devote her time to the socialist cause, "the highest most important work"; and partly because "it is a very difficult matter to advocate certain things in theory, and to have the courage to put one's theories into practice. Probably many of the good ladies in the club would be much shocked at my becoming a member of it."[50] The couple shared an avid interest in the theater; Eleanor had actually trained for a while as an actress, and Aveling was a playwright of dogged determination, but, says Kapp, "sterling insignificance, whom nothing could discourage."[51] They began to travel together, to speak together and separately at political rallies too.

In 1886, they collaborated on an essay on "the woman question" for the *Westminster Review*. It was an extraordinarily high-minded, confident, and lyrical piece about the emancipation of women and the evolution of marriage under socialism. In the ideal socialist society of the future, they wrote, "monogamy will gain the day . . . the highest ideal seems to be the complete, harmonious, lasting, blending of two human lives. Such an ideal, almost never attainable today, needs at least four things . . . love, respect, intellectual likeness, and command of the necessities of life." When these were achieved, they promised, "there will no longer be one law for the woman and one for the man. If the coming society, like European society today, regards it as right for man to have mistresses as well as wife, we may be certain that the like freedom will be extended to women. Nor will there be the hideous disguise, the constant lying, that makes the domestic life of almost all our English homes an organized hypocrisy."[52]

This passage would surely come back to haunt and shame Eleanor Marx, for the domestic life she shared with Aveling would prove to be one of disguise, lying, hypocrisy, and betrayal. Having committed herself in print to such a utopian vision, and to such implicit complacency about her own relationship, it would be humiliating as well as hurtful to discover how much Aveling had deceived her.

Meanwhile, she was beginning to realize that her partnership with Aveling was at the least a social handicap, and that they were ostracized and boycotted. Sometime in 1887, she attempted suicide by taking an overdose of opium, but she was discovered and revived. But she continued to support him, encourage him in his playwriting efforts, plead with her political colleagues to overlook his faux pas, bad judgment, lack of scruples, and irresponsibility, defend him against charges of swindling the party, and get theatrical friends to read his work. In 1886, they staged a private reading of Ibsen's *Nora*. Eleanor was also translating Flaubert's *Madame Bovary,* and identifying with its heroine. "This strong woman," she wrote in her preface, "feels there *must* be some place for her in the world; there *must* be something to do—and she dreams."[53] Why did she stay with Aveling? She later was reported to say: "One alternative is to leave Edward and live by myself. I can't do that; it would drive him to ruin and it wouldn't really help me. . . . Our tastes were much the same. . . . We agreed on Socialism. We both loved the theater. . . . We could work together effectively." Yvonne Kapp adds, "He did not exact subservience from her as his housekeeper and bedfellow but gave her encouragement and self-confidence to become a writer, an able speaker, and a brilliant organizer in her own right. Of how many clever, vain, and selfish men could this be said?"[54]

Eleanor involved herself wholeheartedly in socialist labor activities. "Life seems to be becoming one long strike," she wrote to her sister in 1889. "First there was the Dock Strike. No sooner was that over than I was summoned to Silvertown, and for 10 mortal weeks, I travelled daily to that out-of-the-way place; speaking every day—often twice a day, in all weathers in the open air. I began to hope for peace—when lo! the Gas Strike begins."[55] She maintained her concern for poor women and in 1890 hired a Russian woman to tutor her in Yiddish to supplement her German. "Eleanor explained to me," the woman recalled, "that she was active among the Jewish working women in Whitechapel, and that in the interests of socialist propaganda it was more sensible for her to learn Yiddish than to wait for the ignorant masses of immigrants from Eastern Europe to become Anglicized."[56] Moreover, she felt in her soul that although an atheist, she was a Jew and the descendant of rabbis.

Nonetheless, the Marx-Avelings celebrated Christmas, even if Eleanor felt that "Christmas without children is a mistake."[57] She had always loved children, but would never have them. In 1895, they bought a house at No. 7 Jews Walk, and she wrote to her sister at Christmas, "This is a stupid & sad time where there are no children. I sometimes wonder if it is worse to have had & lost little ones or never to have had them." Kapp comments, "One cannot but ask why Eleanor, with her strong maternal feelings, should have remained childless. It could not have been her wish; it may have been her incapacity. But Aveling's early marriage had been without issue, and never in a life of extensive lechery and in an era of primitive contraception is a paternity suit ever known to have been brought against him, from which it would not be unfair to draw the conclusion that he was sterile."[58]

Aveling's wife had died in 1892, and he was legally free to remarry; but with Eleanor, he continued only to demand more in the way of money and inheritance. On June 8, 1897, while Eleanor was at the International Congress of the Miners, Aveling, under the alias Alec Nelson, married an actress named Eva Frye at Chelsea Register Office. For several weeks he continued to keep the marriage a secret. Then suddenly, at the end of August, he walked out on Eleanor, taking everything that he could sell. On September 1, he returned, without apology or explanation, but that evening may have threatened her with some form of blackmail; she paid him, and he stayed with her for a while, desperate for money. He had borrowed all he could get from everyone they knew; "his exploits as a borrower," wrote George Bernard Shaw, "have grown into a Homeric legend."[59]

Eleanor continued to make excuses for him, and to live with him. When he became seriously ill with pneumonia, she tenderly and patiently nursed him through an expensive surgery, and through his recuperation at a seaside resort. But on March 31, 1898, Eleanor received a letter telling her about Aveling's secret marriage to Eva Frye. No one really knows what happened next, but there may have been an agreement between them of a suicide pact. Eleanor sent her maid to the chemist for chloroform and prussic acid "for the dog." When it arrived (Aveling having mysteriously dashed off to town), she took a bath, ritually dressed in white, like a bride, took the poison, like Emma Bovary, and lay down on her bed. Before noon she was dead. She was forty-three.

Aveling's behavior after the suicide was not gentlemanly, and

Eleanor's friends did not even know about his marriage. It was rumored that he went to a cricket match the next day. At the inquest, he quibbled in all his answers about their relationship and about her suicide threats. At the funeral he was dry-eyed. He inherited, went to live with Eva, in Battersea, where he died four months later.

THE AFTERLIFE

Olive Schreiner believed that her struggles were helping to forge the freer choices of a new generation of men and women. In a message to future generations, she wrote in *Woman and Labor:*

"You will look back at us with astonishment! You will wonder at passionate struggles that accomplished so little; at the, to you, obvious paths to attain our ends which we did not take . . . at the great truths staring us in the face, which we failed to see; at the truths we grasped at, but could never quite get our fingers round. You will marvel at the labor that ended in so little;—but, what you will never know is how it was thinking of you and for you, that we struggled as we did and accomplished the little which we have done; that it was in the thought of your larger realization and fuller life, that we found consolation for the futilities of our own."

Looking back at the New Women, at Schreiner and Marx, from the perspective of the late twentieth century, how should we sum up their lives? Did the future fulfill their dreams? Do women today have a larger realization and fuller lives? And if so, were the rule-breaking New Women martyrs to our freedom? In his book *The New Spirit* (1890), Havelock Ellis predicted that the New Woman will announce "a reinvigoration as complete as any brought by barbarians to an effete and degenerating civilization."[60] Certainly, as we shall see, they inspired the women who came directly after, especially the suffragists who read Schreiner's allegories aloud in Holloway Prison, and the radicals of the 1920s like Vera Brittain.

But feminist intellectuals returned to Schreiner and Marx with a sense of discovery in the 1970s. The politics and preoccupations of the decade seemed right for these voices from the past. In 1970, Ruth First, a South African antiapartheid activist, member of the Communist Party, and wife of exiled South African Communist Party leader Joe Slovo, broadcast a BBC program about Olive Schreiner. In 1963, First had been arrested for treason and imprisoned in solitary confinement without trial, an experience that led to her book *117 Days,* and her daughter Shawn Slovo's film *A World Apart.* First had known of Schreiner since childhood, but her interest was sparked by the women's liberation movement. It led to a book contract, and then to a collaboration on the biography with Ann Scott, an editor of the feminist magazine *Spare Rib. Olive Schreiner* was published in 1980; in September 1982, while teaching at the Centre of Southern African Studies in Mozambique, First was killed by an assassin's letter bomb. The British feminist Liz Stanley eulogized First as "a direct successor of Olive Schreiner. These two women . . . both concerned to live, to practice, their convictions and not just to preach them, show the power, insightfulness, and humanity of feminism in action."[61]

In the joint biography, First and Scott concluded that Schreiner's personal and political isolation, her refusal to join a party, her constant traveling, and her preachiness restricted the impact of her ideas. "Her social science was too nervously evolutionist; her analysis of South Africa intuitive and unsystematic. . . . For women as for Africans she was an advocate of an alternative life and politics, but like the tracts of the abolitionists pleading for the subjected, her writing on the women's question was didactic and rhetorical." Moreover, Schreiner could not settle in any place long enough to put her theories to the test. "The absence of an involvement in any one community for any length of time meant inevitably that she lived at one remove from the investigative work being done at the turn of the century by socialists interested in the condition of women, or from the local work of a sustained campaign on demands that she supported like adult suffrage and equal pay. This actual distance gave to her writing on women a certain benevolence, perhaps even the benevolence of someone from a mission station." Schreiner, they felt, was a woman who took "gigantic leaps," but who never was able to "resolve those issues of personal and productive relationships—her needs and her sense of self as a woman with those of her work as a writer—and the tension persisted to the end."[62]

Yet *Every Secret Thing* (1997), the memoir of Ruth First and Joe Slovo written by their daughter Gillian, suggests that indeed Ruth First was herself insecure and divided about her political and feminine roles, a woman who wore designer clothes, made regular visits to the hairdresser, and tried to juggle the fierce, conflicting expectations of her mother, husband, and three daughters, as well as her underground political work. No more able to resolve the tensions between the different parts of her life than Schreiner a century before, First was more continually invested in a political movement but made costly compromises in marriage and family.

Meanwhile, those involved in the race struggle of modern South Africa tended to be scornful of Schreiner's feminism. When the First-Scott biography came out in 1980, one of the reviewers was the South African novelist Nadine Gordimer, who judged that in "South Africa, now as then, feminism is regarded by people whose thinking on race, class, and color Schreiner anticipated as a question of no relevance to the actual problem of the country—which is to free the black majority from white minority rule."[63] Gordimer was impressed, nonetheless, with the way the two biographers combined "the two dominant aspects of Schreiner's character, her feminism and her political sense, and each writer provides a corrective for the preoccupational bias of the other."[64] Was Ruth First, she wondered, able to take a psychoanalytic approach to Schreiner's life "because of the new attitude to psychoanalysis that has been penetrating Marxist thinking through the work of Lacan and others since the failure of the 1960s student uprising in Paris?"[65] But by the time Gordimer's review became the foreword to a paperback edition of the

Schreiner biography in 1989, Schreiner's work was having something of a revival in South Africa, and Gordimer had modified her assessment of feminism "South African style" and saw it as "an essential component in the struggle to free our country from all forms of oppression, political and economic, racist and sexist."[66]

During the 1970s, Yvonne Kapp (1903–99) was also writing her two-volume biography of Eleanor Marx. In many respects, Kapp too personified the division between ideology and style that seemed to pervade British feminism. As Eric Hobsbawm noted in his obituary of Kapp for *The Guardian,* she struck new acquaintances as an elegant "lady of impeccable breeding," who served a delicious cake at afternoon tea and had once worked for Paris *Vogue.* In fact, she was a communist of sixty years' standing, "tough as oxhide," and a "spectacular rebel against patriarchy" who had nonetheless supported her feckless artist husband and daughter as a freelance journalist. After the marriage broke up during World War II, Kapp set up a household with Margaret Mynatt, the editor of the *Collected Works of Marx and Engels.* Yet out of this temple of Marxist scholarship, Kapp produced a biography of Marx's daughter that is funny, humane, and free from "ideological loyalty."[67] Summing up Eleanor's tragic life, Kapp concluded that while "some may think that throughout Eleanor's years with Aveling she had been sublimating an unsatisfactory relationship in compulsive political activity . . . that is to misinterpret the story of a life molded and directed from earliest youth to that end."[68] Kapp was still feisty and witty in March 1998, when she sent a letter to the Eleanor Marx Centennial Conference at the University of London, wishing she could be present to hear about the distance traveled in the spheres of socialism and feminism, not only since the late nineteenth century but also since her own biography.

In an article published at the time of the conference, Faith Evans described Eleanor Marx as "a symbol of the woman who is almost free."[69] But that "almost" has to be stretched very far. To my mind, however, Schreiner and Marx were victims of a feminism that was still confining, Victorian, and self-punishing.

That Schreiner's manifesto should be called *Woman and Labor* was emblematic of the period's emphasis on work as the route to freedom. Impossible to think of the humorless Schreiner writing about women and play, or imagining pleasures, let alone joys, outside of the twin spheres of principle and duty.

Schreiner did not get from the conflicted Ellis, the "sexologist," the kind of liberatory advice Margaret Fuller got from Adam Mickiewicz. She and Marx were at home with the kind of political engagements Fuller had to travel abroad to find, but in many respects they too were oddly women of the word and the book, living through literature. *Punch* was not totally off the mark when it satirized the New Woman in April 1894 as "Donna Quixote," buried in a mound of radical books with Tolstoy and Ibsen at her feet and the Yellow Book close to hand. Along with her books, Donna Quixote brandishes above her head a large key, the latchkey, sign of her freedom to come and go as she pleased. A third essential accessory of the New Woman was the cigarette.

But in comparison to their dashing and dangerous male contemporaries, the New Women generally were a somber lot. Decadent or aesthetic men mocked the moral earnestness of New Women and were convinced of the intellectual and artistic superiority of men. Olive Schreiner, according to Wilde, moved to the East End of London "because that is the only place where people do not wear masks upon their faces," but, he went on, "I have told her that I live in the West End because nothing interests me except the mask."[70] Wilde's theory of style, surface, and artifice could not have been more different from Schreiner's gray realism. New Women in the theater, such as Elizabeth Robins, dreamed of a profound theater of the future, unlike the polished drawing-room comedy of Wilde's hits, but when their production of *Hedda Gabler* opened, Wilde mocked the dowdiness and political correctness of the enterprise. "The house was dreary," he wrote to Ethel Greenfell, "the pit full of sad vegetarians, and the stalls occupied by men in mackintoshes and women in knitted shawls of red wool."[71]

On their side, New Women writers on both sides of the Atlantic often deplored the frivolity, self-indulgence, and immorality of Wilde and the aesthetes and recorded their horror of the mask and the performance. In the essay "Art for Truth's Sake," the American writer Elizabeth Stuart Phelps recorded her opposition to art for art's sake, and her belief that "the province of the artist is to portray life as it is; and life *is* moral responsibility."[72] Most New Women were shocked by male homosexuality and harshly condemned the moral behavior of gay men. In an unpublished letter of August 1891, the novelist Sarah Grand recorded her responses to the English bible of decadence: "I am just reading *Dorian Gray,* and find it only exasperating so far—the outcome of an unlovely mind, I should say—poor, forced stuff, conceited, untrue to all that is elevating in nature & in art, and not improved by being polished up in passages to a laboured smartness, which one's head acknowledges but one's heart abhors. The personality of the writer oppresses one all through. I know very little of him personally, & feel now that I should certainly hate him if I knew more."[73]

By the trial they did hate him. A few, very few, New Women offered Wilde support. In an article for a Russian journal in 1895, Eleanor Marx defended Wilde against the abuse of the press and the cynicism of theater owners who profited from his plays but would not use his name.[74] But the English feminist newspaper, *Woman's Signal,* welcomed "the fall of Mr. Oscar Wilde and the malodorous decadents," which "must hearten every mother who, in the love of God, is training her sons to habits of purity and manliness."[75] Olive Schreiner made no comments on the Wilde case, although she would probably have sympathized with him. In her friendship with Edward Carpenter, she was relaxed and open-minded about homosexuality. But she too had little taste for aestheticism or the sophisticated word-play of the Wildean style.

Of course, Wilde's career ended as abruptly and tragically as that of the most puritanical or depressed New Woman. But he was never, as they were, the prisoner of principle. In her excellent study of this generation, Ruth Brandon shrewdly points out how thoroughly they were governed and mastered by "the notion of living strictly according to one's principles. The myriad societies and groupuscules that flourished among the radicals of the late nineteenth century reflected, indeed, a positive obsession with principle: to each man his own ruling principle, whether it be militant vegetarianism, universal suffrage, or free love. In those circles every move one made was, in some sense, a matter of principle. This habit of thought came particularly easily to Olive, reinforcing as it did her tendency to set herself stern goals and standards, which, of course, she invariably failed to attain."[76] In the life of Olive Schreiner, this obsession with principle could be suffocating. In the life of Eleanor Marx, it could be noble and magnificent. "In many ways," Brandon asserts, "the uniquely tragic and brave figure of Eleanor Marx dwarfs her contemporaries. She is altogether more serious, more heroic, than they are."

Yet somehow the men of this generation seemed to fare better. Marx's male contemporaries, Brandon observes, "saw themselves as the architects of a new social order," and the most they could do for it was to "live their lives according to the newly forged ideals," which they did by living for themselves and without guilt. The men "used principle . . . to free themselves from any feelings of guilt," and "to displace guilt . . . onto others." The women, by and large, could not suppress guilt for behaving in "unfeminine" ways, no matter how strong the pull of the principles to which they were committed.[77]

The New Women of the nineteenth century did not have the vocabulary to analyze this "great truth staring them in the face." But in the next wave of rule-breakers, newer women would imagine a fuller life.

FIVE

Transition Woman

Charlotte Perkins Gilman

In the United States, more than in Europe and England, the nineties were a decade of hope for women. American women writers greeted the new century with optimism and excitement and believed that they were at the brink of a new era of opportunity and emancipation. In 1893, the Woman's Pavilion at the Chicago World's Fair celebrated women's achievements; in 1894, the National American Women's Suffrage Association first proclaimed the principle of "equal pay for equal work." At the same time, black women intellectuals, who called themselves "race women," were organizing women's associations with racial progress as the agenda: the National Colored Women's League in 1892; the National Federation of Afro-American Women in 1895; and the National Association of Colored Women's Clubs (NACW) in 1896. "Race women argued black women had a special mission in the elevation of race—tied it to the family or tropes of the family: moral perfectibility, economic prosperity, political autonomy of the black family."[1]

The most influential American feminist at the turn of the century was Charlotte Perkins Gilman (1860–1935). Gilman's great intellectual contribution was to apply Darwinian thought and anthropological theory to the questions of the home, the family, and the sexual division of labor. While an earlier feminist generation had appealed to Victorian anthropology to support their beliefs in a golden age of matriarchy, Gilman used the theory of natural selection and survival of the fittest to argue that women's human development had been restricted and repressed by economic dependency on men, and that reforms in education and the home could free them to evolve intellectually through the natural process of conflict and testing.

Through her lectures, her fiction, and her books, Gilman, one contemporary noted, became "a beacon light to girls and women struggling to find themselves in a changing world. . . . Since Mary Wollstonecraft's *Vindication* no book had spoken to women—and to men, on women's problems—so clearly, so authoritatively, with such revolutionary fervor and common sense as her famous *Women and Economics*."[2] Like Olive Schreiner, whom she admired and imitated, Gilman saw herself as a "transition woman," a member of a generation of feminists who would have to make difficult choices and set strict priorities in the interests of women of the future. "The 'transition woman' of this age," she wrote, "has a difficult position, and I've met my share of the difficulties. A few generations more and it will be easier. And I know I've helped it on a little." As she exhorted herself, "Work first—Love next."[3]

Like her British contemporaries, Gilman struggled constantly with the conflict between her longing for independence and her need to be nurtured. Her journals, says editor Mary Hill, were a "story of underlying battles with almost every women's issue she discussed."[4] Yet Gilman was not a tragic martyr like Schreiner or Eleanor Marx. She was the first of the fin de siècle feminist intellectuals to find both work and love, and to live a full and happy life on her own terms. For her, being a transition woman did not mean choosing between love and work, but setting priorities. Despite a restricted, dysfunctional childhood, she bided her time until she was old enough to be independent. Gilman was not about to suffer endlessly in unhappy or suffocating relationships, or to prefer misery to responsibility. She would not torment herself with unrequited love or endure endless frustration, no matter what others might think. Thus she courageously ended an unhappy marriage to a kindly man and willingly shared custody of their daughter with him and his second wife. Her own second marriage, to an affectionate younger man, was a lasting success, and she had close, sometimes romantic friendships with several women.

Although she suffered from depression and nervous illnesses, Gilman was prodigiously active and productive. At the age of fifty, she was single-handedly writing every word of a feminist journal, *The Forerunner*. She traveled and lectured widely, had a large international circle of distinguished friends, and wrote fiction and poetry as well as essays. Most striking, she maintained her rational principles to the end, correcting the proofs of her autobiography during her final illness with breast cancer, and choosing how to die as she had chosen how to live. When her work was complete, Gilman committed a painless suicide with chloroform in 1935.

The bare outline of her life may sound chilly and cerebral, but Gilman's life, amply documented in her diaries, letters, and published writing, is full of humor, grit, and pleasure. As her biographer Ann J. Lane writes, "She survived—no, more, she soared in a world that conspired to deny her flight. She ultimately accomplished much of what she set out to do: create a loving and sustained intimate relationship with a partner and leave behind a legacy of a lifetime of valuable work."[5] Gilman was a utopian thinker who imagined a new society based on maternal values, and who tried to construct her own life in accordance with her theories.

AN UNCUDDLED CHILDHOOD

Why did Gilman succeed? If the answer lay with her family, it came from their opposition rather than their support. Gilman despised the very notion of an unconscious and lectured on "The Fallacy of Freud," but she always wrote about herself as a child who had been deprived of affection and could never feel secure in it: "You see all my life I haven't had what I wanted in the way of being loved. . . . It is not clear grief . . . but a choked, thwarted, fiercely unreconciled feeling—an accumulated revolt—both mental and physical. And they all pile up together—I want them all—from Child to Mother—Sister—Brother—Father—Lover—Husband—Friend."[6] Her messianic goals as a feminist thinker came in part from her revolt against the family she had known and a fierce wish for love.

She was born in Connecticut, a descendant of the celebrated Beecher clan. Her father, Frederick Beecher Perkins, had trained to be a lawyer, but became a professional librarian and linguist, an erratic and dilettantish man with many talents and little staying power. When Charlotte was a baby, Frederick left home. "He was an occasional visitor, a writer of infrequent but always amusing letters with deliciously funny drawings, a sender of books, catalogues of books, lists of books to read, and also a purchaser of books with money sadly needed by his family."[7] The parents divorced in 1873; Charlotte's mother, Mary, raised her two children as a hardworking single parent, borrowing from relatives, moving nineteen times in eighteen years.

But Mary Perkins was equally denying of nurturance, and even more prohibitive of creativity. She deliberately withheld physical affection from Charlotte as a baby, so that "she should not be used to it or long for it." She would not kiss her daughter unless she was asleep, and Charlotte feigned sleeping to feel her mother's kiss.[8] Her older brother, Thomas, was a bully as a child, and in adulthood, while Charlotte was actually supporting him and his family, he always took care to remind her that he never read her books, while he boasted of his own futile plans to write for the Hearsts.

A photograph of Charlotte aged four shows an unsmiling little girl with a furrowed brow. Part of Mary Perkins's puritan regime was to withhold compliments as well as affection, although in secret she treasured her baby. Charlotte recalled that "if I was a pretty child no hint of it was allowed to enter my mind.

Mother cut off the fat little brown curls at an early age, lest I should be vain—and kept them as long as she lived." Deprived of pleasure in the beauty of her own body, she sought it in her environment and longed for it in her clothes: "My passion for beauty dates far back; in picture books the one or two that were really beautiful; in the colors of the worsted mother used, loving some and hating others; in bits of silk and ribbon, buttons—children used to collect strings of buttons in those days; I keenly recall my delight in specially beautiful things. There was a little cloak of purple velvet, deep pansy-purple, made over from something of mother's that enraptured my soul."[9]

Moreover, Charlotte had little formal education—she did not even finish high school—and faced many family obstacles in her efforts to educate herself. In adolescence, in Providence, where she studied drawing, attended women's gymnasium classes, and became a physical-fitness enthusiast, Charlotte was forbidden to read novels or to have intimate friends and ordered to stop making up stories and daydreaming. When she tried to write, she was discouraged: "For instance, at sixteen, I wrote the first bit of verse that seemed to me real poetry, a trifling thing about white violets. I went with it at once to mother. She listened with no apparent interest, and as soon as I had finished said, 'Go and put on the tea-kettle.' As a matter of fact she thought the verses beautiful, and kept them carefully, but at the time the tea-kettle was vividly in mind and the sensitiveness of a budding poetess was not. A trifling incident, but it hurt so that it was never forgotten, and I did not go to her so readily with later verses."[10] Her mother refused to let her go to the theater, although she longed to be an actress; turned down invitations to dances.

But for Charlotte, all these prohibitions against fantasy, sexuality, beauty, writing, and independence backfired. The effect of her uncuddled childhood was to make her fiercely self-reliant, disciplined, and determined as a teenager. In one argument, when her mother slapped her, Charlotte realized that she could not be forced to obey: "I was realizing with an immense illumination that neither she, nor any one, could *make* me do anything. . . . I was born."[11] She commenced a rigorous mode of living that involved strenuous physical exercise, cold baths, disciplined reading, and moral self-development—being polite and kind to everyone—and she followed this program until she was twenty-one.

All the bottled-up emotions of her adolescence erupted that year when Charlotte fell romantically in love with another girl, Martha Luther, and formed a "compact of mutual understanding," a kind of engagement. In her autobiography, Gilman carefully ruled out any implication of lesbianism in the friendship: "In our perfect concord there was no Freudian taint, but peace of mind, understanding, comfort, deep affection—and I had no one else."[12] She was franker, however, in her letters and diaries. When Martha married in October 1881, Gilman wrote about her grief in "knowing the sweetness of a perfect friendship" and losing it forever.[13] On New Year's Eve, she wrote a poem of farewell to Martha, "Unsent": "Think of those days when we could hardly dare / Be seen abroad together lest our eyes should speak too loud, / There is no danger now."[14]

In the painful aftermath of Martha's desertion for the world of wives, Charlotte vowed that she would never marry. In her private journals she inscribed a vow:

> Now that my head is cool and clear, now before I give myself in any sense to another; let me write down my Reasons for living single.
>
> In the first place I am fonder of freedom than anything else— I love to see & be with my friends, but only when I want them. I love to have pleasant faces in my home, but only when I want them. I like to have my own unaided will in all my surroundings—in *dress, diet, hours, behavior, speech, and thought.*
>
> I increasingly like to feel that my home is *mine*, that I am free to leave it when I will & for as long as I will.
>
> I like to select for myself, to buy for myself, to provide for myself in every way.
>
> I like to start out in joyous uncertainty of where I am going, &

with no force to draw me back—like it beyond words. I like to go about alone—*independently.*

I like to be *able* and *free* to help any one and every one, as I never could be if my time and thoughts were taken up by that extended self—a family.

. . . For reasons many and good, reasons of slow growth and careful consideration, more reasons than I can now remember; I decide to *Live*—Alone.

God help me![15]

AN UNCUDDLED MARRIAGE

Two weeks later, Charlotte met Charles Walter Stetson, who would become her husband. Walter Stetson, who was two years older than Charlotte, was also a rebel. He had decided when he was eighteen to be a painter; self-taught, he emphasized color, mood, and personal feeling and had begun to receive good reviews, exhibit his work, and meet wealthy patrons. In addition, he was handsome, in a bohemian, dandyish style. "He was," wrote Charlotte in her autobiography, "quite the greatest man, near my own age, that I had ever known. . . . In courage, in aspiration, in ideals, in bitter loneliness, we were enough alike to be drawn together." Within three weeks of their meeting, he asked her to marry him; she declined, reconsidered, and told him that "if he so desired he might come to see me for a year and we would find out—which he was very willing to do." She found in his company "the pleasure of association with a noble soul . . . the natural force of sex-attraction between two lonely young people . . . [and] on my part, periods of bitter revulsion, of desperate efforts to regain the dispassionate poise, the balanced judgment I was used to."

But beneath his glamorous cape and artistic pose, Walter was the product of his own cheerless puritan upbringing. He was tormented by his sexual drives and wanted his wife to be pure, angelic, and sexually innocent. In his journal he wrote of Charlotte, "She was innocent, beautiful, frank. I grasped at her with the instincts of a drowning heart—was saved for the time."[16] Marrying Charlotte would provide a moral and legitimate outlet for the sexual desires he felt to be "almost overpowering."[17] So Walter was persistent and persuasive, agreeing to Charlotte's ideas about domestic freedom, signing a pledge that she would "never be required, whatever the contingency, to DUST!"[18]

But he did not understand how serious she was about working and writing, and on her side, Charlotte was the victim of her own exaggerated ideas about marital duty and romantic adoration. The question of marriage threatened the divide she had established between work and love. "On the one hand I knew it was normal and right in general, and held that a woman should be able to have marriage and motherhood, and do her work in the world also. On the other, I felt strongly that for me it was not right, that the nature of the life before me forbade it, that I ought to forgo the more intimate personal happiness for complete devotion to my work."[19] Just as she could not imagine continuing her friendship with Martha Luther after Martha's marriage, she felt that agreeing to marriage meant a sacrifice of personal interests, and as she and Walter came closer to a commitment, she gave up going to the gym, art lessons, intellectual independence. In his journal, Walter noted that she had changed and "was not the strongly independent creature she was a year ago." Indeed, she had regressed, "wants to be treated more as a child now than as a woman. I could scarcely have foreseen so complete a subjugation of self—or rather abnegation. She is willing to do anything, go anywhere, so long as I am with her."[20]

What was happening? For a woman of Charlotte's upbringing, the combination of ardent attention and sexual attraction was compelling, disorienting, and new. For years she had fought her emotions and desires; now they seemed to be sanctioned, but at the price of her independence. Her adolescent romantic dreams of a masterful lover, a Heathcliff or Byron, were not only projected onto her husband but internalized in her submissive behavior. On their wedding night in May 1884, Charlotte recorded an ecstatic message: "The bed looks like a fairy bower with lace, white silk and flowers. Make myself a crown of white roses.... Go to my husband. He meets me joyfully; we promise to be true to one another, and he puts on the ring and the crown. Then he lifts the crown, loosens the snood, unfastens the girdle and then—and then. O my God! I thank thee for this heavenly happiness!"[21]

But the months following the wedding were chaotic. First of all, Charlotte's awakened sexuality alarmed her husband, and within a month, she was finding herself "too affectionately expressive" and vowing to "keep more to myself and be asked."[22] Holding back her feelings made her feel unloved and produced a riot of psychosomatic symptoms: fatigue, depression, inertia. By the end of July she suspected that she was pregnant, and morning sickness complicated her unhappiness. Despite their agreement about housework, Charlotte felt that she should be cooking and cleaning, and when Walter had to take over, she felt guilty and inadequate. She tried to study and write, with little success. She seemed to be stuck back in the prison of her childhood.

In March 1885, Charlotte gave birth to a daughter, Katharine. Now, with the arrival of the baby, all the insights and choices of her declaration of freedom seemed to be reversed. The pregnancy had been difficult emotionally and physically; she was exhausted caring for the infant, anxious about eating the wrong things, sinking into a serious postpartum depression: "Every morning the same hopeless waking. Every day the same weary drag. To die mere cowardice. Retreat impossible, escape impossible."[23] In her autobiography, she described this period of her life as "the breakdown": "The only physical pain I ever knew, besides dentistry and one sore finger, was having the baby, and I would rather have had a baby every week than suffer as I suffered in my mind. A constant dragging weariness miles below zero. Absolute incapacity. Absolute misery. To the spirit it was as if one were an armless, legless, eyeless, voiceless cripple. Prominent among the tumbling suggestions of a suffering brain was the thought, 'You did it yourself! You did it yourself! You had health and strength and hope and glorious work before you—and you threw it all away. You were called to serve humanity, and you cannot serve yourself. No good as a wife, no good as a mother, no good at anything. And you did it yourself!' . . . The baby? I nursed her for five months. I would hold her close—that lovely child!—and instead of love and happiness, feel only pain."[24]

In the fall and winter of 1885–86, Charlotte left the baby with her mother and Walter and spent several months recuperating with her friend Grace Channing and her family in California. When she returned in April 1886, she made a determined effort to lead an active life, to row, paint, and write a newspaper column and contribute poems and articles to the progressive women's magazines. She also began a more active involvement with the women's suffrage movement, attending a convention in October 1886, visiting the dress reformer Dr. Mary Walker ("she has no feeling for beauty in costume; thinks it beneath intelligent beings"[25]), got a new library card to start a "course of reading about women," and checked out several books, including Margaret Fuller's *Woman in the Nineteenth Century*. But this feminist program was no protection against the emotional strain of her situation. Caring for the baby made her weepy, exhausted, irritable, in a depressive spiral that finally led to collapse.

In April 1887, Charlotte undertook a rest cure under the supervision of Dr. Silas Weir Mitchell, a celebrated Philadelphia specialist in "neurasthenia," a form of clinical depression, chronic fatigue, and hysteria. The rest cure involved complete bed rest, isolation, rich diet, and passivity; and Charlotte coped pretty well with a month of the regime at Mitchell's clinic. The trouble began again when she was sent home, "with this prescription: 'Live as domestic a life as possible. Have your child with you all the time. . . . Lie down an hour after each meal. Have but two hours intellectual life a day. And never touch pen, brush or pencil as long as you live.' "[26] Typically, Charlotte followed the prescription with fanatical and masochistic devotion; the prohibition of intellectual and artistic labor nearly destroyed her sanity; by June she felt suicidal.

By fall, Charlotte had come to a daring decision: to separate from her husband. "There was no quarrel, no blame for either one," she wrote, ". . . but it seemed plain that if I went crazy it would do my husband no good and be a deadly injury to my child."[27] The break took a full year to arrange, but in September 1888, Charlotte took Katharine and returned, with Grace Channing, to California, determined to support herself and to make a life on her own. As Ann Lane observes, "With her flight to California—and it can only be seen as the desperate flight of a desperate woman—Charlotte Stetson began a new phase of her life."[28] With the separation, Charlotte took control of her destiny and ended what seems to have been more of an allergy to the internalized Victorian roles of her marriage than a reaction to motherhood. Living single, she was reborn; and at the age of twenty-eight, she began her professional career.

A NEW LIFE

In her first year on her own, Charlotte lectured, tutored, acted in community theater, and wrote a vast number of stories, poems, articles, and satirical pieces. The most important, the text by which she has become known today, was her short story "The Yellow Wallpaper," a fictionalized protest against her experience with the rest cure, written in Pasadena in 1890 and published the following year in the *New England Magazine*. The story gives a powerful sense of Gilman's hidden conflicts about mothering and service. Depressed after the birth of a child, the unnamed heroine of the story has been taken for a summer's rest cure in the nursery of a rented country house by her physician husband, who has also forbidden her "story-making." He is the voice of science and reason, while the woman represents the imagination and unconscious. In her secret journal entries we see that she believes her sickness is her wish to work and write in a society that limits women's creativity to the domestic and the maternal. The conflict between her wishes for self-expression and her guilt about failing her husband and child finally drives her mad; she begins to see faces in the patterned wallpaper of her attic bedroom, then to see women creeping in the gardens outside, and finally to merge her identity with the ghostly women erupting from the walls. While some critics have speculated that the story expressed Charlotte's real anger at her husband, certainly putting her anger in writing was a relief.

Witty and imaginative, Charlotte nonetheless distrusted fiction as too womanish, regarded her stories and poems as sugar-coated pills, in the tradition of such other feminist intellectuals as Wollstonecraft and Fuller. Despite the success of "The Yellow Wallpaper," she did not write more fiction for several years. "I have never made any pretense of being literary," she declared in her autobiography; "my real interest is in ideas." Yet as a critic Gilman foresaw the subjects of modern women's writing. In *The Man-Made World* (1911), she both questioned the themes of what she christened "masculine literature" and outlined a "feminine literature" that would deal seriously with women's lives. "The humanizing of women," she wrote, "opens five distinctly fresh fields of fiction." The five plots Gilman presented were very different from the standard plots of Victorian marriage-fiction, or even of the Edwardian problem-novel. The first was "the position of the young woman who is called to give up her 'career'—her humanness—for marriage and who objects to it." Second was the story of the "middle-aged woman who at last discovers that her discontent is social starvation—that it is not more love she wants, but more business in life." "The Yellow Wallpaper" was one of the models of this new kind of story.

But the three last plots were more visionary and remote. Gilman called for fiction "about the inter-relation of women with women—a thing we could never write about before because we never had it before, except in harems and convents." She described a novel about maternity, "not the eternal 'mother and child' wherein the child is always a baby, but the long drama of personal relationship; the love and hope, the patience and power, the lasting joy and triumph, the slow eating disappointment which must never be owned to a living soul—here are grounds for novels that a million mothers and many million children would eagerly read." More abstractly, she imagined a novel about "the new attitude of the full-grown woman, who faces the demands of love with the high standards of conscious motherhood."[29]

Meanwhile she was working out some new plots in her own life. Walter came to Pasadena in hopes of a reconciliation; but what actually happened was that he fell in love with Charlotte's closest friend, Grace Channing. For some months their courtship was kept secret, but when Walter and Grace went back East to be married, Charlotte was much more disturbed by the loss of her friend. "Do you know," she wrote to Grace, "I think I suffer more in giving you up than in Walter—for you were all joy to me. . . . It is awful to be a man inside and not be able to marry the woman you love! When Martha married it cracked my heart a good deal—your loss will finish it."[30] Yet instead of breaking off the friendship, Charlotte used the marriage to cement it. In 1894, she sent Katharine back to live with Walter and Grace, visited, corresponded, and throughout their lives reiterated her love and gratitude to Grace for raising her child. But public disapproval of this act haunted her up to her death, and much of her autobiography is given to defending and justifying the decision as one for the child's own good, and to explaining how much the pain of separation hurt Gilman herself. Gilman writes that she felt confident that Grace would care better for Katharine than she could, but she also notes that "there were years, years when I could never see a mother and child together without crying or even a picture of them." Her bouts of depression may have been an unconscious self-punishment for the urgent needs that forced her to make the break.

Historians wisely warn against applying the sexual assumptions and conventions of one era to another, and certainly tender, emotional, passionate, even physical relationships between women were more conventional in the nineteenth century than they would be today. Charlotte's love for Martha Luther and Grace Channing may never have been translated into sexual acts. Nonetheless, her denials of a "Freudian" element in these friendships demonstrates that she herself understood something about their erotic potential, and like many other feminist pioneers of this century, including Margaret Mead and Simone de Beauvoir, Gilman appears to have been bisexual and capable of deep erotic and emotional attachments to both women and men. In 1891, she began a new love affair with a San Francisco journalist, Adeline Knapp. On May 21, Charlotte wrote in her diary, "I love her." They began to spend nights together, and on June 7, Charlotte wrote, "We are very happy together."[31] Together they moved to Oakland and commenced a turbulent relationship that ended badly—Knapp was possessive, drank, fought. But in setting up house with Knapp, and in sharing Katharine with her ex-husband, Charlotte was experimenting with a variety of communal living arrangements and extended families.

The next four years were major ones for Charlotte's career. The San Francisco Bay area was a center of political, progressive, and feminist reform. Charlotte quickly became involved in the Nationalist movement inspired by Edward Bellamy's best-selling utopian novel, *Looking Backward,* which had been published in 1889, and which presented an idyllic American socialist society of the year 2000, based on Christian cooperation rather than violent class struggle. While Eleanor Marx was supporting labor unions, strikes, and Marxist organization in the United States, Charlotte was working with the Nationalist Club in Oakland, and writing for the movement's publications. Like Margaret Fuller, she also began to organize seminars for women, on themes of economic independence. When she returned to the East in 1895, she had achieved a significant intellectual reputation.

For five years, she was "At Large," lecturing all across the United States, and also traveling to England. Her life at this stage seemed to follow the patterns established by Wollstonecraft's journey to France and Fuller's sojourn in Italy—a broadening of experience, and a deepening feeling of internal revolution against the conventional expectations for a woman's life. Learning to speak effectively before large audiences of women and men gave her confidence in her ability to cope with disapproval and controversy. "When one is propagating truths deeply radical and desperately unpalatable," she observed, "one can not expect an eager and convinced audience."

Lecturing also made her aware of the limitations in women's education and intellectual training, and the way American women's culture could be constraining. "The reason women aren't smart about 'two-masted sloops' and such like, is from lack of associative ideas. They have nothing to tack the information to, and it slips out easily; as perhaps it would with you if you were given names of feminine decorations or crochet stitches." Yet she often felt impatient and frustrated by her audiences, and unable to share their superstitions. "The occultists of the place stick out all over," she wrote at one stop. "There goes the Swami Sardananda even as I write, a portly broadshouldered black man. I am not occult." Her own interests, which included the labor movement, were broader than the legalistic ones of suffrage groups. "I was to speak on Woman Suffrage pure and simple," she wrote in 1897, "and that never did interest me. I can only fire up on that subject when I apply it to other things in life."[32]

Gilman's intellectual interests could not be furthered or deeply sustained by her itinerant life and her speeches to a variety of women's clubs, literary groups, and social organizations. She had read widely in sociology, economics, psychology, anthropology, and other social sciences, but she was always an autodidact, cut off from a real intellectual community. Her thinking was a feminist amalgam of an optimistically American social Darwinism, a belief that although heredity and genetics determine human "nature," human beings can also speed up the evolutionary process through education and environment. Overall, Gilman believed, the progress of humankind was retarded because women still lived "in a prehistoric state of sub-social domesticity." The sexual division of labor, women's economic dependency on men, was holding back their intellectual devel-

opment. Until women had equal access to education, information, experience, work, and responsibility, men would be mating
with their evolutionary inferiors, as if "Mr. Horse were mated to
Mrs. Eohippus." Thus, she believed, various forms of social engi-
neering that would accelerate women's evolutionary development would also accelerate the overall intellectual and moral
progress of the human race.

Relatively indifferent to class differences, Gilman also overlooked the racial divisions in American society, and the voices of
a new generation of African-American feminist intellectuals in
the 1890s. Anna Julia Cooper (1858–1964), for example, received
her BA and MA at Oberlin College and in 1887 was recruited to
teach math and science at the all-black Dunbar High School in
Washington. In *A Voice from the South* (1892), Cooper encouraged black women to seek higher education, criticized the racism
of the labor movement, and devoted an entire chapter to attacking the white supremacist ideas that had crept into the women's
movement. For Cooper, the greatest potential of the women's
movement lay not with white women but with the women who
were "confronted by both a woman question and a race problem."[33] Ironically, however, living in New York among various
immigrant, racial, and ethnic groups convinced Gilman of their
inferiority in terms of her Darwinian program of human evolution, and her writing about them was always maternalistic and
elitist.

A NEW MAN

In January 1897, in the annual summing-up of the year's
accomplishments that Charlotte wrote in her journal, she felt
that a corner had been turned. She could support herself, pay off
her debts, find time to write. She also felt that she was ready to
address the psychological issues that had prevented her from
forming a stable relationship with another person. Having a
daughter intensified her desire to become a role model, to blaze

a trail for the next generation. In this annual self-assessment, Charlotte commits herself to the task of living an exemplary life: *"I must come out forever* from the feelings of shame and regret. Must leave off the past more fully than ever before. Must feel and be a strong brave happy useful honorable woman." Above all, she vowed, she would "live as I would wish my daughter— as I would wish all women to live."[34]

By spring that year, she had begun a friendship with the man who would become her second husband, the strong partner of her life. G. Houghton Gilman was her first cousin, a Wall Street lawyer, seven years younger, a scholarly, quiet, gentle man. Charlotte was much aware of the age difference, and of Houghton's relative obscurity in the public world she was beginning to conquer. She explored these differences in the hundreds of letters she wrote to him during the three years of their courtship, letters that compare to those of Wollstonecraft, Fuller, and Schreiner in the way they attempt to confront and transcend gender stereotypes in the interests of forging a true bond between women and men. Fuller was an important precursor to Gilman: "I love you considerable," she wrote Houghton. "It seems ever so much more reasonable than it did. Margaret Fuller married a man younger than she."[35]

The difference in age and in fame helped to cancel out the power differences that Charlotte still experienced in relationships with men. But like Fuller, Charlotte also wanted to be honest about the possibility that their marriage would shock her friends or expose him to pity and ridicule. "I always smile to think of the anguish of my Socialist admirers when I marry a man from Wall St.! You know it is Sodom and Gomorrah to them." She recognized the disparity in their public reputations as a topic for gossip: "My public will think I have married a quiet inconspicuous young man and wonder why I should do it. . . . Your public will think that you have married a cold queer rebellious unnatural sex-failure—old at that—and marvel at your foolishness; you knowing the while that this unnatural monster is—well, is not bad to take!"[36]

Indeed, in her determination to be completely open with Houghton before their marriage, she was sometimes brutally direct about the psychological effects on both of them that she was much more famous. "Whatever the evenness of stature of our souls inside—and there's no disparity there you splendid true man!—outside I make the bigger noise, and you'll be considered of small account beside me. That'll hurt you and hurt me. A woman so loves to have her husband seem her Master and her Lord—that's heredity."[37]

They courted primarily through letters, and with Houghton, Charlotte felt secure enough to share the conventionally feminine tastes and insecurities she had suppressed in adolescence. She wrote to him from Memphis about her delight in being called "pretty"; she told him about her pleasure in buying beautiful clothes; she confessed that she would like him to work out and do bodybuilding ("I want you to get at dumbbell and chest-weight work. I want another inch to lay my head on—my steadily enlarging head! . . . I want a little more Romanness in your neck—if you please—dear husband!"[38]); she wrote about her wishes that he would be more sexually aggressive: "You are so gentle, so tender, and so exquisitely self-restrained that passion does not show in you as it does in some men—either to plead or to demand; but I am beginning to read it in beneath and behind . . . and I like to see it—as a woman must. I like to feel the force and fire of it—as a woman must."[39]

Above all, she was insistent about her need for space and leisure to think, write, and speak. "Now it may yet appear that I shall develop a new power—a man's power; and learn to detach my personal from my professional life; learn to be the strong free helpful spirit in my work—giving due time to it; and yet come home to you, a happy wife for the rest of the time. Come now! This is what women have got to learn to do, if my new world is to come true! It may be part of my work to accomplish just this thing! To do world's work and live large and glad in it; to love and wed and be great mothers too—this is before the women of the world; and I must at least try at it. The most hampering cir-

cumstance is the mechanical detail of household life. . . . You
will have to give up a certain ideal of home; and I shall have to
give up even more—for I have had it, I know it, I love it, and
every tingling nerve of endless hereditary use just jumps to be at
work at it again!"[40]

When they married in June 1900, they had decided together
not to have children, despite Charlotte's half-wish to begin again
and make up for the disaster of her first marriage. In their happy
life together, which lasted until his death in 1934, Houghton
took as much responsibility as Charlotte for establishing domestic boundaries and refusing to slip back into conventional, or
"hereditary," marital roles. Charlotte never entirely abandoned
the fantasy of a tempestuous, dominant Byronic lover with a
Roman expanse of muscular chest; but she learned to accept
Houghton as he was, and to appreciate his support in maintaining her balancing act between her personal and public lives.

THE NEW HOME

In the wake of her romance with Houghton, Charlotte settled
down to the writing that would make her reputation as a feminist
thinker. In her books *Women and Economics* (1898), *The Home*
(1903), *The Man-Made World* (1911), and *His Religion and Hers*
(1923), and in her articles and stories for *The Forerunner,* a peri-
odical she edited and wrote from 1909 to 1916, Gilman outlined
her Darwinian agenda. She argued that women's liberation is the
prerequisite for the liberation of all humankind. The most pragmatic and original aspect of Gilman's work was her analysis of
the domestic household as the source of women's oppression.
From her reading of Darwin, Veblen, and other social theorists, as
well as from her own experience, she understood that women's
maternal drives and economic dependence on men would combine to keep them prisoners of the private world of the home,
unless the social structure could be changed to value the work
done by women in the home, including child care, by making it

a true profession, and by breaking down its privatization. In this way, women's traditional contributions to society could be shared by both sexes and compensated like any other highly skilled work, and individual women would be free to make real choices about their work in the larger society outside the home. Her many suggestions of reform in housekeeping, family life, and child care were radically ahead of their time, and some have yet to be achieved today.

First of all, if women were to be relieved of drudgery and freed to go out in the world, and yet maintain the comfort and security of The Home, with all its traditions, homemaking had to be radically redesigned. As Ann Lane comments, "College education was just opening to women. But she longed for more. She longed for the release of the married through professionalized house service. No one could get decent ice-cream, pastry, preserves, tinned stuffs in that day, save through the individual kitchen, and the woman who stitched her own husband's shirt bosoms was still more highly appraised than the one whose husband bought his shirts, as was possible even then. A public laundry was disdainfully regarded no matter how well the work was done. As for cooked food ever being served to the home instead of raw materials, or ready-made dresses worn—either was ridiculed. An early advocate of quality time, Gilman argued that women would be more patient and loving parents if they were not full-time mothers. Her most prophetic solution to the problem was to centralize and industrialize cooking and childcare, with communal kitchens and nurseries servicing neighborhoods or high-rise apartments."[41]

In *The Home,* Gilman argued, "The home has not developed in proportion to our other institutions, and by its rudimentary development it arrests development in other lines."[42] In her crusade for a kitchenless home, collective housekeeping, and feminist architecture, Gilman tried to resolve some of the practical contradictions between her love of domestic comfort and her advocacy of women's freedom. She envisioned apartments in a complex with a central dining room and kitchen. Although the individual kitchen would go, the private dining room would remain; singles, couples, or families would order their meals from the central kitchen, which would provide tempting, varied menus and professional cooks.

"This establishment, it will be observed, is not a restaurant. It does not have to pay rent for eating space in the business part of the city, nor to allow for an immense margin of waste with varying customers. It has a steady number of patrons, who can order their preferred dishes in advance if they choose, or pay somewhat less for a well arranged menu which shall make of the weary housewife a cheerful guest, or both. You carefully order your dinner—by telephone, of the manager—all at once, instead of ordering it of a number of tradesmen after discussion with the cook. That dinner, perfectly prepared and hot, comes into your pantry by the dumbwaiter as it does now. What difference does it make to your family happiness that it was not steaming through the halls beforehand? It is better food, far better cooked. If your devout regard for the privacy for the family leads you to insist on a stranger in the room to wait on you, that may be had by paying for it."[43]

Yet for all its convenience, the image of the kitchenless home is symbolically harsh. The kitchen stood not only for the essence of Home itself, but also for an idealized maternity. It was the warm heart of the house, the place where Mother dispensed nurturance and love. In the best-selling sentimental novels of nineteenth-century America, such as *Uncle Tom's Cabin,* the kitchen was to the house as the womb is to the woman.

Thus Gilman's ideas, however scientifically and rationally explained, seemed cold and unappealing to younger women. In 1915, Henrietta Rodman, a leader of the radical Greenwich Village Feminist Alliance, proposed a new kind of housing for professional women, incorporating many of Gilman's suggestions. An architect drew up plans for a model apartment building on Washington Square that would utilize the latest technology and include space for a central kitchen and day nursery. Professional cooks and teachers, hired by the families in the apartments, would take over food preparation and child care, freeing the mothers for their careers. Rodman understood that child care would become the central issue in twentieth-century feminism: "The care of children, particularly those under five years of age, is the point at which feminism is most open to attack. We must have this apartment house before we can become honest feminists."[44]

But the apartment was never built, and the deliberate centralized planning Gilman envisioned was displaced by capitalist economic development. Her plans for efficient food preparation and delivery anticipated the boom in fast food, takeout, and professional catering that accompanied women's participation in the workforce. In London at the turn of the twenty-first century, some new apartment complexes are being constructed with a central dining facility, while in cities like New York, young professionals, women and men, group together in buildings with vestigial kitchenettes, close to food outlets. Professional cleaning services abound, but these options are still seen as personal choices and luxuries rather than social necessities.

Gilman's ideas about professional child care were equally ahead of her time. True, the rich had always been able to afford nursemaids and nannies, but those were not the New Women she wanted to address. Further, she saw child-rearing as a major task of each civilization. "As we, collectively, establish great universities, colleges, and schools for our children, so we should prepare child gardens, numerous and convenient, where all our little ones could have their special guardians, special playgrounds, special care, and special educational environment—beyond that of the home."[45]

HERLAND

Gilman's utopian novel, *Herland* (1915), is an attempt to imagine an Amazon matriarchal society constituted on feminist principles. Herland is a country about the size of Holland, with a population of 3 million women, located in the Southern Hemisphere. It originated in volcanic explosions that cut the country off from the rest of the civilized world, followed by a war in which all the men were killed. The founding Herlanders were "hysterical girls," and some old slave women. They not only rebuilt their country but also developed parthenogenetic modes of reproduction. At the age of twenty-five, the best five women spontaneously gave birth to five daughters. Thereafter, the society limits reproduction according to its needs; when Herlanders enter their phase of conception and are "filled with concentrated desire for a child," they repress the desire for the good of the nation by taking cold showers, working hard, and caring for babies in the nursery.

Because they are women, Herlanders are maternal, sisterly, cooperative, reasonable, and nurturant. Because there are no men, they are not hierarchical, aggressive, competitive, or sexual. Gilman argues that the dualism of sex underlies all dualistic struggles. There is no nationalistic feeling, "no interplay of warring nations," no sport. Moreover the women have no sexual drive, feel no desire, and have no overt lesbianism. Gilman imagines a whole country as an Edenic garden, "a land in a state of perfect cultivation . . . a land that looked like an enormous park, only it was even more evidently an enormous garden." The state religion is not based on war and plunder, but on nature, vegetation, plenitude, cooperation, and nurturance: "Here was Mother Earth, bearing fruit. All that they ate was fruit of motherhood, from seed or egg or their product. By motherhood they were born and by motherhood they lived—life was to them, just the long cycle of motherhood."

This all-female society, in which women reproduce without insemination, is invaded by three American men—a capitalist, a doctor, and a sociologist. In developing these submerged metaphors of male invasion of the secret and forbidden maternal body, Gilman was drawing on several nineteenth-century literary models. In Rider Haggard's *She,* and Kipling's *The Man Who Would Be King,* for example, men penetrate and conquer the Dark Continents of Africa and Asia and find at the center, core, or heart of the darkness a mysterious, powerful queen. Gilman was also responding to the radical utopian movements of nineteenth-century America: the celibate, matriarchal Shakers; the Oneida Colony of free love and sexual experimentation; the polygamous Mormons and apocalyptic Seventh-Day Adventists. Many utopian groups believed that God was androgynous, and that the Messiah might be male or female. The sects challenged the family, marriage, and sexuality and included many female leaders and advocates of women's rights. Finally, Gilman was writing her own version of feminist ethnography.

She also used the novel to dramatize her ideas about the evolution of human sexuality. As the invading men discover, intercourse with a Herland woman is a violation of a deep psychological taboo, except for the holy ritual of reproduction. The appropriate emotion for a man toward a Herland woman is reverence, what Gilman calls "loving up": "a very good sensation which gave . . . a queer feeling, way down deep, as if the stirring of some ancient dim prehistoric consciousness . . . like coming home to mother." By the end of *Herland,* heterosexuality has been restored, but only on the women's terms of maternal superiority. It's a creepy, quasi-incestuous vision of female moral dominance, and a regression to a moralistic insistence on women's essential purity and sexlessness.

Indeed, in part because of her reading of Olive Schreiner's *Woman and Labor,* Gilman had become convinced that human sexuality was also evolving toward a higher and more altruistic form and could be helped along by the efforts of women. Schreiner's view had been that when sex was separated from reproduction, it would become more aesthetic and beautiful, more complete an expression of love. Gilman took a different approach; sex, she argued, was nature's way of assisting reproduction, and its biological justifications were diminished in modern society. In the article "Birth Control" she wrote for *The Forerunner* in 1915, she argued that the emphasis human beings placed on sexuality was abnormal and excessive, and that it was an evolutionary throwback, harmful to the "parental emotions and capacities. When the human species, gradually modifying its conduct by the adoption of changed ideas, becomes normal in this regard, it will show a very different scale of emotional and functional demand; the element of sex-desire greatly reduced in proportion to the higher development of parental activities worthy of our race; and of a whole range of social emotions and functions now impossible because of the proportionate predominance of this one process and its emotions."[46] In *Herland,* even the men slowly realize that they are less interested in sex than they used to be. In the fully evolved society Gilman dreamed of, sex would take place only during an annual mating period, and there would be no need for birth control.

A FEMINIST ENDING?

As we see in *Herland,* and in her letters to Houghton, Gilman never really came to terms with female sexuality as a force in either her own life or in culture. She never claimed female sexuality as a right, as part of individual self-expression, and she never managed intellectually to separate it from male desire or male adoration or reproduction. Freud's concepts of the unconscious and the libido were anathema to her, just at the moment that they began to have a serious impact on American society. Thus in the 1920s, after the war and the women's suffrage amendment, Gilman's hyperrational feminism was increasingly out of synch with her time, and with a younger generation. In 1922, in her sixties, she and Houghton moved to Norwich, Connecticut, and her writing took on a nagging elderly and suburban tone. She disapproved more and more of the casual lifestyles, free sexual behavior, and fashions of the flappers and denounced "the physical indecencies of our misguided young people" and "the mental indecencies of a sex-sodden psychoanalysis."[47]

But while she was uncomfortable with birth control because it might encourage sexual license, Gilman was unequivocal in her support of death control. She had always believed in euthanasia. "Human life consists in mutual service," she wrote. "No grief, pain, misfortune or 'broken heart' is excuse for cutting off one's life while any power of service remains. But when all usefulness is over, when one is assured of unavoidable and imminent death, it is the simplest of human rights to choose a quick and easy death in place of a slow and horrible one. . . . Public opinion is changing on this subject. The time is approaching when we shall consider it abhorrent to our civilization to allow a human being to die in prolonged agony which we should mercifully end in any other creature."[48] In 1932, when she discovered that she had breast cancer, she began to stockpile supplies of chloroform, which she thought provided a neat and painless death. Rational to the end, she read the proofs of her autobiography, chose the photographs, and approved the cover; then, on August 17, 1935, three months before the date of publication, she carried out her plan to "go peacefully to sleep with my beloved chloroform."[49]

THE AFTERLIFE

The Living of Charlotte Perkins Gilman sold fewer than a thousand copies when it was published. But Gilman was rediscovered by feminist critics and historians in the 1960s, and "The Yellow Wallpaper" and *Herland* have become standard reading for courses in American literature and women's writing, and Gilman has become the subject of numerous biographies, a feminist Mother of Us All. Yet biographical research has also revealed an ironic twist to Gilman's life—her own daughter's anger and resentment toward this famous mother. When Mary Hill interviewed Gilman's daughter, Katharine Chamberlin, in 1975, she discovered, to her dismay, that Katharine resented her mother for abandoning her, did not admire her work, and did not see her as a feminist heroine at all. Katharine Stetson Chamberlin, a mother of two children, had been a sculptor, painter, and professional genealogist. In her nineties, she was still angry with her mother and saw her as an irresponsible "Amazon." "Mama was always scurrying," always "too tired or too distracted" to cook, to comb her daughter's hair. Katharine felt that Gilman had been selfish and preoccupied, "too absorbed in expressing herself, making a career for herself, or in her causes."[50] In her view, Gilman preached rather than listened, and "would talk to people but it was more in the form of giving than thinking that they had anything to give her."[51]

Ann Lane also met Katharine Chamberlin in 1978, when she was living in a nursing home in Pasadena. "She seemed unable to comprehend the point of my visit: why would I want to write a book about her mother?" Lane concluded that "her reluctance to understand my visit had to do with her reluctance to acknowledge the growing respect for her mother's work." When they began to talk, Lane was struck by Chamberlin's anger toward her mother, and her insistence that her mother had abandoned her when she was nine years old. Reading Chamberlin's own unpublished memoir, and the letters between mother and daughter, Lane concluded that despite her good intentions, Charlotte patronized Katharine or ignored her. "When Katharine turned to her mother for help, Charlotte did try to support her, but Charlotte's insensitivity and self-centeredness often got in the way. When Katharine was strong and capable, her mother became competitive and critical."[52]

Yet overall, Chamberlin's bitterness seems more indicative of her own failure to overcome childhood conflicts and divided loyalties than Charlotte's failure to love. On one side, there are extraordinary letters from Charlotte to her adult daughter, testifying to her love and affirmation: "I can send honor and admiration for a brave strong life, for splendid talents, for magnificent motherhood and wifehood and friendship. . . . You are a very noble woman, Katharine, my dear."[53] On the other side, there are Katharine's many letters to scholars denigrating Gilman's accomplishments: "To my mind my father had the greater gifts. . . . My mother went to pieces over my birth—not a difficult birth—but a few months in Pasadena, acting in plays, etc.—she thought she was cured."[54] Katharine was unable to do her mother justice, or to forgive.

Gilman's feminist daughters, who stand outside the oedipal hothouse, can do both. Mary Hill explains that when she first started working on Gilman, she was looking for a flawless icon: "Many years ago, when I first came across her published works—witty, insightful, radical feminist critiques—I was looking for a heroine, for closer contact with a woman who could articulate my own frustrations and explain women's problems in ways directly relating to my life. Her concerns were mine as well: how to reconcile family responsibilities with professional ambitions; how to be a responsive mother to two small children and still have time to teach and write; how to satisfy the human need for love and work. Undoubtedly, I was looking for historical roots as well, for intellectual precedents to feminist ideas of the 1960s, which to many even now seem unsettling and new."[55] But, Hill writes, "as the heroine image disappeared, a very human woman came to light."[56]

SIX

Heterodoxy in America

A Feminist Tribe

In 1919, Florence Guy Woolston, a Manhattan settlement-house worker, wrote a learned study of the advanced women of New York: "Remains of the early Heterodites, a tribe of women living on the Island of Manhattan in the North Seas, are still to be found by the ardent traveller. Relics of their former civilization are fairly well preserved although dates are difficult to obtain owing to the shape of the Island and the great difficulty of moving in either a north or south direction."

Like the anthropologist Elsie Clews Parsons, whose iconoclastic study *The Family* had compared marriage customs and taboos in various cultures, Woolston analyzed the varied marriage customs of the Heterodites: "Three types of sex relationships may be observed, practiced by those who call themselves monotonists, varietists, and resistants. Most of the monotonists were mated young and by pressure of habit and circumstance have remained mated. (*Sometimes sheer inertia and the difficulty of un-mating keeps the monotonist as such.) The varietists have never been ceremonially mated but have preferred a succession of matings. The resistants have not mated at all." Nonetheless, she noted, "True resistants are rare. As virginity is an asset outside of monotony many varieties assume an outward resistancy. I recall one resistant who had cleverly concealed 18 varieties of mating, because, as she confessed, her economic status depended upon her virginity." Finally, "the tribe of Heterodites is known as a taboo-less group. There is the strongest taboo on taboo. Heterodites say that taboo is injurious to free development of the mind and spirit. Members of the tribe suspected of a tendency to taboo are frequently disciplined. (A favorite method of discipline is to avoid sending them notices of anarchistic, Bolshevikistic or pacifist meetings, and to prevent them from obtaining platform seats for revolutionary gatherings.)"[1]

"Marriage Customs and Taboo among the Early Heterodites" was a satiric celebration of Heterodoxy, a remarkable women's club that flourished in New York from 1912 to 1920. Charlotte Perkins Gilman was a member, but the worlds of Herland and Heterodoxy seem centuries apart. According to Mabel Dodge Luhan, Heterodoxy was a club for "unorthodox women, women who did things and did them openly."[2] Most Heterodites were sexually active and believed that their freedom depended upon birth control. Woolston explains, "Heterodites are not fecund because undoubtedly Neo-Malthusianism and Sangerism is thoroughly familiar to them."[3] Margaret Sanger spoke at a meeting of Heterodoxy in 1914, and members of the National Birth Control League, including several of the Heterodites, backed her during her various arrests and trials for distributing birth control information. Moreover, Heterodites included women living in openly lesbian relationships. To Elizabeth Gurley Flynn, the club was "a glimpse of the women of the future, big spirited, intellectually alert, devoid of the old 'femininity' which has been replaced by a wonderful free masonry of women."[4]

Heterodoxy had started as a lunch gathering at a café and remained "the easiest of clubs. The meetings were almost invariably addressed by members. It entailed no duties or obligations. There was no press. Everything that was said was off the record." Dues were two dollars a year. At the meetings, "a member told whatever she chose to reveal about her childhood, girlhood, and young womanhood," sharing experiences in a way that anticipated the consciousness-raising groups of the 1970s.[5] Inez

Haynes Irwin recalled that Heterodoxy "talked about everything. Heterodoxy members came from many states of the Union. Most of them had traveled with amazing extensiveness. Among them were Democrats, Republicans, Prohibitionists, Socialists, anarchists, liberals, and radicals of all opinions. They possessed minds startlingly free of prejudice. They were at home with ideas. All could talk; all could argue; all could listen. . . . Our occupations and preoccupations ranged the world. Many of our members were working for various reforms. A sizable proportion were always somewhere else. During the First World War, when no Americans were supposed to enter Russia, always, at least two members of Heterodoxy were there writing articles."[6] Irwin herself was a war correspondent, and others were political activists and Marxists, who wrote for *The Masses,* the radical journal edited by Max Eastman.

Florence Woolston's parody captured the iconoclastic anthropological and tribal quality of the new feminists. Mainly Greenwich Village bohemians, during a time when the Village was a sanctuary for the avant-garde, they borrowed their ideas about feminism from the new studies of society and culture. Even the word *feminism* first came into use in the United States around 1911, when male and female writers began to use it in place of the nineteenth-century terms *woman movement* and *woman question* to describe "a new moment in the long history of struggles for women's rights and freedoms." The new feminism went beyond the specific goals of the suffrage movement and the social-purity and moral-uplift campaigns of the woman movement in a high-spirited quest for intellectual, political, and sexual self-determination. Feminism, said the radical Edna Kenton, was a revolt "as much against Woman as Man." It stood for "a troop of departures from the established order of women's lives."[7] The historian Mary Ritter Beard insisted that women were "people of flesh and blood and brain, feeling, seeing, judging and directing equally with men, all the great social forces."[8]

Marie Jenney Howe, a minister who was the leader of Heterodoxy, also organized the first public mass meetings to discuss the new term and the new vision of liberated women. In February 1914, at Cooper Union, more men than women came to hear talks titled "What Feminism Means to Me" and "Breaking Into the Human Race," which included such topics as "the right to work," "the right of the mother to her profession," "the right of her convictions," "the right to organize," "the right to her name," "the right to ignore fashion," and "the right to specialize in home industries." Howe summarized the meeting's main theme: "We're sick of being specialized to sex. We intend simply to be ourselves, not just our little female selves, but our whole, big, human selves." Feminism, Howe wrote, is "woman's struggle for freedom. Its political phase is woman's will to vote. Its economic phase is woman's effort to pay her own way. Its social phase is woman's revaluation of outgrown customs and standards. . . . Feminism means . . . a changed psychology, the creation of a new consciousness in women."[9] Feminists expected to serve their society, but they also expected to be having "a better time than any woman in the world ever had before." Following the tenets of the influential Parisian philosopher Henri Bergson, who attracted intellectual women to his lectures in 1910–11 as Jacques Lacan would sixty years later, they defined their aims as turning "away from the intellectualism of life to life itself."[10] "To me," wrote the novelist Rose Young, "feminism means that woman wants to develop her own womanhood. It means that she wants to push on to the finest, fullest, freest expression of herself. She wants to be an individual."[11]

The goal of modern American feminism was a balance of the needs for love and achievement, individual fulfillment and political or social commitment; but it seemed terribly difficult to achieve. The first decades of the twentieth century were a period of troubled introspection for women all along the political spectrum, and a period of turning back for inspiration to the great feminist icons of the past. The Heterodites were the first feminist generation with genuine access to higher education, and many of them had not only college degrees but doctorates and professional qualifications in medicine and law. Looking at the examples of other cultures, writing biographies of their heroines, and using the methods of Freudian psychoanalysis and contemporary ethnography, they tried to integrate women's participation in economic and public life with private and personal fulfillment.

In November 1911, Emma Goldman, the notorious anarchist nicknamed Red Emma, gave a lecture in New York called "Mary Wollstonecraft, the Pioneer of Modern Womanhood," using Wollstonecraft as a template against which to compare herself and from which to distance herself. The historian Alice Wexler calls the lecture "the most revealing short self-portrait [Goldman] ever wrote." Goldman declared that "the Pioneers of human progress are like the seagulls, they behold new coasts, new spheres of daring thought, when their co-voyagers see only the endless stretch of water." Like all pioneers, Mary Wollstonecraft had also been "isolated, shunned, and repudiated," and "her search and yearning for love . . . hurled her against the rock of inconsistency and despair." But, she went on, Wollstonecraft was still ahead of her time, because she recognized the split between women's rights and women's longings. "The woman's movement of today and especially the suffrage movement," Goldman proclaimed, "will find in the life and struggle of Mary Wollstonecraft much that would show them the inadequacy of mere external gain as a means of freeing their sex. No doubt much has been accomplished since Mary thundered against women's economic and political enslavement but has that made her free? Has it added to the depth of her being? Has it brought joy and cheer in her life? Mary's own tragic life proves that economic and social rights for women alone are not enough to fill her life, nor yet enough to fill any deep life, man or woman."[12]

I was surprised by Goldman's choice of Wollstonecraft as her precursor, rather than Eleanor Marx. A Russian immigrant who arrived in the United States in 1869, Goldman had been politically awakened by the Haymarket riots of 1886, in the aftermath of which five anarchists and socialists had been executed. Inspired by Sonia in Dostoyevsky's *Crime and Punishment,* she had even ventured into prostitution to raise money for her lover Alexander Berkman's plot to assassinate the executive Henry Clay Frick. Frick lived, but Berkman was convicted of attempted murder, and Emma was convicted of inciting to riot and sentenced to a year in prison. In 1911, she was the best-known woman radical in America, and a leading figure in the international anarchist movement, lecturing on literature, drama, and politics around the country, editing the literary journal *Mother Earth,* and working for various causes including women's suffrage and birth control.

Yet Goldman too was tormented by her feelings in an unhappy love affair with a younger man, Ben Reitman, a doctor from Chicago who worked with hoboes and homeless men. Habitually unfaithful, Reitman confronted Goldman with "her own feelings of helplessness before emotional forces she could neither understand nor control."[13] Despite all her political activism and anarchist convictions, Goldman also feared the death of the inner life. In her essay "The Tragedy of Woman's Emancipation" (1906), she insisted that "modern woman must emancipate herself from emancipation—break loose from customs and prejudices." In 1925, she wrote to her old comrade Alexander Berkman, "The tragedy of all emancipated women, myself included, is that we are still rooted in the old soil, though our visions are of the future and our desire is to be free and independent."[14]

Other feminists and Heterodites also looked to the past in an effort to imagine the future. Marie Jenney Howe wrote a biography of George Sand; Katherine Anthony, a University of Chicago Ph.D. who had studied in Germany, wrote a number of "psychobiographies" of notable women. Her 1920 biography of Mary Wollstonecraft tried to define a "broader kind of feminism," and she also wrote about Fuller and Susan B. Anthony. Katherine Anthony "found chaotic personal lives a source of both interest and inspiration . . . she admired Fuller's life for its turbulence and its passions." One of the Heterodites living in a long-term lesbian relationship, Anthony "used Freudian tools to explore and defend Fuller's intimate bonds with other women, the implicit eroticism of which she regarded as healthy and vital."[15]

THE FEMINIST ANTHROPOLOGISTS

In the teens and twenties, many American New Women turned to the sciences of anthropology and psychology to understand themselves. As Ruth Buzell commented, "Some of us went into anthropology, hoping that there we might find some answers to the ambiguities and contradictions of our age and the general enigma of human life."[16] Feminist anthropologists wanted to lead large and intrepid lives, to break out of small towns and conventional jobs, to explore the world, and to experiment with a variety of living arrangements from the solitary to the communal. Anthropology seemed to offer the opportunities for both adventure and self-discovery. Moreover, as Gilman and Woolston both felt, women had a culture of their own, a wild zone within society, which had never been fully explored. But while Gilman, denied access to the university, approached it through the romantic feminist utopianism of *Herland,* the Heterodites turned to scientific method, comparative fieldwork, and extensive research. Out of all the forms of femininity, family, and culture in the world, they were asking, were there common elements, or rather such variations that American women could be free to reinvent themselves?

The beginning of the twentieth century was a golden age in the development of American anthropology. At Columbia University, the German Jew Franz Boas was the chairman of a celebrated department. His school of anthropology rejected the Victorian view that white Anglo-Saxon male civilization represented the apex of cultural evolution and contested the notion that non-Western societies were "primitive" and backward. Moreover, Boasian anthropology challenged assumptions about gender as well as race and pioneered studies of the lives of women, and the rearing of children. Boas and his students "made no moral judgments about differences in custom from culture to culture. Instead they accepted them as alternate possibilities of human life formed from the particular circumstances unique to each culture's history."[17]

Boas himself was a charismatic figure whose women students called him Papa Franz. Margaret Mead described him as "a surprising and somewhat frightening teacher. He had a bad side and a good side of his face. On one side there was a long dueling scar from his student days in Germany—an unusual pursuit for a Jewish student—on which his eyelid drooped and teared from a recent stroke. But seen from the other side, his face showed him to be as handsome as he had been as a young man."[18] Boas was tirelessly energetic and fearless in defending views, however unpopular, he believed were right. By the time Mead came to Columbia in the early 1920s, the anthropology department, she writes, "was a small embattled group. Boas had been a pacifist during World War I, and as a German, had also been the focus of rancor."[19] In the 1930s and 1940s, Boas was a leading liberal voice against racist theories of heredity. Even when he was in his seventies, he went into the field to experiment with the new technology of film.

Boas was supportive of women students and attracted many to his program. In 1920, he said, "All my best students are women." Yet this generation of female anthropologists had to struggle for professional recognition, settle for lower-level university positions, or work outside academia. They needed an extra dose of daring and initiative in order to do their research. "For a woman to be able to travel in the early days of anthropology," notes anthropologist Ruth Behar, "she had to have not a room of her own but plenty of spunk and money of her own."[20] We should not be surprised to discover among them women who were truly heterodox and flamboyant, who devised their own marital and domestic arrangements, who crossed boundaries of race and sex, and who brought literary technique and poetic vision to their fieldwork and research. Their iconoclasm was disciplinary and stylistic as well as personal, and the popularity of their work with general audiences made them suspect to the academic community. At the same time, their use of ethnographic methodologies to analyze their own urban social communities made them controversial and even scandalous figures.

ELSIE CLEWS PARSONS: THE PIONEER

Elsie Clews Parsons (1874–1941) was among the most remarkable social scientists in heterodoxy. Parsons was the oldest of three daughters in a rich and prominent New York banking family, but she attended Barnard College and earned a Ph.D. in sociology from Columbia University in 1899. She married in 1900 and gave birth to six children, four of whom survived to adulthood. While the children were growing up, Parsons also lectured at Columbia and NYU, traveled extensively in Europe, South America, and Mexico, and helped found the New School for Social Research. By 1915, she had become interested in cultural anthropology and began a series of annual field trips to Arizona and New Mexico, where she lived with and studied the Zuni, Hopi, Taos, Tewa, Laguna, and other Native American tribes. Near the end of her life, in 1941, she became the first woman president of the American Anthropological Association.

But Parsons's contribution to the heterodox community of American New Women went far beyond her professional accomplishments. She had a gift for living, a sense of dynamic improvisation and witty experiment accompanied by a fearless will to make her life exemplary of the modern. These are the qualities that led Florence Woolston to dedicate "Marriage Customs and Taboo" to her for her "courageous researches" and "continual inspiration." Her biographer, the Australian-born sociologist Desley Deacon, was first attracted to Parsons's "cool, level gaze" in a period photograph: "her exquisite dress, which I now know probably came from Worth; and—more than anything—the baby on her lap" were signs across the years of another "pioneer of new gender arrangements."[21]

Deacon situates Parsons in the context of the American modernist rebellion against rigid nineteenth-century beliefs, values, classifications, hierarchies, systems, and codes of social relationships. Both in her work as an anthropologist and in her life as a Heterodite feminist, Parsons argued for a more flexible, tolerant, and embracing social organization that excluded no group, tribe, or caste. Most of all, Deacon writes, Elsie Clews Parsons was modern "in that she put her ideas into practice in her own life, testing the new relationships and moralities she advocated. Her 'experimental life,' which included marriage, children, lovers, and friends, adventurous and arduous travel, and professional commitment and distinction, demonstrated to an interested public the practical working out of modernism by one of its pioneering theorists."[22]

As a child, Elsie Clews grew up in the fashionable New York society satirically depicted by Edith Wharton as the "Reservation" for a vanishing aboriginal tribe. "It used to seem to me," Wharton wrote in her autobiography, *A Backward Glance,* "that the group in which I grew up was like an empty vessel into which no new wine would ever again be poured."[23] But Wharton, who was fifteen years older than Elsie Clews, also recorded the social evolution of this seemingly moribund and sterile culture in such novels as *The House of Mirth* (1905) and *The Custom of the Country* (1913).

Clews was young enough to be part of that change. Although girls in her social circle did not attend college, Elsie had been such a diligent student that when Barnard College opened in 1889, she set her sights on passing its entrance examinations. By 1892, she had mastered Greek and mathematics and entered Barnard. As an undergraduate, her life took a different path from that of Wharton and Gilman, brilliant women who were denied higher education, and who went through long periods of depression and breakdown before they could find their vocation. Instead, Elsie began to study sociology under the direction of Franklin Giddings, an iconoclastic thinker and scholar. Following his guidance, she became involved with the settlement-house movement in New York, and with public-education reform. After graduation she enrolled in a Ph.D. program in education at Columbia, supervised by Nicholas Murray Butler.

To her mother, still hoping Elsie would be a socialite and shopping companion, this intellectual determination was a trial, especially when Elsie spent the summer of 1896 in Paris translating a book by the influential French sociologist Gabriel de Tarde. But Elsie was also being courted by the progressive young Republican lawyer Herbert Parsons, whose enthusiasm for social reform and charity work was as keen as her own. In September 1900, having completed her dissertation, published her first article, and won his agreement that she would continue to work, Elsie married Parsons. Six weeks later, she was pregnant.

For the first six years of her marriage, Parsons managed to keep up her settlement-house work, teach sociology at Barnard, and give birth to three children, while Herbert pursued his political career. But in her first book, *The Family* (1906), she also advocated sex education, birth control, and trial marriage, subjects so shocking to women of her class that she was stricken from the Social Register. The press coverage embarrassed her husband, who was by then chairman of the Republican Committee of New York County, and a political ally of Theodore Roosevelt. Parsons promised the president that in the future "authorship is going to yield to statesmanship." She published her next book, *Religious Chastity,* under a pseudonym, and her memoir, *The Journal of a Feminist,* was not published until 1994. Between 1907 and 1912, Parsons went through a difficult phase of her life. Two babies died at birth; she had a series of miscarriages; and the marriage was showing signs of strain as her husband became involved with other women. Parsons wrote little for several years.

As the new feminist movement took off, Parsons was attracted to it along with other New York intellectuals. She joined Heterodoxy in 1912 and began an involvement with the movements for suffrage and birth control and with the new ethnographic ideas about sex, marriage, and the family. From 1912 on, according to Deacon, she was attempting to "reconstruct herself as a totally new woman." She "deliberately cultivated an adventurous life, physically, intellectually, and emotionally, and exposed herself to a variety of situations that forced her to interact in personal rather than conventional ways."[24] Every year she took field trips, defining her own priorities and independence. In her journal, she addressed the question of how women might live with men, but not through men, recommending frequent separations to avoid boredom, staleness, and dependency. In her work, Parsons had always rebelled against categories, insisting that "the more thoroughly a woman is classified the more easily she is controlled. . . . The new woman is the woman not yet classified, perhaps not classifiable."[25] But inventing this unclassifiable new woman was a harder task than she had supposed. In *The Old-Fashioned Woman* (1913), she compared the experience of women from a wide range of cultures with women of the present, discussing parallels in menstrual taboos, marriage customs, and the trade in women. In "The Exclusive Sex," a chapter on male zones in various societies, she commented that "women are quite generally excluded from a share in public affairs. The Nagas have a war stone no woman may look upon and live. In anti-suffrage argument a voting-booth seems to be nearly as dangerous a spot for women."[26] She explained to her anxious mother in 1914 that she had always been a feminist: "When I would play with the little boys in Bryant Park, although you said it was rough and unladylike, that was feminism. When I took off my veil or gloves whenever your back was turned or when I stayed in my room two days rather than put on stays, that was feminism. When I got out of paying calls to go riding or sailing, that was feminism. When I kept regular hours of work in spite of protests that I was selfish, that was feminism. When I had a baby when I wanted one, in spite of protests that I was not selfish enough, that was feminism."[27] Parsons developed a clear and consistent theory of open, experimental marriage with sexual freedom for both partners, based on her study of sex and gender across cultures.

In her writing, Parsons wittily examined codes of good behavior, social decorum, and etiquette, showing how they encoded sexual stereotypes and perpetuated female subordination, as "women try hard to live down to what is expected of them." She herself had no intention of doing what was expected. A sophisticated bohemian who could look like the central casting image of the New Woman, in heavy Indian jewelry and long, droopy cardigans, she wore tennis shoes with a dinner gown, avoided all greetings from "hello" and "good-bye" to "merry Christmas," and refused offices, honors, and full-time jobs. In her journal in 1913–14, she wrote about her frustration with confining sexual roles: "This morning perhaps I may feel like a male; let me act like one. This afternoon I may feel like a female; let me act like one. At midday or at midnight, I may feel sexless; let me therefore act sexlessly. . . . It is such a confounded bore to have to act one part endlessly." While women suffered most from having always to act like women, she could also imagine that "men may rebel sometime against the attribute of maleness. . . . Some day there may be a 'masculism' movement to allow men to act 'like women.' "[28]

By 1915, Parsons had started attending meetings of the American Anthropological Association and was beginning to think of herself as a specialist in folklore, American Indian culture, and ethnology. During the war years, she took long trips in the field, studying the Indians of the Southwest and collecting African-American folklore in the Bahamas. As an outspoken pacifist, she was an embarrassment to her patriotic family; but in her work on changing Native American cultures and acculturation in the Southwest, she was becoming one of the best-known anthropologists in the United States. In 1919, she became one of the supporters of the Free School of Political Science in New York—later the New School for Social Research—and taught there herself. She used her private income to pay secretaries for Franz Boas and to help fund his women graduate students. Her Southwest Society financed the research of dozens of young anthropologists.

Within her own marriage, Parsons tried to practice what she preached about sexual freedom for both partners, but she suffered

intense jealousy and unhappiness over Herbert's companionship with other more conventionally feminine women, and she
was shocked and dismayed to find how little her high-minded
ideals helped her control her feelings. Gradually, she adjusted to
a more detached marital relation, with frequent separations, and
invested most of her energy in her work. She also had affairs of
her own, including a prolonged relationship with the novelist
Robert Herrick. Yet when Herbert died in an accident in 1925,
Elsie was devastated and indeed felt "revived respect and regard
for her dead husband which she had not felt when he lived and
thwarted and irritated her."[29] In keeping with her impatience
with polite social ritual, she did not attend his funeral; but she
ended her affair with Herrick. After Herbert's death, she devoted
more time to travel and research and published a series of distinguished anthropological studies of culture and folklore.[30] She
followed to the letter her lifelong views on meaningless conventions, ordering in her will that she should be cremated, that
there should be no funeral, and no gravestone. As her friend
Karl Kroeber recalled in an obituary, "She was an unflinching
person, grappling and pushing steadfastly toward what seemed to
be the fundamentals."[31]

RUTH BENEDICT: THE POET

Parsons never held a formal university position, but she certainly had a significant intellectual influence on other women.
One was Ruth Fulton Benedict (1887–1948), who took Parsons's course "Sex in Ethnology" at the New School for Social
Research in 1919. The course surveyed a number of societies,
looking at sex roles and especially the sexual division of labor;
and in Parsons, Benedict found "a kindred spirit and a courageous role model," whose theories provided Benedict with
another perspective on her own concerns.[32] Never an activist,
Benedict lived a life that, according to biographer Margaret Caffrey, was nonetheless "a case history in cultural feminism, a fem-

inism derived from other than political sources, focusing on changing the values and beliefs that make up the framework of a culture rather than working for change through laws or the courts . . . a feminism that concentrates on internal questions, such as definitions of masculinity and femininity, and questions of selfhood, of individuality, of independence."[33]

Benedict had made her way to the study of anthropology by a desperate and tortuous path. Her father, a homeopathic surgeon, had died when she was not quite two years old, and she was raised in upstate New York by her mother and maternal grandparents in an atmosphere of both hardship and religious hyperemotionalism, a "cult of grief." Her mother became to her "an object of fear and disgust, her father a symbol of calm and repose, and both together an incitement to alienation from life and to a yearning after death."[34] Handicapped by partial deafness produced by an attack of measles, Ruth grew up withdrawn, unwilling to be touched, susceptible to fits of depression and attacks of nervous vomiting. She also suffered from a hormonal imbalance that affected her menstrual cycle; as an adult, she could not have children.

But Ruth was a brilliant student who won scholarships to private school and then to Vassar, where she graduated Phi Beta Kappa in 1909. One of her biographers speculates that her hearing impairment may have protected her from some messages about the feminine role, since many role reinforcers are verbal.[35] After college, however, she worked aimlessly as a social caseworker and teacher and began to despair of her future. "So much of the trouble," she wrote in her journal, "is because I am a woman. To me it seems a very terrible thing, to be a woman. There is one crown which is perhaps worth it all—a great love, a quiet home, and children. . . . A great love is given to very few. Perhaps this make-shift time-filler of a job is our life work after all. It is all so cruelly wasteful. There are so few ways in which we can compete with men—surely not in teaching or in social work. If we are not to have the chance to fulfill our one great potentiality—the power of loving—why were we not born men?"[36]

In 1914, she fell in love with Stanley Benedict, a young bio-chemist who would become a professor at Cornell Medical School. The romance and their marriage seemed transforma-tive. In her journals she rapturously wrote about her new happi-ness: "This satisfying comradeship, this ardent delight, this transforming love—now that I have it, it is what gives meaning to all of life."[37] Perhaps no marriage could sustain such a weight of intense need. But quickly her dependence and the differences between their views of marriage renewed her depression. Stan-ley did not want her to work outside the home and, because of his interests and hobbies, they lived in suburban New York, in Bedford Hills. She was bored with being a housewife, and like Charlotte Perkins Gilman, one of her heroines, she struggled to find some deeper purpose for her life.

In her diary of 1914, Benedict outlined a plan to analyze her-self by writing a book about "New Women of Three Centuries," Mary Wollstonecraft, Margaret Fuller, and Olive Schreiner. She intended "to steep myself in the lives of restless and highly enslaved women of past generations and write a series of biogra-phical papers from the standpoint of the 'new woman.' My con-clusion so far as I see it now is that there is nothing 'new' about the whole thing except the phraseology and the more indepen-dent economic standing of recent times—that the restlessness and groping are inherent in the nature of women and this gen-eration can outdo the others long since past only in the frank-ness with which it acts upon these."[38] According to Margaret Mead, the project was a search for "a key to the meaning of cre-ativity for human beings who happened also to be women."[39]

Benedict's book, so much like the one I am trying to write myself, was never finished. In her journals, she tormented her-self with her inability to do the subject justice. But she did write the section on Mary Wollstonecraft, a moving and sensitive essay that captured the tragedy and immediacy of Woll-stonecraft's ideas and life. "The story of Mary Wollstonecraft," Benedict writes, "is that most precious of human documents: the story of a life that achieved an idea. She was one of those few and valuable persons who are born with a pitiless thirst for understanding afresh. For her, life had no axioms; its geometry was all experimental. She was forever testing, probing; forever dominated by an utter unwillingness to accept the pretense, the convention in place of the reality."

Benedict emphasized the experimental quality of Wollstonecraft's life, her determination to test her ideas through experience: "She lived with all the alertness of her brain focused upon the abrupt experiences of her life; the knowledge she won, the price she paid, her books may hint to us, but it is her life through which we understand. It is there that we can measure that passionate attitude toward living out of which all the restlessness of modern womankind has grown. It is her life story that makes her our contemporary."[40]

Working on her book in 1916, Benedict became more and more feminist in her convictions. She sent the Wollstonecraft essay and a prospectus of the book, titled "Adventures in Womanhood," to Houghton Mifflin. But they rejected it; her views were ahead of her time. Afterward, she "jammed drafts, notes, and sketches into a carton."[41] With the writing project in limbo, she wrestled again with the prospect of motherhood. But then she learned that she would not be able to have children, a "mixed source of great pain and of relief." In her journals, she imagined a Feminist Messiah or "Woman-Christ," whose message to women was that they must live for themselves and not through their sons: "Those visions which you saw," the Woman-Christ tells her followers, "they were given for the guidance of your own life, you had no other, nor can attain one. Go! Live the life you covet for your child."[42] She had made the decision to live for herself, to become her own daughter.

By 1919, when she enrolled at the New School for Social Research, Benedict and her husband had already become estranged, and he remained in Bedford Hills while she rented a room in Manhattan, so austere that she had not even a picture of her own on the walls. Elsie Parsons introduced her to anthropology, then recommended her to Boas at Columbia, where she received her Ph.D. in 1923 at the age of thirty-six. As Benedict told one of her classmates, "I don't have children, so I might as well have Hottentots."[43]

But she was really attracted to anthropology because of its unconventionality and tolerance of the many roles that men and women could take in various cultures, and its respect for the deviants and misfits. In Margaret Mead's view, "anthropology made the first 'sense' that any ordered approach to life had ever made to Ruth Benedict."[44] Benedict initially did her field research on Native American tribes, then the tacitly understood special territory of American anthropologists, but her deafness hindered her in learning languages and she had to rely on intermediaries. Moreover, her academic standing was marginal and precarious. Teaching and lecturing were difficult for her, and she had a series of part-time lectureship appointments at Barnard and Columbia. Boas was always short of research funds and assumed that married women should manage on lower pay. She tried to conceal her femininity and her extraordinary beauty by adopting a professional uniform, wearing the same dress to lecture every day, as Boas wore the same suit.

Boas's requests to the Columbia administration and to various foundations for support for Benedict were rejected until 1931, when, at the age of forty-four, officially divorced from her husband, and already editor of the *Journal of American Folklore,* she was hired as an assistant professor at an annual salary of $3,000. Once she and Stanley had separated, Boas accepted her urgent need for regular work. Benedict's life blossomed intellectually and psychologically as she attained financial independence. Her beauty emerged as her hair turned prematurely white and framed her serene face and strong, dark brows. In part, she had come to recognize her bisexuality, commencing affairs with women lovers in the 1930s and, in 1939, establishing a permanent household with a psychologist, Ruth Valentine.

The personal and psychological themes of Benedict's life led her to develop an influential theory of the social construction of personality, arguing in such important books as *Patterns of Culture*

(1934) and *The Chrysanthemum and the Sword: Patterns of Japanese Culture* (1946) that every culture creates its own hierarchy of temperament and value, but that the outcasts and deviants of one culture, including homosexuals, might be the heroes of another. Her work for the Office of War Information in 1943–45 made officials aware of the importance of understanding complex modern societies, and after the war she received a massive government grant to direct a Columbia research center in contemporary cultures.

Always she insisted on the humanistic elements in anthropology. While she was writing *Patterns of Culture,* she was reading Virginia Woolf's *The Waves;* and in a lecture titled "Anthropology and the Humanities" in 1947, she declared that "long before I knew anything at all about anthropology, I had learned from Shakespearean criticism—and from Santayana—habits of mind which at length made me an anthropologist."

MARGARET MEAD: THE EARTH MOTHER

These literary and modernist habits of mind also attracted Margaret Mead. In the autumn of 1922, in her senior year at Barnard, Margaret Mead met Ruth Benedict, who was assisting Boas in his teaching, and taking groups of Barnard anthropology students to the Museum of Natural History. Mead encountered Benedict at a time when Benedict was most uncertain and unprepossessing, and even her beauty "was completely in eclipse. We saw her as a very shy, almost distrait, middle-aged woman whose fine, mouse-colored hair never stayed quite pinned up. Week after week she wore a very prosaic hat and the same drab dress. Men wore the same clothes every day, she said. Why shouldn't a woman, also? She stammered a little when she talked with us and sometimes blushed scarlet." But Mead was captivated by Benedict's enthusiasm for anthropology, and her interest in modern poetry: "The intensity of her interest, combined with the magnificent clarity of Boas' teaching, made anthropology, as such, something of a revelation to me."[45] In fact, Mead was so enthusiastic about the course and talked about it so much that the enrollment doubled.[46]

Margaret Mead (1901–78) was fifteen years younger than Benedict, but she would take the theories of the feminist anthropologists furthest in understanding the patterns of American women's culture, and in arguing that the sex roles and behaviors of Americans were culturally specific rather than biological or universal. "I have spent most of my life," Mead wrote in her autobiography, "studying the lives of other peoples, faraway peoples, so that Americans might better understand themselves."[47] Her use of anthropology as a method for explaining fundamental human behavior made her as controversial as she was famous.

Even as a little girl in rural Pennsylvania, Margaret had been strong-minded, passionate, and robustly individualistic. At the age of eleven she horrified her agnostic, intellectual parents by becoming a baptized and fanatically devout Episcopalian. Athletic, plain, and bookish, she became engaged at sixteen to a local ministry student four years older, Luther Cressman. Later she explained that she "never had to live through that period of being rejected by a man. . . . If you had a man, you weren't continually thinking about them."[48]

She had hoped to go to Wellesley, but her father could not afford it and even tried to persuade her not to go to college at all. To back him up, he called in the local doctor, who told Margaret, "Look at those useless little hands! Never did a day's work in their life and never will! You'd maybe make a good mistress, but a poor wife. You'd better study nursing." Margaret exploded "in one of the few fits of feminist rage I have ever had."[49] In 1919, she went to her father's alma mater, DePauw, in Greencastle, Indiana, where she was shocked to be treated as a social misfit and rejected by the sororities. She accepted the rejection as a challenge, but she felt she was "in exile. I used to sit in the library and read the drama reviews in *The New York Times*. Like so many other aspiring American intellectuals and artists, I developed the feeling that American small towns were essentially unfriendly to the life of the mind and the senses. I believed that the center of life was in New York City."[50]

In 1920, Margaret transferred to Barnard College in New York, where she quickly became a leader and a standout. With the poet Leonie Adams, she created a semi-sorority of artists and bohemians, the Ash Can Cats, which also became a surrogate family with an elaborate kinship system. Luther Cressman was in New York attending theological seminary, and Margaret saw him every week; she was planning to become a minister's wife, studying psychology, and hoping to become a writer.

But at Barnard she was emotionally and intellectually seduced by Ruth Benedict. Mead believed that, to Benedict, "I was the child she never had. I had all the things she wanted in a child: joy of living, positive affirmation of life—I worried that she'd lose interest in me because of the age discrepancy."[51] Benedict introduced Mead to the fascinations of anthropology and got her admitted to the graduate seminars taught by Franz Boas. Working with Boas, who was constructing the entire graduate discipline of American anthropology, and with the Canadian linguist Edward Sapir, Mead was excited by anthropology's potential to cut across disciplinary lines, and to understand what was normal in human behavior. "I was accustomed to regard all the races of man as equal and to look at all human cultures as comparable. What was new to me was the vista that was opened up by discussions of the development of men from their earliest beginnings."[52]

She was particularly interested in the prospect of using Freudian psychoanalysis along with ethnological fieldwork to understand the meaning of culture. She gave up the notion of being a novelist: "Once I had satisfied myself that human cultures were far more complex and interesting than anything I could create and that in my attempts to write fiction I had actually been trying to understand real situations that I had encountered as a child, I had no further desire to write fiction."[53] Finally, as she realized, choosing anthropology was a kind of intellectual commitment to Ruth Benedict. They would share "our hopes and worries about Boas, about Sapir, about anthropology, and in later years about the world. When she died, I had read everything she had written and she had read everything I had ever written. No one else had and no one else has."[54]

Mead began her graduate research in New York. Nevertheless, she married Cressman in 1923 as planned, although she kept her own name and they had separate bedrooms on their honeymoon so that she could work on an article. But Mead was not uninterested in sex. Indeed, she was eager and had discussed it extensively with her Barnard friends. But, as she hinted in her autobiography, the honeymoon was a bit of a letdown. There were moments of "strangeness and disappointment. . . . We had read so many books written by the sex specialists of the 1920s, who believed that sex was a matter of proper technique—that men should learn to play on women's bodies as if they were musical instruments, but without including in their calculations the idea that women must be very good musical instruments in order to please the men who played on them."[55] Whether or not Luther, after years of training for the ministry, was a talented sexual musician, Margaret, with lots of theory and no practice, was not a particularly tuned instrument. She later wrote that her marriage had been "unclouded by fear of pregnancy," but that was news to Cressman: " 'Not *much* we weren't afraid of it!' he said. 'Only once a month, that's all.' "[56]

Mead still faced the decision on her thesis topic and fieldwork. She was bored by the idea of studying the Zuni or the Pueblo, even alongside Ruth Benedict. At the time, Phyllis Grosskurth explains, "the Americans concentrated on the American Indian, the English concentrated on the South Pacific and West Africa." Mead's intention to go to Samoa to study adolescence among the Polynesians would bring her into conflict with the English anthropologist A. R. Radcliffe-Brown, "for venturing into territory that had already been implicitly staked out."[57] But Boas backed her up and helped her get funding. The ever-faithful Cressman offered to come along, but she decided that she would be more efficient unencumbered. Instead, he went to London for a year on a fellowship to study delinquency. Mead was by far the stronger of the two personalities; she had already persuaded Cressman to change religious denominations and then to give up the ministry. "My going to Europe," he noted mildly, "had been . . . far more a device to facilitate M's Samoan plans than a carefully thought-out educational program."[58] He was depressed and lonely in London and sought comfort from a friend who would become his second wife; Mead meanwhile met her second husband, Reo Fortune; and so Mead's departure for Samoa alone in 1925 turned out to be the end of her first marriage, and the beginning of her own life journey. She spent nine months living in Samoa, a length of time that became controversial among anthropologists as insufficient for serious study, but which also hints at the way the experience represented an intellectual gestation and personal rebirth for Mead herself.[59]

Mead returned from Samoa famous, and the book she wrote about her fieldwork there made her reputation and became a classic. The experience also changed her life and the way she thought about herself and about women in general. *Coming of Age in Samoa: A Psychological Study of Primitive Youth for Western Civilization* (1928) is primarily a study of adolescent girls in the American Samoan islands. Based on her interviews with twenty-five girls, Mead concludes that in Samoa "adolescence represented no period of crisis or stress, but was instead an orderly development of a set of slowly maturing interests and activities. The girls' minds were perplexed by no conflicts, troubled by no philosophical queries, beset by no remote ambitions. To live as a girl with many lovers as long as possible and then to marry in one's own village, near one's own relatives, and to have many children, these were uniform and satisfying ambitions."[60] The Samoans, moreover, regarded sex as an art requiring experience and technique. They accepted homosexual practices as play; masturbation was almost universal, and rape extremely rare. Promiscuity seemed to protect the girls against pregnancy, but if they did have a child, it was welcomed. Sexual adjustment in marriage was smooth and uncomplicated; frigidity and impotence were unknown; and adultery, while not sanctioned, was tolerated.

But what made these observations so sensational was the concluding chapters of the book, in which Mead, only twenty-seven years old, used the Samoan example to criticize the sexual mores and marriage customs of American society. If adolescence was not biologically disruptive for Samoan girls, why was it such a problem for American girls? If the puritanical sexual taboos and conflicting choices confronting American girls led to neurosis, the fear of spinsterhood, and an inability to make a commitment to work, were they too costly? Should the social environment be changed? In fact, she uses Samoa as an "allegory,"[61] an opportunity to raise important questions for American society.

In 1983, a book by an Australian anthropologist, Derek Freeman, rocked the academic world with its attack on Mead's Samoan fieldwork. In *Margaret Mead and Samoa: The Making and Unmaking of an Anthropological Myth,* Freeman took no prisoners in his demolition of Mead's reputation and ideas. Arguing relentlessly point by point that Mead's facts were mistaken, Freeman insinuated that her book was part of a Boasian conspiracy to establish culture, nurture, and environment rather than biology, nature, and heredity as the determinants of human behavior.

But actually Mead's view of Samoan girls is more nuanced and ironic than Freeman's version suggests, and her tone more speculative than didactic. Her interests were as much personal, feminist, and exploratory as they were ideological efforts to produce a document in the Boas school. Anthropologists have hotly debated Freeman's charges about Mead's scholarship, while noticing that Mead also used anthropology as a form of literary and cultural criticism. What she saw in Samoa certainly responded to her own questions and concerns about growing up female. Samoan culture became a kind of Herland with sex, in which homosexuality was part of the erotic repertoire, men were expected to develop sexual expertise before marriage, and birth control and adultery were not a problem. In short, Samoa seemed to have everything that Mead was needing in her own sexual life and in her marriage. Indeed, on the return trip from Samoa, she began an affair with another anthropologist, Reo Fortune, who became her second husband.

Mead was told that she was unable to bear children and had accepted the verdict as one that freed her to do anthropological research anywhere in the world. "I wrote to Professor Boas that he could send us anywhere he would send a man, since I would no longer need any special protection."[62] Her work in the South Pacific and in Bali and an appointment as a curator at the prestigious Museum of Natural History gave her the opportunity to write several books that became popular best-sellers as well as anthropological statements. But in Bali in 1939, with her third husband, Gregory Bateson, Mead discovered that she was pregnant. Dr. Benjamin Spock was her pediatrician, and she made careful plans to have a natural delivery and to feed the baby on demand—a program antithetical to the theories of infancy dominant at the time. Her ideas about child-rearing influenced many thousands of other women.

Between 1925 and 1975, Margaret Mead published more than thirteen hundred articles, books, reviews, and prefaces in a wide range of scholarly and popular publications.[63] In her postmenopausal years, years that she celebrated as a time of women's renewed energy and zest, she was the best-known anthropologist in the world. She relished being a mother and eventually a grandmother and, almost alone among feminist thinkers, wrote about the fascination of this new role in her autobiography, *Blackberry Winter.* When Mead discussed the problem of women divided between "work and child care," Bateson noted, "she quoted Harriet Beecher Stowe as saying that she was distracted from her novel because 'the baby cries so much,' but she pointed out that the real problem is that the baby smiles so much, that the care of an infant is a perfection of creativity and delight that few can achieve in any other kind of work."[64] Yet she was open-minded and ingenious in ways of finding solutions to allow women to devote themselves to both babies and work.

Mead's daughter, Mary Catherine Bateson, grew up to be a distinguished anthropologist and writer, the author of a number of books about her parents, and about contemporary women's lives. In her account of Mead, she stressed her mother's lifelong concern not to dominate Mary or interfere with her choices. In 1947, Mead wrote a poem for her daughter expressing this determination:

> *You must be free to take a path*
> *Whose end I feel no need to know;*
> *No irking fever to be sure*
> *You went where I would have you go.*

Unlike the daughter of Charlotte Perkins Gilman, Bateson grew up to be a friend and even a colleague to her parents, and to understand the ways in which she had been shaped by them.

In the 1950s, Mead became a celebrity who wrote a monthly column for *Redbook* magazine; in the 1960s, she appeared frequently on radio and TV talk shows with hosts such as Johnny Carson. Like Dr. Ruth or Clare Rayner, she presented herself as a comfortable motherly woman who could write frankly about sexual matters and offer advice in every crisis. Such activities did not endear her to her peers. Many of her male colleagues and her female contemporaries were offended by this persona and dismissed her as a popularizer, a moralizer, a tyrant, or worse. Senior British anthropologists such as A. C. Haddon and E. E. Evans-Pritchard mocked her ethnographic writing as the effusions of a romantic lady novelist. The anthropologist Marshall Sahlins sneered that Mead "made parenthood, menopause, and other experiences of her adult life into *Redbook* magazine articles that taught middle-class American women how to live theirs."[65] In her brief biography of Mead, Canadian academic Phyllis Grosskurth portrays her as an archetypal American egomaniac, primarily concerned with being famous and thus fitting in perfectly with the narcissistic and shallow values of her society. In many respects, Grosskurth thinks, Mead was a secular religious figure, "the female counterpart of Norman Vincent Peale," who dressed in a flowing red cape and carried a forked cherrywood stick, like a prophet or benevolent "grandmother to the world."[66]

This stumpy feminist messiah (Betty Friedan said Mead's students called her "God the Mother") was not asexual. After Mead's death, Catherine discovered that her mother had continued late in life to have love affairs with both men and women. To her daughter, Mead had frequently expressed her conviction that one could sustain "more than one deeply loving intimacy at a time," and that each kind of relationship offers unique pleasures, with relationships with women "providing the comfort of the known and relationships with men as always containing the element of arbitrary and mysterious difference."[67]

Predictably, Mead had thought a great deal about death in the abstract, and about her own death. She had written what we now call a living will, stipulating that she did not want to live with reduced mental capacities. But when she discovered in 1978 that she had pancreatic cancer, she resisted the diagnosis. Some found it hypocritical that in her own final months she turned to healers and denied the seriousness of her illness. Catherine Bateson suspects that Mead was also maintaining and reaffirming choices about women, work, and love she had made throughout her life. Mead insisted that Bateson return to her work in Iran, rather than sit by her bedside, in a recognition that "the impulse to be present beside a deathbed is a repetition of the attraction of the cradle." In her death, as in her life, she was determined to be free herself, and to defend the cause of freedom in others.

ZORA NEALE HURSTON: THE BLACK QUEEN

But Mead did not have to surmount the problem of race as well as sex. The fourth woman in this group of Columbia-educated anthropologists was the novelist Zora Neale Hurston (1891–1960).

While Parsons, Benedict, and Mead had all had to overcome family discouragement to follow their careers, Hurston's presence at Columbia was almost miraculous. She had grown up in the all-black community of Eatonville, Florida, five miles from Orlando, where her father was the mayor. When her mother died and her father married a woman she despised, she was sent to school and studied first at Morgan Academy, then Howard University, where she studied with the poet Georgia Douglas Johnson and the philosopher Alain Locke. Her first story, "John Redding Goes to Sea," was published in Howard University's literary magazine in 1921.

In 1925, Hurston arrived in New York with $1.50 in her pocket. She had hopes of becoming a writer, and of studying writing at a college in New York. Two years later, her quick wit, distinctive style, and assertive talent had won her visibility and popularity among the mostly male writers, intellectuals, and artists of the Harlem Renaissance, where she irreverently called herself the Queen of the Niggerati. At the same time, Hurston was given a scholarship to Barnard College, where she was the only black student. The abyss between these two cultural worlds would characterize her career.

At Barnard, she too was a protégée of Ruth Benedict and Franz Boas, who encouraged her to work on African-American folklore in the South and in the Caribbean. She was immensely proud to have been chosen by Boas, "the greatest anthropologist alive," and to be acknowledged as another of his daughters. ("Just one of my missteps," he joked.[68]) Combining anthropology and art gave her an intellectual advantage and put her into a difficult position as a participant observer, even a native informant, in the cultures she studied. The tensions and contradictions between her positions as outsider and insider were particularly fraught in the Harlem Renaissance, when black identity and aesthetic autonomy were being celebrated. Moreover, Hurston also came into conflict with the male dominance of the art world and with her own demons and desires.

Hurston's personal life remains shadowy, although its outlines suggest that despite—perhaps because of—her glamour and success, she could not work out egalitarian and lasting relationships with men. At Howard, she had met Herbert Sheen, a jazz musician who was working his way through Howard and planning to go to medical school. After a six-year engagement, and many separations, they married in May 1927 while Hurston was in Florida studying black folklore. She kept the marriage secret from her academic advisers and sponsors, but in any case it did not last long. By August, Sheen had returned to Rush Medical School in Chicago, and Hurston went back to New York. She told Langston Hughes that "Herbert holds me back," and he reported that "the demands of her career doomed the marriage to an early, amicable divorce."[69] Her second marriage in 1939, to a man fifteen years younger, survived less than a year. Hurston's secretiveness about her personal life may have reflected the uneasiness black women intellectuals felt about their professional image in racist America, and their difficulty in finding partners who both respected their work and provided passion and love.

Although she did fieldwork in Florida, Louisiana, Jamaica, and Haiti, Hurston never finished her Ph.D. Part of the reason was her difficulty in finding financial support. When she received a meager six months of funding from the Rosenwald Foundation to write her dissertation, she used it instead to write a draft of her first and most famous novel, *Their Eyes Were Watching God*. But a major part of her ambivalence about an academic career was pressure to conform to the demands of two very different worlds. The funding for her work came from white patrons and mentors such as Boas and Benedict, Carl Van Vechten, and especially Mrs. Rufus Osgood Mason, a wealthy New Yorker who had done some ethnographic study of her own among the Plains Indians. Each had a different agenda about the importance of African-American folklore—for creating an anthropological discipline, establishing a popular view of black folk, or building the basis for an aesthetic of high culture.[70] In her fiction and essays, Hurston had the freedom to be heterodox.

THE EVOLUTION OF DISENCHANTMENT

By the late 1920s, after the passage of the suffrage amendment, many American women who were finding it hard to live the feminist dream of love and work entered a period in which the lessons and joys of feminism were repressed. Their problems were as much practical as theoretical or political. Psychologist Leta Hollingworth, who dedicated her career to a study of gifted children, found that her "time and energy were chiefly consumed by housework, cooking, dressmaking, mending, washing, ironing, making her own hats and suits and endless other domestic duties in the frugal apartment home. Almost always she effectually stifled her own eager longing for intellectual activity like that of her husband. . . . She led her solitary life in the meagerly furnished quarters . . . once in a while she would unexpectedly and for no apparent cause burst into tears."[71] By 1926, "confessions of ex-feminists" had begun to appear in the women's magazines, reporting their failure to live by feminist ideals without shared parenting, good child care, or professional support systems.

That year, *The Nation* invited seventeen "modern women" to discuss anonymously the personal sources of their feminism and its realization. The "new-style" feminist wanted a life of commitment and social activism, a career and a family. Crystal Eastman explains that the modern woman "is not altogether satisfied with love, marriage, and a purely domestic career. She wants money of her own. She wants work of her own. She wants some means of self-expression, perhaps, some way of satisfying her personal ambition. But she wants a husband, home and children, too. How to reconcile these two desires in real life, that is the question."[72] Some of the women saw resistance to domestic drudgery as the only solution. Inez Haynes Irwin regarded the Sunday dinner as the symbol of everything she "hated and dreaded about the life of the middle-class woman. That plethoric meal—the huge roast, the blood pouring out of it . . . the many vegetables, all steaming; the heavy pudding." She made a vow that she would never learn how to cook. But Cornelia Bryce Pinchot, wife of the Republican governor of Pennsylvania, defined all aspects of a woman's life, including homemaking and maternity, as the basis of an adventure: "Personally I would not change, abate or sacrifice any part of my own job. My feminism tells me that woman can bear children, charm her lovers, boss a business, swim the Channel, stand at Armageddon and battle for the Lord—all in the day's work!"[73]

The *Nation* series was the brainchild of the young managing editor Freda Kirchwey (1984–1976), the Tina Brown of her day. Daughter of George W. Kirchwey, the dean of Columbia Law School and warden of Sing Sing prison, Freda Kirchwey seemed born to lead a charmed life. As a teenager she adopted George Bernard Shaw and H. G. Wells as her heroes; at Barnard College, she campaigned for women's suffrage and led the fight to abolish sororities. When she graduated in 1915, her classmates voted her "best looking, the one who has done the most for Barnard, most militant, and the one most likely to be famous in the future." In her private life, she was also a role model for the new lifestyle of marriage and career. When she married Evans Clark, a history instructor at Princeton, in 1915, she kept her name and commuted from Princeton to New York, where she worked for the *Morning Telegraph.*

Kirchwey's lifestyle as a Princeton faculty wife would have been avant-garde even fifty years later, when I was living in Princeton faculty housing and going to the obligatory ceremonial round of tea parties and houseplant tours. In 1915, it led to disaster. Both husband and wife were sexually inexperienced despite their radical ideas; she quickly became pregnant, and her son Brewster was born in 1916. The strains of maintaining the marriage, jobs, and parenting overwhelmed them both. Clark lost his position at Princeton, and tragically, the baby died at the age of eight months.

The couple moved to New York, and Kirchwey joined the staff of *The Nation* under the great editor Oswald Garrison Villard. She gave birth to her second son, Michael, in 1919 and went home from the office every day to nurse him. A third son was born soon after. Meanwhile, Kirchwey's socialist interests, intelligence, and ambition contributed to her rapid rise at *The Nation*. By 1922, she was managing editor. But her marriage was in tatters; by 1924, both partners were having affairs, and Clark began a Jungian analysis with Beatrice Hinkle.[74] When Kirchwey edited *These Modern Women,* she asked Hinkle to write a comment, which proved discouraging:

"Although our group of feminist women appear . . . to have achieved some kind of fulfillment . . . they have not achieved an inner freedom, or a real solution of their personal problems. They are weak on the side of their woman's nature. Several of them are married, but children are few; and taking them as a group, the general deduction to be drawn is that the love life is meager and that little enrichment of the personality through the love experience has been gained."[75]

But a dominant theme of the essays was the equation of disillusion and maturity. "Growing up" was defined as a loss of faith in movements and ideologies, and a greater reliance on individual solutions and individual success. Psychologist Lorine Pruette called her essay "The Evolution of Disenchantment." At the age of thirty-one, she explained, she had "lost all my motivating faiths, faith in the righteous cause of women, faith in the re-creating powers of science, faith in the ennobling possibilities of education."[76]

Although they experimented boldly with new lifestyles and careers, the Heterodites of the 1920s did not create a feminist revolution. Their radical programs left intact the idea that women, rather than both parents, were responsible for maintaining the home and the family. In an eloquent and farsighted article called "Why Women Fail," published in 1931, Lorine Pruette saw women as conditioned to lead lives as vicarious achievers, channeling their needs and aggressions through others. "Most women," she wrote, "still lead contingent lives. It is not quite nice for them to be greedy and grasping for themselves, but they can be shameless for another—a man or a child. Great numbers of them prefer to work through another person and to find their own joys and compensations in the success of another."

But these contingent lives could lead to bitterness and frustration and could put an unbearable weight on the relationship. Until women could cease to live contingent lives, they would never compete successfully with men or find their own strength and joy. "The woman who wishes to be famous," Pruette recommends, "should not marry; rather, she should attach herself to one or more women who will fetch and carry for her in the immemorial style of 'wives.'"

Married and divorced twice herself, Pruette too had experienced the temptations of love and the contingent life. But her final thoughts about feminism were hopeful, and like others before her, she used a fable to imagine the coming generations of women who would be free. In the fable, Atalanta loses her race and marries the man who has defeated her:

"After they were married, Atalanta said nothing at all about those other races which she had won, although she heard a great deal about the one that she had lost. She never told that she had grown weary of winning them, nor that she could see no real reason why she should take great pains to arrive always first at the myrtle tree, nor did she ever deny that the gold apples which were brought to her on all future occasions were her favorite fruit. And when her husband competed in other races she came and cheered for him, until presently she forgot that she had been the fleetest runner on any island in the sea. But when upon that first smiling morning after her wedding Atalanta's old nurse had chid her because she had lost the race which she certainly would have won, had she cared enough, even though she had paused to gather all the apples, Atalanta put her quickly out of the room as she whispered finally, 'Do not think that I was vanquished—I was diverted.'"[77]

American women in the 1920s were diverted but not vanquished, and they taught their daughters to work for the time when the golden apples of love, family, sexuality, and security would not come at the price of losing the race.[78]

SEVEN

Heterodoxy in Britain

"I think your hallmark is that you have always disliked people who wanted approval," an interviewer said to Rebecca West in her old age. "You like the heterodox." Surprisingly, West vehemently denied it. "I should like to be approved of," she said. "I hate being disapproved of. I'd had rather a lot of it."[1] British feminists in the 1920s faced a very different environment than the American Heterodites and Atalantas. They had endured the losses of the war. Many women who had been active in the suffrage movement and optimistic about the future before the war had had love affairs and families shattered. They were shocked out of stability, angry at the Victorian values that had precipitated the war and wrecked their lives, and determined to invent new ways to live. In Bloomsbury and beyond, they were experimenting with new models of sexuality including bisexuality, open marriage, and "semi-detached" marriage; with single parenthood and communal housekeeping.

But at the same time, these women wanted social approval for their heterodoxy; they were rebels who also needed the understanding and acceptance of their parents, the cooperation of their spouses, and the tolerance of their children. "I don't believe you realise how much the war has stung our generation," the Scottish novelist Naomi Mitchison wrote to her mother. "We have had the bottom of things knocked out completely, we have been sent reeling into chaos and it seems to us that none of your standards are either fixed or necessarily good because in the end they resulted in the smash-up. We have to try and make a world for ourselves, basing it as far as possible on love and awareness, mentally and bodily, because it seems to us that all the repressions and formulae, all the cutting off of part of our experience, which perhaps looked sensible and even right, in those calm years, have not worked. Much has been taken from us, and we will stick like fury to what is left, and lay hold on life, as it comes to us."[2]

In the postwar years, British feminists won a number of victories. Women over thirty got the vote in 1918; in 1920, women at Oxford got degrees, and the feminist magazine *Time and Tide* began publication. There were two active feminist groups, the Six-Point Group, battling for women's social and economic rights, and the National Union of Societies for Equal Citizenship (NUSEC), whose leader, the Labour MP Eleanor Rathbone, called for a "New Feminism" shifting from equal opportunity to women's special needs. But equality of opportunity was still far from achieved. Over half the women in their late twenties at the beginning of the war never married, and they faced barriers in their professional and vocational lives.[3] For postwar feminists, battling against Victorian standards of femininity, domesticity, and maternity they had internalized despite their efforts to be modern led to stressful decisions. "Of recent years," writes Vera Brittain, "intelligent women in ever-growing numbers have been faced with an intolerable choice. . . . In effect it is this: shall a woman who loves her work for its own sake continue it throughout her life at the sacrifice of marriage, motherhood, and all her emotional needs? Or shall she marry and have children at the cost of her career, and look forward for the rest of her days to an existence which, for a highly-educated woman, means intellectual starvation and monotony?"[4]

Brittain and her contemporaries felt the pressure to live exemplary feminist lives, to prove, by their successful examples, what women could do. "I feel it to be . . . important to the women's movement," wrote Brittain during her first pregnancy, "to supply the fullest possible proof that one can be a normal woman as well as a good feminist."[5] Brittain came as close to leading an exemplary feminist life as any of the women I discuss; that is, a life deliberately viewed as historic, public, adventurous, and experimental. "For Vera Brittain," writes her biographer Deborah Gorham, "feminism was more than a cause she espoused. It was the central organizing principle of her personality, the belief that gave direction to her energies, that enabled her to make the best possible use of her talents as a writer, and through which she defined her personal relationships and her own sense of self."[6] But unlike their American counterparts, Brittain and the feminists of her generation were trying to be modern without the intellectual framework of anthropology, or the support of a feminist community. And they depended to a degree they could not always acknowledge on a sympathetic understanding from those immediately affected by feminist lives—parents, friends, lovers, husbands, children. When these unacknowledged dependencies went awry, they had problems making the transition to the emotional autonomy of the truly heterodox.

REBECCA WEST

Rebecca West (1892–1983) was the most celebrated and contradictory of these icons. The story of Rebecca West, according to her biographer Victoria Glendinning, "is the story of twentieth-century woman. She was both an agent of change and a victim of change."[7] Her real name was Cicely Fairfield, and she grew up in London and Edinburgh, where, as a fourteen-year-old schoolgirl, she was already interested in women's suffrage. Like many rebellious daughters, she wanted to go on the stage, and left school to attend the Royal Academy of Dramatic Arts in London, where she lasted only three terms. But when she realized she would not make it as an actress, she broke into journalism by writing theater reviews for the *Evening Standard,* in exchange for free tickets. In November 1911, she began to write for the radical feminist journal *The Freewoman* and decided to adopt a pseudonym from Ibsen's *Rosmersholm* to protect her parents' feelings. Thus on February 15, 1912, "Rebecca West" was born. After all, she had decided, Cicely Fairfield was not the name for a serious writer, but for someone "blond and pretty like Mary Pickford."[8]

As a journalist and critic, West was forthright, funny, and irreverent. She did not bear fools gladly, and she had no patience with the pious, even when the piety was feminist. In one feud, she called housework "rat poison" and was then taken to task as an elitist unlike the normal woman, who should find joy in domestic tasks. West was unrepentant. "Domestic work is the most elementary form of labor," she replied. "It is suitable for those with the intelligence of rabbits." She was just as dismissive of Olive Schreiner's "humorless" and "depressing" allegories, with their "absurd" and portentous air of enlightenment over commonplace facts: "Then the sun passed down behind the hills: but I knew that the next day he would rise again."[9]

Among West's sharp satiric reviews was one of H. G. Wells, a famous and wealthy novelist of forty-six. "Mr. Wells's mannerisms are more infuriating than ever in *Marriage,*" she wrote in September 1912, going on to describe his bad habits of "spluttering at his enemies" and reveling in sex like a scientific old maid with "a mind too long absorbed in airships and colloids."[10] Wells was amused and intrigued; he invited her to tea at the home where he lived with his second wife, Jane, and his two sons; and in part since he was between mistresses, they began to have an affair. Although West was nineteen, and beautiful, with thick, dark hair, strong eyebrows, and a wide mouth, she regarded the short, stocky Wells as a matinee idol, the maestro: "Being in his company, she recorded half a century later, was 'on a level of seeing Nureyev dance or hearing Gobbi sing.'"[11]

Wells had arranged his life satisfactorily to enjoy both the comfort and security of marriage and the excitement of affairs. Indeed, he shared the details of his conquests and romances with his wife, who uncomplainingly acquiesced. But the stakes were of course much higher from West's point of view. As a feminist journalist she had made bold statements about woman's autonomy, but when Wells tired of the affair after a year, she wrote him letters from the same self-abasing model as had Margaret Fuller and Eleanor Marx: "I would give my whole life to feel your arms around me again. I wish you had loved me. I wish you liked me."[12] Her passion attracted him back, and in the main phase of their affair, Wells was careless, and Rebecca became pregnant.

What was to be done? She could not get an abortion; he refused to leave his wife. For months, Wells paid for her to live secretly in the country. On August 5, 1914, just before the start of the war, she gave birth to a son, Anthony Panther West. They had planned that she would give the baby up for adoption, but when she held him, she was unable to do it. With great courage, West determined to keep the child and raise him herself. Wells was willing to provide financial support. "Well, I'm a rich man," he wrote to her sister, "and can give her that. At least I can let Rebecca keep her baby."[13] Her mother, to whom she was very close, wanted to take her home, even if it meant acknowledging the fatherless child; but Rebecca refused.

Wells was generous with money, and with affection; he moved her around, first to a rented farmhouse in Hertfordshire, then to a house in the London suburbs with a nurse, two servants, and a housekeeper, where she posed as "Miss West," with her infant nephew. For the next few years, Wells moved back and forth between the two households, while Rebecca wrote, reviewed books, made new friends, and visited with her family. In 1917, when he was three, she sent Anthony away to board at a Montessori school in London, supposedly for his own good.

But this peculiar masquerade was even harder on Anthony than on Rebecca. He did not know who his parents were; for the early years of his childhood he called his mother Auntie Panther, and his father Wellsie. Wells never visited for longer than three days at a time and to the little boy was "someone enormously buoyant, cheerful, and energetic, who blew in and out of my already sufficiently bewildering existence quite inexplicably and unpredictably."[14] At the age of six, when his grandmother died, Anthony started asking questions, and Rebecca told him that she was his mother but asked him to continue to call her Auntie Panther. Not until Anthony was eight did HG begin to sign letters "Your affectionate Daddy Wellsie."[15] Throughout Anthony West's life, he would blame Rebecca for his unhappiness, although she was the one who made sacrifices for him and who took responsibility for him.

In March 1923, West broke off the affair, with the proviso that Wells would give her five hundred pounds a year and child support for Anthony and would no longer see his son. Nevertheless, Wells and West continued to see each other for some time. In October, she went to New York on a book tour, lecturing on feminism and the modern novel. Here she met new lovers and made new friends, including Emma Goldman, Doris Stevens, and the best-selling novelist Fannie Hurst, later to become the patron of Zora Neale Hurston.

In New York, she had a fling with the London press magnate Max Beaverbrook, publisher of the *Daily Express* and the *Evening Standard*. West was infatuated, but, humiliatingly, he seemed to have taken the affair much more lightly than she did. In April 1924, she sent him a macabre comic fable, about a "wicked newspaper proprietor" with a "pure young enemy" and four demanding wives, each with a baby. The proprietor has the wives poisoned and the babies "parked in a row on the lawn." He arranges to make the deaths appear accidental, but then it turns out that they have been insured with his company, and he will be bankrupt. In the end, he commits suicide in his pond while the pure young enemy revives the corpses and promises to take the wives to Salt Lake City, where everyone is a Mormon.[16]

That summer, she adapted the fable as a silent movie script, *They Forgot to Read the Directions,* which Beaverbrook had made at his country estate Cherkley. West starred in its production along with Beaverbrook, Wells, and various other friends and relations. Hamming it up as befits a onetime student at RADA, West plays "gentle little" Hannah Bella, one of three innocent girls seduced and abandoned by the charming but unprincipled

tycoon Jasper Habbakuk (Beaverbrook). The girls arrive, carrying their illegitimate babies ("little blossoms, fallen untimely
from the tree," writes West in the garrulous subtitles), at Habbakuk's estate, where the Reverend Jeremiah Honeydew (a sleek
and debonair H. G. Wells) is trying to redeem the evil tycoon.
But Habbakuk orders his black retainers, George Washington
Abraham Lincoln General Grant Snowball and Peter, to poison
the women by putting prussic acid in their cocktails. They collapse, writhing, on the lawn, and then the faithful retainers
throw their babies into a pool called the Infanticidium.

But a visiting Utah politician, Senator Smoot (Isaac Bell),
brings the women back to life with the American miracle remedy Yadil, and Hannah Bella insists on going at once to the
Infanticidium. There she sees the babies floating upside down.
"That baby has two feet!" she cries. "My baby had two feet! It is
my child!" Smoot dives in and saves two of the infants. Hannah
looks them over and grabs one by the leg. "I am not interested in
babies as such," she exclaims. "This one is mine. Throw the
other one back." He does; but then he also comes up with a plan
to rescue the three women: he will take them all back to Utah as
his polygamous Mormon brides. Meanwhile Habbakuk marries
Florence Flightingale (Lady Hulton), a tough-looking matron
who will keep him in check.

Luckily, Anthony never saw this Ortonesque farce of polygamy
and infanticide. Given their lighthearted attitudes toward sexual
misalliance, it's a wonder that Beaverbrook, Wells, and West
didn't get him to play a bit part. By this point, Anthony, who had
been shuttled around to a variety of boarding schools and progressive schools, was clearly unhappy and troubled. He knew that
he was illegitimate, and that the other students would bully him;
he cut up his bedsheets with scissors, wrote plaintive letters
home, and wished to become a Roman Catholic. In one sense,
the film is a hilarious tribute to West's gutsiness and ability to
make fun of herself. In another sense, this sophisticated adult
humor was not much use to an unhappy child.[17]

Over the next few years, West traveled back and forth to New

York, where she had a number of affairs, and spent a summer in Florence, where she began psychoanalysis with an American lay analyst, Mary Wilshire—a wasted opportunity in which West quickly began to recover memories of childhood sexual abuse by her father.[18] Wilshire also spent some time with Anthony and told Rebecca that he had a mother fixation.[19] These expensive "discoveries" did not do much to advance Rebecca's understanding of herself. Throughout the 1920s, West was planning a book called *Second Thoughts on Feminism*. She never wrote it, but we can surmise that it would have been angry and bitter. She was also rethinking her political positions, moving away from her youthful socialism to be strongly critical of communism; and realizing that despite her radical bravado, she had "a steady monogamous nature and would have been the most wifely wife on earth."[20] Although West became highly successful as a novelist, the affair with Wells was so painful that even in her eighties she could not bear to reread their letters.

In 1929, through her friend Vera Brittain, West met Henry Andrew, a banker working in Germany. By November 1930, they were married. The marriage was long-lasting and stable, but also emotionally disappointing. Within a few years, she had realized that he was losing interest in her, and their sex life ended in 1937. Her relationship with her son worsened to the point of a feud, especially after Wells died in 1946, and they battled over his legend. As she received more and more honors as a novelist, journalist, and woman of letters, celebrated for her books on Yugoslavia, and on the Nuremberg trials, West also had to face the disintegration of her youthful and defiant dreams.

In 1970, widowed, and by now a "Dame," West allowed the American scholar Gordon Ray, the president of the Guggenheim Foundation, to read more than eight hundred letters from Wells, which she had kept in an old suitcase. Only five of her letters to him had survived. Over the next three summers, she read drafts of Ray's study of her relationship with Wells. The process was agonizing; she had vowed not to profit from her relationship with Wells, but the appearance of new biographical data revealed how much he had concealed from her and how much he had lied to her. It was, Victoria Glendinning writes, "a sad time bomb exploding in the 1970s when she was old."[21]

As the women's liberation movement gained momentum in the 1970s, a new generation of feminist writers and critics became interested in Rebecca West; but seeing herself through their eyes was also difficult and troubling for her. In 1973, in an interview on the BBC, she talked about her life as a woman writer in terms of constant interruptions: "It's a terrible handicap to be a woman."[22] Yet in an essay on contemporary English women writers in the *TLS* the following year, she took an ironic, resigned stance about the way "they all lived unhappily ever after": "It is the time-scales of the universe which put us all wrong. A baby takes nine months to bring to birth, and a woman can have a baby a year; yet it will take centuries before the sexual life of a woman, which produced these babies with such speed, becomes guaranteed against the humiliation and insecurity described by contemporary women novelists. But we were never promised otherwise."[23]

I met Rebecca West in the winter of 1977, when she invited me to tea at her large flat at Kingston House across from Hyde Park. She was eighty-five, deaf, with a bad leg and cataracts in both eyes, but she was astonishingly gallant and witty. "I'm terribly dilapidated," she told me, along with much gossip about Wells and other writers, especially Iris Murdoch. When Victoria Glendinning talked with West about her biography, Glendinning felt that it had "turned out to be a sadder story than I expected, on account of the way she felt about the things that had happened to her. She felt, like Job, persecuted by God (and by man, woman, and child) and any friend who played the part of Job's comforter got short shrift from her."[24]

West had become an icon, sought out by scholars and biographers whom she befriended. The American feminist scholar Jane Marcus set about editing West's early journalism, and Carmen Callil and Ursula Owen of Virago Press "arranged a meeting with Rebecca, approaching Kingston House almost as if it

were a fortress. . . . Ursula regarded Rebecca as deeply daunting—even frightening. Rebecca could almost literally take your
breath away, Ursula remembered, in the way she condemned
people."[25]

VERA BRITTAIN

One of the women she had condemned was Vera Brittain
(1893–1970), who had introduced West to her husband, but fell
out with her over the issue of pacifism during World War II. In
1933, Brittain's *Testament of Youth: An Autobiographical Study of
the Years 1900-1925* had been an international best-seller. Both
a record of her own intellectual development as a feminist, and a
personal history of the catastrophic war years, the book had a
strong political message about pacifism and moral awareness.
Brittain wanted to write "history in terms of personal life," and to
use her experience to awaken her readers to the temptations of
blind patriotism and heroic fantasy. For biographer Deborah
Gorham, Brittain's book was "one of the intellectual milestones"
of her adolescence, the story of a "girl who defies the voices
which tell her that she will never achieve anything of importance
because she is female, and who goes on to become a woman
who is able to use her talents and achieve genuine autonomy."[26]
But in researching Brittain's life, Gorham also discovered more
contradictions and tensions than this inspiring self-portrait
revealed. Those contradictions are what make Brittain relevant to
women today.

BEFORE THE WAR

As the oldest child growing up in a prosperous upper-middle-class
family in Buxton, in Derbyshire, Vera Brittain seemed destined for
a traditionally feminine life. She was pretty and petite and, along
with her mother, enjoyed games, shopping, housekeeping, and

clothes. Her parents confidently expected her to play a significant role in local society, and to make a good match, and they sent her to St. Monica's School when she was thirteen with the idea that an excellent education would be a good investment in these roles. At school in 1910, Vera had her first romantic friendship with another girl, Stella Sharp. When the headmistress called her in to question her about this forbidden "GP,"or Grand Passion, she defended her feelings in intellectual and literary terms: "I told her of all the shadows of the greater things of life & my wish to write about them. I told her that Stella was necessary to me not only because I loved her but because she understood these things."[27]

Brittain's adolescent sense of herself as a writer and intellectual, someone different from other girls, was inspired by her reading and encouraged by her encounter with women teachers at St. Monica's. Reading Shelley's "Adonais" at sixteen, she was determined to become a writer, and her English teacher, Miss Fry, influenced both her literary tastes and her early feminism. "My . . . writing tends towards a purpose now," she wrote. "I believe that this is greatly due to Miss Fry's teaching, and her understanding of Carlyle and Ruskin, about whom she taught us, so differently to the dull, hackneyed type of 'literature' that so many English mistresses make use of today." In an essay on Thomas More's *Utopia,* Brittain wrote, "Women's rights are a burning question not only in their own, but in male minds, and not infrequently their voices are heard in our streets demanding of the age a speedy reparation for the injuries done to them by the 'centuries that are gone.'"[28]

Brittain was also reading Olive Schreiner's *Woman and Labor,* which seemed to respond to her own needs to break away from provincial society and live an epic life. The book, she later observed, "sounded with a note that had the authentic ring of a new gospel" and "supplied the theory that linked my personal resentments with the public activities of the suffragettes."[29]

In her last year of school, Brittain was longing for independence, and the wider life of the university. But instead she went home to Buxton for her social debut, and the daily life of a young lady. She acted in amateur theatricals, played bridge, paid calls, and changed her clothes: "I put on my new white serge and the Paris hat with the white tulle bows, white shoes & stockings & a low necked blouse, and looked quite a dream."[30]

She was eighteen, but, as she bitterly reflected many years later, innocent about sexuality and much more driven by ambition and dreams of literary success. Although she adored her brother, Edward, she also felt that she was brighter, and that she should earn her own living, ideas that shocked her old-fashioned parents: Father "has nothing but contempt for me & my knowledge, just as he has at heart for all women because he believes them for some unknown reason to be inferior to him." Her mother supported Vera's intellectual ambitions, but had been "brought up in an age which taught that a wife was *always* subservient to a husband."[31]

Meanwhile there were possible and impossible suitors on the scene—the tutor, the curate—who bothered her by their yearning glances and confused her with their physical overtures. When Vera's mother finally told her about sex, she was disgusted: "On the way to golf I induced Mother to disclose a few points on sexual matters which I thought I ought to know, though the information is always intensely distasteful to me & most depressing—in fact it quite puts me off my game!"[32]

Her golf game was even more undermined in June, when a friend of her brother Edward's was expelled from his public school, Uppingham, for what Edward described as the "one unpardonable sin at a public school—immorality." Again, Vera demanded answers from her mother, and learned about homosexuality. "Now I *know*," she wrote in her diary. "I feel as if I don't want ever now to marry—it is all such confusion, the union of our physical & spiritual nature & to know just where longing becomes temptation and is wrong."[33]

With these feelings of confusion, Brittain refused a proposal of marriage and persuaded her parents to let her go up to Oxford. By today's standards, she was astonishingly innocent and naive for a girl of nineteen, confiding to her diary, "How I wish I could meet a good strong splendid man, full of force & enthusiasm, and in earnest about his life! There *must* be such!"[34] While she had thought enough about women's roles to rebel against the expectations of her family, she had never questioned the equally restrictive and unnatural roles assigned to men. The terrible contrast between that girlish innocence and the Great War that would change it forever is part of the reason for Brittain's value and impact as a woman witness.

Moreover, those feelings of hero worship, once Vera had expressed them, soon attached themselves to a real person. In the spring of 1914, she met Roland Leighton, a school friend of her brother's. He was two years younger, even more inexperienced than she; but he was a serious, confident young man who both lived up to prewar public school ideals of manly virtue, patriotism, and service, and also came from a family that appealed to Vera's romantic, rebellious side. His mother, Marie Leighton, was a popular novelist, the Barbara Cartland of her day, who dressed in sable and ermine and maintained a bohemian, literary household very different from Vera's own. Roland gave her a copy of Olive Schreiner's *The Story of an African Farm,* with a letter: "When you have read it let me know what you think of it, and whether you agree with me that Lyndall is rather like you— only sadder perhaps and not so charmingly controversial." Vera writes back, "I think I am a little like Lyndall, and would probably be more so in her circumstances, uncovered by the thin veneer of polite social intercourse." She writes in her diary, "It is a great book, and it has made my head almost ache with thinking."[35] Her thoughts also drifted toward love: "I so desire a sympathetic companionship. I do so want as Lyndall did in Olive Schreiner's book, 'something to worship.'"[36]

By April 1914, Vera believed that Roland Leighton was that destined companion, that object of worship: "beside these newly-born dreams," she wrote in her diary, "my old dreams and aspirations grew pale, as would the moon's cold splendour beside the passionate flames of the sun."[37] These passionate flames seemed even hotter in July, at Roland's graduation, when they wandered in the school's beautiful rose garden, and she wore "pink ninon" and a rose-trimmed lace hat. Afterward, he wrote her a love poem called "In the Rose-Garden," which she kept forever.

And if Vera had become infatuated with Roland's stoic personality and glamorous mother, Deborah Gorham suggests that, unconsciously, Roland may also have been attracted to Edward and have been compensating for those feelings in his courtship of Vera, "perhaps as a move toward heterosexuality."[38] Without the catalyst of the war, the romance might quickly have faded, as the stolid and conventional Roland and the ambitious, mercurial, competitive Vera got to know each other better. But under the circumstances of the time, "the abnormal wartime situation encouraged them to proceed more quickly than they would otherwise have done in moving from an initial mutual attraction to intense love."[39] In the end, Vera and Roland would meet only seven times, for a total of seventeen days.

DURING THE WAR

By the time Vera entered Somerville College in the fall of 1914, the war had begun, but she was shielded from it in the early months. "Current events," she later explained, "represented something that must be followed rather reluctantly in the newspapers, but would never, conceivably, have to be lived. What really mattered to us were not these public happenings, but the absorbing incidents of our own private lives—our careers, our ambitions, our games, and our love-affairs."[40] As an adult, Brittain would become famous, even notorious, for her pacifist beliefs, but in 1914 she was unthinkingly supportive of the public school ideals of manly duty and courage, and quite ready to play her part in urging her brother and male friends to enlist for the noble cause of war. She had been thrilled to see her brother Edward's participation in the school's Officer Training Corps and was proud when he joined the Officers' Senior Training Corps at Oxford.

Moreover, Brittain's feminism was more rhetorical than real. She joined the Oxford Women's Suffrage Society, but also found herself ill at ease in a community of female students, so closely chaperoned that not even her brother could come to her room. "Strange how one can feel as I do about some women & be an ardent feminist still!" she wrote in her diary. "A feminine community is always appalling to anyone like me who gets on much better in the society of men."[41] Feminism for Brittain in 1914, Gorham explains, meant "not a sense of identification with other women, but rather a desire to enter the world of men." Her own ambition was to become the secretary to a famous literary man, and she was already thinking of studying typing and shorthand when she finished her degree.[42]

Brittain projected these conservative views of femininity onto her favorite women dons. She admired Miss Hayes Robinson, but thought "she has somehow missed her vocation in life . . . she ought to have been married. I should say she is very clever indeed & very self-reliant, without being either violently original or aggressively independent, and these qualities . . . would have made her an excellent wife & really the ideal and equal companion of some brilliant man." Perhaps, she speculated, Hayes Robinson was "nearer to the ideal type of woman—to the woman we hope the future will bring. . . . She is an instance of a woman who has spent her life in the pursuit & imparting of knowledge . . . without ever losing an atom of her womanliness or feminine attractiveness."[43]

Roland had enlisted, and in one of their brief meetings, they became engaged, "for three years or the duration of the War." Vera did not wear a ring; it is "a symbol of the old inequality & therefore hateful to me."[44] By March 1915, he had been sent to the front. That summer, after her first year at Oxford, Brittain left school and joined the Voluntary Aid Detachment (VAD), an auxiliary association of ladies that provided support to the trained professional nurses. When she entered nurse's training, Brittain had led such a protected life that she did not know how to boil an egg. Sexually, she and Roland had shared one romantic kiss. By April 1919, when she left the VAD, she would have witnessed the unprecedented carnage of the Western Front and become familiar with the bodies of men. "Towards the men," she wrote in *Testament of Youth,* "I came to feel an almost adoring gratitude for their simple and natural acceptance of my ministrations. Short of actually going to bed with them, there was hardly an intimate service that I did not perform for one or another in the course of four years, and I still have reason to be thankful for the knowledge of masculine functioning which the care of them gave me, and for my early release from the sex-inhibitions that . . . beset many of my female contemporaries."

Roland and Vera corresponded on the same lofty level of romantic and literary idealism that had characterized their courtship. She called him "Roland of Roncesvalles" and turned him into the soldier hero of British patriotic fiction. But over the months, Roland's letters from the trenches took on a very different tone, suggesting the gulf of experience that lay between them. "Do I seem very much of a phantom in the void to you?" he writes. "I must. You seem rather to me like a character in a book or someone whom one has dreamt of & never seen. I suppose there exists such a place as Loewstoft and that there once was a person called Vera Brittain who came over there with me."[45]

Just before Christmas, 1915, as Vera was expecting him home on leave, Roland Leighton was killed at Hédauville. He was only twenty years old; Vera was twenty-two. "This year dawned differently from any other I have known," she wrote on New Year's Day, 1916. "It marks the completion in the change of my outlook on life from a child's or even a girl's to a woman's."[46]

For the rest of the war, Vera worked as a nurse, under dire conditions, and mourned the loss of Roland and his friends. "Nursing," according to Deborah Gorham, "represented the antithesis of her wartime experience with love; if her romance with Roland was largely based on fantasy sustained by literary illusion, nursing plunged her into forceful contact with blood, flesh, pain and dirt."[47] The war experience made Brittain a lifelong pacifist and put steel into her romantic feminism. But in 1918, she and her family suffered a further terrible loss: her brother, Edward, was killed in action in Italy. In some ways, they never entirely recovered; Brittain's father became seriously depressed and, despite periods of recovery, committed suicide in 1935. Vera requested before her death that her daughter scatter her ashes on Edward's grave on the Asiego Plateau, where for nearly fifty years she had left her heart.[48]

AFTER THE WAR

After the Armistice, Vera returned to Oxford to finish her degree, changing her concentration from literature to history. Although she made friends and began to take serious steps toward a literary career, she often felt depressed and out of place among the younger women. When one of her new Oxford friends died of heart failure, Vera began to have symptoms of serious depression, insomnia, and breakdown. Looking into her mirror, she hallucinated that her face was disfigured, and that she was growing a witchlike beard, the external sign of her survivor's guilt, and also of her confused emotions. For months, "with a sense of incommunicable horror," she could not keep herself from anxiously checking mirrors and rubbing her face for signs of this "sinister and peculiar change."[49]

But she was able to get through this period of postwar traumatic stress largely because of the patience, support, and affection of another woman at Oxford who would become her closest friend—Winifred Holtby. Holtby, who was almost six years younger, had worked in a woman's auxiliary army corps during the war and was also an aspiring novelist. The relationship was the most intense and idealized of Brittain's life, second only to her doomed romance with Roland; she wrote *Testament of Friendship* to commemorate it after Holtby's death of kidney disease in 1935; and most of the women who have written about the friendship describe it as a lesbian love affair.

But while Brittain loved and depended upon Holtby for emotional and intellectual support, she was adamant in denying any sexual component. Any gossip of their friendship as a lesbian liaison, she insisted, was just "too, too Chelsea!" In her diaries, she indicates her distaste for lesbian sexuality. In 1929, she was planning to write "a longish article called 'Who Are the Feminists?'—a reply to the oft-repeated statement . . . that feminists come from the ranks of the inverted . . . my argument being based on an analysis of the anti-feminism of *The Well of Loneliness* and *Extraordinary Women* in contrast to the sexually normal qualities . . . of such leading feminists as Mrs. Josephine Butler, & Olive Schreiner & Mrs. Pankhurst. . . ."[50]

Holtby may have felt differently, but if so, she kept it to herself. She accepted the role of old maid aunt next to the dazzling Vera and learned to take vicarious pleasure in Vera's romances and family, to put herself second, and to put up with Vera's demands while expecting little in return. But they shared literary and political ideals, and a feminist vision of the modern woman. When they left Oxford, they shared a flat together in London, working for feminist organizations, getting started as freelance journalists, and working on their novels. Together they went to hear Rebecca West lecture on the modern novel at the London School of Economics, where they found her "exquisitely funny, brilliant and often wise," and wonderfully dressed in a smoke-gray dress and sable coat.[51] They were jubilant when Winifred's novel *Anderby Wold* was published in 1923, followed by Vera's *The Dark Tide.*

Both supported the "Old Feminism" of equal rights rather than the "New Feminism," which asserted that women had been emancipated and looked beyond questions of gender. In an article for *Time and Tide,* Holtby argued that while the Old Feminism might seem "conservative, hysterical, or blindly loyal to old catchwords," that was not "the real truth. The New Feminism emphasizes the importance of the 'women's point of view,' the Old Feminism believes in the primary importance of the human being." Holtby was an Old Feminist because she desired "an end of the whole business, the demands for equality, the suggestions of sex warfare, the very name of feminist. I want to be about the work in which my real interests lie, the study of inter-race relationships, the writing of novels, and so forth. But while the inequality exists, while injustice is done and opportunity denied to the great majority of women, I shall have to be feminist, and an Old Feminist, with the motto Equality First. And I shan't be happy till I get it."[52]

But these ideals of autonomy and woman's full humanity were abstractions that became much more complex within marriage. Both Holtby and Brittain had preached the doctrine of modern egalitarian marriage, but they had always expected that Vera—the fragile, pretty one—would marry and that Winifred—the hulking, hearty one—would not. In the summer of 1924, Vera met the Oxford-trained political philosopher George Edward Gordon Catlin, and they married a year later. During the engagement, she had negotiated frankly with him over terms, insisting that she regarded the first year of marriage as an experiment, and that he would have to respect her feminist convictions and professional priorities. Their wedding was traditional, with Vera in orange blossoms and a veil; and the bride, at thirty-two, was still a virgin. But in other respects, it marked the beginning of an attempt at a marriage of true minds and equal partners.

SEMI-DETACHED MARRIAGE

Initially, Brittain, who kept her own name, agreed to follow Catlin to Cornell University in Ithaca, New York, where he had a professorship in the Department of Government. But the arrangement soon began to fray. She hated being a faculty wife in the provinces and could not translate her journalistic success in England to work in the United States. By 1926, she had decided to return to London and initiate the "modernist experiment" of what we would now call a commuting marriage—commuting between London and upstate New York. In an article for the *Evening News* in 1928, Brittain outlined her proposal for "semi-detached marriage." "One of the strongest of traditions," she wrote, "is that which regards marriage as a day-by-day, hour-by-hour, unbroken and unbreakable association. Our grandparents were wont to boast that they had been married for thirty years and had never spent so much as one night under different roofs." But "under such circumstances marriage soon becomes a bondage, with mutual jealousy for chains. Nothing could be further from the free, generous, and intelligent comradeship which is the marriage ideal of the finest young men and women of today." Instead, she recommended comradeship, and "intermittent reunions," with "children, for obvious reasons, under the care of their mother." In an optimistic tone, Brittain concluded that although semi-detached marriage was not perfect, the more advanced men and women "have found that the advantages of living under one roof do not outweigh the disadvantages of one partner being deprived of her beloved occupation, and being thereby made dependent, restless, and discontented."[53]

Brittain and Catlin put the idea into action in the summer of 1927, when their son was born, and maintained a joint household, with Vera, Winifred, and the children living in London, and George joining them for part of the year, until Winifred's death. Like the domestic arrangements of Eleanor Marx and Edward Aveling, the arrangement won plaudits as a model for the avant-garde. Winifred reported that Lady Rhondda, the editor of *Time and Tide,* "thinks what you & Gordon are doing supremely important. She says it may happen that you as an artist & thinker won't accomplish as much as you might have done unmarried, because so much of your time will be taken up in fighting for your career, but that only by doing what you are doing will it be possible for people in the future to live normal lives, and that it is immensely important to humanity."[54]

But actually living in a semi-detached marriage brought unexpected tension and bitterness. The chains of jealousy were not so easily broken, and one major set of problems was sexual. Catlin felt free to have extramarital affairs while Brittain did not; and despite her earnest efforts to educate herself about modern sexuality, and to overcome what was now disapprovingly labeled "frigidity," they never completely resolved the issue. For years, she tolerated his affairs and had unrequited sexual fantasies about her American publisher, George Brett. Catlin became even more estranged after Winifred's death, when Vera became her literary executor. "You preferred her to me," he wrote to her. "It humiliated me and ate me up. . . . The point is, not sex but preference is what matters."[55]

Secondly, the arrangement did not prevent conflicts over their careers, and both felt resentful of and limited by the professional demands of the other. Catlin was jealous of her great success as a writer and wanted to have a career in Labour Party politics. He left Cornell in 1935, "trying to run a semi-detached career as well as a semi-detached marriage."[56] But he was not a successful politician and blamed Vera's involvement in pacifism for his problems.[57] Vera was immensely courageous in maintaining her pacifist stance during World War II, when it became not just unpopular but suspect; her own readership dramatically declined. But she had little sense of humor and took herself and her ideas seriously; even her literary agent, David Higham, privately called her most famous book "Testicles of Youth" to amuse himself.[58]

Third, and most painful, Vera worried that she had made decisions that had a negative effect on her son. While her daughter, Shirley, born in 1930, demonstrated even as a child the intelligence and resilience that would bring her a distinguished political career, her son, John, had problems that got out of control during the war when both of the children were sent to the United States to escape the Blitz. When they came back three years later, Shirley made a rapid readjustment, but John's life was disrupted for years, and much like Anthony West, he blamed his mother. Brittain too saw the separation as irrevocable: "The small gallant figures which disappeared behind the flapping tarpaulin of the grey-painted Duchess of Atholl have never grown up in my mind, for the children who returned and eventually took their places were not the same; the break in continuity made them rather appear as an elder brother and sister of the vanished pair."[59]

Yet in 1950, Catlin and Brittain were still together to celebrate their twenty-fifth wedding anniversary, and Brittain managed to convey to her daughter the unconditional support she had longed for herself. In a letter to Shirley Williams, she wrote that she was "conscious all my life that I had disappointed *my* mother because, as she once told me, what she really wanted was the kind of daughter who was happy just to stick around the house and do the flowers—and if you had turned out to be the flower-doing kind I didn't want you to feel that you had disappointed *me*."[60]

Brittain was no longer a literary celebrity when she died in 1970; but in the late 1970s, *Testament of Youth* was rediscovered by Carmen Callil, one of the founders of Virago Press. At first, Sir George Catlin was unwilling to have the reprint go forward by a company trading under "the deplorable title" of Virago. "I think it an extremely *bad* title (!!Lesbian)," he noted.[61] But he was mollified, and the book went on to become a best-seller again, and a hit when it was dramatized by the BBC starring Cheryl Campbell as Vera Brittain.

Rebecca West too made a final dramatic appearance in the 1980s, appearing in the film *Reds* (1981) to talk about Emma Goldman. While making the film, the director, actor Warren Beatty, asked West about her sex life. She immediately answered: "I have some time free on Thursday afternoons."[62] At her funeral in 1983, her friend Bernard Levin quoted from *Rosmersholm:* "Live, work, act. Don't sit here and brood and grope among insoluble enigmas."[63]

EIGHT

The Dark Ladies
of New York

Zenobia on the Hudson

In an essay in the *Partisan Review* in 1941, Philip Rahv singled out Zenobia in Hawthorne's *Blithedale Romance* as "the most resplendent and erotically forceful woman in American fiction." For Rahv, Zenobia epitomized not only Hawthorne's fascination, but also his discomfort, with the feminist intellectual: "He wants to destroy the dark lady as at the same time that he wants to glorify her; hence his indictment of her is never really driven home."[1]

When the editor Norman Podhoretz wrote *Making It,* his memoir of fame and status among the Jewish intellectuals of New York, he seemed to recall Rahv's image of the sensuous, powerful, and brilliant dark lady. Each generation of American intellectuals, Podhoretz declared, has had a slot for a female writer, preferably a "dark-haired one with supreme intellectual self-confidence and a keen desire for prominence."[2] Like the Fisher King of the Grail legends, the Dark Lady ruled alone until she became too old, and then she was retired as Dark Lady emerita, or symbolically slain by a younger and perhaps even darker lady. In the tribe of New York intellectuals to which both Rahv and Podhoretz belonged, the Dark Lady held her place by tacitly endorsing the prejudices and attitudes of the male members of the group, including their contempt for popular culture, their reverence for alienated high modernism, their left-wing political engagement, and their disdain for feminism. This token woman, the Dark Lady of New York, was also erotically forceful and sexually magnetic; and a century after Zenobia, the Dark Lady of Salem, those who glorified her still also wanted to destroy her.

Both men and women writing about the New York intellectuals of the 1930s and 1940s have emphasized the difference between the experiences of men and women.[3] The men came from families where adoring parents cherished their intellectual aspirations, pampered and admired them. Lionel Trilling, the son of Polish immigrants, for example, was considered so irresistible by his doting mother that she put a sign on his carriage reading, "Please Don't Kiss the Baby." At the age of six, Trilling's proud parents decided he should go to Oxford, and his father changed trades to spare the infant genius the "embarrassment of having to say that his father was a tailor."[4]

Trilling became a prominent professor at Columbia University, but many male intellectuals were not expected to earn a living. All over Greenwich Village were *Luftmenschen*—"air men"— without visible means of support. The cafeteria was their salon, the park bench their seminar room. "To read and talk all day was considered a respectable profession—especially when a rich or hard-working wife kept up the amenities."[5] As Irving Kristol said, "It was a tradition among the New York intellectuals to marry money."[6] Some of them married it again and again.

The women grew up with different expectations. Trilling's wife, Diana Rubin, the daughter of Polish immigrants, was "never complimented" on her looks or intelligence and was told that her college education was to provide "mental diversion" as she went about her domestic chores in the future. After her marriage to the genius, Diana Trilling suffered for twenty years from panic attacks and other debilitating phobias and did not write her first book until after her husband's death.

After 1934, belonging to the crowd around the magazine *Partisan Review* virtually defined membership in the New York intellectuals. Edited by two young radicals, Philip Rahv and William Phillips, the *Partisan Review* thrillingly attempted to unite American left politics with literary modernism and aesthetic sophistication. No longer "the masses," but the intellectual elite were to be the hope of progress. Although there were other magazines and other crowds and coteries in New York—the *New Republic, Dissent, Commentary, The Nation, The New Yorker*—in its heyday, the *Partisan Review* and the "family" of writers around it was "possibly the most influential little magazine ever"; the "house organ of the American intellectual community."[7] Its writers shared various common characteristics: they were communist anti-Stalinists, "non-Jewish Jews," dissident modernists.[8] The magazine represented an allegiance to "cosmopolitan values . . . a spirit of openness and striving—openness to variety and to change, striving for a fuller understanding of the world and for higher and more inclusive means of expression . . . suspicious of dogma and quick to lash out against the narrowing of cultural responsibilities."[9]

Acceptance by the *Partisan Review* was the crucial initiation rite for aspiring New York intellectuals. But while the writers of the *Partisan Review* distinguished themselves from other left-wing American intellectuals by their admiration for literary modernism and the avant-garde, even in literature they excluded women from the club. Over a fifty-year period, only 12 percent of the essays in the *Partisan Review* were by women.[10]

MARY MCCARTHY: HER OWN WOMAN

Among the New York intellectuals, the Dark Lady was Mary McCarthy (1912–89). McCarthy's combination of elegant style and macho bravado not only made her the first of the New York Dark Ladies, but also the most feared. William Barrett, a minor figure in the New York postwar milieu, recalls that two men recoiled when she appeared at a party as if "an ogress, booted and spurred, had entered the room brandishing her whips." To him, McCarthy was "a Valkyrie maiden, riding her steed into the circle, amid thunder and lightning, and out again, bearing the body of some dead hero across her saddle—herself unscathed and headed promptly for her typewriter."[11] Alfred Kazin thought she owed her rise to a "wholly destructive critical mind," and his wife, Ann Birstein, complained that McCarthy regarded the wives of the New York intellectuals as nothing but Tootsie Rolls.[12] Yet without a feminist movement to offer an alternative intellectual community, or a group like Heterodoxy to unite them, women intellectuals in New York internalized many of the values of the *Partisan Review,* competed for its recognition, and measured themselves against its moral and political standards. When she got drunk and spent the night with Edmund Wilson, Mary McCarthy's first waking thought was "Oh, God, I've disgraced *Partisan Review.*"[13]

When I was growing up in the 1950s, Mary McCarthy was the epitome of the woman who was both glamorous and smart, both dangerously sexy and relentlessly self-mocking. Her confident motto, ironically spoken by the deluded heroine of *The Company She Keeps,* was taken from Chaucer's Criseyde: "I am myn owene woman, wel at ease." She had also modeled herself on the ardent intellectual heroines of Turgenev; and her portrait of the young professor Domna Rejnev in *The Groves of Academe,* my longtime secret role model for the woman intellectual, is a version of this ideal. Domna is a Radcliffe BA, twenty-three years old, who teaches Russian literature and French at a small experimental college. She is a "smoldering anachronism, a throwback to one of those ardent young woman of the Sixties, Turgenev's heroines, who cut their curls short, studied Hegel, crossed their mamas and their papas, reproved their suitors, and dreamed resolutely of 'a new day' for peasants, workers, and technicians." She smokes a lot, likes to drink three little jiggers of whiskey neat before dinner, and has spectacular looks: gray eyes, "dark, straight, glossy hair, cut short"; a "severely beautiful, clear-cut profile, very pure ivory skin, the color of old piano keys." Moreover, Domna has a sophisticated fashion sense. "Unlike most advanced young women, she dressed quietly, without tendentiousness—no ballet-slippers, bangles, dirndls, flowers in the hair. She wore dark suits of rather heavy, good material, cut somewhat full in the coat-skirts: the European tailor-made." In her office, "to deter familiarities, she wore a plain smock . . . that gave her something of the look of a young woman scientist or intern."[14]

Old piano keys! A smock! I have to say that Domna and I had little in common; but this description of the feminist intellectual as elegant, austere, mannish—the whiskey, the coat-skirts—both motivated and alarmed me, and after all, my ancestors came from Kiev. I tried drinking a few jiggers of neat whiskey—bourbon actually—when I was sixteen and passed out. I tried to pursue the fashion decisions at Peck & Peck and Best & Co. and ended up as surely the most weirdly dressed member of the 1959 Jordan Marsh College Board, in a Pendleton tweed outfit that was as close as I could get to the European tailor-made. I even studied Russian intellectual history at Harvard Summer School.

But to those who knew her, Mary McCarthy was more in the American intellectual tradition than the Russian one. When she died in October 1989, Elizabeth Hardwick said of her intellectual lineage: "If there were any real ancestor among American women for Mary McCarthy, it might be Margaret Fuller. . . . Both women have will power, confidence, and a subversive soul sustained by exceptional energy." But as Hardwick also pointed out, "A career of candor and dissent is not an easy one for a woman. . . . Such a person needs more than confidence and indignation. A large measure of personal attractiveness and a high degree of romantic singularity are necessary to step free of the mundane, the governessy, the threat of earnestness and dryness."[15]

McCarthy certainly had romantic singularity. Her young parents died in the flu epidemic of 1918, leaving their four children in the care of a sadistic aunt and uncle, who starved and beat them. She was rescued from this Dickensian experience by another aunt and uncle, but in some ways never recovered completely and compensated her whole life for childhood sensory deprivation by a delighted pleasure in the sensual, the visual, the tactile, the luxurious, in her surroundings and food.

She lost her virginity in high school, with a series of older men. She was also intellectually precocious. "I . . . was an ardent literary little girl in boarding school on the West Coast, getting up at four in the morning to write a seventeen-page medieval romance before breakfast, smoking on the fire-escape and thinking of suicide, meeting a crippled boy in the woods by the cindery athletic field, composing a novelette in study hall about the life of a middle-aged prostitute."[16] One of her English teachers, whom McCarthy remembered as "the cool essence of blue-stocking," suggested that she should go to Vassar; and she entered in 1929, the autumn of the stock-market crash, feeling immediately "the pride and joy of belonging to the very best class in the very best college in America." For McCarthy, "Vassar supplied . . . a pedigree, by osmosis."[17]

At Vassar, while she worshiped her favorite teachers, Miss Kitchel and Miss Sandison, McCarthy was not entirely at home among the society girls and the politicos. "The difference," she told a journalist in 1964, "was not a matter of clothes, proms, men, but was mainly a matter of what they would call 'breeding.' I was not ill-bred, but 'untrained' and 'wild,' which meant not just living-with-a-man-before-marriage and drinking . . . and breaking the rules, but being very outspoken and extreme in all my enthusiasms and dislikes."[18] As her classmates saw it, she "was not a class leader, nor was she an editor on any of the official school publications. To many, she was just a tall, skinny girl from Seattle with straight black hair, which sometimes needed washing, and lovely green eyes. Some felt she had a Cheshire-cat grin. A couple thought she was good-looking. One says now that she looked like Charles Addams' Morticia."[19] In the 1933 class yearbook, though, McCarthy is stunning, looking like a young model, with wide-set eyes, a large, unsmiling mouth, a dramatic gaze, a severe and glossy boy's haircut. Like Margaret Fuller, she was often feared by her classmates. "She could be sharp in her comments in class, and if she didn't care for you she could be abrupt. . . . If you were in her dormitory freshman year, and shared the same bathroom, she would tell you about the older actor she was sleeping with in New York or lecture you on douching. In her sophomore year she was not chosen for the Daisy Chain."[20]

The actor McCarthy was sleeping with was Harold Johnsrud, whom she had met in Seattle; she married him the week after she graduated from Vassar Phi Beta Kappa. In New York, McCarthy began reviewing for the *New Republic* and *The Nation,* while Johnsrud struggled to find work. But during their marriage, she recalled, he "only found work in productions of 'social significance.'" Without having strong political convictions, they both, "through our professional connections, began to take part in a left-wing life"; and without ever joining the Communist Party, they participated in some of the Marxist activism of the thirties. McCarthy describes the atmosphere of these years with deadly wit: "We went to parties to raise money for the sharecroppers, for the Theatre Union, for the New Masses. These parties generally took place in a borrowed apartment, often a sculptor's or commercial artist's studio; you paid for your drinks, which were dispensed at a long, wet table; the liquor was dreadful; the glasses were small, and there was never enough ice. Long-haired men in turtle-necked sweaters marched into the room in processions and threw their overcoats on the floor, against the wall, and sat on them; they were only artists and bit-actors, but they gave these affairs a look of gangsterish menace, as if the room were guarded by the goons of the future. On couches with wrinkled slipcovers, little spiky-haired girls, like spiders, dressed in peasant blouses and carapaced with Mexican jewelry, made voracious passes at baby-faced juveniles; it was said that they did it 'for the Party,' as a recruiting effort."[21]

Marxism, she decided, "was something you had to take up young, like ballet dancing." The marriage to Johnsrud—the first of four for McCarthy—broke up in 1936, and she went to consult the oracular Miss Sandison at Vassar, who told her: "You must learn to live without love if you want to live *with* it." Alas, wrote McCarthy, "I have seldom been capable of living without love, not for more than a month or two."[22]

While the Moscow Trials were on in the midthirties, McCarthy was in Reno. When she returned to New York, in November, she went to a publisher's party in honor of Art Young, cartoonist for *The Masses,* and found herself in the midst of a debate about Trotsky. Did he deserve a hearing? she was asked. Did he deserve the right of asylum? As McCarthy tells the story, she was only vaguely aware of who Trotsky was, but could not imagine that anyone could dispute these basic rights. Four days later, she found herself on the Committee for the Defense of Leon Trotsky and, almost by accident, became an anticommunist. But accident or destiny had its consequences; she began to read more about politics in order to defend herself and discovered, to her shock, that she was on the right side.

The Trotskyites led her naturally to the *Partisan Review,* which she had thought was "over my head," but "kept . . . trying my best to read."[23] Rahv and Phillips soon decided to make her the theater critic of *Partisan Review* because they "thought the theater was of absolutely no consequence"[24] and mistrusted her "critical skills in other fields."[25] But her reviews, says Joseph Epstein, "established her formidability as someone sharp, authoritative, clearly not to be fooled with."[26]

The Trotskyites, moreover, "were said to have all the beautiful girls." As one of McCarthy's friends observed, "To make it with these men a woman had to be good-looking . . . otherwise she didn't exist—she was just like an old rug. Mary was pretty."[27] According to Epstein, "So intrinsic were Mary McCarthy's good looks to her career that everything about the literary persona at the center of that career seemed to proclaim: 'I am not your standard emotionally crippled, intellectual female who has drifted into art or criticism because nothing better was available to her.'"[28] Yet McCarthy did not seem obsessed with her looks; on the contrary, William Barrett remembered, "she did not seem to worry about her clothes or her appearance generally" and did not bother to shave her legs.[29]

She was, however, going through a period of sexual experimentation. McCarthy soon realized that she was sleeping with as many as three men in the same day. "Though slightly scared by what things were coming to, I did not *feel* promiscuous. Maybe no one does. And maybe more girls sleep with more men than you would ever think to look at them."[30] She was also enjoying the substance and surface of her life. It's easy to mock McCarthy as the Martha Stewart of the New York intellectuals and to make fun of her eye for detail. In McCarthy's memoirs, every cocktail has its proper name: Singapore Sling, Daiquiri, Manhattan, Old-Fashioned, Martini, with the Russell Wright aluminum cocktail shaker prominent on the table. She remembers the decor of every apartment she lived in—Beekman Place in 1933, painted apricot with white trim, with good closet space, elevator boys and a doorman, Hepplewhite chairs, L-shaped twin bed–sofas, upholstered in dark brown sateen, van Gogh prints on the walls, and English ivy in white cachepots from Macy's. Another Beekman Place sublet in which she lived during a love affair with Philip Rahv had "elegant modern furnishings, all glass, steel, and chrome on thick beige rugs."[31]

In 1937, in the offices of the *Partisan Review,* McCarthy met Edmund Wilson, who was forty-two while she was twenty-five. He was already the most powerful literary critic in the United States; and the *Partisan Review* crowd was eagerly courting him. Wilson, however, was smitten by McCarthy, "the goyisha princess" among the men, and immediately began to take control of her literary career.[32] They began a clandestine affair, and in 1938, McCarthy married him, leaving her official lover, Philip Rahv, devastated. For the rest of her life, McCarthy revisited this decision and wondered whether she had really loved Rahv more after all; but however badly the marriage to Wilson turned out, she was beginning to feel constrained by the political correctness of the *Partisan Review* environment.

Wilson promised her an upper-class life of glamour and leisure. But he turned out to be an alcoholic, and when he was drunk, he sometimes hit her. On one occasion, while she was pregnant with their only son, Reuel, he hit her and then had her committed to a psychiatric clinic. They stayed together, more or less, for seven years, during which time McCarthy began to write and publish fiction.

During this period, McCarthy also began to create a new image for American women—the woman well at ease. The novelist Alison Lurie writes that "before Mary McCarthy, if an educated girl did not simply abdicate all intellectual ambitions and agree to dwindle into a housewife, there seemed to be only two possible roles she could choose: the Wise Virgin and the Romantic Victim. . . . Clearly there were serious drawbacks to both of those roles . . . but most of us couldn't imagine any alternative until Mary McCarthy appeared on the scene. Her achievement was to invent herself as a totally new type of woman who stood for both sense and sensibility; who was both coolly and professionally intellectual, and frankly passionate."[33]

HANNAH ARENDT: PALLAS ATHENE

By the late 1940s, McCarthy, by this time a well-known writer, was living in New York with a new husband, Bowden Broadwater, and had a new group of European friends. Chief among them was Hannah Arendt (1906–75). In her edition of the McCarthy-Arendt letters, Carol Brightman calls their correspondence "an epistolary romance . . . because it frames the tale of a passionate friendship that was improbable on the face of it. . . . The tenderness found in their letters, however, bespeaks a friendship that borders on romance, not sexual romance, but not totally platonic either. A longing for one another's physical presence runs throughout the correspondence of the 1960s," when McCarthy settled in Europe with her fourth husband, James West.[34]

Indeed, wrote Alfred Kazin, Hannah Arendt was McCarthy's "first real love."[35] In their letters, McCarthy and Arendt discussed each other's work, confided, sought and gave romantic advice, and gossiped. "I was away from New York," Arendt wrote in 1960, "an idiotic affair at Baltimore, honorary degree together with Margaret Mead, a monster, and Marianne Moore, an angel . . . she certainly is not a woman."³⁶ "Dearest Hannah," McCarthy wrote from Paris, "I do miss you tremendously. I am really homesick for you."³⁷ According to Norman Podhoretz, the mutual devotion of Arendt and McCarthy was so great that when McCarthy revealed in her autobiography *Memories of a Catholic Girlhood* that she had a Jewish grandmother, New Yorkers joked behind her back that it was Hannah Arendt.³⁸

Like McCarthy, Arendt was "impatient with feminism, dismissing it as merely another (mass) movement or ideology. She believed strongly that feminism's concern with gender identity, sexuality, and the body were politically inappropriate. She worried that these issues might overwhelm the public sphere and she herself approached them through indirection and allusion."³⁹ But Arendt also felt a strong awareness of her own identity as a woman and had her own history of political and emotional contradiction.

Unusually among these women, Arendt came from a family that appreciated and recognized her intelligence, specialness, and ambition to succeed. Her parents, assimilated German Jews (as a child, Arendt would later recall, she did not know that she was Jewish and never heard the word *Jew* in her home), kept a detailed journal of their daughter's development called "Our Child"—*Unser Kind*. In it, her mother recorded that by the age of three, Hannah could speak correctly "on any subject . . . even if it is not always intelligible for those who aren't familiar with it." By the age of six, she was lively, impetuous, very warm, even with strangers, and "apparently gifted, particularly in mathematics."⁴⁰

For Arendt, growing up was a positive experience, one of strong self-esteem and confidence. From early childhood, she seemed to be a philosopher, an intuitive stoic. Although she adored her father, Paul, and her grandfather Max, she displayed almost no emotion when they both died in 1913. According to her mother, "She told me that it wasn't necessary to think so much of sad things, that there wasn't time to let oneself become sad." At the funerals, she cried, but said it was because of the beauty of the music.

But when her mother remarried in 1920, Hannah did not get along with her stepfather and stepsisters. Like others before her, she developed an intense adolescent friendship with another bright girl, Anne Mendelssohn, a descendant of the composer Felix Mendelssohn, and a member of a distinguished family of Jewish activists. Anne's influence led Hannah to decide to study philosophy at Marburg, where she was known among her friends as the Green Girl because she often wore a beautiful green dress. Even as high-minded a figure as Hannah Arendt knew that beauty could mean power in a woman's career. "In a woman," she wrote in her study of the eighteenth-century German intellectual Rahel Varnhagen, "beauty creates a perspective from which she can judge and choose. . . . Neither intelligence nor experience can make up for the lack of that natural perspective."[41]

At this vulnerable stage of her life, the fresh and blooming Hannah was transformed by a romantic and sexual encounter with a male mentor, Martin Heidegger, the most popular teacher at the university, and a philosopher on the brink of his major work. Heidegger was an adept stage manager of his teaching persona and knew how to use his clothes and his lecturing style to create an image of mystery and glamour. According to Arendt's biographer Elizabeth Young-Bruehl, "He was a figure out of a romance—gifted to the point of genius, poetic, aloof from both professional thinkers and adulatory students, severely handsome, simply dressed in peasant clothes, an avid skier who enjoyed giving skiing lessons."[42] He dressed in dark brown, in knickerbockers and a Black Forest coat, and Karl Loewith, another student, noted that "the dark color of the cloth matched his jet-black hair and dark complexion. He was a dark little man who knew how to cast a spell."[43] He was also thirty-five, seventeen years Arendt's senior; of Catholic background; married to the formidable Elfriede, whom he had no intention of divorcing; and the father of two young sons.

For Arendt he was a satanic temptor who kept her in thrall for the rest of her life. Heidegger initiated the affair with his young student in the usual way, by inviting her to a conference in his office. He then wrote her a long and eloquent letter describing his deep respect for her intelligence and his own profound loneliness. "It is an emotional letter," Elzbieta Ettinger writes, "lyrical, beautifully phrased, a subtle caress and a firm statement. It contains no wavering, no doubts, not even reflections or questions."[44] Within a month they were lovers. "The first-year student found in Heidegger a lover, friend, teacher and protector. He promised to love her forever, to help and guide her. Carried away by his seductive declarations, she let down her defenses as never before: in an unpublished confessional piece called 'The Shadows' (Die Schatten) 1925 . . . she described for him the terrors of her childhood and girlhood, her insecurity and vulnerability."[45] She willingly played the shy maiden to his commanding presence. She persuaded herself that she was the most important woman in his life, although later Heidegger himself made clear that he wished he had confided the affair to Elfriede at the time and shared it with her.

In her stunning dissection of the affair in 1995, based on the correspondence between Arendt and Heidegger, Elzbieta Ettinger stressed its oddness in the formal environment of the German university, where professors and students were miles apart. But in another sense it sounds all too familiar, even classic, even a cliché. He is the famous professor, she is the devoted student, he the master, she the willing disciple. Heidegger dominated her, set the terms of the relationship, initiated their meetings, took what he needed. He dazzled her with his rhapsodies to the spirituality of the German intellectual life, all the while writing cagey letters to Karl Jaspers about academic politics and financial wheeling and dealing in the university. He trivialized her work and pressured her to leave Marburg to complete her dissertation elsewhere—a move convenient for his reputation—claiming she "had failed to establish herself and did not fit in."[46] In 1928, Heidegger broke off the affair; apparently, although she did not know it, another woman was waiting in the wings. Arendt suffered but accepted his decision, writing to him in the words of Elizabeth Barrett Browning, "But if God please, I shall but love thee better after death."

Arendt had passionately colluded with his efforts to make her his audience, his worshiper, and she seems to have enjoyed it. Ettinger says, "Throughout their love affair Arendt understood and accepted Heidegger's rules. She did everything in her power to ease the burden of his split life, followed every one of his often shifting and complicated instructions concerning their meetings; she was uncomplaining, undemanding, available when he wanted her, patiently waiting when he did not."[47]

Unlike Edward Aveling, whom he resembles in his hypocrisy and vanity, Heidegger was admired and defended throughout his life not only by besotted women, but also by his students, such as Karl Jaspers. Not only as a woman, but as a philosopher, Arendt had been conditioned to respect and believe this genius who proclaimed his integrity. All her life, she insisted that she had internalized not only his philosophical formulas, but his ideas, that he was the inspiration, source, and genesis of her finest work.

The relationship with Heidegger severely undermined Arendt's personal, intellectual, and sexual development. In 1928, having finished her dissertation on Augustine, she began a biographical study of the eighteenth-century German-Jewish saloniste Rahel Varnhagen, dedicated to her friend Anne Mendelssohn. The project was obviously a way to analyze herself. Margaret Fuller had identified with Varnhagen's intellectual and social ambitions a century before; now Arendt used Varnhagen's career to explore her own emotions about the affair with Heidegger. Varnhagen had had an unhappy affair with the gentile Count von Finckenstein and, like Arendt, had experienced existential despair. But Varnhagen had been able to recover and to make a life for herself under even more difficult circumstances for women. Arendt was so determined to view her study of Rahel Varnhagen as an objective scholarly analysis that she insisted it be accepted as her doctoral thesis after the war.

Meanwhile she was becoming more involved in the political scene, and in the situation of European Jews. She was also working for the Jewish agency Youth Aliyah, which helped European Jews emigrate to Palestine. "Among her Zionist colleagues . . .

Arendt was much admired for her intellectual abilities—enough to be known by the quite non-Zionist title 'Pallas Athene.'[48] But the serenity was all on the surface. In 1929, "absolutely determined never to love a man again," she married Guenther Stern, a fellow graduate student she did not love. They had been living together in Berlin, and her mother was fond of him. Moreover, he was having a hard time with his thesis because of his politics. She was "a bundle of inhibitions and fears."[49]

The relationship with Heidegger was over, but in the spring of 1933, after Heidegger had been appointed rector of Freiburg University, Arendt wrote to him in distress over rumors that he "excluded Jews from his seminars, didn't greet his Jewish colleagues on the campus, rejected his Jewish doctoral students and behaved like an antisemite."[50] He denied it all, in a sarcastic response, as he would continue to deny his actions and attempt to minimize his participation in the Third Reich. Arendt never knew that as early as 1929, Heidegger had written an official in the Ministry of Education about the danger of "Judaisation" in the German university. By August 1933, when Arendt decided to leave Germany, he had joined the National Socialist Party and made a notorious pro-Hitler inaugural address.

By this time, Arendt had recognized the passivity that was the occupational hazard of intellectuals: "The problem, the personal problem, was not what our enemies might be doing, but what our friends were doing. This wave of cooperation—which was quite voluntary, or at least not compelled in the way it is during a reign of terror, made you feel surrounded by an empty space, isolated. I lived in an intellectual milieu, but I knew many people who did not, and I came to the conclusion that cooperation was, so to speak, the rule among intellectuals but not among others. And I have never forgotten that."[51] She came to a significant personal and political decision: "When one is attacked as a Jew, one must defend oneself *as a Jew*."[52]

With her mother, she escaped to Prague, where she met Heinrich Blucher, a Communist who had fled from Berlin to Prague in 1934, disguised as a bourgeois tourist. He loved popular music and movies and loved to argue and talk. The marriage to Stern ended amicably in 1937; in January 1940 in Paris, Arendt and Blucher married.

But their honeymoon was brief. On May 5, 1940, all men and women from Germany were required to report to French internment camps. On May 23, Arendt went by train to Gurs, "a camp that had been used since April 1939 for Spanish refugees and members of International brigade. . . . By June there were 6,356 internees including some children." Arendt "insisted that her barracks-mates should keep up their appearances as best as they could, that their morale would decline if they took on the ugliness of their surroundings." At one point, there was talk of a mass suicide. But "the general mood turned suddenly into a violent courage of life." Two-thirds of the internees left; Arendt walked and hitchhiked to a house rented by a friend in Montauban and was reunited with Blucher, whose labor camp had been evacuated when the Germans reached Paris. They stayed in Montauban, watching the Vichy government's "progressively more stringent anti-Semitic measures," and in October began to seek visas for the United States. By May 1941, they were in New York.

Their marriage seemed ideal, a partnership, a "dual monarchy." But they did not have children. Arendt told her friend Hans Jonas, "When we were young enough to have children, we had no money, and when we had money, we were too old."[53] In 1949, when Arendt published *The Origins of Totalitarianism,* she was forty-three and Blucher was fifty. Only in this year did they move out of their small rooms on the Upper West Side to a larger apartment, neat and monochromatic, "tending towards a mute shade of beige in its appointments," where she served coffee and drinks, and German-style cakes, chocolates, and nuts from the bakery.[54] There was a photograph of Kafka on the wall. Blucher said that "we decided not to have children in times such as these. We were sad about it, but a sense of responsibility for those who might be innocent sufferers is a valuable thing." Their old German friends tended to be childless too and became a surrogate family of friends.

Yet in 1950, Arendt resumed her relationship with Heidegger, in a way she could never have done if she had been a mother. Still married to Elfriede, Heidegger needed Arendt's friendship after the war to rehabilitate his reputation. Domineering as always, he wanted her to be a brown girl, to wear a brown dress, not only the color in which *he* remembered her as a girl but oddly symbolic of a sort of German national mythology of the earth and the earth mother—"the brown of a freshly-sown field when it bathes in the light of dusk."

By now she was famous. In 1951, she wrote to her old friend and teacher Karl Jaspers, "A week ago I became a 'cover girl' and had to look at myself on all the newsstands."[55] In 1953, she gave the Christian Gauss seminars at Princeton University, the first woman to do so. When Princeton offered her a full professorship in 1959, she threatened to refuse because the university stressed the token woman aspect in their publicity. "I am not disturbed at all about being a woman professor," she commented, "because I am quite used to being a woman."[56]

The beginnings of the 1960s were difficult and turbulent for both McCarthy and Arendt. Arendt, acknowledging that Heidegger still did not read any of her work, was getting fed up with playing dumb and pandering to his insatiable vanity. "I know that he finds unbearable that my name appears in public, that I write books, etc.," she wrote to her husband in 1961. "Always, I have been virtually lying to him about myself, pretending the books, the name, did not exist, and I couldn't, so to speak, count to three unless it concerned the interpretation of his works."[57] Then she was hit by a truck in Central Park in 1962 and bedridden for two months with a concussion, lacerations, and nine fractured ribs.

In August 1963, McCarthy's novel *The Group* became both a best-seller and the center of a literary controversy. McCarthy described the book as "a mock-chronicle novel . . . about the idea of progress seen in the female sphere." Eight Vassar graduates deal with "home economics, architecture, domestic technology, contraception, childbearing, the study of technology in the home, in the playpen, in the bed. It's supposed to be the history of the loss of faith in progress, in the idea of progress, during that twenty-year period."[58] Norman Mailer, among other young male critics, lampooned her materialism and obsession with surface detail, as a "cold lava of anality, which becomes the truest part of her group, her glop, her impacted mass."[59]

Meanwhile, Hannah Arendt was dealing with the furor over *Eichmann in Jerusalem,* and especially with a hostile review by Lionel Abel published in the *Partisan Review.* Both women felt offended and betrayed by their treatment. Still, neither McCarthy nor Arendt declared themselves to be feminists. Carolyn Heilbrun recalls that she met Arendt "only once, when we were both members of a large special seminar at Columbia. . . . She mentioned to me that this was one of the few occasions in her life when she had not been the only woman in such a gathering. I did not respond, having heard from other women who had approached her on the subject that she scorned feminism."[60] In 1993, Carol Brightman's biography of McCarthy, *Writing Dangerously,* won the National Book Critics Circle Award. Like so many other women biographers of women, Brightman had been drawn to McCarthy by parallels between their lives, and by her own unconscious quest for a model. She was Catholic and had gone to Vassar; as a graduate student in the sixties, she had written a master's thesis on Simone de Beauvoir and Anaïs Nin; and she had been an activist during the Vietnam War. She reports that in her interviews with Mary McCarthy, she was repeatedly startled by the vehemence of McCarthy's denunciation of the women's movement and of the "self-pity, shrillness, and greed" of contemporary feminism.[61]

In the later years of their lives, McCarthy and Arendt continued to be troublemakers and rule-breakers, taking unpopular political stands, quarreling with some friends, grieving deeply for others, losing their own health. McCarthy went to Vietnam in 1967, and wrote a six-part series for the *New York Review of Books,* later published as *Hanoi.* And from the middle 1970s on, she struggled with a series of debilitating illnesses: breast cancer, shingles, cardiac episodes. Arendt too refused to slow down her pace, or even to stop smoking, despite attacks of angina. In 1975, she was traveling, lecturing, visiting Heidegger for the last time. She died suddenly that fall. McCarthy's last years were not so peaceful. In 1979, on Dick Cavett's television show, she bantered about "overrated" writers, then said that Lillian Hellman was "dishonest" and that "every word she writes is a lie." Hellman sued for $2.25 million, and the case dragged on until her death, creating controversy and much anxiety for McCarthy.

Paradoxically, McCarthy's reputation as the Zenobia or Scarlet Lady of the Hudson seemed to pass with her death in 1989. But Hannah Arendt has become an increasingly perplexing and divisive figure. After her death, the revelations of Arendt's affair with Heidegger shocked those who had been defenders of her observations on the banality of evil. "How is it," asked Richard Bernstein, "that the shrewd observer of the banality of evil could have failed to see the banal evil of a man like Heidegger?"[62]

The question is the silent subtext of the study by Julia Kristeva, who takes Hannah Arendt as the subject of the first volume of her trilogy, *Le génie féminin* (1999). Revealingly, Kristeva, herself a Dark Lady and the devoted student of the French maîtres, more or less glosses over this central paradox in Arendt's life. Rather than blaming Heidegger for deceiving Arendt, Kristeva emphasizes Arendt's attraction to the image of the master, and the way she became masculinized herself in achieving philosophical mastery.

Analyzing a series of photographs of Arendt from 1927 to 1950, Kristeva argues that as Arendt became a celebrated philosopher, she took on the image of the master she had internalized in youth: "Maturity and intellectual conflict had made the soft young girl with long hair who had seduced the Plato of Marburg at the age of eighteen disappear. The boyish young woman with the cigarette who addressed the public with a concentrated profile at a New York conference in 1944, is abruptly established."[63] By 1950, at the age of forty-three, captured in a photograph smiling with cropped hair and a mannish dark suit,

Arendt seems androgynous to Julia Kristeva, as if she were an older version of Domna Rejnev. Kristeva sees evidence in the photo of Arendt's "psychic bisexuality . . . the witness of a virile blooming. We no longer see neither the feminine masquerade, designed to facilitate the integration of a woman in a man's profession, nor simply the unconscious revelation of an unrecognized homosexuality." Not until Kristeva's own French feminist generation would female philosophers present themselves as elegant and chic, with Kristeva as famous for her suits as her stories, and Cixous an eyeliner queen.

For Arendt, Kristeva concludes, Heinrich Blucher was the partner who "allowed her to stabilize her emotional life and to consecrate herself entirely to the world of ideas, but to remain always in contact with the world of life." He was also the shadow, the missing male double—different, foreign, gentile, German, working class—who supplied the missing elements for her in an environment that allowed him to display feminine traits as well, and that allowed her to develop what was regarded as masculine. Passionate, sexual, devoted, he provided sanctuary for Arendt.[64]

But the images that seem so masculine to Kristeva seem reassuringly feminine to other eyes. Another woman philosopher, Linda Zerilli, keeps the 1944 photograph of Arendt next to her computer as a comforting image of reality. "Reclined on what appears to be a bed, she is cut off at the waist, dressed in black and looking very existential. Here is the model of the thinking woman: high forehead, short hair, serious and sad eyes that reflect the weight of the world. Framing this curiously disembodied image of female intellect is a shadow that her impressive head casts on the wall. . . . Then I notice that she is smoking a cigarette. Judging from the ashtray, she has smoked several. For a fleeting moment, this paper seems possible."[65] If Hannah Arendt, the most brilliant female thinker of all, was a chain-smoker, there is hope for the rest of us.

NINE

The Lost Sex
and the Second Sex

Simone de Beauvoir

"In January, 1947," wrote Mary McCarthy, "the leading French *femme savante* alighted from an airplane at La Guardia Field for a four months' stay in the United States. In her own eyes, this trip had something fabulous about it, of a balloonist's expedition or a descent in a diving bell. Where to Frenchmen of an earlier generation, America was the incredible country of *les peaux rouges* and the novels of Fenimore Cooper, to Mlle. de Beauvoir, America was, very simply, movieland—she came to verify for herself the existence of violence, drugstore stools, boy-meets-girl, that she had seen depicted on the screen."[1] The *Partisan Review* crowd, having looked forward with excitement and trepidation to visits from the French existentialists, found Beauvoir a great letdown as an ambassador. "It is hard to say whether her literary or political opinions were more arrogant," wrote William Phillips. Hannah Arendt thought the problem was that Phillips should simply have flirted with Beauvoir, instead of treating her as a thinker.[2]

On her side, Simone de Beauvoir (1908–86) was disappointed in American women as well. Seeing the wives of the writers and intellectuals such as Nancy MacDonald and Ellen Wright taking care of their men, she realized for the first time how unusual she was. "I didn't think there was anything special about myself in regard to these other women except that I had more willpower and a much stronger understanding of myself than they did," she told biographer Deirdre Bair. "No man had ever asked me to fetch the coffee or iron the clothes, because I had no intention of doing it for anyone, myself or others, and they probably sensed that."[3] Having expected that American women would be exceptionally free, Beauvoir was shocked by their dependence on men and their obsession with clothes, decor, and beauty. She took an instant dislike to the women of the *Partisan Review,* especially "the beautiful cold novelist"—McCarthy?—"who has already devoured three husbands and many lovers in the course of a cleverly managed career."[4]

Their mutual enmity is no surprise. Beauvoir, according to her companion Sylvie Le Bon, "could live in filth, surrounded by garbage, and it never bothered her at all"; McCarthy reveled in interior decoration and liked nothing better than to rearrange the furniture.[5] Beauvoir had come to the United States with a few blouses, a skirt, and a navy blue wool dress that she wore everywhere, often to the discomfort of her hosts; McCarthy loved clothes and wore a black silk dress "with tiers of fagoting" and a long silver-fox fur when she met Edmund Wilson.[6] Beauvoir despised all the bourgeois ceremony of dining and, like Sartre, could eat almost anything; McCarthy, according to Elizabeth Hardwick, "felt the command to prepare and serve a first course at dinner ought to be put in the Bill of Rights." Beauvoir rejected the idea of marriage; McCarthy "believed in marriage, or rather in being married." Beauvoir was humorless and ideological; McCarthy was an ironic iconoclast and often wrote about the "clash of theory and practice, taste and ideology."[7]

But as studious, literary, left-wing, ex-Catholic, feminist intellectuals and Dark Ladies, they had much more in common than either realized. McCarthy's *Memories of a Catholic Girlhood,* which she was beginning to write in 1947, has similarities to Beauvoir's *Memoirs of a Dutiful Daughter.* Beauvoir's austere life of intellectual severity and hotel-room transience was an unnecessarily prolonged, self-punishing reaction against a conventional domestic life, but after the American trip, she moved into her first Paris apartment and was able to enjoy comfort and even some luxury. For women intellectuals of this generation, deprived not only of creative space but also of privacy, a room of one's own, with a door they could shut, walls they could paint, and colors they could choose themselves, was much more than a metaphor. And both McCarthy and Beauvoir had images of America, violence, and love formed by Hollywood. Ironically, McCarthy would later spend a long period in Paris, involved in anti–Vietnam War activities similar to those of Beauvoir.

But in 1947, Beauvoir was still adjusting to the aftereffects of the war and to the shock of prosperity after the poverty of the Occupation. Moreover, she arrived in the United States at a tense moment for feminism. In 1947, as the GIs came home, *Modern Woman: The Lost Sex* by Ferdinand Lundberg and Dr. Marynia F. Farnham, was a best-seller. Farnham, a psychiatrist and mother of two children, had graduated from Bryn Mawr in 1921 and trained at the University of Minnesota Medical School, the Children's Hospital at Harvard Medical School, and abroad in London and Vienna. At the time she wrote the book, she was in private practice and a consultant at Payne Whitney Clinic in New York. In her book-jacket picture, at forty-seven, she looks easily sixty, with severe, graying hair, no makeup, wrinkled brow, and grim half-smile. Farnham should have been the model of the modern professional woman. Yet the book, based on her personal observations, and written by journalist Lundberg, was a Freudian diatribe against women's emancipation from the home.

In a chapter on feminism, Farnham and Lundberg traced the problems of the current era to "a single fateful book": *A Vindication of the Rights of Woman*. Mary Wollstonecraft, they insisted, "hated men. She had every personal reason possible known to psychiatry for hating them. Hers was hatred of creatures she greatly admired and feared, creatures that seemed to her capable of doing anything while women to her seemed capable of doing nothing whatever."[8] To their view, "Mary Wollstonecraft's life reads like a psychiatric case history," as do "the lives of many later feminists."[9] Basically, they found Wollstonecraft a victim of penis envy, acting out her grievance against her parents in the form of feminist radicalism. In a lengthy appendix, they listed quotations from a variety of feminist thinkers, including Charlotte Perkins Gilman, Olive Schreiner, Victoria Woodhull, and Margaret Sanger, organized under the categories of penis envy, masculinity complex, vaginal superiority, oppression, free love and promiscuity, unmarried mothers, the dreadful child, homosexual women, a new golden age, the end of war, passive-feminine males, and feminist "science."

Beauvoir certainly read *Modern Woman: The Lost Sex* and noticed its "irritating features." In her introduction to *The Second Sex,* she wrote, "Most assuredly the theory of the eternal feminine still has its adherents who will whisper in your ear: 'Even in Russia women still are women,' and other erudite persons—sometimes the very same—say with a sigh: 'Woman is losing her way, woman is lost.' "[10]

But in 1947 these ideas were only beginning to dawn upon Beauvoir. "I had not yet settled on the idea of woman as the other—that was to come later. I had not yet decided that the lot of woman was inferior to the allotment of men in this life. But somehow, I was beginning to formulate the thesis that women had not been given equality in our society, and I must tell you that this was an extremely troubling discovery for me. This is really how I began to be serious about writing about women—when I fully realized the disparity in our lives as compared to men. But [in 1947], none of this was clear to me."[11]

How had Beauvoir managed to reach the age of thirty-eight without noticing the disparity between the lives of women and men? It's a question that engaged her, as she wrote the four volumes of her memoirs, and that has engaged and troubled her biographers, some of whom have even accused her of self-deception and bad faith. Throughout her life to this point, Beauvoir had regarded herself as exceptional, and as exceptionally free. She had broken away from the prudery and narrowness of a Catholic girlhood to become La Grande Sartreuse, the high priestess of existentialism. She lived at the center of postwar French intellectual ferment and had made a reputation as a gifted novelist of ideas. In 1947, French women had finally received the vote, a sign that could be taken as a guarantee of political equality.

But however confident and closed-minded she seemed to the New York intellectuals, Beauvoir was actually on the brink of a personal awakening that would change the way she thought about herself and about women in general, and by the end of her career she would write six novels in addition to books on America, China, old age, sickness, and death; and *The Second Sex*. To the Norwegian feminist literary critic Toril Moi, "Simone de Beauvoir is the emblematic intellectual woman of the twentieth century," "a mythological figure . . . that has made its presence felt in the thoughts and dreams of every intellectual woman in the Western world."[12] To the British anthropologist Judith Okeley, "she was our mother, our sister, and something of ourselves."[13]

BECOMING A WOMAN

"One is not born a woman, one becomes one," Beauvoir would write in *The Second Sex*. How did she become the intellectual woman who arrived in the United States in 1947? Her autobiography, especially the first volume, *Memoirs of a Dutiful Daughter,* provides some of the answers. In these reminiscences Beauvoir seems to have total recall of every day of her life; and because she is also a novelist and a passionate reader of fiction, the major phases in her intellectual evolution seem to echo those feminist archetypes we've seen before: education in the father's library; adolescent loss of faith; rejection of the mother; meeting with the male muse/double; vocational commitment; female friendships. While the posthumous publication of Beauvoir's letters and journals has made clear that she concealed much about herself in these books, even the myth she deliberately constructed explains a lot about the way she managed to evade the realities of her own existential situation as a woman for so much of her life.

Beauvoir's father supervised her reading and introduced her to the French and English fiction she adored. For him, she remembered, in an unconscious echo of Margaret Fuller, she was not a little girl, but "simply a mind." When the family fell into financial difficulties after World War I, Simone found a sanctuary and secret hiding place under her father's desk, where his letter opener, pens, blotter, scissors, and inkpot became icons of patriarchal magic. Her fantasies of adult fulfillment, maintained until her death, were always of herself and another shadowy person sitting at their desks writing in a sun-filled room. When, as a teenager, Beauvoir read a magazine article about Leontine Zanta, the first woman *doctorat d'État* in philosophy in France, "sitting at her desk" in a "grave and thoughtful posture," while her 'niece,' whom she adopted, hovered nearby, it seemed like a perfect and idyllic life—the desk a sort of barricade against the outside world, and another woman, a child, or a lover, or a servant, in the household. Mademoiselle Zanta, Beauvoir decided, had "thus succeeded in reconciling her intellectual life with the demands of female sensibility."[14] At the end of her life, with her adopted daughter–partner, Sylvie Le Bon, Beauvoir would actually achieve this ideal.

But the dutiful daughter who worshiped her father's intelligence learned not to expect his love. He never embraced his daughters, and indeed, Beauvoir later said, there was "no human rapport" with him. Affection, touch, physical attention, came from her mother, but she also represented all those Catholic, bourgeois, expressive, and feminine values that Simone despised. Like the Heterodites, and other women of her generation, Beauvoir regarded housework and cooking as repulsive domestic drudgery: "One afternoon I was helping Mama to wash up; she was washing the plates, and I was drying; through the window I could see the wall of the barracks, and other kitchens in which women were scrubbing out saucepans or peeling vegetables. Every day lunch and dinner; every day washing-up; all those hours, those endlessly recurring hours, all leading nowhere: could I live like that?"

Growing up in Boston, Inez Haynes Irwin had taken a vow never to learn how to cook; in Paris, Simone de Beauvoir managed not to learn how to cook until her thirties during the war. She would live the first half of her life in hotel rooms. And as a girl, she consoled herself by thinking that she would never have to do housework simply because she was too poor to attract a husband: "Fortunately I was not dedicated to a life of toil at the kitchen sink. My father was no feminist . . . but after all, necessity knows no law: 'You girls will never marry,' he often declared. 'You have no dowries; you'll have to work for a living.'"[15]

This view of their attractions was not exactly flattering to Simone and her sister, Hélène. Moreover, when Simone reached puberty, the intellectual bonds with her father began to fray. When she was twelve, he told her she was ugly, and sixty years later this was still a painful memory for her. "I was going through a difficult patch: I looked awful; my nose was turning red; on my face and on the back of my neck there were pimples which I kept picking at nervously. My mother, overworked, took little trouble with my clothes: my ill-fitting dresses accentuated my awkwardness." This was also when she began to menstruate, and menarche was another awkward event. Simone's mother had never told her about menstruation but, when her periods began, told her matter-of-factly how to cope with them. As an old woman, Beauvoir would tell her biographer Deirdre Bair that she "was never much troubled by my hormones; both menstruation and menopause came and went and that was that."[16] But clearly she *was* troubled. She developed nervous tics, shrugging her shoulders, twitching her nose, unable to drink twice from the same glass.[17] The conviction of her ugliness would recur often throughout her life and make her ashamed to mother or pamper herself.

Clumsy, shy, disgusted by her changing body, and repelled by her parents' sexuality ("forty-two then and they were still fucking," she said to Bair), she turned to fiction for escape and for ideals.[18] In Louisa May Alcott's *Little Women,* Simone believed she had caught a glimpse of her future self. "I identified myself passionately with Jo, the intellectual. Brusque and bony, Jo clambered up into trees when she wanted to read; she was much more tomboyish and daring than I was, but I shared her horror of sewing and housekeeping and her love of books. She wrote; in order to imitate her more completely, I composed two or three short stories. . . . But the thing that delighted me most of all was the marked partiality which Louisa Alcott manifested for Jo. . . . Jo was superior to her sisters, who were either more virtuous or more beautiful than herself, because of her passion for knowledge and the vigor of her thought."[19]

If Simone was the ugly sister, perhaps she might also be the brilliant and literary sister. In reading *Little Women* and George Eliot's *Mill on the Floss,* Simone began to fantasize that eventually her superior intelligence would win her not only prominence but love. Jo March had attracted the handsome, dashing Laurie; Maggie Tulliver was irresistible to Stephen Guest. Simone dreamed of a perfect lover for whom she would feel "a passionate admiration . . . I should be in love the day a man came along whose intelligence, culture, and authority could bring me into subjection. . . . I should not marry unless I met someone more accomplished than myself, yet my equal, my double."

Despite her father's cruel comments and her mother's preoccupation, Simone was an attractive and desirable young woman, and she was courted by her cousin Jacques. But she rejected his marriage proposal for reasons both romantic and ambitious. "I want my life to be an all-consuming passion. I need to act, to give freely of myself, to bring plans to fruition: I need an object in life, I want to overcome difficulties and succeed in writing a book. I'm not made for a life of luxury. I could never be satisfied with the things that satisfy him."[20] At the same time, she was frustrated by the lack of privacy and comfort in the cramped room she shared with her younger sister, Hélène; "outside my bed, there wasn't a single corner I could call my own; I didn't even have a desk to put things in . . . I found it painful never to be on my own."[21]

What sort of work might she do? How could she live on her own? As much as she admired Jo the writer, Simone never imagined herself as a novelist or actress. Instead, remembering Mademoiselle Zanta, Simone decided that she wanted to study philosophy. "In those days the women who had a degree in or a doctorate in philosophy could be counted on the fingers of one hand: I wanted to be one of those pioneers. From a practical point of view, the only career that would be open to me if I had a degree in philosophy was teaching: I had nothing against this."[22] Moreover, in the intellectual environment to which she aspired, philosophy was the "queen of disciplines, the undisputed champion in the pecking order of academic subjects."[23] Parisians idolized the philosopher as Jewish New Yorkers idolized the intellectual, and in similar terms. According to the literary critic Albert Thibaudet, writing in 1927, "The philosophical vocation is in principle analogous to the vocation for the priesthood."[24] Beauvoir's role model Leontine Zanta had proclaimed, "To teach philosophy is not at all the same thing as to teach literature, mathematics, or English. In order to be worthy of this task, it is not enough simply to know and explain systems of thought . . . one must also have an elevated soul, galvanized by struggle and constant self-mastery."[25]

LADY WITH A TURBAN

In 1928, Simone made the first major break with her family when she took the entrance exams to the Sorbonne to study philosophy and to enter its sacred priesthood, one that had only recently admitted women at all, and in which she was still marginal. She was intensely serious, dressed always in shabby black. Her university friends gave her the nickname Castor, or Beaver, for her studiousness. She had recently had her straight, fine hair cut in a short bob she hoped would be fashionable, but it looked terrible on her, and she habitually hid it under a turban, which became her feminist fashion statement. As a French journalist,

Gérard Lefort, commented after her death: "There are vesti-
mentary details that, when they become systematic, have the
quality of a lifestyle and a way of thinking. The Beauvoir style,
her trademark signature, was always and everywhere the turban. Beauvoir traveling, Beauvoir writing, Beauvoir on the
podium, Beauvoir on vacation, Beauvoir on television, Beauvoir
in the Élysée Palace, Beauvoir young, Beauvoir old, from the
beginnings to our own times, not an official portrait, not a personal snapshot, without that turban."

He made a sharp guess that she had started to wear it because
she had something to hide. "Was Beauvoir ashamed of her hair?
Did her zealous feminism require of her that, as a penitence,
this classical emblem of feminine adornment should disappear,
disposed of once and for all?" But the effect of the turban, like a
nun's headdress, was to signal commitment to a priesthood, a
life of the mind: "Beauvoir, a strong-minded woman, bound her
skull. But for what purpose? To keep her head from exploding
under the pressure of ideas? Or more simply, barricaded at the
top, to prevent the world's disorders from gaining entry? In this
obsession with the headband, there is something of a warrior's
determination. As if protected by an Amazon's headgear, Beauvoir advanced helmeted, emblem of discipline, almost an addic-
tion, which one imagines must have brooked no infractions (did
she sleep in it?)."[26]

The following year, Beauvoir moved out of her parents' house
and into a room at her grandmother's. It was an epochal event.
"From the moment I opened my eyes every morning I was lost in
a transport of delight. When I was about twelve I had suffered
through not having a private retreat of my own at home. . . . It was
wonderful to be able to shut my door and keep my daily life free
of other people's inquisitiveness. For a long time I remained
indifferent to the decor of my surroundings. . . . To have a door
that I could shut was still the height of bliss for me."[27] She also
enjoyed buying her own clothes, putting on makeup, "smother-
ing my face in powder, dabbing a patch of rouge on each cheek,
and applying lipstick liberally."[28] For the first time in her life, she

felt pleasure in her surroundings and her body. Despite the turban, or because of it, her classmates found her mysterious and pretty. Lefort notes that, on her, "the turban beautifies and enhances, exposing the maximum of skin for the incredible beauty of her severe face ('intellectual' forehead, and a statue's gaze) and crowning it with a halo of impeccable elegance."

One of these classmates was Jean-Paul Sartre, already a legend at the age of twenty-two. He was famous for failing his exams (in his efforts to achieve dazzling and unprecedented originality he had neglected to answer the questions), for cutting classes, for throwing water bombs out the window and crying, "Thus pissed Zarathustra!" and for his prowess with women. Unlike the insecure Simone, Sartre was confident that he was a genius. On their first date, he invited her to his squalid rooms to discuss Leibniz, and although he was tiny, walleyed, pockmarked, dirty, and badly dressed, she was thrilled to be singled out. Sartre, she believed, "corresponded exactly to the dream-companion I had longed for since I was fifteen: he was the double in whom I found all my burning aspiration raised to the pitch of incandescence."[29]

When Sartre took first place in the philosophy exams and she took second, the myth of his intellectual superiority was established forever, although the members of the examination committee later agreed that Sartre came first mainly because he had failed before. Yet Beauvoir would always insist that while Sartre was a philosopher, she was only someone who liked philosophy. Therefore she hid or played down her own intellectual tastes and deferred to his. For example, she was reading the American Transcendentalists at university, including Margaret Fuller, but could not persuade Sartre to take a look at their work.[30] Similarly, she loved the novels of Rosamund Lehmann, while Sartre "would laugh at me for wasting my time."[31]

Meanwhile, despite her proud claims of self-sufficiency for each, she served Sartre. She took his laundry to the washerwoman; put up with his absence while he went off to do his military service; suffered agonies of jealousy over his affairs with other women; taught at various lycées and visited him on the weekends; read the books he recommended and spent hours reading Hegel and Heidegger so she could help him edit his articles. She enjoyed hikes and long walks in the country, but Sartre did not share these cheap dates with pleasure. "He was allergic to chlorophyll, he said, and all this lush green pasturage exhausted him."[32]

Sartre proposed that they not be monogamous, but remain essentially faithful to each other in spirit: "What *we* have is an essential love; but it is a good idea for us also to experience *contingent* love affairs." What this came to mean was that Sartre was essential for Beauvoir, while she was contingent for him. He suggested that they "sign a two-year lease"—that is, stay together in Paris for two years, then separate and take teaching jobs apart elsewhere. Beauvoir accepted. They decided to call their relationship a "morganatic marriage," an odd term that would be used when the Prince of Wales married Wallis Simpson. "As a couple we possessed a dual identity. In the ordinary way we were Monsieur and Madame M. Organatique, unambitious, easily satisfied, not very well off, the husband a civil servant. But sometimes I dressed up and we would go to a cinema on the Champs-Élysées, or dancing at La Coupole, and then we were an American millionaire and his wife, Mr. and Mrs. Morgan Hattick."[33]

They made a pact of total honesty: they would share with each other every aspect of their lives, including feelings about other lovers. Sartre seems to have enjoyed his side of the bargain. He told or wrote Beauvoir about his sexual conquests in excruciatingly graphic detail and often asked her to play the heavy whenever the women wanted too much from him. In his amorous relations, Sartre comes off as comic, an affectionate little guru who preferred his girlfriends to be short (Beauvoir wore low heels and stooped), young, and willing to fit into his life. Moreover, he readily admitted to his friend Olivier Todd that he coped with his many women by lying to them. "You lie to them all?" inquired Todd. "To them all," replied Sartre with a smile. "Even to Castor?" "*Especially* to Castor."[34]

Beauvoir explained in her memoirs that since she did not want to have children, this arrangement made perfectly good sense: "There was only one consideration that could have carried sufficient weight to make us pass under the yoke of so-called legitimacy: the desire for children. This we did not possess. I have so often been taken up on the point, and have been asked so many questions concerning it, that an explanation is, perhaps, desirable. I had not then, and have not now, any prejudice against motherhood as such. Small babies had never interested me, but I often found slightly older children charming, and had intended to have some of my own when I was thinking of marrying my cousin Jacques. If now I turned aside from such a scheme it was, primarily, because my happiness was too complete for any new element to attract me. . . . In any case, I felt such absence of affinity with my own parents that any sons or daughters I might have I regarded in advance as strangers; from them I expected either indifference or hostility—so great had been my own aversion to family life."[35]

However, pregnancy and children did not really come into the picture. The erotic bond between Sartre and Beauvoir was never strong (he was "never enthusiastic in bed"[36]), and they stopped sleeping together after eight years, leaving her with awakened sexual feelings that shamed her. She took no precautions against pregnancy, leaving it all to the men, and never became pregnant or had to face an abortion. Like Arendt and Heidegger (one of Sartre's philosophical mentors), Beauvoir and Sartre seem in retrospect to have had an unbalanced bond. Sartre set the terms of their relationship and felt free to violate it. "There is a question every thinking woman in the Western world must have posed herself one time or another," Angela Carter once wrote: "Why is a nice girl like Simone wasting her time sucking up to a boring old fart like Jean-Paul? Her memoirs will be mostly about him; he will scarcely speak of her." Indeed, while Sartre figures on virtually every page of Beauvoir's biography, Sartre's biographer Annie Cohen-Solal speaks only briefly of Beauvoir.

THE WAR: QUEEN OF DENIAL

During World War II, Beauvoir's life, and her relationship with Sartre, changed relatively little; she let his interests, work, and needs take precedence over hers. At first he was a private in an artillery group stationed in Alsace and Lorraine, playing chess, and writing for up to twelve hours a day in beautiful little notebooks that Simone sent him from Paris; at his insistence she started a journal too in cheap children's exercise books. Meanwhile she was working hard on her first novel and struggling with food shortages and lack of heat. She worked every day in heated cafés, writing two novels, a play, and two philosophical essays, even after France surrendered to Germany in 1940 and her favorite cafés became haunts of the Nazi propaganda staff.

In March 1941, Sartre, who had been a prisoner for nine months in a German camp, was suddenly released and returned to Paris. He had managed to do a lot of writing in the prison camp too, but he had also made up his mind to start a resistance group and berated Simone for her unthinking acceptance of the Occupation. Over the next few months, Sartre, with her support, made a variety of futile attempts to organize a resistance— futile and silly, because other French citizens without his philosophical gifts had already been resisting and risking their lives for quite a long time and either distrusted him (had the Nazis deliberately released him from the camp?) or considered him a lightweight.

Both of them went back to supporting themselves by teaching. Simone also taught herself to cook as an intellectual challenge: "I turned my culinary worries into a full-blown obsession, and stuck to it for the next three years. I watched while the coupons were clipped from my ration book, and never parted with one too many. I wandered through the streets, rummaging behind the dummy window displays for unrationed foodstuffs, a sort of a treasure hunt, and I thoroughly enjoyed it;

what a windfall it was if I stumbled on a beetroot or a cabbage! The first lunch we had in my room consisted of 'turnip sauerkraut,' which I tried to improve by pouring tinned soup over it. Sartre said it wasn't at all bad."[37]

The description doesn't make one eager to read a Simone de Beauvoir cookbook. But in some sense, after years of denigrating everything about domesticity, she found cooking gratifying. Partly, she thought, it was the pleasure of "alchemy," of making something edible out of unpromising ingredients; partly, though, it was also about comfort, nurturance. One night, with a "savory-smelling vegetable soup" simmering on the stove, she had "a glimpse of the housewife's joys."[38]

She was tasting other joys as well. In addition to an affair with Sartre's student Pierre Bost, she had secret affairs with three of her women students, Olga Kosakievicz, Natasha Sorokine, and Bianca Bienenfeld. All three became Sartre's mistresses too, in a series of elaborate triangles. These were risky adventures; in 1943, Natasha's mother complained to the Lycée Molière in Paris that Beauvoir had corrupted a minor, and although by this time the affair was over and Natasha was living with a young Algerian, Beauvoir was dismissed from her job. Beauvoir always denied that she had had sexual relationships with women; in an interview with the journalist Alice Schwartzer in 1984, she said that every woman is "a bit homosexual," but insisted that she herself had never felt "erotic passion" for a woman. In her correspondence and conversation, she frequently referred to homosexuals as pansies or dykes. Toril Moi suggests that Beauvoir may never have thought of herself as lesbian because she also had sex with men, and in her mind, lesbianism was an exclusive sexual choice.[39]

Still, during the war Beauvoir managed to sustain a set of moral, political, and sexual definitions that made it possible for her to sleep with her students, publish her writing, produce her plays, and make her way in occupied Paris without any anxiety about collaborating with the Germans or guilt about putting her own needs first. She also worked hard at maintaining the image of herself and Sartre as a couple. According to Deirdre Bair, "Throughout their years together, Simone de Beauvoir insisted that the one aspect of her life which had never disappointed her was her relationship with Sartre, and she unleashed her fury on anyone who dared to question it." But as soon as he was free to travel, in January 1945, Sartre flew to the United States—his first plane trip, and one that Beauvoir had assumed they would take together—and embarked on an ecstatic affair with another woman, leaving Beauvoir to supervise the publication of their new journal, *Les Temps Modernes*. She was drinking heavily, missing a tooth knocked out in a bicycle accident, shabbily dressed, and convinced that she was "old, far beyond passion, too old to be with men."[40] She was suffering from excruciating headaches, and smoking so much that her hands trembled. She had crying jags. She was thirty-seven.

This was the Simone de Beauvoir who claimed never to have noticed that women's lot was inferior to that of men. In June 1946, Beauvoir began to think about writing her memoirs and had to confront the question of gender: "I realized that the first question to come up was: What has it meant to me to be a woman? At first I thought I could dispose of that pretty quickly. I had never had any feeling of inferiority, no one had ever said to me: 'You think that way because you're a woman'; my femaleness had never been irksome to me in any way. 'For me,' I said to Sartre, 'you might almost say it hasn't counted.'" Sartre mildly disagreed and sent her to investigate further, and, she says, she had a sudden epiphany: "This world was a masculine world, my childhood had been nourished by myths forged by men, and I hadn't reacted to them in at all the same way I should have done if I had been a boy."[41] But the effect of this astonishing and belated epiphany was to send her to the Bibliothèque Nationale to do research on "Woman." Her personal sense of identity remained unshaken. Not until after her trip to the United States did Beauvoir connect her abstract generalizations about Woman with her own experience.

THE FROG WIFE

What happened to her on that trip? For one thing, she fell passionately in love with a sexually competent man. In 1947, a friend in New York put her in contact with the novelist Nelson Algren, a year younger, who she hoped would act as her tour guide to Chicago. They met at the Palmer House; Beauvoir told him that she would be carrying a copy of the *Partisan Review.* Despite this bad omen, Algren, who looked like a young Sylvester Stallone, found her "attractive at first glance."[42] He courted her with a tour of Chicago, including the heroin addicts and the electric chair, and took her to his cold-water flat on Wabansia Street, where they made love all night and Beauvoir (as she revealed to her biographer Deirdre Bair) had her first "complete orgasm."[43]

Beauvoir's feelings for Algren were the most romantic of her life. Unlike Sartre, he gave her presents and wrote her a love poem, over which she cried on the plane back to Paris. But their transatlantic affair was as much epistolary as real. He could not abandon Chicago; she could not give up Sartre and Paris. Nonetheless, their passionate love affair continued erratically throughout the years that both were doing their most important writing, Beauvoir completing *The Second Sex* and Algren his best novels, *The Man With the Golden Arm* and *A Walk on the Wild Side.*

With Algren, the personal meaning of being a woman, its pleasures and pains, at last hit home for Beauvoir; the affair acted as a catalyst to release feelings she had stifled for years. One of the male myths she had wept over as a child was Hans Christian Andersen's little mermaid, who "exchanged her fishtail for a woman's legs for love, and then found herself walking on needles and burning coals."[44] In her playful letters to her lover, Beauvoir called herself his "frog wife," his "loving little frog." Although it echoed his tough-guy slang about their Franco-American romance, the phrase has the ring of feminist fable. Now, having fallen in love, she was also losing her amphibious, hybrid identity as an intellectual, and the armor or shell that had protected her from the consciousness of her own emotions.

She spent time fussing over him, "just like all the American women I had ridiculed for the way they catered to men's needs. I was surprised by how much I enjoyed it."[45] To please Algren, she had her missing tooth replaced, bought pretty dresses, wore lipstick, nail polish, and jewelry. On her fortieth birthday she wrote him a letter of reminiscence about her adolescence as a "serious student who never flirted with men, poorly dressed, wearing no makeup," returning from the library to her parents' ugly flat. "Today I turned forty, twice as old as I was in those days. I am ashamed of it, and I wish I could offer you a younger girl's love."[46]

In addition to grooming herself, she offered even to cook and clean. She gave up her affairs with other men, but encouraged him to feel free: "Don't make your life too dull, honey. I should not like to deprive you from the least thing. You can indulge gambling and women a little, there is no harm in it." She wrote him long letters about her life, feelings, and work even when she was tired and when he did not write back. "You have to love much a man to write such a letter," she notes in the middle of a magnificent description of postwar Berlin, "and in a foreign language too." She helped him with his career in France, getting his work translated and published, excused his failings, and bolstered his self-esteem. When she was attacked by American critics, she offered Algren a flattering erotic rebuttal: "I suggest you say to Bromfield, 'I know Simone de Beauvoir and when she is in bed with me, she does not look hopeless or nihilistic, but with *you,* I don't know what would happen.'"

Like an epistolary novel, the 350 letters she wrote to Algren, in English, record the rise and inevitable fall of their affair; and they are also great love letters, spontaneous, funny, inventive, wise, and sad. In the beginning she writes joyfully, "I love airplanes. I think, when you are at a high pitch of emotion, it is the only way of travelling which fits with your own heart." But she would spend many hours weeping in airports and on planes, as Algren could not bring himself to accept her life or to modify his own. She tried to bridge the gap between passion and reality: "I want so much to make a link between my frog life in Wabansia and my working life." She tried unsuccessfully to get him to learn French ("Suppose you should write to me ten lines in French in each letter and I tell you your mistakes?"), and to help plan their infrequent holidays together so that they could combine travel and work. As she wrote on July 3, 1947, "I want everything from life, I want to be a woman and to be a man, to have many friends and have loneliness, to work much and write good books and to travel and enjoy myself, to be selfish and to be unselfish. . . . You see, it is difficult to get all which I want."[47]

Algren sent her Gunnar Myrdal's book on the race problem, *An American Dilemma,* which impressed her very much: "I would like to write a book about women as important as [Myrdal's] is about blacks," she wrote to Algren.[48] He also introduced her to his black American friends in Chicago, urging them to share their experiences with her. She adopted Algren's view in part because of her own friendship with the black American writer Richard Wright and his white wife, Ellen. Seeing the problems they encountered as a couple convinced her that white men had succeeded in relegating both black men and all women into positions of "altérité" or "otherness." Algren also insisted that she read American literature of the 1920s and 1930s, with its strong political and social content. When he was in Chicago and she in Paris, their correspondence often contained discussions about such writers as James T. Farrell, John O'Hara, John Dos Passos, Frank Conroy, Tess Schlesinger, Meridel LeSeuer, and others.[49]

Algren and Beauvoir planned to spend four months together traveling. But Beauvoir, much as she longed to be with Algren, also wanted to work on her book about women. "Of all my books that was truly the easiest to write, especially in the beginning. The material just seemed to arrange itself naturally into patterns of analysis."[50] Although she had to shorten the trip by two months, she had a marvelous time. In New York, en route to meeting Algren, she asked her friend Stépha Gerassi to advise her about birth control, which her male lovers had always taken responsibility for. Beauvoir had written to Algren: "Honey, there is something I wanted to speak about. I am just a little afraid you'll laugh at me. Well, you are my husband we have to discuss some wife and husband matters." She asked Algren to decide on the method of contraception. "I don't want any chance to be trapped by a baby. . . . I'll do exactly what you decide—just don't choose the most unpleasant for you."[51] For the first time ever, she was fitted for a diaphragm.

Algren came to see her in Paris, and Beauvoir, dramatically, moved out of her hotel into a three-room apartment with a view of Notre Dame. She furnished it with "souvenirs of their travels together, brightly colored fabrics, rugs and pottery from Central America, and the frequent presents he sent from Chicago."[52] He was insistent that she should join him there. However, she tried to explain her family history, her feelings about Sartre, her commitment to her writing, her ideals, and her country: "I should give up friends and the sweetness of Paris to be able to remain forever with you; but I could not live just for happiness and love. I could not give up writing and working in the only place where my writing and work may have meaning."

THE SECOND SEX

In 1949, the first volume of *The Second Sex,* dealing with women's status, history, and literary representation, was published in Paris. From the very beginning, it was sensational and controversial. "How courageous you are!" one of Beauvoir's friends said. "You're going to lose a lot of friends!"[53] Its sexual explicitness shocked some readers and illuminated others (the American feminist critic Jane Gallop says she learned how to masturbate by reading Beauvoir), but overall it is deeply pessimistic about woman's place and woman's fate. Although Beauvoir thinks some of the problems of women's conflict will disappear under socialism and after patriarchy, she also sees the condition of woman as psychoanalytically determined. From girlhood to old age, she asserts, women are subject to the dictates not only of patriarchal society, but also of their own timidity, and their own bodies.

Despite her sudden feminist notoriety, however, Beauvoir had no interest at all in the work of other feminist theorists and anthropologists such as Margaret Mead. She had read Lévi-Strauss, but when Mead came to Paris, and Blanche Knopf set up a forum between the world's two most famous theorists of women, it was a disaster. Beauvoir thought Mead was an unpretty, "horrible American woman" and swore never to read a single word of her writing.[54] Yet here too was a missed opportunity, for Mead's *Male and Female* (1949) covered similar ground to Beauvoir's book. Mead had also responded to the blatant misogyny of the postwar period: "We have had a spate of books that claim women are being masculinized, to their ill, to men's ill, to everybody's ill, and another spate, or sometimes the same spate, of books that insist men are being feminized. When one follows the shrill insistencies of books like *Modern Woman: The Lost Sex,* which end by attacking men as well as women, one realizes that we are passing through a period of discrepancies in sex roles which are so conspicuous that efforts to disguise the price that both sexes pay are increasingly unsuccessful."[55]

While Mead and the feminist anthropologists saw sex roles as evolving and changing, Beauvoir approached the question of womanhood philosophically, through a set of universal axioms and principles. Her major idea was that women were compelled by men "to assume the status of the Other." While the woman, like the man, is an autonomous human being, she writes in her introduction to *The Second Sex,* men turn her into an object, and claim superiority over her. Women's dilemma lies in the conflict between their aspirations as autonomous human beings and their social situation as secondary and defined by men.

The Second Sex is a monumental and difficult book; while

many readers regard it as the greatest feminist treatise of our century, nobody ever wished it longer or more theoretical. But in its more than seven hundred pages, there are passages of remarkable wisdom, eloquence, and insight about women's situation, even when Beauvoir is wrong. Women, she writes, "have no past, no history, no religion of their own; and they have no such solidarity of work and interest as that of the proletariat. . . . They live dispersed among the males, attached to certain men—fathers or husbands—more firmly than they are to other women." While she underestimated the significance of women's history, Beauvoir predicted correctly that in most situations, women would identify with their class or race before their sex.

More problematically, having traced the obstacles placed in the way of the development of the girl and young woman, Beauvoir nonetheless tends to blame adult women—women different from herself in their choices and actions—for their inadequacies. The professional woman, she writes, "rarely uses her opportunities with simple directness, and thus she will often be handicapped later by a bad start. The conflicts I have spoken of do, in fact, reach their greatest intensity between the ages of eighteen and thirty, precisely the time when the professional future is at stake. Whether the woman lives with her family or is married, her family will rarely show the same respect for her work as for a man's; they will impose duties and tasks on her and infringe on her liberty. She herself is still profoundly affected by her bringing up, respectful of values affirmed by her elders, haunted by her dreams of childhood and adolescence; she finds difficulty in reconciling the heritage of her past with the interests of her future. Sometimes she abjures her femininity, she hesitates between chastity, homosexuality, and an aggressive virago attitude; she dresses badly or wears male attire; and in this case she wastes much time in defiance, playacting, angry fuming. More often she wants to emphasize her feminine qualities: she is coquettish, she goes out, she flirts, she falls in love, oscillating between masochism and aggressiveness. She questions, agitates, scatters herself in every way. These outside activities alone are enough to prevent complete absorption in her enterprise; the less she profits by it, the more tempted she is to give it up."[56]

To Beauvoir, nothing that a woman might choose or do could compensate for the disadvantages of her existential position. "We rarely encounter in the independent woman," she writes, "a taste for adventure and for experience for its own sake or a disinterested curiosity; she seeks 'to have a career' as other women build a nest of happiness; she remains dominated, surrounded, by the male universe, she lacks the audacity to break through its ceiling, she does not passionately lose herself in her projects."[57]

Worst of all, no matter how much they accomplish, Beauvoir believes, women are in a losing race with time. Menopause is a form of "mutilation," and "long before the eventual mutilation, woman is haunted by the horror of growing old . . . to hold her husband and to assure herself of his protections, and to keep most of her jobs, it is necessary for her to be attractive, to please; she is allowed no hold on the world save through the mediation of some man. What is to become of her when she no longer has any hold on him? This is what she anxiously asks herself while she helplessly looks on at the degeneration of this fleshly object which she identifies with herself. She puts up a battle. But hair dye, skin treatments, plastic surgery, will never do more than prolong her dying youth. Perhaps she can at least deceive her mirror. But when the first hints come of that fated and irreversible process which is to destroy the whole edifice built up during puberty, she feels the fatal touch of death itself."[58]

But despite this pessimistic message, when *The Second Sex* appeared in the United States in spring 1953, it was a huge popular success, and within two weeks it was on the best-seller list. Beauvoir became a celebrity; at last she had reached a point where she might write and work in the United States and be with Algren. But by this time, he had ended their affair: "One can still have the same feelings for someone and still not allow them to run and disturb one's life. To love a woman who does not belong to you, who puts other things and other people before you, without there being any question of your taking first place, is something that just isn't acceptable. I don't regret a single one of the moments we had together. But now I want a different kind of life."[59]

He remarried and redivorced; he became more suspicious and demanding; finally, when he read Beauvoir's account of their relationship in her novel *The Mandarins* (1955) and her memoir *Force of Circumstance* (1963), he was bitter and enraged. He told a journalist that between them, Beauvoir had always accepted "the secondary status of the female in relation to the male. . . . I thought posterity ought to know that."[60] Certainly Algren could not tolerate being the second sex. As he told a reporter in May 1981, "I've been in whorehouses all over the world and the woman there always closes the door . . . but this woman flung the door open and called in the public and the press." The next day, as he was about to be inducted into the American Academy of Arts and Letters, he died of a heart attack. Although Beauvoir suffered needles and burning coals from Algren, she wore the ring he gave her to her grave.

Clearly, Beauvoir made the right decision about Nelson Algren. She should not have given up her life in Paris to go to Chicago and wash Algren's socks in the kitchen sink. After their breakup, she got her driver's license and bought a car, a Simca, the new love of her life. But she was convinced again that at forty-four she was an aging woman too old for sex or passion. And she repudiated the lessons she had learned about the pleasures of domestic life, and the rewards as well as the disadvantages of living with and for someone else. To her surprise and delight, in 1952, Beauvoir began an affair with a man seventeen years her junior—the handsome and intense journalist Claude Lanzmann, who would later become known as the director of the film *Shoah*. Lanzmann gave her new confidence and renewed youthfulness, but also accepted the pre-Algren lifestyle whose terms she dictated. "Throughout the seven years they were together, each took care of his or her own needs. She never ran his errands and she never asked him to run hers. It was unthinkable to her that either should perform any kind of domestic service for the other. Yet they were truly a couple in a highly visible sense."[61] Beauvoir would never allow herself to become a vulnerable frog wife again.

But meanwhile Sartre began a series of hectic, overlapping affairs with adoring young women and groupies, among them Lanzmann's sister, a beautiful young actress who used the stage name Evelyne Ray, for whom he wrote *The Condemned of Altona*. Because of his other entanglements, Sartre asked her to keep the relationship secret. Moreover, Beauvoir explained to Deirdre Bair, Evelyne "was getting old, and she had trouble accepting the idea of aging." Evelyne was almost thirty. She also wanted children, and "of course, that was out of the question." After a long period of depression, Evelyne wrote a series of "very nice little letters" to Sartre, Simone, and her brother and then killed herself.[62]

FINALLY FEMINIST

From the mid-1960s until her death, as she herself was aging, Beauvoir began to experience the kind of political and emotional solidarity with women that, in *The Second Sex,* she had denied existed. A series of events in her personal life initiated the transition. In 1963, her mother died, and Beauvoir was stunned by the depth of her feeling. "Why did my mother's death shake me so deeply?" she asked in *A Very Easy Death.* "Since the time I left home I had felt little in the way of emotional impulse towards her. . . . Generally speaking I thought of her with no particular feeling. Yet in my sleep (although my father only made very rare and then insignificant appearances) she often played a most important part; she blended with Sartre, and we were happy together. And then the dream would turn into a nightmare—why was I living with her once more? How had I come to be in her power again? So our former relationship lived on in me in its double aspect—a subjection that I loved and hated. It revived with all its strength when Maman's accident, her illness, and her death shattered the routine that then governed our contacts."[63]

This reunion with the maternal side of her emotional life was followed by Sartre's sudden decision in 1965 to adopt one of his young women, Arlette Elkaim. Beauvoir herself had been getting to know a young philosophy student thirty years her junior, Sylvie Le Bon, and by 1965, Sylvie was her closest friend. They traveled together, had meals together, established a kind of family. Both women denied vehemently that their friendship had a sexual component, or even that it resembled a mother-daughter bond.

Although she had mixed feelings about the student revolutions of 1968, Beauvoir nonetheless felt herself revitalized by this uprising of passionate protest, and with Sylvie's presence, the old age she had feared and dreaded for so long seemed much less devastating. Young women wanted her advice, support, and participation in their movement as its "spiritual mother." In 1970, Beauvoir began to go public as an activist and feminist in the women's liberation movement, first in the fight for legalized abortion, then through feminist journals and meetings with feminists from other countries. As Bair notes, Beauvoir, who "spent most of her life in male groups centered around Sartre's political concerns, found herself more comfortable in communal situations with women in her last fifteen years. Previously, she had been only a satellite to Sartre's shining star; now she was in a leadership role and happy to have assumed it on her own."[64]

She and Sartre led distinctly separate but parallel lives. Nonetheless, his death in 1980 was the one time, Gérard Lefort observed, that she seemed publicly destroyed: "The day of Sartre's burial . . . Simone de Beauvoir appeared with her hair unkempt, her famous turban unwound. And there, for the first time, the photographic machine-gunners delivered her to us literally undone." After his death, she spent many years editing and publishing his letters to her (although not hers to him). But when the letters were published, she "concentrated on the two things that gave her the greatest pleasure in the world: working on behalf of women, and traveling with Sylvie," whom she had adopted as her daughter and heir. According to Le Bon, "It was love between Castor and myself. What made it complicated is that neither one of us was prepared, especially me, to love someone who was a woman." Their life together seems to have been the marriage of loving, faithful, yet independent equals Beauvoir could not achieve as the frog wife of Algren or Sartre.[65]

Beauvoir died in April 1986, acknowledged as the modern feminist messiah, the mother of the modern women's liberation movement, a revered figure whose funeral in Paris was a great public event. At the cemetery in Montparnasse, Elisabeth Badinter declared, "Women, you owe her everything!"

TEN

Writing Well Is the Best Revenge

Susan Sontag

One of the women who owed her feminist consciousness to Beauvoir was Susan Sontag (1933–). Throughout her life, Sontag has always felt that Beauvoir "wrote the best feminist book in all of feminist literature."[1] In 1951, eighteen years old, married and pregnant, she read *The Second Sex* for the first time. "That's the moment I really became militant," she later recalled. "I feel I've had these ideas on a conscious level for twenty years and unconsciously all my life. I tried as much as I could to put them into practice in my own life."[2] Before reading Beauvoir, she had thought of her decisions as purely personal acts of principle. "I didn't even know I was a feminist, so unfashionable was that point of view at the time, when I married at the age of seventeen and kept my own name."[3]

In 1972, along with Beauvoir, Sontag answered a questionnaire about women from the Spanish literary quarterly *Libre*. Her reply, published in the *Partisan Review* in 1973 under the title "The Third World of Women," is her most personal and explicit statement about herself as a feminist intellectual and therefore an exception: "Every generation produces a few women of genius (or at least of irrepressible eccentricity) who win special status for themselves. But the historical visibility of . . . that small band is understood to follow precisely from their possessing qualities that women do not normally have. Such women are credited with 'masculine' energy, intelligence, willfulness, and courage."[4]

Susan Sontag herself became part of this small band of women of genius. Yet feminism as an ideology has also been second to her belief in personal autonomy. Sontag has written that she "never felt consciously or unconsciously that there was any conflict between my vocation and being a woman. Writing is the one art, perhaps, where there are a great many first-rate women. So that's the one activity where one would probably have, even in the benighted bygone days, the least problem. . . . I never thought, There are women writers, so this is something I can be. No, I thought, There are writers, so this is something I want to be."[5] In her best-selling novel *The Volcano Lover,* Sontag's nineteenth-century intellectual heroine, Eleanora de Fonseca, feels the same way: "I had read and admired Mary Wollstonecraft's book when it was published in Naples in 1794, but I did not, in my newspaper, ever raise the issue of the rights of women. I was independent. I had not sacrificed my mind to some trivial idea of my sex. Indeed, I did not think of myself as a woman first of all. I thought of our just cause. I was glad to forget I was only a woman . . . I wanted to be pure flame."[6]

When she became famous as a New York intellectual in the 1960s, however, men saw Sontag as a woman rather than a flame, and as the heiress to the American feminist tradition. Some reacted with jealousy, condescension, and spite. At the time, as Sontag's biographer Sohnya Sayres points out, few women intellectuals had won the right to "be a handsome, near beautiful woman with a never spoken of, but never hidden bisexuality; to keep from being disliked as a woman for not lampooning one's own power."[7]

Sontag never apologized, never explained, never made fun of herself, and thus intimidated and antagonized some of her male rivals. In a 1966 review of *Against Interpretation,* one Burton Feldman wrote: "Miss Sontag is the latest . . . and perhaps leading example today of that strenuously intellectual woman starting with Margaret Fuller and coming forward to Mary McCarthy.

She shares with these a quick mind, a good education, a high-handed manner, and an inability to stop nagging."[8] Among the New York intellectuals, Norman Podhoretz in 1968 attributed her rapid rise to "the coincidental availability of a vacant position in the culture" for the "Dark Lady of American Letters." That role, he claimed, had been "carved out" by Mary McCarthy; but since McCarthy was now too old for the role, "a public existed when Sontag arrived on the scene which was searching for a new Dark Lady, and she was so obviously right that a spontaneous decision was made on all sides to cast her for the role."[9]

When Sontag met Mary McCarthy in the late 1960s, McCarthy declared, "Oh, you're the imitation me." To Sontag, the idea of a preordained role for a woman was "grotesque. You can have one smart woman and you can have one talented, passionate black. Then, obviously, if there is a slot and you're waiting for the next woman to come along that has a bit of pizzazz and authority, then she's going to be praised beyond her merits because, look, she's finally arrived."[10]

Moreover, Sontag, with her long dark hair, later marked by a striking streak of white, was beautiful, and thus even more alarming and arousing. Like Woody Allen fantasizing about the Whore of Mensa, a floozy with a high IQ available to discuss Proust and Strindberg, the editor and critic Joseph Epstein also notes that Susan Sontag is "the model of the bohemian graduate-student lover every bookish man feels he ought to have." Moreover, he argues, "good looks in a woman, especially an intellectually gifted woman, can seem more than a touch anomalous: it is almost as if beauty would make a woman's possession of intellectual ability appear surprising." Would Sontag have had such a great career, he asks, if she had been "4'10", weighed 165 pounds, had sandy-colored hair, and wore largish round spectacles?"[11] Similarly, in the French-Canadian film *The Decline of the American Empire,* a lascivious academic confides that he secretly longs to sleep with Susan Sontag. And in *Bull Durham,* Kevin Costner spars with Susan Sarandon by declaring that Sontag's novels are "self-indulgent, overrated crap."

But Sarandon retorts, "I think Susan Sontag is brilliant!" To women, Sontag was a feminist icon of independence and spirit, a heroine—"like meeting Joan of Arc on her day off."[12] "Think of the things I don't do," she told *New York Times* critic Richard Bernstein in 1989. "I don't appear on television. I don't write for any newspaper or magazine regularly. I'm not a journalist. I'm not a critic. I'm not a university teacher. I don't speak out on most public issues. If I wanted to play a pundit role, I would be doing all these things. . . . My life is entirely private."[13]

"THAT LONG PRISON SENTENCE, MY CHILDHOOD"

Although she said in 1972 that she had "never been tempted to write about my own life," Sontag has discussed herself in interviews and a few essays, and we can splice together at least some of the story of her private life.[14] She was born Susan Lee Rosenblatt in New York on January 16, 1933, the daughter of Jack and Mildred Jacobson Rosenblatt. As a little girl, she told classmates that she had been born in China, but this exotic story was not entirely true. She was conceived in China, where her father was a fur trader, but her mother returned to New York for medical care when her daughters, Susan and Judith (1936), were born. The girls were left in the care of relatives in New York when their mother returned to China; Susan rarely saw her parents "because they spent almost all their time in the Far East."[15] She has described herself as a "psychologically abandoned child."[16]

In "Project for a Trip to China" she meditated upon her memories of this background. "Chinese forms placed about the first living-room I remember (we moved away when I was six): plump ivory and rose-quartz elephants on parade, narrow rice-paper scrolls of black calligraphy in gilded wood frames, Buddha the Glutton immobilized under an ample lampshade of taut pink silk. . . . Trophies brought back, left behind in homage to the other living-room, in the real Chinese house, the one I never saw. . . . The birthday gift of a bracelet made of five small tubular lengths of green jade, each tiny and capped in gold, which I never wore."[17] When she was four, her father's partner Mr. Chen taught her how to eat with chopsticks and said that she looked Chinese.[18]

In 1938, her father died of tuberculosis in Tientsin. His death, however, was never discussed with the children; when her mother returned to the United States in early 1939, Sontag recalled, "it took several months for her to tell me that my father wasn't coming back."[19] As an adult, Sontag confessed, "I still weep in any movie with a scene in which a father returns home after a long desperate absence, at the moment when he hugs his child. Or children."[20] A year after her father's death, Susan began to have symptoms of asthma, and the family moved first to Miami, and then to Tucson, Arizona, along with their Irish Catholic nanny. By the age of three, Susan had already started reading and formed her passionate identification with books. When she started public school, Susan was so advanced for her age that she skipped immediately to the third grade. "I was a terribly restless child, and I was so irritated with being a child that I was just busy all the time."[21] By the age of seven, she was reading the biography of Madame Curie. For many years she intended to become a scientist or a doctor.

But Mildred Rosenblatt was no Madame Curie, and Susan's feelings toward her cold, morose, and "bony" mother were very different from her loving memories of her father.[22] "My mother was a very withholding woman. . . . I would leave my report card by her bed at night and find it signed at the breakfast table in the morning. She never said a word. . . . I have a vision of my mother lying on her bed, with the blinds drawn, and a glass next to her that I thought was water, but I now know was vodka. She always said she was tired. As a consequence, I am happy to sleep four hours a night."[23]

Meanwhile Susan lost herself in books. "I can remember my first bookcase when I was eight or nine. This really speaking out of my isolation. I would lie in bed and look at the bookcase against the wall. It was like looking at my fifty friends. A book was like stepping through a mirror. I could go somewhere else.

Each one was a door to a whole kingdom."[24] A "demon reader," she devoured fairy tales, comic books, the Bobbsey Twins, "books about astronomy, chemistry, China, biographies of scientists, all of Richard Halliburton's travel books, and a fair number of mostly Victorian-era classics."[25] She was also "writing up a storm."[26] By the age of ten, she had discovered the Modern Library at a Tucson stationery store and immersed herself in great names. "I sort of understood these were the classics. I used to like to read encyclopedias, so I had lots of names in my head. And here they were! Homer, Virgil, Dante, George Eliot, Thackeray, Dickens. I decided I would read them all."[27]

In 1945, Mildred Rosenblatt married Army Air Corps captain Nathan Sontag, "a handsome, bemedaled, and beshrapneled" ace who had been shot down five days after D day; and the girls took their stepfather's last name. The following year they moved to Canoga Park, California, to a "cozy shuttered cottage with rosebush hedges and three birch trees." Susan finally had a bedroom with a "door of her own." "Now I could read for hours by flashlight after being sent to bed and told to turn off the light, not inside a tent of bedclothes but outside the covers."[28]

In North Hollywood High School, she was editor of *Vintage,* the literary magazine; editor of the student newspaper; and a member of the student council. Even in high school she had developed leftist inclinations. "There was a little communist group in my high school, and they gave me the 1936 Soviet Constitution to read. I read it, we talked about it—and I never asked myself any questions; I was sure that it corresponded to reality."[29] But the ordinary details of American life in the forties drove her crazy, led her to grind her teeth, twirl her hair, bite her nails, overeat. Especially popular culture: "the weekly comedy shows festooned with canned laughter, the treacly Hit Parade, the hysterical narratings of baseball games and prizefights—radio, whose racket filled the living room on weekday evenings and much of Saturday and Sunday, was an endless torment."[30] Later, she would attach the same feelings of exasperation to television—unless it was French.

In December 1947, at fourteen, Sontag was an intense, somewhat humorless girl, in love with books and music, "steeped in
vehement admirations and impatience for the reality to which I
would travel once released from that long prison sentence, my
childhood." Many of the details of her adolescence seem paradigmatic of the feminist as a young woman. Her closest friends
were boys, Peter and Merrill, but Sontag did not seem to befriend
other girls—"Elaine," a senior who played the flute, was an
exception—and she was distant from her own younger sister,
Judith, although they became close as adults. With Merrill, she
shared her breathless discovery of Thomas Mann's *The Magic
Mountain* and realized that the tuberculosis that had killed her
father was "the very epitome of pathetic and spiritual interest!"[31]
The perception would resurface years later in *Illness as Metaphor.*

Immersed in the novel, she read and reread it, then loaned it to
Merrill, who loved it too. But Merrill embarrassed her by insisting that they go together to pay a call on the elderly Thomas
Mann, living nearby in Pacific Palisades. The episode is at the
center of Sontag's autobiographical essay "Pilgrimage," which
begins, "Everything that surrounds my meeting with him has the
color of shame." For her, the visit to Mann seemed impertinent
and hubristic, like visiting a god. But what actually shocked her
was that Mann, who was working on *Dr. Faustus,* did not talk like
a god, or like a book; he "talked like a book review," in what
sounded to her like "sententious formulas." When Mann's wife
served an elaborate German tea, she was almost paralyzed with
self-consciousness. Mann asked them about Hemingway, who to
these snobbish young high school aesthetes was not a serious
artist, merely "a very popular author of novels that had been
made into romantic movies."

Worst of all were his questions about American youth, which
revealed that he "hadn't the faintest idea what a high school in
southern California was like. Did he know about Driver's Education (compulsory)? Typing courses? Wouldn't he be surprised
by the wrinkled condoms you spotted as you were darting across
campus for first period (the campus was a favorite nighttime

trysting spot)? . . . And by the 'tea' being sold by a pair of pachukes (as the Chicano kids were called) stationed along the left wall of the assembly building every morning recess? Could he imagine George, who, some of us knew, had a gun and got money from gas-station attendants? Ella and Nella, the dwarf sisters, who led the Bible Club boycott that resulted in the withdrawal of our biology textbook? Did he know Latin was gone, and Shakespeare too, and that for four months of tenth-grade English the visibly befuddled teacher handed out copies of the *Reader's Digest* at the beginning of each period—we were to select one article and write a summary of it—then sat out the hour at her desk, nodding and knitting? . . . He couldn't, and I hoped he would never find out." He seemed very far away from Europe; she did not want him to know how far.

Even years later, when she knew many writers and had learned to be more tolerant, Sontag found the memory of her pilgrimage to see Thomas Mann deeply embarrassing—she will not say "disillusioning." And she never seems to have realized how very much more serious, authentic, vivid, and engaging these gothic details of her American high school life in southern California were than the faint ghostly echoes of Mann's elite European civilization. What could have happened to those dwarf sisters? To George, who went off to do time in prison as she went off to college? Perhaps, however, in some way this unconscious realization about her material is at the heart of the story, since Sontag remembers it so clearly and tells it so dramatically. "Pilgrimage" is the most emotionally immediate piece she has ever written about growing up female in America, her equivalent of McCarthy's *Memories of a Catholic Girlhood* or Beauvoir's *Memoirs of a Dutiful Daughter.*

But at the time, the incident seemed to signal the need for escape from "America" and from girlhood. In 1987, Sontag writes, "I still feel the exhilaration, the gratitude for having been liberated from childhood's asphyxiations. Admirations set me free. And embarrassment, which is the price of acutely experienced admiration. Then I felt like an adult, forced to live in the body of a child. Since, I feel like a child, privileged to live in the body of an adult."[32] She would also transform herself rapidly into a person more suitable to meet the idealized novelist "Thomas Mann," the kind of cosmopolitan, deracinated American intellectual Elizabeth Hardwick called a "good European . . . international, too respectful of the cultures and peculiarities of nations, to be rooted but not small or provincial or too native for curiosity."[33]

CHICAGO

By the time Sontag was a teenager, she had already become an American version *avant la lettre* of the feminist intellectual—a young Simone de Beauvoir. Hardwick writes, "It is easy to imagine her as a prodigy at the École Normale and no accident that, being an American, she turned up at sixteen at the University of Chicago."[34] At fifteen, she was freed from the prison of childhood, her sentence reduced for good behavior. Her high school principal told her she was wasting her time and allowed her to graduate and go off to Berkeley, her mother's choice.

But Sontag's heart was set on the University of Chicago, the opposite of everything that was popular, loud, crude, and competitive in American culture. "What led me to Chicago?" she later asked herself. "It was reading an article in, I believe, *Collier's* magazine in 1946 or 1947. It was either by Robert Hutchins, explaining their aims and curriculum of the college, or it was an article about this eccentric place, which didn't have a football team, where all people did was study, and where they talked about Plato and Aristotle and Aquinas day and night. I thought, that's for me." And "Chicago was exactly what I expected it to be."[35]

For Sontag, it was like finding home, amid people like herself. She welcomed the discipline it imposed. "Until Chicago, I'd been a gluttonous reader. But the kind of intellectual work I was doing until I came to Chicago was simply *taking in;* I didn't have a method. The method practiced at Chicago was comparative and basically ahistorical. . . . There was a constant dialogue of texts; and the method of comparing them, which I learned at Chicago, is one I still practice in my essay writing." She wrote very little fiction because "writing comes from a kind of restlessness and dissatisfaction. And I was so satisfied at Chicago." Although she did not notice at the time, there were no women role models for her at Chicago. She took courses with Joseph Schwab, Kenneth Burke, Richard McKeon, and Leo Strauss and became friendly with Mike Nichols and Allan Bloom. "At Chicago I was handed an invaluable set of tools, and my enthusiasm and my natural respect for seriousness and for learning were confirmed. The University of Chicago was the single most important part of my education. My entire life has been a development of a debate with the education I received there."[36]

As Sontag recalled, professors at the University of Chicago, like Thomas Mann, were "gods, and we couldn't imagine that we could have a social relation with them."[37] But in December 1950, at the urging of friends, she went to hear a young instructor, Philip Rieff, lecture on Freud. When the lecture was over, she was the last to leave. "He was standing at the door," she recalled, "and he grabbed my arm and asked my name. I apologized and told him I had only come to audit. 'No, what's your name?' he persisted. 'Will you have lunch with me?'"[38] Ten days later they were married. Rieff was twenty-eight, a "dapper Anglophile," while Sontag was a young-looking seventeen in blue jeans with long hair. Visiting one of his lectures soon after the wedding, she overheard his students gossiping that Rieff had married "a fourteen-year-old Indian."[39] As Sohnya Sayres dryly observes, Sontag's beauty had something to do with this whirlwind courtship: "Men do not usually grab the arm of merely brilliant women."[40]

A MARRIED WOMAN

The marriage was intellectual and cosmopolitan; they were both "eccentric, intense people."[41] Sontag graduated with an accelerated BA in 1951, and they moved to Boston, where Rieff taught at Brandeis. Their son, David, was born in September 1952, two weeks after she had enrolled as a Ph.D. candidate in philosophy at Harvard. She received an MA in philosophy from Harvard in 1955, then commuted to the University of Connecticut at Storrs to teach English and taught philosophy for a year at Harvard.

Sontag has written and said little about this period of her life, little about the shock of faculty wifedom, motherhood, and responsibility at such an early age. But clearly she was restless. Remember that she read *The Second Sex* during the first year of her marriage and suddenly awakened to an understanding of the female predicament. From then on, she said, she tried to apply Beauvoir's principles of existential freedom and choice in her own life. In 1957–58, she won an AAUW fellowship to St. Annes in Oxford. Rieff had won a fellowship too, but at the last moment, for unknown reasons, he decided not to go. Sontag went without him, and, according to the novelist Judith Grossman, without her child. Grossman, who was at Oxford at the same time, wrote sympathetically about Sontag's impact on the Oxford literati in her novel *Her Own Terms:* "This woman, there!" raves one of the young men to the narrator, Irene. "American! Brightest woman ever met, drank me under the table. . . . Calls herself Sontag." But before he can try to seduce her, she is off to Paris for a term at the Sorbonne—not for the art but for the philosophy. The women gossip about Sontag's scandalous independence: " 'Did you know there was a husband *and* a child, in the States? . . . We wouldn't *imagine* doing something like that.' I said nothing; it occurred to me that we weren't very strong in imagination around here."[42]

At the Sorbonne, Sontag was exposed to the *nouveau roman* and to the *nouvelle vague* in film. But she also began to enjoy popular music, and the pleasure and sexual liberation it implied. "Rock and roll really changed my life," she told Jonathan Cott of *Rolling Stone* in 1978. "It was Bill Haley and the Comets. I really had a revelation, and I can't tell you how utterly cut off I was from popular music because being a child in the forties, the only things I ever heard were crooners, and I loathed them. And then

I heard Johnnie Ray singing 'Cry.' I heard it on the jukebox, and something happened to my skin. Several years later there was Bill Haley, and then I went to England in 1957 as a student and heard some of those early groups who were influenced by Chuck Berry. It was the beginning of what would lead to the Beatles.

"You know, I think rock and roll is the reason I got divorced. I think it was Bill Haley and the Comets and Chuck Berry that made me decide that I had to get a divorce and leave the academic world. At that time, the late fifties, I lived in a totally intellectual world. I didn't know one single person I could share this with. I didn't talk about it. People say a lot of stupid things about the fifties, but it is true that there was this total separation between the people who were tuned into the popular culture and those who were involved in the high culture. There was nobody I ever met who was interested in both, and I always was."[43] Sontag learned to dance for the first time at the age of twenty-six.

When she returned to New York, she asked Rieff for a divorce. "It was in many ways a good marriage," she said. "But I didn't want to go back to that. I thought there were other lives to live."[44] Twenty years later, she explained to Cott: "I did have the idea that I'd like to have several lives, and it's very hard to have several lives and then have a husband . . . somewhere along the line, one has to choose between the Life and the Project."[45] In 1958, Rieff got custody of the book they had worked on together, *Freud: The Mind of the Moralist,* and Sontag got custody of David. Her lawyer told her she was the first person in California history to refuse alimony.[46] "It seemed to me an equally 'personal' act of principle on my part, when I divorced my husband seven years later, to have indignantly rejected my lawyer's automatic bid for alimony, even though I was broke, homeless, and jobless at that moment and I had a six-year-old child to support."[47]

Sontag never forgot that she had been a single parent: "I was divorced when my child was five years old and I raised him myself. I had all kinds of responsibilities that a man would not have. I had to take care of the apartment, raise the child, put the shoes on him in the morning, take the laundry, and so on. You have to be stronger than a man."[48]

But despite these responsibilities, after her divorce Sontag's real adolescence began. "I had a very enjoyable adolescence from the age of twenty-seven to about thirty-five, which coincided with the sixties—I enjoyed them in a way people much younger experienced them." As Bob Dylan sang in the sixties, she had felt so much older in high school and was younger than that now.

NEW YORK INTELLECTUAL

Sontag plunged into the life of New York, working as an instructor at various colleges, and as an editor for *Commentary*. She was also writing her first novel, *The Benefactor.* When she finished it, she simply "took it to a publisher. I made a list: Farrar, Straus and Giroux was my first choice in 1962, because they had published *The Djuna Barnes Reader;* second was New Directions, but somehow I had the impression they were less accessible; and third was Grove Press, because they were publishing Beckett. It was ridiculous!"[49] Two weeks later, Farrar, Straus called and offered her a contract—like her marriage, it was another whirlwind courtship.

Indeed, Sontag's rapid rise in New York intellectual circles aroused gossip and jealousy. Many young women writers wanted the chance; in her journals for winter 1960, Sylvia Plath records a dream of being discovered by her brother in bed with a man named the *Partisan Review.*[50] William Phillips recalled that he first met Susan Sontag at a Farrar, Straus and Giroux party in 1962. "She walked up to me and said, 'How do you write a review for the *Partisan Review*?' I said, 'You ask.' 'I'm asking,' she said. 'O.K.,' I answered. 'What do you want to do?' I do not know whether it was the whiskey or the fact that my guard was down or that there was something immensely attractive about Susan. I prefer to think that I was open to new talent and that I was mes-

merized by the intelligence one could detect in her eyes."[51] Philip
Rahv, however, was not so mesmerized. "Susan Sontag. Who is
she?" he demanded of Mary McCarthy. "Above the girdle, the girl
is a square."[52]

But Rahv's image of Sontag was not widely shared. Contrary to
his view, she quickly became a celebrity for the avant-garde, and
also something of an iconoclast in her passion for popular culture.
"I made a few jolly references to things in popular culture that I
enjoyed," she explained. "I said, for instance, one could enjoy
both Jasper Johns and the Supremes. It isn't as if I wrote an essay
on the Supremes." In 1964, she published the supremely hip
"Notes on 'Camp'" in the *Partisan Review,* introducing the subject
of the gay aesthetic, and defining the importance of artifice, style,
androgyny, theatricality, and extravagance in camp sensibility.
Written at a time when Oscar Wilde and the decadent movement
were seen as dated and irrelevant, "Notes on 'Camp'" came well
before its time in drawing attention to Wilde as a literary theorist,
and to aestheticism as a serious artistic category. In another sense,
attention to camp was a prelude to feminism. "Camp's extremely
sentimental relation to beauty is no help to women, but its irony
is," Sontag later remarked. "Ironizing about the sexes is one step
toward depolarizing them. In this sense the diffusion of camp
taste in the early 1960s should probably be credited with a considerable if inadvertent role in the upsurge of feminist consciousness in the late 1960s."[53]

Meanwhile Sontag was raising her son, David, alone, in an
atmosphere he recalls as "amiable squalor" but intense loving
intimacy. Mother and son were extremely close and shared many
interests. Along with the children of Harry Belafonte, Robert
Rauschenberg, and Zero Mostel, he attended the "ultraprogres-
sive, ultra-rad, and boho New Lincoln School" on 110th Street.
Here the students included red diaper babies, as well as the rich
and famous. As classmate Michele Wallace recalled, their assem-
blies "featured peace activist folksingers, speakers from SNCC
and the Civil Rights Movement. We listened to the music of
Leadbelly and John Cage and we sang the songs of Pete Seeger in

our classes."[54] Among Sontag's friends were artists such as Jasper Johns, and doctors such as Jonathan Miller and Oliver Sacks, with whom she talked about medicine and went to autopsies.[55] But despite her brief fling with popular culture, Sontag's intellectual interests seem once again to have separated her from women, and from a younger generation, and allied her with more elite circles of the arts—PEN International, the New York Film Festival, grants from Rockefeller and Guggenheim. She wrote brilliantly about film, including Ingmar Bergman's *Persona.* She was active in the antiwar movement, and in May 1968 went to North Vietnam—by then almost a cliché among the old New York intellectuals such as McCarthy and Arendt, and not the center of radical energy during the Prague spring and the *événements* of Paris.

A "LIBERATED" WOMAN

The years between 1968 and 1973, pivotal for many feminist intellectuals during the late twentieth century, were also years of rootlessness and wandering for Sontag—back and forth to Stockholm, where she learned Swedish and made two films, *Duet for Cannibals* and *Brother Carl;* to Paris, where she began living for extended periods with David, who had dropped out of Amherst; to Vietnam, China, and Israel. In 1972, she was living in a penthouse apartment overlooking the Hudson, "with the Spartan, uncluttered look of a place you've just moved into," although it had been her home for five years.[56] Sontag described this period of her life as a crisis. "Where am I, what am I doing, what have I done? I seem to be an expatriate, but I didn't mean to become an expatriate. I don't seem to be a writer anymore, but I wanted most of all to be a writer."[57]

By 1972, she had also become aware of the American women's liberation movement and had read the books. "I like them all because the main thing is to make a fuss," she told Victoria Schultz. Still, she found *The Female Eunuch* "essentially reactionary," and *Sexual Politics* to have "tremendous limitations."[58] In terms of her own life, Sontag, like Beauvoir, still did not see any direct relevance of women's disadvantage. "The feminist movement has been important to me because it's made me feel less odd and also because it has made me understand some of the pressures on women which I was lucky enough to have escaped, perhaps, because of my eccentricity or the oddness of my upbringing."[59]

She elaborated this view in her most complete feminist manifesto, "The Third World of Women" (1973), where she states her credo: "The first responsibility of a 'liberated' woman is to lead the fullest, freest, and most imaginative life she can. The second responsibility is her solidarity with other women. She may live and work and make love with men. But she has no right to represent her situation as simpler, or less suspect, or less full of compromises than it really is. Her good relations with men must not be bought at the price of betraying her sisters."

From her perspective above the struggle, Sontag took some loftily remote intellectual positions. She described the legalization of abortion, and the establishment of free day care, as "reformist" demands, "and as such, suspect. History shows that the anger of women, when channeled into pressing reformist demands only, is all too easily defused . . . such reform tends to narrow and then abruptly disperse, militant energies. It can also be argued that they directly bolster the repressive system, by ameliorating some of its hardships."[60] She criticized other successful women in the arts and professions for their misogyny and complacency, without seeming to notice that she too was complicit in the circle of blaming the victims. Sohnya Sayres sees this essay as forced and evasive: "The essay gives one the sense that she was never there when women were shaking each other free from victimization to empowerment . . . she writes about what she is attracted to but does not wish to be, because she is troubled by what it reveals about herself as well as her times."[61]

CANCER

Sontag's life and values were permanently changed in 1975 when she was hospitalized with breast cancer and told that she had a 10 percent chance of living two years. "Becoming ill, facing one's own death, being in the company of people who are suffering terribly—and many of them dying—for several years is, of course, a watershed experience. You are not the same person afterwards. I was told that very likely I was going to die. I didn't die, I was lucky. But the fact is that I have survived, that I am not now ill. I'm in remission and perhaps that means I am cured. It doesn't mean I can cancel that experience. One is on the other side of something that changes your relation to life, that brings you close to death in such a way that you can never come completely back.

"And it has changed a lot of things for me. In some ways it has been a strengthening experience. It's like any one of the great emergencies that bring out the best and worst in people, and that's very impressive. I saw it in other people, not just in myself—other people with the most extraordinary amount of courage, intelligence beyond anything that they were capable of before. It's also weakening, because you realize in a very painful way your own mortality and once again the extent of all this needless human suffering, which enraged me."[62]

Sontag responded to the news of her cancer with fierce intelligence and determination to survive. She had five operations, a mastectomy, several rounds of chemotherapy, and went back to France for the aggressive cancer treatment unavailable elsewhere. She also had to accept help from others. Robert Silvers, coeditor of the *New York Review of Books,* raised money from her friends for treatment since she had no medical insurance. She has said many times that surviving cancer left her with a renewed sense of the centrality of human relationships and a deepened compassion for human suffering. "When I got sick," she told a journalist, "I wanted to be closer to people, to accept consolation, and talk about life and death. For the sake of my self-respect, I continued to work, but if I were a less conscious, driven person, I would have simply been with people. I didn't want to write—I wanted to hold hands."[63]

In an interview with Jonathan Cott in 1978, she described the illness as both terrifying and oddly exhilarating. "Well, of course, I was told it was likely that I'd be dead very soon, so I was facing not only an illness and painful operations, but also what I thought might be death in the next year or two. And besides feeling the physical pain, I was terribly frightened. I was experiencing the most acute sense of animal panic. But I also experienced moments of elation. A tremendous intensity. I felt as if I had embarked on a great adventure."[64]

The experience of illness led to her most original and groundbreaking book, *Illness as Metaphor,* and its sequel, *AIDS and Its Metaphors.* Facing the prospect of death also freed Sontag to break away from the political shibboleths of the intellectual left. In 1982, she created a firestorm by declaring at a public meeting that the American left had underestimated the evil of Communism. It was a declaration of political independence that shocked her former friends. Sontag felt that she was finally expressing feelings she had had since the midseventies, when she started to meet exiles from Communist countries such as Joseph Brodsky, who described the horror of life under Communism. But Elizabeth Hardwick attributed the venom of the subsequent attacks to Sontag's position as "a woman, a learned one, a *femme savante. . . .* As an intellectual with very special gifts and attitudes, it was somehow felt that this made her a proper object for ridicule of a coarse kind. I believe the tone was different because she was seen as a very smart, intellectually ambitious woman." In Hardwick's view, Americans felt "an inclination to punish women of what you might call presumption of one kind or another."[65] Sontag herself shrugged the episode off; "*writing* well is the best revenge," she told an interviewer.[66]

She continued through the eighties to put her own advice

into action, breaking away from male-dominated intellectual institutions to take her own stance on political, aesthetic, and sexual issues. When PEN met in New York in the winter of 1986, women members protested to Norman Mailer, the president, because there were virtually no women on the panels. "Since the formulation of the panels is reasonably intellectual," Mailer explained, "there are not that many women like Susan Sontag, who are intellectuals first, poets and novelists second. More men are intellectuals first, so there was a natural tendency to pick more men than women."[67] Sontag, however, established her solidarity with the feminist protester group that walked out of the congress and indeed attended the formative meetings of the PEN women's group. At the next election, she became president of PEN.

In other ways too she was beginning to assert herself as a professional, and to make demands for herself. In 1989, a fire broke out in her apartment. "Firefighters chopped through the roof to extinguish the blaze," wrote journalist Paula Span, "which caused at least as much psychic as physical damage. What horrified her, Sontag says, was the realization that she didn't have enough money in her checking account to take refuge in a decent hotel. The landlord put a tarp over the hacked-open hole, and she spent the night in her roofless apartment." Sontag realized that she had no money of her own and was unprotected against the future. At the age of fifty-six, she decided that "it's not so much to own an apartment and have all your books out of storage and have time to write. These are not unreasonable demands; they're not corrupt." She acquired her first agent, Andrew Wylie, who arranged a four-book deal with Farrar, Straus that gave her financial security. She also received a MacArthur Fellowship for $340,000, which allowed her to buy a sunny co-op. "I ask myself all the time," Sontag said, "why did it take me so long?" She speculates, "I didn't have access to this kind of expressiveness, of inner freedom."[68]

WRITING FICTION

Meanwhile, she was struggling with the effort to be a writer. "I have to come out of the closet of the third person and speak in a more direct way," she said in one interview.[69] After many years of producing learned essays about difficult European writers such as Calvino and Barthes, Sontag realized that she had always felt constricted by the demands of the essay form and had found writing essays difficult and limiting. For years she had been trying to write in a way that would give expression to her volcanic feelings. Yet again, Sontag did not connect these discoveries with anything about her socialization as a woman, or with the experience of women intellectuals in the past, from Wollstonecraft and Fuller on, who had feared that writing a certain kind of fiction was too feminine, and that they needed to adapt to masculine standards of intellectual style.

One night in 1987, Sontag received a phone call telling her that a close friend had AIDS. She was unable to sleep that night and took a bath. In the bathtub, the first words of a story came to her: "At first he was just losing weight, he felt only a little ill." "It was given to me, ready to be born," she says. "I got out of the bathtub and started writing standing up. . . . I wrote the story very quickly, in two days, drawing on experiences of my own cancer and a friend's stroke. Radical experiences are similar."[70] The story, "The Way We Live Now," describes the illness of an unnamed man through the reactions of his wide circle of friends; "We're learning how to die," says one. It was published in *The New Yorker* and included in a number of collections of the best fiction of the year. In its emotional depth and accessibility, "The Way We Live Now" went far beyond anything she had written before and seems like a kind of rebirth.

At last, in 1992, she published *The Volcano Lover,* her first novel in twenty-five years, and an unexpected best-seller. For three years, she had "worked . . . in a delirium of pleasure" on the book. With its publication, she felt freed from the "kind of one-note depressiveness that is so characteristic of contemporary fiction. I don't want to express alienation. It isn't what I feel. I'm interested in all kinds of passionate engagement. All my work says be serious, be passionate, wake up."[71]

The following year, Sontag published a play, *Alice in Bed* (written, she says, in 1990), that is her most feminist and personal work. "Alice" is both Alice in Wonderland and Alice James, Henry James's brilliant and neurotic sister, who died of breast cancer at the age of forty-three. The play is perhaps the first of Sontag's works to locate itself explicitly in the tradition of women's writing. Much influenced by the theater of Caryl Churchill, especially *Top Girls, Alice in Bed* brings together Alice James, Margaret Fuller, and Emily Dickinson in a surreal tea party. In a note on the play, Sontag begins by recalling Virginia Woolf's fantasy of a female Shakespeare in *A Room of One's Own* and suggests that Alice James was an American equivalent—a woman of thwarted genius. The play, she explains, is about "the all too common reality of a woman who does not know what to do with her genius, her originality, her aggressiveness, and therefore becomes a career invalid." More generally, it is a play about "the grief and anger of women," which she claims "to have been preparing to write all my life."[72]

Sontag's 1990s thus began with an affirmation of her feminist identity and ended on a similar note in her introduction to *Women* (1999), a book of photographs of women by her friend Annie Leibovitz. The introduction is wry and thoughtful about the way in which women are scrutinized and scrutinize one another: "Whether well-known or obscure, each of the nearly one hundred and seventy women in this album will be looked at (especially by other women) as models: models of beauty, models of self-esteem, models of strength, models of victimhood, models of false consciousness, models of successful aging." Perhaps because she herself is now sixty-six, Sontag emphasizes the scrutiny of aging. "Nobody looks through a book of pictures of women without noticing whether the women are attractive or not," but women "are judged by their appearance as men are not, and women are punished more than men by the changes brought about by aging. Ideals of appearance such as youthfulness and slimness are in large part now created and enforced by photographic images. And, of course, a primary interest in having photographs of well-known beauties to look at over the years is seeing how well or badly they negotiate the shame of aging."[73]

The "shame" of aging seems like too strong a term, but certainly this is very different language from the woman who for a long time thought of herself as a child, rather than a girl, in an adult, rather than a female, body. The last photograph in *Women* is of Susan Sontag herself—her famous hair now totally white, and boyishly cropped. She has never been more beautiful.

ELEVEN

The Inner Revolution
of the 1960s

Before the Revolution

In the late 1950s and early 1960s, intellectual girls were fascinated and excited by the life of Simone de Beauvoir, but also puzzled and alarmed by feminism. Helene Wenzel, a freshman at Barnard College in 1961, read *The Second Sex* and "was not favorably impressed; on the contrary, much of what she had to say was truly terrifying to me; who would want to become one of those belea-guered creatures she called a 'woman'?"[1] Juliet Mitchell read *The Second Sex* at Oxford and "thought it brilliant but somehow applicable only to some inexplicable predicament of French women."[2] The Parisian life certainly looked glamorous, especially to the critic Rachel Brownstein and her friends in Brooklyn, who hoped that "ideally one would be Simone de Beauvoir, smoking with Sartre at the Deux Magots, making an eccentric domestic arrangement that was secondary to important things and in their service. One would be poised, brilliant, equipped with a past, above the fray, foreign not domestic." Of course, the lover would look a lot more like Albert Camus than Sartre, but that was a fine point.[3] The main thing was *la vie existentielle*.

I too read *The Second Sex,* in 1958 while I was in high school in Brookline, Massachusetts, but my fantasies did not quite extend to

Paris; and as an admirer of Mary McCarthy, I saw myself more ironically and comically than romantically, as the heroine, at best, of a screwball tragedy. Like Susan Sontag in her memoir, "Pilgrimage," I was "still serving out my long prison sentence of childhood." When I was sixteen, I discovered that one of my literary idols, Isaac Asimov, actually lived in Boston and taught at the Boston University Medical School. He agreed to let me interview him for the school newspaper, and we met for lunch near the Charles River, where he casually offered to buy me a cheeseburger. My parents were not very observant Jews; we ate shrimp, bacon, and Chinese pork strips. But I had never had a cheeseburger. Eve eating the apple, Sophie Portnoy with her first lobster, had nothing on my feelings as I ate that cheeseburger, the forbidden fruit, so to speak, that would launch me into the adult world.

Meanwhile I was plotting my escape to the women's college farthest away from home, Bryn Mawr. M. Carey Thomas, the first president of Bryn Mawr College, had been a feminist fireball. "Women are one half the world, but until a century ago," she said in 1908, "women lived a twilight life, a half life apart, and looked out and saw men as shadows walking. . . . Now women have won the right to higher education and economic independence. . . . We have gone so far, we must go farther. We cannot go back."[4]

When I actually did go to Bryn Mawr in the fall of 1958, however, my dreams of becoming a free woman met a severe disappointment, and in some sense I did feel as if I had gone back. By the late 1950s, the college had reached a nadir of gentility, snobbery, authoritarianism, and puritanism. M. Carey Thomas's original vision of educating women to take on the challenges of the world had been watered down to mean educating women as if they were sexless. There were no college counseling services, and, since Bryn Mawr was Quaker, not even a chaplain. Although we often quoted Thomas's motto that "our failures only marry," no one ever talked with us about how we were going to combine careers with family life. We were required to bring tea sets to college and, I suppose, intended to use them. I still remember a terrifying freshman tea given by my appointed "big sister," at which she served Camembert and panettone, foods of a sophistication I had never seen or tasted before. I was equally alarmed and impressed by the residents of the French house, who smoked Gauloises, wore tailored suits like those in the wardrobe of Domna Rejnev, and could be heard in the college tea shop drawling, "Tu piges, chérie?"

Yet despite this cosmopolitan surface, our lives were as restricted as if we had been living in a convent. We were not allowed to drive cars and had to be in early at night unless we were accompanied by a male. With our mobility thus curtailed, we devoted much of our energy to finding an escort with a penis and wheels, a time-consuming task given Bryn Mawr's geographical isolation and reputation at nearby men's colleges and universities for bluestocking weirdness. Sex for most of us was still secretive, mysterious, and taboo. There was no sex counseling or birth control, but students could be expelled for getting pregnant, and many of my classmates disappeared abruptly that way, leaving red-eyed roommates refusing to talk. The most exciting and seductive of the lesbians disappeared abruptly too. Despite these restrictions, my friends displayed great courage and resourcefulness in our so-called sex lives. One girl came back from her junior year in Paris and regaled us with her account of how she and her boyfriend had become lovers in France, cheerfully describing the details, down to using spit as a lubricant. Some of my friends managed to obtain diaphragms by telling doctors that they were about to be married. But in fall 1961, the birth control pill was marketed for the first time, and the sexual revolution flooded over us like a tidal wave. It seemed as if everyone in my dorm "lost" her virginity that fall, even the lesbians. And the unspoken code was actually to find as unthreatening and disposable a boy or man for this significant initiation as possible, a cruel decision that equalized what we all felt was the power differential in sex.

The situation was not very different elsewhere. At Cambridge University in the 1960s, Judith Okeley recalled, "a woman student was sent down from university for being found in bed with her boyfriend *during* the male visiting hours (2–6 P.M.). She lost her grant and could not obtain a reference to any other university. The man, by contrast, was sent away from his all-male college for two weeks. . . . A lecturer in English, David Holbrook, wrote an article in our university magazine *Isis* in 1962 defending the college's decision to send down our colleague for premarital sex and declared that the experience of sexuality should be restricted to the purposes of reproduction."[5]

At Bryn Mawr, we were also served our meals by black maids and porters who lived in the dormitories and called us "miss." Small wonder that the one black girl in my class dropped out at the end of her first year. Some of the maids at Bryn Mawr were followers of the black evangelist Father Divine, and on a sociology field trip, they escorted us to his Divine Peace Mission Headquarters in Philadelphia. Father Divine's followers believed that he was God and that they would live forever if they had the faith. But by this time, the Father Divine community was dwindling from its glory days in the Depression; Father Divine was an old man who rarely made appearances, and the interracial group of followers, which preached and practiced celibacy, was aging and shrinking like the Shakers. But they could still put on an amazing show. The evening began with a Holy Communion banquet; for $1.50 each, we were taken into a room with a long, narrow table set with a white cloth, flowers, and place mats printed with excerpts from Father Divine's speeches, which were also broadcast from a loudspeaker during the meal. The food was handed out on platters and in huge glass bowls through a window at one end of the table, and we passed it around; the ritual included not letting a dish touch the table until it was empty. There were salted and unsalted versions of the same dish, including fried eggplant, which I had never seen before, chicken and meat and every imaginable kind of vegetable. For dessert, we had a huge glass bowl of chocolate ice cream, piled up in petals like a brown rose.

After the banquet, we went downstairs to the chapel, where Mother Divine led the prayer services. She was youngish, blond, a Canadian who had become a secretary in the movement headquarters, originally named Edna Rose Ritchings, known as Sweet Angel, and who had married Father Divine in 1946. They claimed to have a celibate marriage, and their anniversary was the occasion of a major banquet attended by representatives of the Divine Peace Mission worldwide. The men's choir, called the Crusaders, and the two women's choruses, the Rosebuds and the older Lilybuds, were dressed like usherettes at the Paramount movies, complete to the white cotton gloves. They sang the same verses again and again, clapping and swaying until the congregation caught the spirit: "Father knows the way where there is no way, when you're in harmony with hi-i-im." Then people would stand and testify or speak in ecstatic tongues.

Although the moment in the service when guests were expected to feel the spirit and speak was always horribly embarrassing for me, I was fascinated by the group and went back on my own every week for the next two years. I was trying to write a novel about what would happen when Father Divine died—an honorable project but way over my head. And I never guessed that what would actually happen when Father Divine died in 1965 was that Mother Divine would rise to the occasion, rally the remnants of the movement, and even start serving healthier food.

I was engaged the fall of my senior year to a graduate student in mathematics at Princeton. But during the Christmas break, I had a frightening, belated epiphany of how little we had in common, and how blindly I had been shepherded into choosing early marriage. I broke off the engagement and applied to attend graduate school in English at Brandeis University. It seemed like an ideal compromise. To my parents, Brandeis was less a university than a Jewish philanthropy and synagogue extension, and they hoped it was a place where I would meet the right sort of men. To me, Brandeis was the New England outpost of the New York intellectuals. Irving Howe and Philip Rahv were teaching there. Moreover, I would be able to support myself by working as a dormitory counselor.

The scary near-miss of my engagement had made me aware that I had a lot to learn about myself before I settled down, and I was trying to keep my distance from men for a while. But in the early winter of 1962, I met English Showalter, a young French instructor at Haverford, who came from Roanoke, Virginia, and had attended Yale and the École Normale Supérieure in Paris. His roommate, a chaplain hired by the local Protestant community to minister to the unchapeled Quakers of Haverford and Bryn Mawr, was helping to start an ecumenical, interracial coffeehouse in the town of Bryn Mawr, and as the head of the college Arts Council, I was invited to participate in the planning. English and I were assigned to sand the old church pews we used for seating. The coffeehouse was a huge success, although the chaplain enjoyed the street life and atmosphere so much that he lost his faith and left the church. Meanwhile, English and I spent a lot of time together that spring. I took him and the chaplain to the Father Divine Mission, where they both performed brilliantly in the talking-in-tongues and hallelujah part of the service.

At my Bryn Mawr graduation, the situation was tense. My parents were horrified by my relationship with English—a Southerner and Episcopalian with floppy hair—and ordered me never to see him again. "Now you're finished with those not-conforming people," my father said triumphantly as we drove up the highway back toward Boston. Instead, English and I met secretly at Tanglewood for a weekend and decided that we wanted to get married. The news so outraged my parents that after a summer of quarrels, scenes, and futile attempts to negotiate with English ("Do you realize that if you marry this Jewish girl, you'll never be able to stay in a nice hotel again?" one of my uncles warned him), they disowned me. At summer's end, I moved into my dorm at Brandeis, never to go home again. I had my tuition, room, and board, and a stipend of $300 for the year. Despite my parents' hopes, I never dated any nice Jewish men at Brandeis, although I did briefly hang out with a Mormon who was studying Arabic.

After the docility and decorum of Bryn Mawr, I was unprepared for the clamorous debate of the Brandeis seminars; intimidated by the boldness of the men in my classes, especially one named Sharkey; and terrified by the harsh brilliance of Rahv and his confident young disciples. All the faculty in the English department were men, and for the first time in my life I began to feel stupid, inadequate, and slow, and to doubt whether I could succeed at all in the academic world.

Politically the year was clamorous too. During the Cuban missile crisis, hundreds of panicked Brandeis students tried to flee the country to avoid nuclear attack. Herbert Marcuse was one of the campus gurus. In the midsixties, students were again becoming politicized. At Cambridge, noted Judith Okeley, "despite the conservatism of the university authorities and Macmillan's government, the student societies experienced a socialist renaissance. Despite the rigid politics syllabus, we were reading Marx, Luxemburg, Goldman, Trotsky, Nkrumah, and Marcuse out of school hours. We listened to Nelson Mandela and Bertrand Russell and I spent a morning with Malcolm X. Each year, another colonized nation broke free."[6]

Malcolm X came to Brandeis as well. The lecture was controversial because we had to be frisked by the Black Muslim bodyguards, and also because he spoke to the Brandeis community with a mixture of camaraderie and menace, both as another oppressed group on the margins of American society that might join his radical cause, and as privileged whites who were an obstacle to his vision of black pride and nationality. One of half a dozen black undergraduates at Brandeis, Angela Davis recalls that evening as the first moment she felt the stirrings of black nationalism. "I might have said that I felt 'empowered' by Malcolm's words," she recalled, "except that that notion of power had not yet been understood in a way that separated the exercise of power from subjective emotions occasioned by an awareness of the possibility of exercising it. But I recall that I felt extremely good . . . momentarily surrounded by, feeling nurtured and caressed by black people who, as I recall, seemed to have no particular identity other than that they were black." Davis remembered that Malcolm X "offended the white people in attendance," but created a new identity for her. Indeed, she noted, "no one could have convinced me then that Malcolm had not come to Brandeis to give expression to my own inarticulate rage and awaken me to possibilities of militant practice."[7]

Meanwhile, English and I managed to meet in Philadelphia or Boston once a month and joked about having our wedding in the middle of the pool around which Brandeis had built its interfaith chapels. We actually married, though, in the Unitarian Church in Philadelphia the morning of June 8, 1963. The young minister read a passage from George Eliot, who had also lost her faith and defied her family to run off with a man. Then we returned to our apartment in Haverford for a wedding breakfast prepared by my Bryn Mawr friends. After breakfast, our friends departed, and English's family left for the drive back to Virginia. Feeling that the occasion required something special and festive, English and I went to the movies. Perhaps George Eliot would have expected something more uplifting.

The next day we left in our VW Beetle to drive to Mexico for two months. It was an unpropitious time for a honeymoon. George Wallace had called out the National Guard in Alabama, and we drove through the Deep South in our VW along highways crowded with military convoys and stayed in Faulknerian rural motels whose segregated cafés served "wop salad" alongside the fried catfish. In Mexico, we drove all the way to Yucatán before I succumbed to amoebic dysentery and landed in a jungle hospital run by nuns. The summer was often terrifying and disorienting, but I felt that my life had at last begun.

In addition to the civil rights movement, other signs of violent social change in 1963 included the Kennedy assassination, church bombings, the beginnings of protest against the escalation of war in Vietnam. Doris Lessing's novel *The Golden Notebook* (1962), which dealt profoundly with the fragmentation of women's political and sexual identity, was a Bible for prefeminist intellectual women in the 1960s. I read it in Davis, California, where English was teaching and I was enrolled in graduate school and working as a TA. Here our daughter Vinca (named for the heroine of a novel by Colette) was born in 1965, while English read *The Feminine Mystique* in the hospital waiting room; and we witnessed the free speech movement at Berkeley, the beginning of Cesar Chavez's grapeworkers' strike, and the early days of the rock scene in San Francisco. I had always had close women friends, but at Davis I formed a lasting bond with my classmate Wendy Martin, who became a surrogate sister. Wendy was a Californian who had been an undergraduate at Berkeley, and who seemed both my opposite and my twin. She too was married, to a reporter on the *Sacramento Bee,* and we shared both a passionate interest in the lives of women writers and a sense that we were making up our own lives as we went along, unable to predict the future.

Many years later, when Wendy was remarried and a mother, settled in Berkeley and teaching at Claremont, she was invited to lecture at Davis and wrote to me about the trip back:

> The drive up to Davis seemed long and hot in the late afternoon sun. After the Carcinas straights, the land begins to flatten out and there are no longer any vistas of the Bay. The towns becoming increasingly smaller: Vacaville, Dixon, Woodland—do you remember them? As I drove into campus on a back road and saw all of the experimental agricultural projects in greenhouses and gardens, I wondered how the hell we ever found ourselves in Davis and how we managed to stay sane while we were there. But when I got to the Library and inner quad, the campus began to look quite spacious and substantial—very civilized really. And I began to think that it looked like a serious quiet place to get some work done which, of course, is what we all did—get work done and lots of it.
>
> The lecture went well and I had a chance to drive around town while it was still light. Of course, I drove by the small frame house on J street which was right next to the railroad tracks. It is considerably worse for wear; it needs paint badly and the shingled roof is actually shredded in places. A bearded fellow was sitting on the porch and when I told him I once lived there, he asked if I'd like to see the inside. Yes, I would I said repressing

any thought that it might be dangerous to enter this house in which a strange man now lived. The rooms were exactly as I remembered them, but the place wasn't nearly as pleasantly furnished or well maintained. I remembered the homebrew we made on the back porch, the long dark oak table where we all spent many an hour eating and talking, the parties where we danced to the Beatles, the Rolling Stones and the Grateful Dead, the good and bad things about being married to Arthur (mostly bad it seems now but there are a few positive memories too).

When I went around the back of the house, I could remember exactly what it felt like to be a married graduate student in my midtwenties, and I realized that I was very much the same person I am now. The difference is that then I didn't know very much about life or how to live. I was certainly in the center of myself and my life, but I had no idea where I was going really or what the rest of my life could possibly be. My extraordinarily limited sense of possibilities is quite distressing really. Here I am a person who some people say has an unusually vivid imagination; yet, I could not construct a life for myself beyond being a graduate student at UCD or beyond the walls of that little house. Terrifying really. Surely, young women are not so limited and self-limiting today.

When I look back on what seems an incredibly impoverished vision of the future, it seems miraculous that I have had such a rich and varied existence. Yet, it may be this very inability to envision possibilities that resulted in what seems to some an adventurous life. I never really knew where I was going so I just chose what seemed best at the moment rather than waiting to see if what I thought I wanted might come along. Since I had no idea that I could decide what I wanted, what there was to want even, or that there might be something worth waiting for, I took the opportunities as they came. This does make for a rather episodic life to say the least. Maybe this is the way a lot of Americans live when you get right down to it—they take chances as they come along. Maybe other people are better at creating the illusion of orderly progression toward a goal or goals than I am.

Even now, I have a difficult time imagining how I want to live as an older person. But last night I was actually counting the probable number of years I have left if a dread disease doesn't get me or if an accident doesn't do me in. And I wondered how much work I might get done in that span of time—say twenty years or so. 75 is exactly as far in the future as 35 is in the past. It's something to think about.[8]

DURING THE REVOLUTION

I have always been grateful that I was the right age for the sixties, and at least in some of the right places at the right time. The year 1968, as Angela Carter wrote in one of her essays, "felt like Year One . . . all that was holy was in the process of being profaned. . . . I can date to that time . . . and to that sense of heightened awareness of the society around me in the summer of 1968, my own questioning of the nature of my reality as a *woman*. How that social fiction of my 'femininity' was created, by means outside my control, and palmed off on me as the real thing."[9]

Richard Holmes, the biographer who went to Paris in search of Mary Wollstonecraft, was there in 1968 and recognized in the spirit of that moment the kind of revolutionary fervor that had transformed Wollstonecraft's imagination. "The whole ethos of the Sixties," he wrote, "—that youthful explosion of idealism, color, music, sex, hallucinogenic states, hyperbolic language and easy money . . . was based on a profoundly romantic rejection of conventional society, the old order, the establishment, the classical, the square—and also, in fact, austerity."[10]

Like Richard Holmes, I too was in Paris during the revolutionary summer of 1968. English and I, along with our three-year-old daughter, Vinca, had rented an apartment on the Left Bank, in the Place du Président Mithouard, so that he could do research for his book. I was trying to finish my dissertation on Victorian women writers, a project that seemed both hopeless and futile; I had a part-time job teaching freshman composition at Douglass College, but there did not seem to be any full-time teaching jobs available for women in the vicinity of Princeton University, where English was an assistant professor. We shared our large, sparsely furnished apartment with a horde of guests who arrived in the hopes of seeing the remnants of the student uprisings before they disappeared. In the back bedroom were a poetic couple of English anarchists who had dropped out of Oxford and who sometimes spent their lunchtime francs on anarchist pamphlets instead of baguettes. In the *chambre de bonne* were two French students, English's French "sister" and her fiancé, and we scrambled around to hide him like characters in a French farce when Papa made unannounced visits. Our Princeton friend Bert Sonnenfeld took up residence on the folding bed next to the big dining-room table, and a friend from the States arrived in tears in the middle of the night from a lovers' quarrel with a boxer in Barcelona to sleep on the sofa. With English's graduate students and their Parisian lovers added to the list, I had an enormous crowd to cook for in the evenings before we went out to sit in the cafés, to watch the police clear the last groups of student protesters out of the École des Beaux-Arts, to debate the declarations and counterdeclarations, and to talk excitedly about the future.

Richard Holmes wrote about Paris in 1968 that its excitement came not from destruction, but from "the sense of something utterly new coming into being, some fresh, immense possibility of political life, a new community of hope, and above all the strangely inspired note—like a new language—that sounded in the voices of those who were witnessing it. It was a glimpse of 'the dream come true,' the golden age, the promised land."[11]

For French feminists, May '68 was a significant turning point. Antoinette Fouque, one of the leaders of the French women's liberation movement (MLF), recalls that she "experienced '68 as a real revolution and as time goes by, I'm more and more convinced of this."[12] She was beginning her third year of graduate study, "working with Roland Barthes on my thesis, which I never finished, on the notion of a literary avant-garde. I had arrived in

1960 from the Aix-en-Provence, was married to an intellectual the same age as I. My daughter was four. He and I were working for François Wahl at *Le Seuil*. . . . My future seemed clear; everything seemed to point me toward publishing, criticism, writing.

"But in fact, I was very rebellious. A woman's economic independence, professional equality, intellectual competence, were not really valued. The milieu in which I found myself was very conservative in the way it operated. . . . I was constantly made aware of the false promise of equality, symmetry, and reciprocity that a university education had for so long held out. To have had a baby was almost shameful."

Although she had read *The Second Sex,* Fouque had never been politically active. "I was concerned about social and political struggles, but at a distance. I observed them as though through a pane of glass. . . . I didn't know what feminism was and now I can say that I regret that. It was a sign of my ignorance of the struggles of women in history."[13] But in May '68, at the Sorbonne, she and Monique Wittig "formed a Cultural Action Committee that drew filmmakers, actors, writers, intellectuals: Bulle Ogier, Michèle Moretti, André Téchiné, Danièle Delorme, Marguerite Duras—these are just a few of the names that come to mind." Fouque was thirty-two, but felt that in the MLF "we were all young and beautiful. For most of us it was our first involvement in politics. We felt as though we had grown fifteen years younger. We all felt in '68 as though we had come down with a healthy case of adolescence."

She was surprised to find herself behaving like an activist and a leader. "The truth is that if Monique hadn't dragged me by the scruff of the neck, I would never have gone to the Sorbonne. I was very intimidated. I had never spoken in public, except in class." Overall, her memories of the beginning of the French women's movement were a mixture of confusion and exhilaration. "We felt so small, so inexperienced, so clumsy. . . . And yet, at the same time, it was like a Ferris wheel, a moment of destabilizing but also joyous giddiness, a chaotic and productive education, and exhausting and exalting apprenticeship to life and history."[14]

Nancy Miller had lived in Paris during much of the sixties, but in 1968, she was coming out of a divorce and deciding to go to graduate school. "I missed '68 . . . if we think of '68 narrowly as a single apocalyptic event, or even a network of events with specific locales: the Sorbonne, Berkeley, Columbia. But '68, we know, can be seen as . . . the figure of diffuse political movements, including feminism. . . . In this sense '68 didn't miss me."[15]

When I returned to the United States in September 1968, the American women's liberation movement was beginning, and the dissertation I had labored over seemed already out-of-date; I had to begin rewriting it again. Information circulated on broadsides and mimeographed pages, passed from hand to hand at conferences; in pamphlets, available by mail; and in discussions face-to-face. Radical feminism in the United States was not puritanical or didactic. In the Redstockings' broadside titled "Women and Consumerism," Ellen Willis declared, "There is nothing inherently wrong with consumerism. Shopping and consuming are enjoyable human activities and the marketplace has been a center of social life for thousands of years." Willis herself was a rock critic for *The New Yorker* and a connoisseur of popular culture. While she opposed "the pervasive image of the empty-headed female consumer," she believed that "we must stop arguing about whose lifestyle is better (and secretly believing ours is)."

In their revolutionary manifesto, the Women's Liberation Collective of Palo Alto announced in 1969: "Let us join together in groups (fifteen or less) to discuss all aspects of womanhood. To understand the nature and extent of our oppression, we must discuss everything from diapers to orgasms, from political economy to the woman's page, from the desire to have children to the desire to be married to the desire to own a house. We must analyze everything we talk about."

The New York Redstockings put out their "Principles": "1. We take the woman's side in everything. 2. We ask not if something is 'reformist,' 'radical,' 'revolutionary' or 'moral.' We ask is it good for women or bad for women? 3. We ask not if something is 'political.' We ask: is it effective? Does it get us closest to what we really want in the fastest way? 4. We define the best interests of women as the best interests of the poorest, most insulted, most despised, most abused woman on earth. Her life, her suffering and abuse is the threat men use against all of us to keep us in line. She is what all women fear being called, fear being treated as and yet what we all really are in the eyes of men. She is Everywoman: ugly, dumb (Dumb broad, dumb cunt), bitch, nag, hag, whore, fucking and breeding machine, mother of us all. Until Everywoman is free, no woman will be free. When her beauty and knowledge is revealed and seen, the new day will be at hand." The feminists of the New England Free Press wrote: "Not all women will want to work in the women's movement. We should encourage each other to love and act in our own best interests."

In England, Juliet Mitchell had broken away from the New Left and written *Women: The Longest Revolution* in 1966. "At that moment," she recalls, "I felt, for all sorts of personal and intellectual reasons, that I would not be able to think freely if I stayed within that environment."[16] Mitchell had grown up in an intellectual family, with a mother who was a scientist and a socialist. She had attended King Alfred's, a coeducational progressive school in London, and had grown up "in a communal atmosphere with different people—artists, journalists, teachers—living in the same house." When she was twelve, she heard Margaret Mead lecture; "Margaret Mead was the first major model of an intellectual woman for me."[17]

At Oxford, Mitchell had read English and started a Ph.D., but the honors syllabus stopped with the Romantics. "The only way you could do a thesis on twentieth-century literature even as a graduate student was to work on manuscripts, so I started to do one on Joyce Cary (all of the manuscripts were in the new Bodleian Library). So I started out. But after a year I got a job as an assistant lecturer at Leeds University."[18] She also married Perry Anderson, one of the prominent intellectual leaders of the New Left. But by the end of the 1960s, Mitchell had begun to rethink the basic assumptions of left-wing politics and its attitudes toward the woman question. She began to wonder, could you be "a creative, intellectual woman if you don't have a kind of power of aggression somewhere?" And she started "wondering about Mary Wollstonecraft again. She had a lot of political aims: in education, law, social structures, etc. But she felt that there was a place you couldn't touch—something that was personal. She exempted the sexual relationship, in fact, from the politics of feminism."[19] With these questions in mind, Mitchell turned to Freud and psychoanalysis.

By 1969, as Hillary Rodham graduated from Wellesley College, the questions of female identity and feminist adventure had become much more than remote abstractions in the writing of Simone de Beauvoir. Once again they were words in a new language, a glimpse of the promised land.

TWELVE

✦✦✦

Talkin' 'Bout My Generation

The 1970s

ONLY THE CONCEPTION

April 1970. A letter from Margery Somers Foster, dean of Douglass College, to Kate Millett: "Dear Miss Millett: Things are all set here, all in the lines you and I discussed. We will expect you here on Monday . . . at 5.30, on the Public Service bus. . . . There will be time for brief drinks, partly with the Liberationists and partly with the Departments of Bacteriology and Education, the latter being my dinner guests. The Liberationists will take you to dinner and keep you as long as you can take it in the evening. You will stay at my house and have the morning free until your talk at 11.10. . . . After the luncheon Mrs. Showalter would like to have you attend her course on 'The Educated Woman in Literature,' to which she will be inviting a few extra people. . . . We certainly look forward to the whole visit."

A letter on the same day from Elaine Showalter, part-time instructor at Douglass College, to her mother-in-law in Virginia: "Dear Jean, Everything is looking better, if only temporarily. We have had several conferences with the Dean and it now appears that our proposals will definitely be incorporated into the co-ordinate program, and voted upon by the faculty Tuesday. . . . On Monday, Kate Millett, a radical feminist who is the

Founder's Day speaker, is coming and we're arranging meetings between her and young faculty, hoping she can persuade them to support us. She is the author of the *Token Learning* pamphlet, and when the alumnae hear her, there should be some fireworks."

In spring 1970 I was teaching freshman composition in the Douglass English Department, seven and a half months pregnant with my second child, and a member of the central New Jersey chapter of the National Organization for Women. The women's liberation movement was just beginning to surface in the mass media, in part because the media themselves became subject to feminist protests about discrimination in hiring and demeaning stereotypes in representation. In March the women employees at *Newsweek* demonstrated against the magazine, with *Time,* NBC, and CBS soon to follow; and on March 19, a coalition of feminist groups had staged a sit-in at the *Ladies' Home Journal* to demand serious coverage of women's issues and options rather than sunny prescriptions for saving hopeless marriages. The seventeen women and one man in my NOW chapter in Princeton were working on setting up a day care center, desegregated help-wanted ads, employment and housing discrimination, sexism in children's books, abortion rights, and the Angela Davis Defense Fund. The Supreme Court had agreed to hear two cases on abortion, one of which became Roe v. Wade. In a huge feature story on education in the 1970s in the *New York Times,* Margaret Mead, one of only three women out of sixty-five respondents, foresaw the demands for self-determination the decade would bring: "There is a questioning all over the world, by colonized peoples, by minorities, by women, of an order of life in which others—teachers, administrators, social workers, members of other classes and races, and of the other sex—care for them, no matter how well-intentioned the care may be."

But on April 14, 1970, when Kate Millett came to Douglass for Founder's Day, *Sexual Politics* had not yet been published, and Millett was a little-known activist I had met at the Congress to Unite Women in New York, an instructor in the English department at Barnard College—the women's college at Columbia

University—and the author of a scathing indictment of American women's colleges called *Token Learning* (1968), which documented the ways that even the best women's colleges in the country had betrayed their trust, and which showed how their founders' original goals of opening the fullest range of opportunities for women had declined through the fifties into a tacit feminist mystique of gentility and service, educating followers rather than leaders. It was an alarming moment for women's higher education in general, for the situation in traditionally or newly coeducational colleges and universities was if anything worse; shunted into a limited number of academic fields, shackled by restrictive social policies, and subject to harassment and prejudice, women students were nowhere offered the full educational opportunities available to men.

When she spoke at Douglass, Millett shocked some of us with her evidence of the second-class status of women's education and of women within society. But at least women's colleges had a motive to lead in rethinking higher education in the twentieth century. While she saw coeducation in the classroom as the obvious direction of the future, Millett argued that American women's colleges could serve a major function "as centers of hope and encouragement devoted exclusively to the encouragement of excellence in women."

At Douglass we were in the midst of a heated debate about this very subject. When Rutgers College decided to accept women, as Princeton had done that same year, most of the Douglass faculty initially thought that the only way the college could survive would be to accept men. Those who wanted it to stay a women's college were regarded as old-fashioned, spinsterish, and provincial, defenders of inevitable mediocrity and respectability. The Southern style of Dean Foster, whose dinners for faculty followed the Victorian mode of having the ladies withdraw for chitchat and coffee while the gentlemen stayed behind for brandy and cigars, did not inspire much confidence in the progressive agenda of women's colleges.

But there was another way of looking at the problem. Along

with another young instructor, Mary Howard, in the sociology department, I had written and circulated a mimeographed report called "The Future of Douglass College: Women and Education." Mary and I had criticized the description of a Douglass education, as it was then defined by the catalog: "to enable students to find the fullest satisfaction in rich and responsible personal lives and to serve usefully as citizens," and argued that the college could do a lot more to "provide students and faculty with a genuine sense of identity and leadership." We called for the development of courses dealing with women's history, status, and achievements; for a day-care center; for programs for women in the community; for an emphasis on women artists and writers; for improved career counseling; for the sponsorship of research on women; for sexual counseling and information; and for the abolition of inequities between male and female student life at Rutgers.

Politics makes strange bedfellows, and rarely stranger than our alliance with Dean Foster. Together we brought Kate Millett to the campus to help us publicize the idea, and she made a great impression on the older women faculty, rather than the young. On the day after her visit, the Douglass faculty decided that the solution was not to admit male students, as Vassar and other women's colleges had done, but rather to try a bold experiment in feminist education. They voted 90 to 32 to adopt the basic recommendations of our report. At the meeting, Doris Falk, the feisty chair of the English department, and the author of a book about Lillian Hellman, made the speech that turned the tide, describing the way she had come to realize that the old-style feminism she opposed—"the bluestocking, seven-sister type oriented toward preserving chastity and cultivating femininity"— had been replaced by a new-style "liberation of body and spirit for women and for all people," and that while she had once thought she herself was liberated, she now realized that was "a foolish mistake." For she had been part of a generation of academic women ghettoized in women's colleges, and unable to develop their talents to the fullest degree.

"My own universities," she told us, "had openly stated to me that they would not hire women on upper-level positions—so I was conditioned and poor and therefore adjusted to the situation. I am still trying to adjust. But," she went on, "I want to liberate my students from this imprisonment—or rather, I want to give them the tools to liberate themselves—to create a job market in which men and women receive equal pay for equal work, and have equal opportunity and mobility. I think it is possible now that Douglass must take the lead in research—yes, *research*—to find the ways to make this happen. It must also find ways to make women think of themselves as free to fulfill themselves as people, not just as women. I wonder how different life would have been for many women of my generation, if they had not been subjected to sexual stereotypes of what a lady did or did not do, and inhibited by the very real threat of disaster (social, emotional, physical) through unwanted pregnancy. . . . We at Douglass College must support equal rights for women and men to sexual development and to freedom from fear: fear of social disgrace, or of a forced wrong marriage, or of perilous traumatic abortion. But the fight for freedom can only be fought by women who think of themselves as free, and who can cut their 'mind-forged manacles'. . . . We have the obligation to our students to nurture such freedom." Within a few days of the vote, Dean Foster asked Mary Howard and me to chair an ad hoc committee setting out what needed doing "to do right by women's education." The letter was addressed to Mrs. John Howard and Mrs. English Showalter, but we were thrilled nonetheless.

The excitement of those few days was abruptly overshadowed by chaos. At the beginning of May, Nixon ordered the invasion of Cambodia, and all over the country demonstrations exploded against the Vietnam War. At Kent State and at Jackson State, student demonstrators were killed by inexperienced National Guard soldiers, and Rutgers, like many other campuses, went on strike, canceling classes and final exams as students and faculty participated in teach-ins, protests, and a day of mourning. These were exhilarating but also disturbing days, too close to the edge between revolution and terror to feel entirely positive. A student radical from Kent State came to speak at the college and described the demonstrations leading up to the shootings; the night before, she said, someone had torched a campus building, and it was intoxicating. "Have you ever seen a really big fire?" she crooned. At Princeton, students and faculty staged a sit-in at the Institute of Defense Analysis, a campus think tank reputed to be doing planning for the war, although they said they were doing pure mathematical research. Rumors spread through the group that night riders from nearby Trenton, working-class patriots with baseball bats and maybe guns, would come through on pickup trucks to attack the student radicals, and the event took on the slightly goofy macho feeling of a western, or *Desert Song,* as young male faculty masked themselves with purple scarves and ordered the women and the children into the library.

Still, when the Cambodia protest came to an end, a sense remained that many previously silent groups in American society—students, women, homosexuals—would follow the lead of the civil rights movement in demanding their rights as full social participants. That summer also saw the first gay pride parade in New York and huge marches all over the country to celebrate the fiftieth anniversary of the women's suffrage amendment. In August, *Sexual Politics,* which argued that all societies were patriarchal and that relationships between the sexes as well as the races were political, hit the best-seller list, and Kate Millett was on the cover of *Time.* Somehow, between meetings, classes, and sit-ins, I managed to finish my dissertation on Victorian women writers, and in June, the week that I gave birth to my son, Michael, I received my Ph.D. from the University of California, with a diploma signed by Governor Ronald Reagan. I was twenty-nine.

WOMEN'S STUDIES

The summer of 1970 was a turning point for many young women in the academy. The historian Lois Banner was one of my friends at Douglass; she too had a husband who taught at Princeton, and she too received her Ph.D. in 1970, from Columbia University. "Before then feminism hadn't interested me," she recalled, "for it hadn't seemed relevant to my life. I read Betty Friedan's *The Feminine Mystique* soon after its 1963 publication, but . . . I liked taking care of my home, and I had a job. Friedan seemed to have in mind women different from me. It took the militant radical agitation of 1968 and 1969 to shock me into awareness: the sit-in at the *Ladies' Home Journal* offices; the Atlantic City protest against the Miss America pageant. The decisive event for me was Kate Millett's photograph on the cover of *Time* magazine in 1970. . . . Millett's extension of politics to the realm of the personal resonated with something inside of me. . . . I realized that the dearth of female faculty members at UCLA, Columbia, and Princeton wasn't an accident."[1]

In 1971, Adrienne Rich's seventh book of poems, *The Will to Change,* seemed like the slogan and rallying cry for a new generation, although the term *will* also looked back to the rational determinism of Olive Schreiner and Eleanor Marx. Rich had conspicuously changed her own life, leaving her husband, Alfred Conrad, surviving his suicide, raising her sons, joining the civil rights and women's movements. She was publicly working out in her poems the full life trajectory of a woman artist, a woman thinker, a story truncated in my generation's collective memory by the spectacular suicides of Sylvia Plath and Anne Sexton. With each book, Rich took us to a new level of self-discovery, and a new awareness of what life might have in store. As she wrote in her study of motherhood, *Of Woman Born* (1976), "The most notable fact that culture imprints on woman is the sense of our limits. The most important thing one woman can do for another is to illuminate and expand her sense of actual possibilities."[2]

In New York, where Wendy Martin, now divorced, was teaching at Queens College, there was a heady sense of excitement and expansion. She wrote to me in November 1971 about a dinner of "movement heavies" where there was a cross fire of heterosexual, lesbian, and bisexual conversation about "their ex-husbands and

lovers, male and female, intricate sexual and domestic arrangements . . . going to parties in drag etc. etc. There I was trying to
listen to both conversations, unable to decide which group, if any,
to identify with. At the same time I didn't feel at all alienated—
just fascinated with the incredible variety of experiences, possibilities. Life in the twenty-first century will be very interesting
indeed."

For Nancy Miller, in graduate school at Columbia, feminism
was "in the streets." On August 26, 1970, she joined with friends
in the Fifth Avenue march, and in January 1971, after reading
Vivian Gornick's article about consciousness-raising groups in
the *New York Times Magazine,* she started a group: "In particular, we talk about how we don't want to be like our mothers who,
we believe, did not know what they wanted. What do we want?
The specifics are not clear but the project involves taking charge
of one's own life. . . . The point of the group as we see it is to help
each other bring this about: not to be a victim."[3]

There was a growing interest in changing the academic curriculum to include the history and achievements of women. On
December 29, 1970, in Chicago, alongside Adrienne Rich and
Tillie Olsen at a forum organized by Florence Howe and the
Women's Caucus of the Modern Language Association, I shak-
ily delivered my first professional paper, titled "Women and the
Literary Curriculum." "Having their experience dignified by
inclusion in the literary curriculum," I argued, "would not work
miracles for women students, but it would be an important
recognition of the importance of the feminine perspective."
Moreover, "teaching women could be the new frontier of education," for "a generation of confident women students might produce a new and exciting feminist criticism and perhaps even a
new literature."

The pioneers of women's studies began to think of themselves
as a new generation of feminist thinkers. In 1972, in *Female Studies VI,* Ginny Foster wrote that "at this point in the history of education, women are for the first time in a position to influence
institutions of higher learning." Women in universities, she

argued, should become *"femmes de lettres"* and *"intellectuelles,"* following Hannah Arendt's distinctions in *On Revolution*. Rather than limiting themselves to bureaucratic or professional questions about the structure of the university, *"femmes de lettres* must begin to think of what women's studies could be."[4] But the pioneers included political activists such as Florence Howe, who had returned to Goucher College after a summer teaching in the Mississippi Freedom Schools and wondered why her white, middle-class women college students didn't write as well as the black high school students she had taught in Mississippi. The answer, she hypothesized in an essay called "Identity and Expression," was that they too needed to begin by writing about issues in their own lives. Howe's Feminist Press, which she directed with the fervor of an Eleanor Marx and the tirelessness of an Elizabeth Cady Stanton, furnished some of the texts for the new teaching enterprise.

But for the aspiring young *femme de lettres* in the 1970s, being the Dark Lady was still the major career lottery, and I read Norman Podhoretz's *Making It* avidly, trying to figure out exactly how I might apply for the job. I was dark; and William Phillips and Richard Poirier were still editing the *Partisan Review,* now at Rutgers. As one of the miniskirted, finger-cymbaled, rock-music-loving chicks around the English department, I managed an invitation to the annual Christmas party, the most desirable social event of the Rutgers year. After a few drinks, I made my way up to Phillips and tried out Susan Sontag's line about wanting to write for the *Partisan Review,* and I told him about my adventures in the women's liberation movement and its New York conferences. Phillips had no interest at all in feminism, but whether he was mesmerized by the intelligence in my eyes or by my Cossack minidress from the East Village, he was intrigued by my account of the "feminist pornography" Ti-Grace Atkinson and her group were selling at the conferences and insisted that I send it to him immediately. He called several times to follow up, but after I finally sent him the pink mimeographed pages, with stories of women dominating, torturing, and enslaving men, I never heard from him again.

The other members of the New York intellectuals were not interested in feminism or women's studies either. Carolyn Heilbrun recalled that in 1972, "the year in which I became, belatedly by any standards, a full professor at Columbia, Trilling, then almost sixty-seven years old, was named the first Jefferson Lecturer in the Humanities by the National Endowment for the Humanities" and told a reporter for the Columbia student paper, "I always preferred to teach boys."[5] A few years later, Trilling expressed his dismay at the decline of graduate study in English literature: "Virginia Woolf is likely to be the author that a typical Ph.D. candidate today thinks he ought to know best. And now I see that the Modern Language Association had an annual seminar devoted to Doris Lessing."[6] At Columbia generally, Nancy Miller recalls, feminist criticism "was not yet an acknowledged working category." One of her dissertation supervisors warned her, "Don't try to be another Kate Millett."[7]

At the time, according to a survey in the optimistically entitled *Female Studies I,* there were seventeen courses in women's studies in the United States, two of them at Douglass, where we were making up women's studies as we went along on a budget of $300 a year, funding our newsletter and lecture series with a male-faculty bake sale, and answering letters of inquiry from all over the country about our "program" when it wasn't much more than a drawer in a desk and a gleam in our eyes. By 1971, Douglass was featured in the *New York Times* as the center of the new women's studies initiative nationally. Kate Millett had turned down an invitation to become a member of the faculty, but during the 1970s, Adrienne Rich, the novelist Maureen Howard, the feminist literary critics Catherine Stimpson, Janet Todd, and Rachel DuPlessis, and the black feminist writer Cellestine Ware joined our small English department.

I've often wondered what would have happened if circumstances had not come together to make Douglass the right place at the right time to do the right thing by women. What if the faculty vote had gone the other way? What would have happened to my life if I had been too busy or too frightened to get involved in 1970? Did feminist action require a strong dose of youthful idealism and innocence, and an equal amount of youthful energy? Was the solidarity that sparked the Douglass decision an indelible element of the second wave of the women's movement in America, a bygone golden age we will not see again?

But of course those beginnings were not as simple and clear as retelling their outcome makes them seem. In her 1899 masterpiece, *The Awakening,* a book feminist critics were rediscovering in 1970, Kate Chopin describes her heroine's coming to feminist consciousness: "The beginning of things, of a world especially, is necessarily vague, tangled, chaotic, and exceedingly disturbing. How few of us ever emerge from such beginning! How many souls perish in its tumult!" In much less heightened terms, I often cheered myself in the 1970s with a joke from Joan Rivers's nightclub act: "Can we talk about the pain of giving birth? I screamed and screamed—and that was only the conception!"

The beginning of women's studies was not painless. Although the slogan we chalked up on the blackboards during Brotherhood Week was "Brotherhood Weak, Sisterhood Powerful," sisterhood, we knew, was often feeble and far from perfect. The feminist coalition at Douglass was not a profile in courage either. Some faculty were just used to the status quo; some were worried about their jobs or their egos. Many, perhaps most of the students at the time, favored coeducation and regarded the decision as a vote for retrograde feminine protectivism. "Dean Foster's idea," a furious editorial in the student newspaper raged, ". . . is called a guide for the modern girl to be sheltered, Victorian, and stuffy until she settles down with her man at 21."

But it is comforting, I think, to know that important changes don't have to come from perfect people, or be implemented in perfect unanimity by perfect institutions, in order to succeed. We needn't fall into postmodern apocalyptic despair about the futility of political action or the impossibility of theoretical correctness as a precondition for action. Change doesn't have to come from the glittering metropolis, or the Ivy League, or the fancy think tanks; in fact new visions are much more likely to come from outside the bastions of security and complacency.

FULLERITES

Women breaking the academic rules and flying too close to the sun in the 1970s risked crashing and burning. In the early 1970s, I had met Ann Douglas, another assistant professor, who was the first woman hired by the English department at Princeton. A Harvard Ph.D., with a background in Anglo-Saxon, Victorian, and American literature, Ann was also a great beauty, slim, blond, and tanned, in her green Diane Von Furstenberg wrap-dress, with an elegant sexuality that made her stand out in academia. She was a green girl, a Diana, like the young Hannah Arendt. (In her fifties she told a reporter that when she was young, she was often compared to Grace Kelly. "I must say it's been one of the great reliefs of my life to be past that.") Ann was casual about her beauty and told funny stories about life at Princeton, where coeducation was so recent that women's toilets were few and far between. "We hold our water at Princeton," she claimed to have told a female job candidate. When I joined the Princeton faculty a decade later, I used to dash over to the library to use the women's bathrooms since the ones in our office building were so run-down. My first act as department chair was to get the faculty and staff ladies' room renovated. I wallpapered it myself one weekend, with a pattern of ivy—perhaps my only lasting legacy to the university.

Ann and I became close friends, although we could not have been more different. I was the superego; she was the id. I was dressing for success, working hard, playing by the rules. She was a rebel, a genius, a flash of light, a wild streak in the sky. I was the daughter of first-generation Jewish Americans; Ann's childhood had been a fairy tale, until her father died of leukemia when she was eight. Then her mother remarried, and her stepfather, the CEO of a Fortune 500 company, was immensely rich: "We were used to people with millions of dollars and a lovely country estate and maybe a cook at most. All of a sudden, we were in a world with stables and several Rolls-Royces and a Bentley and a huge estate in Maine and another in California and a transplanted German castle from the Rhine in New Jersey." There were private planes, country clubs, and flowing drinks.

Ann defined herself "as a rebel against everything he stood for. I was going to be a champion of the underdog, opposed to all the rules by which the rich prescribe protection for themselves and exposure for everyone else."[8] At Milton Academy, she was suspended for breaking the rules, and at seventeen, she dyed her hair black and ran away to New York under the name of Anna Watsonska, trying to pass as a Russian Jew. She lived at the YWCA until her stepfather had detectives bring her home.

While I was almost an autodidact, a scholarly itinerant, Ann had been educated at Harvard and Oxford. In the early 1970s, I was married and the mother of two small children; Ann was married too, but young men fell madly in love with her as if she were a New Jersey Zuleika Dobson; famous elderly scholars told her they had one great love left in their lives and offered it to her. (At Harvard, she had been "jumped" by one of her professors at the grave of Henry James.)[9] I was awed by the Princeton bigwigs; Ann seemed to have been born without the gene of feminine deference. She had none of the body language of feminine submission, the nods, smiles, cocked head, lowered lashes. Sometimes when I was walking across the Princeton campus with Ann, we would meet young male faculty and I would watch them first bewildered, then irritated, then fuming, as she interrupted them, contradicted them, dismissed them. They didn't know exactly what was happening, but they were fascinated and frightened. Some were also jealous and enraged. One senior professor said to her, "I have never known anyone so hated in any department as you are."[10]

We made a literary pact—I would have all the English women writers to study; she would have all the Americans. There didn't seem to be any competition for the turf. She already had an amazing collection of books by and about nineteenth-century American women, beautifully arranged in floor-to-ceiling wooden bookcases, that inspired me to start my own collection of Victorian women's novels. She called her writers by nicknames— Mrs. Sig—as I called mine by their initials—CB, GE, EBB. In a documentary made by Princeton to recruit prospective students, Ann was shown congratulating an undergraduate advisee on finishing his senior thesis on Havelock Ellis and asking, "But how do you really feel about Ellis? Do you like him?"

Ann's first book, *The Feminization of American Culture,* made a huge impression on me. She signed her copy to me: "For Elaine, my friend, sister, &, in the truest sense, co-labourer." I was struck by her acknowledgment to Alan Heimert and Perry Miller, whose "example taught me the meaning of exhaustive, committed, and heroic scholarship." What Ann meant by heroic scholarship was total immersion in all the literary and cultural data of a period; and Ann embodied it and inspired it. At the same time, she brought a highly personal set of feelings to her research and took her childhood reading seriously: "As a child I read with formative intensity in a collection of Victorian senti- mental fiction. . . . I followed the timid exploits of innumerable pale and pious heroines."[11] She most remembered the death of Little Eva; I had been marked by the sufferings of Elsie Dins- more. But the most stunning chapter of the book was the one on Margaret Fuller, and indeed Ann was Fuller reincarnated, only beautiful as well.

The brilliance and beauty, but also a tinge of the self-destruc- tiveness and manic energy, that came out of Ann's life were already apparent in the seventies, but I never realized that she had started drinking in the winter of 1971. After she had left Princeton for Columbia, been divorced, and embarked on a dif- ferent social life in New York, our phone conversations became infrequent and frustrating; she would spin a web of talk and hang up before I got a word in. Much later, she wrote about her drinking and discussed it with journalists. Working on *Terrible Honesty,* she confessed, "I wrote two whole drafts of this book . . .

but I couldn't write the book as it is as long as I didn't know how my own life was going to turn out. In other words, I didn't know if I was going to drink myself to death, and that was where I was headed." When her partner, Jay Fellows, became more and more disabled by alcoholism and manic-depression, Ann decided to leave him, and in 1988, she "quit drinking with the help of Alcoholics Anonymous and a stay in a psychiatric hospital."[12] She now sees alcoholism as a "twisted version of a spiritual quest, the search for God played as a challenge game."[13]

In her fifties, Ann has become a prominent journalist as well as cultural critic, writing about Hillary Clinton for *Vogue,* and about her childhood reading for the *New York Times.* In a 1999 symposium in the *New York Times Magazine* on the best time in history to be alive, she reiterated her fascination with the age of Margaret Fuller: "I think what matters most to me is to live in an age where there is conscious change going on, and where I as a woman could play a part in it. . . . So the time for me would be in nineteenth-century New England, the 1830s, '40s and '50s, at the time of the abolitionist movement, at the time that women became professional authors in this country. They could actually make a living not only as schoolteachers but also as writers. . . . I don't need to be a leader. I don't need to be a martyr. I just need to have some chance to go from my space, whatever that meant, into a wider world."[14]

But obviously for Ann Douglas, the best time to be alive is now. "No one pretends that physical aging is fun," she writes in *Vogue.* "Yet at fifty-seven, if it's sometimes disconcerting to realize that men aren't turning to watch me go down the street, at least I'm no longer an aging 'golden girl,' ready to dispense smiles and favors, playing stewardess on the airline of life. Rushing into the arms of the nearest man, I broke dates I needed to keep with myself. Today I live by myself, and like many American women, I've found my fifties to be the most intellectually adventurous, politically engaged, happiest time of my life."[15]

BLITHEDALE REVISITED

Like Margaret Fuller, Ann always had intense friendships with women. At Harvard, one of her best friends was Gail Thain Parker, another precocious young Americanist and feminist who by 1972 was already publishing on nineteenth-century American women writers in her anthology *The Oven Birds: American Women on Womanhood, 1820–1920*. The year the book came out, Gail was twenty-nine and an assistant professor of literature and history at Harvard, where she had received her Ph.D. in 1969. The first Harvard faculty member to teach a course on women, Gail was married to Tom Parker and was the mother of a five-year-old daughter. The one time I met her, I found her as impressive, as intense, and as daunting as Ann. Although she came from Chicago, Gail perfectly inculcated the Radcliffe style—lean, brisk, confident—that I remembered or internalized as an under-grad.

In her introduction to *The Oven Birds* (the title referred to Robert Frost's poem about "what to make of a diminished thing"), Parker argued that "something vital went out of the organized woman's movement in the 1890s when Elizabeth Cady Stanton and Susan B. Anthony abandoned the field to the new 'realists' in the suffrage ranks." These were the leaders who had "scorned compromise," while the next generation embraced it. Parker contended that the devolution had begun in the late 1860s and early 1870s, the years after the Civil War, and that her anthology was meant to show "just what it was that had gone out of their lives, leaving them emotionally—and physically—impoverished." In brief, they suffered from an absence of heroines. Indeed, "in the absence of living models, women were dependent upon fictional characters to enlarge their conception of the potentialities of their kind." They envied their grandmothers, who they believed had a confidence in the powers of womanhood that made it possible for them to act and yet attend to their emotions and personal needs. "They could demand their political rights without trying to conceal from the world or from themselves that they had feelings—of love and grief and indignation—because those feelings were in themselves proof that women were the equals of anyone." Finally, the early generation of feminists "could have lucrative careers without being accused of behaving in an unladylike fashion. Whatever success they had was understood to be confirmation of their tender sensibilities and not the mark of unbecoming ambition."[16]

Parker's career seemed uncannily to follow the trajectory of the women she had studied. She was planning a book (never written) about Charlotte Perkins Gilman. But her scholarly career was interrupted in June 1972 when she and her husband were named president and vice president of Bennington College, at a salary of $40,500 a year. Their joint appointment made headlines; she was the youngest college president ever, a young woman who "looked like a student and wore blue jeans." Her appointment ran on the front page of the *New York Times:* "Wife-Husband Team to Head Bennington." *Life* magazine came to fall opening exercises. The Parkers were profiled in *Ms.*

Yet only four years later, the Parkers were forced to resign by a hostile faculty threatened by Gail's administrative style, and scandalized by her affair with another professor. In a story in *Esquire* in 1976, Nora Ephron wrote that among the ways of thinking about what had happened with Parker at Bennington was to "think of it as a modern Hawthorne novel in which hypocritical moral righteousness triumphs over adultery." But Ephron also saw it as an allegory for the American women's movement: "What is not as commonly acknowledged is that the women's movement caused some women to be given power who were . . . unprepared for it."[17]

When Gail Parker arrived at Bennington, the college thought of itself as an academic utopia, in the tradition of Brook Farm. Rush Welter, a history professor who played the role of Bennington gadfly, was a declared utopian: "When I came here, the college was deeply committed to progressive principles. The college looked after the whole person, and it had an imaginative sense of the transaction in the classroom. The idea was not to impart information to students who would become replicas of the faculty, but to encourage the development of students capable of operating on their own inventively. To teach here was a truly exhilarating experience." At faculty meetings Parker made a practice of reading passages about other fictional academic utopias—McCarthy's Jocelyn College in *The Groves of Academe,* for example, and the real Black Mountain College in North Carolina, described by historian Martin Duberman as "a group of squabbling prima donnas."[18] The Bennington faculty was not amused.

Like all American utopian communities, Bennington had its own tradition of sexual customs, food habits, and literary models. Parker immediately began to violate them. She told the faculty wives to stop preparing food for the college meetings. She bypassed entrenched groups to make her own decisions and appointments. She issued a controversial financial report calling for budget tightening and cuts. Hostility against her mounted, and the faculty began to mutter about her behavior. She didn't wear a bra. She didn't go to all the concerts and plays. She watched television. She served unthawed Sara Lee banana cake. The horror, the horror![19]

Meanwhile Bennington people were startled when Rush Welter, the leader of the opposition, began supporting Parker's programs. Soon it emerged that they were lovers, with the tacit consent of Parker's husband and Welter's wife. Welter defended the affair as an intellectual meeting of great minds: "I'd never had anyone to talk to. I'd never had anyone trained in any of my fields. I'd never had anyone whose intelligence was available."[20]

Parker also took a high-minded stand. "I think it's like being the minister who's found to be sleeping with some member of the congregation," Parker said about herself. ". . . What's ludicrous is that this happened in a community that prides itself on sexual immorality. They can't understand that there might be moral adultery."[21] Moral or not, it's hard to see what was in it for Gail

Parker. Twenty years younger than Welter, she was on a career fast track. Rush Welter was a classic Harvard type, unpublished, making the college the center of his life. He was no glamour boy; as one reader wrote to *Esquire,* "Anyone who picks that nerd on p. 56 to have an affair with is obviously no Ted Williams in the peepers department."[22]

But for Parker, the louche atmosphere of Bennington may well have been a heady jolt, a delayed adolescence after the stern decorum of Cambridge, where she had been working hard for years under the eyes of the Fathers, marrying and raising a child when many women her age were off frolicking at Woodstock. And then there was the example of Margaret Fuller. In the spring of 1975, Parker and Welter were teaching a course together on ninteenth-century reform movements called "The Power of Sympathy," which ended with *The Blithedale Romance.* On the last day of class, they told the students that "there's one thing more. Then they removed their shirts to reveal twin T-shirts: his labeled Coverdale and hers, Zenobia."[23]

What brought things to a head was not sex but money, and the faculty's fear that some of them would lose tenure because of the budget cuts. Over a lengthy period of squabbling, a review committee held hearings, then persuaded the trustees that Parker could not run the college, and that there had been "an overall loss of confidence." The Parkers received a visit from trustee Merrell Hambleton and Paul Wickes, the Bennington lawyer, who summarized the findings. At the end of January 1976, the Parkers resigned and moved to Chicago. It seemed for a long time as if Gail Parker's career was over.

But unlike Zenobia, Parker was a fighter. Abandoning academe, she forged a brilliant career in investment banking. And in a wonderfully unexpected twist, she remarried—not Rush Welter, but Paul Wickes.

ENTER CAMILLE

Reading Ephron's 1976 *Esquire* story in the library nearly twenty-five years later, I found another surprise: in the margins of the story, there appears a now-familiar name. Leading the faculty forces of revenge against Parker, or, should we say, at the head of the pack of hounds, was a young English professor named Camille Paglia, who taught at Bennington from 1972 to 1980. "At Bennington you can do it with dogs and no one cares," she told Ephron. "But there was a feeling that educational policy was being made in the boudoir."[24] Paglia told the same thing to the college review committee that recommended Parker's dismissal, and according to Ephron, Paglia was the first Bennington faculty member to raise the question of Gail Parker's personality and personal style in a public meeting: "'My mother sends me clippings about her,' Miss Paglia said. 'She's in Kansas City. She's in Baltimore. How much longer must we put up with these shallow, superficial nothings who are ruling us?' There was an outburst of applause; the faculty had always resented the amount of traveling and speaking Gail Parker did; it also resented her lecture fees."[25] Meanwhile Paglia "complained that it was all very well for Gail to tell the faculty wives not to bring hors d'oeuvres to the cocktail party, but it was very stingy of her then to serve only celery and olives, and carrot sticks."[26]

It's a remarkable entrance, with the personality perfectly formed right from the beginning, and all the themes in place: the allusion to the family as credential of authenticity, the invective, the exploitation and manipulation of the audience's envy and spite, the resentment of another woman, only a few years older, whose achievements had to be trivialized, and whose intelligence had to be denigrated.

Meanwhile, Nancy Miller notes, "the trend in feminist literary studies was moving massively towards the study of women's writing," and women scholars were beginning to realize how much of their own history had been excluded or ignored. When Miller began writing about French women writers in 1978, she felt "a new sense of self-authorization that changed my relation to all of the issues in the profession."[27] In Norway, Toril Moi was writing her dissertation on women writers too, but looking for a new theory. Older feminists too were redefining themselves. In 1979, Gerda Lerner became a "feminist historian." Carolyn Heilbrun wrote *Reinventing Womanhood* during a year's residence at the Bunting Institute at Radcliffe: "I was . . . now, at fifty, provided with the ideal conditions for the work I had undertaken."[28] Heilbrun saw the year as a time of flowering and identified with Charlotte Perkins Gilman, who began *The Forerunner* when she turned fifty. At her thirtieth class reunion at Wellesley, Heilbrun realized that Wellesley was not only "marvelously uncommitted to the problems of women in our time," but also anti-Semitic. Reading *World of Our Fathers,* by the New York intellectual patriarch Irving Howe, Heilbrun decided that "having been a Jew had made me an outsider. It had permitted me to be a feminist."[29] By the end of the 1970s, feminists were outsiders no more.

THIRTEEN

Divas

Germaine Greer
and the Female Eunuch

In December 1970, Mary McCarthy wrote to Hannah Arendt about a recent trip to London. "I saw a lot of fashion-mad people," she explained, "including the current Women's Lib idol, an absurd Australian giantess who made remarks like 'We must make them understand that fucking is a *political* act.'"[1]

The Australian giantess, of course, was Germaine Greer (1939–), the first of the feminist divas. A few months after the publication of *Sexual Politics,* Greer's feminist manifesto, *The Female Eunuch,* was launched at a party attended by the glitterati of the London underground and a sprinkling of feminists. According to biographer Christine Wallace, "Germaine was one of the underground's own, and hip London knew where she was coming from: the counterculture, not a women's collective. A few months before *The Female Eunuch* appeared, she had published a spread on "New Ways with Playclothes" in her incarnation as *Oz* magazine's "Needlework Correspondent," demonstrating original designs including the "Phun City Bikini" and the "Keep It Warm Cock Sock." At Germaine's suggestion, Richard Neville posed for photographs wearing her hand-knitted, multi-striped cock sock and scrotum pouch, which she said could be whipped up in an evening out of odds and ends of colored wool. Few feminist activists at that time were sitting around knitting—and cock socks tended not to be in the pattern books of those who were."[2]

Germaine Greer did not give up her knitting entirely—ten years later I met her at the centennial conference for George Eliot at Rutgers University, where she carried an enormous carpetbag and knitted ferociously throughout the papers—but she had little time for it in the seventies. From the moment she appeared she became a media superstar, the "saucy feminist even men like," as *Life* magazine put it. Gorgeous, exotic, streetwise, adventurous, articulate, witty, and often photographed laughing, Greer gave feminism a subversive sexiness and joie de vivre it needed and had appeared to lack. In Australia, she became a cultural heroine. On her book promotion trip, she had mentioned that she never wore underpants. Australian feminists gamely followed suit. "It was a bit breezy!" remembered Anne Summers. "We were all trying to be incredibly free. That was a much bigger deal than not wearing a bra, I can tell you."[3]

The Female Eunuch labeled itself "part of the second feminist wave," but was always more successful with women who were outside of the movement than those who had been involved. Greer was an academic iconoclast, a sexual libertarian and cofounder of the sex paper *Suck,* who declared that the liberated woman was above all an individual: "The first exercise of the free woman is to design her own mode of revolt, a mode which will reflect her own independence and originality."[4] Greer argued in behalf of an autonomous, assertive female sexuality, and for the pleasure principle as an agent of liberation. "Cooking, clothes, beauty, and housekeeping are all compulsive activities in which the anxiety quotient has long since replaced the pleasure or achievement quotient. It is possible to use even cooking, clothes, cosmetics, and housekeeping for *fun*." The tone was utopian, but her conclusions were broad and inspiring. The revolution would go much further than "equal pay for equal work, for it ought to revolutionize the conditions of work completely." It would go beyond "equality of opportunity," for women would have to be changed so that they desired opportunity. "Women can do almost anything they want," Greer said prophetically on the BBC. ". . . They could probably be prime minister if they want, although a good many people's noses would be put out of joint. What I wrote the book about was why is it so few women *want* to do these things."

Greer was openly disdainful of the British left and its theories of socialism as the way to women's emancipation, at a moment when the British women's liberation movement was an offshoot of the left. Almost four hundred women had gathered for a weekend in February 1970 at Ruskin College, the trade union college in Oxford, to discuss equal rights, the family, and women's history. Organizer Sally Alexander, a historian and former actress, remembered the thrill of this first meeting: "We'd done it. . . . It felt like the culmination of something. It didn't feel like the absolute beginning."[5] These young women were earnestly following in the footsteps of Eleanor Marx and Olive Schreiner and did not identify with Greer.

At the same time, women in the London counterculture were coping with the aftermath of the sixties sexual revolution. Nicola Lane recalls, "You had to fill so many roles: you had to be pretty and you had to be 'a good fuck,' that seemed to be very important. . . . It was paradise for men in their late twenties: all these willing girls. But the trouble with the willing girls was that a lot of the time they were willing not because they particularly fancied the people concerned but because they felt they ought to be. There was a huge pressure to conform to nonconformity. . . . There was supposed to be no jealousy, no possessiveness. What it meant was that the men fucked around. You'd cry a lot, and you would scream sometimes, and the man would say, 'Don't bring me down—don't lay your bummers on me . . . don't hassle me, don't crowd my space.'"[6] Greer was welcomed by these women, who were tired of masquerading as dolly birds and beginning to get tired of following the band. Caroline Coon writes that when Germaine appeared, "she was loud, virile and beautiful, with a fantastic, fearless ability to stand up to the male chauvinist pigs. . . . *The Female Eunuch* . . . at last gave us a language with which we could explain the hostility heaped on us, a label for the men's behavior: sexism."[7]

Finally, British conservatives heaped scorn on Greer and on the assumptions that women needed liberating or that sexism existed. In her book *The Female Woman* (1973), Arianna Stassinopoulos (now Arianna Huffington), who had made her name as the first woman president of the Oxford Union, went after Germaine Greer and feminism. The women's movement, she contended, "is not a movement calling for equal opportunities, equal pay, equal status for woman's role in life, in fact as well as in law; instead it attacks the very nature of women and, in the guise of liberation, seeks to enslave her." In her view, men and women were equal but innately different; sex is more fulfilling within a deep personal relationship; the family is an important institution to be fostered; women should be able to choose their family, their career, or both; and feminists such as Greer were "muddled intellectuals projecting their hang-ups onto all women."[8]

In the United States, as we have seen, feminists were more active in academia than in the counterculture, and Greer's flamboyant style came as a distinct shock. Furthermore, she had been explicitly critical of the American women's movement and had been held up by the mass media and some male critics as everything Millett was not. When she arrived in New York for the American publication of the book, Greer stayed at the Chelsea Hotel, haunt of rock stars. Camille Paglia, then a graduate student at Yale, was awestruck by Greer's "swashbuckling 1971 American book tour, which was as provocative as Oscar Wilde's 1882 visit."[9]

In New York feminist circles, only Gloria Steinem, the closest an American activist at the time came to approximating Greer's superstar image, was truly sympathetic: "It was exhilarating to see a woman who was claiming the right to be sexual without any qualms at all." Steinem remembered a lunch at which Greer loudly compared her vaginal secretions to male erections, to the horror of the other diners. "I remember thinking it was a very valuable piece of information," Steinem fondly recalled, "being very grateful to her and wonderfully entertained at the same time. She was terrific."[10] Later, Steinem tried to recruit Greer as a contributor to *Ms.* But Steinem was committed to feminist politics, and Greer disdained organizations such as the National Women's Political Caucus as futile. "If by the movement we mean women supporting other women," Steinem observed, "then Germaine is not part of the movement because she has, as far as I know, not sought or given that kind of support. But if the movement is defined as 'women moving'—as women 'off our ass,' so to speak, and the movement of ideas—then certainly she's been sometimes interesting and always influential."[11]

On the other hand, Steinem herself refused to debate Norman Mailer at Town Hall; she did not want feminism to be exploited in a media circus. Greer had no such scruples. On April 30, 1971, wearing a slinky black gown and a fox fur, she took on Mailer at a Town Hall debate that became a free-for-all when another panelist, Jill Johnston, staged a clinch with her woman lover.

Susan Sontag was in the audience at Town Hall, along with other New York intellectuals; but she was not a fan of Greer's and considered *The Female Eunuch* "essentially reactionary, though it has some very good descriptive passages. Early on in the book there's a whole passage about the imagery of a woman's body which is brilliant, a very good phenomenological description of the situation of women and their relation to their bodies. Then the book takes off in another direction which I think is ultimately very reactionary—to cite a book which is not one of my favorites."[12]

But feminist journalists such as Claudia Dreifus were outraged by Greer and her book. Dreifus wrote in *The Nation* that Greer was no feminist but indeed "antiwoman," a self-proclaimed "intellectual superwhore" who pandered to male fantasies. "If Germaine Greer didn't exist," she concluded, "Norman Mailer would have had to invent her."[13]

INVENTING GERMAINE GREER

Revolutionary? Reactionary? Feminist? Groupie? Germaine Greer may have been Norman Mailer's fantasy feminist, but she had invented herself out of the contradictory raw materials of her girlhood in Australia, a girlhood with parallels to those of Wollstonecraft, Beauvoir, McCarthy, and Sontag herself. In addition, like Olive Schreiner, Greer had struggled with the added burdens of the postcolonial intellectual far removed from the centers of intellectual life, and with the psychological problems of the ugly duckling who becomes a swan. She was born in Melbourne in 1939, in a Catholic family, with a remote, mysterious father she adored and a clever, angry mother she despised. As a child, Germaine saw a film version of *Il Trovatore* and decided, "I wanted to be a diva. . . . I was going to have thousands of lovers."[14]

From the age of twelve, she dreamed of an escape from Australia. "I used to walk down to Port Melbourne and watch the boats sail away, and I promised myself that I'd be on one just as soon as I could."[15] By the age of fourteen, Germaine was six feet tall, an awkward, studious, theatrical girl who acted in the school play at Star of the Sea College and frightened her classmates and the nuns with her sharp tongue. Here too she had her first passionate romance with a classmate, Jennifer Dabbs, and flaunted the relationship in a way that alarmed her parents, leaving love notes in her pockets for her mother to find. Although she would become famous as an icon of flaming heterosexuality, this first love affair with another girl seems to have been more satisfying than the many affairs with men that followed.

At the University of Melbourne in 1956, Greer suddenly discovered that she was attractive to her male classmates. Stories about these years suggest that she was more unsettled and overwhelmed by this sexual attention than she wanted to reveal. On the one hand, she made a decision to lose her virginity at the age of eighteen, became a sexually exhibitionist undergraduate celebrity, openly discussing her many abortions, and an active participant in Melbourne's avant-garde subculture, the Drift. Nonetheless, the strains of this lifestyle took their toll; she had a breakdown that required hospitalization between her first and second years, and she also revealed in 1994 that she had been the victim of a violent rape when she was nineteen. Although she was known as one of the only women bold enough to stand up to the masculine coterie of the Drift, later she disparaged its artistic pretensions: "It was a lifestyle, it represented a way of just hanging around. It was full of shit, I'm afraid. I always knew that. I knew it was second-rate."[16]

Ill at ease in her own family (she eventually discovered that her father had told many lies about his impoverished background), and aware of being a misfit, even if a popular one, in her society, Greer fantasized that she was actually Jewish. "'A strange thing happened to me at the university,' she said of her Melbourne days. 'I began to gravitate toward the Jewish community, which was interesting because my father was an anti-Semite who found it embarrassing to do business with Jews. I spent all my time rapping with Jewish students, I learned Yiddish, I went out with nothing but Jewish boys, I joined a Jewish theatrical group. Finally, when I was twenty-one, the truth came out. My father told me he'd had a Jewish mother.' She told the *New York Daily News* her father was of Jewish origin, and expanded on Reg's wartime traumas."[17]

From Melbourne, she went to do graduate work at Sydney, where she wrote a master's thesis on Byron. Here the artistic and political avant-garde, the Push, was organized around libertarian, utopian, and anarchist ideas, and Greer found it congenial. She was active in the university theater, and a highly visible figure on the cultural scene, in which once more she stood out as an outspoken woman among a crowd of men. Lynne Segal recalls that "Germaine was such a prima donna eccentric that you couldn't see her as a role model."[18]

In Sydney too women were expected to be sexually available to radical men. According to one Push woman, Elwyn Morris,

"Tremendous social pressure was put on women to be available. Free love was free, in that men didn't have to pay, or even take a girl out, or buy her a beer; for a few of them, it was a new and loveless way of exploiting women. Promiscuity was a virtue, and possessiveness and jealousy cardinal sins."[19] When Greer reflected on her time in Sydney, she thought the most important intellectual influence had been the anarchist philosopher Harry Hooton. He had told her "that he had great faith in me, that he thought I was the woman of the twenty-first century. I didn't know what he meant then, but I think a lot of the things I've done since I've done out of a desire to please Harry Hooton."[20]

In 1964, Greer received a Commonwealth Fellowship and finally left Australia, headed for Byron's alma mater, Cambridge University. Having sojourned in Melbourne's Drift and Sydney's Push, she was now on her way to England's Shove—a much more competitive environment where the glittering prizes of fame and wealth were available to a cultural elite. Here for the first time, as a Ph.D. student in Elizabethan drama and Renaissance studies at Newnham College, Greer worked with inspiring women scholars, especially Muriel Bradbrook, and her thesis supervisor, Dr. Anne Righter, later Professor Anne Barton. Righter was an American, only six years older than Greer, who had graduated summa cum laude from Bryn Mawr and received her doctorate from Cambridge.

At Cambridge, Greer wrote her dissertation on Shakespeare's early comedies, emphasizing *The Taming of the Shrew*. Christine Wallace argues that the thesis already showed Greer's lack of sympathy with women and, in her belief that Petruchio actually rescues Kate from her "fruitless revolt," a tacit acceptance of male domination. "Can Greer's apparent sympathy for Petruchio's scheme and Kate's submission be rationalized on historical grounds—that Greer believed it represented a better deal for women than others on offer in Shakespeare's time?" Wallace asks. "Apparently not. Greer writes: 'There is hardly a woman alive who is not deeply attracted to the notion of a husband of the kind extolled by Kate: the difficulty is to find a man capable of assuming all this responsibility and exercising this kind of sexual and domestic dominion.' How could it be? Why would Greer—highly intelligent, worldly, striking, striving—why would she of all people condone without disclaimer women's longing for men who are capable of exercising dominion over them?"[21]

Greer received her doctorate on May 7, 1968, at the height of the student revolt in Paris. But she herself was involved with the underground libertarian press and preparing to teach at the University of Warwick. For a few brief months in 1968, she was married to a handsome construction worker, Paul de Feu. (He would subsequently marry another feminist diva, Maya Angelou.) And she had started to become known as a journalist in the magazines and on the radio.

This was Germaine Greer's background at the time *The Female Eunuch* was published, and she had few allies or friends among the other feminists of the period. In the United States, Susan Brownmiller writes in her memoir of the women's movement that Greer "soon tired of explaining feminism to Americans. She grew increasingly testy on the lecture circuit, drank more than she should have, snapped at the repetitive questions, ducked the well-meaning professors and earnest students who had arranged her visits. Eventually she went back to London. Most of us weren't sorry to see her go."[22]

In August 1971, while Greer was in Italy writing a contemporary version of *Lysistrata* (it would not be produced until the summer of 1999), Gloria Steinem appeared on the cover of *Newsweek* as the "unlikely guru" of women's liberation. Gloria Steinem (1934–) had grown up in Toledo, Ohio, in a family with a father who was often absent, and a mother who had a series of breakdowns; as a child, Steinem also became a caretaker. She went to Smith College at the same time as Sylvia Plath, who graduated a year ahead, and waitressed to pay the daily expenses while her divorced parents scraped together the money for the college fees. Upon graduation, Steinem spent two years on a government fellowship traveling in India, returning in 1958. By the 1970s, she had become known as a journalist with serious intellectual credentials that belied her beauty-queen looks.[23] An early supporter of the women's movement, Steinem became the media-anointed spokeswoman for feminism and its ideals.

In 1972, when Germaine Greer was sent by *Harper's* to cover the Democratic National Convention, she was very much an outsider to the group of American feminists who were there lobbying to have women's reproductive rights included in the Democratic platform. As presidential scribe Theodore H. White reported, the National Women's Political Caucus "had taken over as headquarters the third floor of the derelict, sea-sprayed Betsy Ross Hotel. One might be amused by the high-octave span of women's voices gathered together, or the rooms with the unmade beds, half-unpacked suitcases, yogurt cartons, chests covered with blue jeans and bras—but only briefly. The Betsy Ross Hotel was a power center."[24] Greer got a lot of publicity from the press as she zipped into bars at the convention looking for prostitutes to interview about women's rights. One of them told her she looked terrible, and she retorted: "I've always had this haggard look and lots of people like it."[25] (Camille Paglia echoed the line twenty-five years later: "An intellectual has an obligation to look haggard."[26])

During the mid-1970s, Gloria Steinem was putting all of her time and energy into editing the new *Ms.* magazine, and to speaking across the country in behalf of feminism. During the decade, while she continued to have a number of serious relationships with men, Steinem maintained her determination not to marry or raise a family. Meanwhile Greer was divorced from Paul de Feu, and increasingly unhappy about her inability to conceive a child. In 1977, she had gynecological surgery at a Harley Street clinic in the hope of enhancing her fertility, but it was unsuccessful.[27]

In 1979, Gloria Steinem was thinking about taking some time away from *Ms.* to focus on the neglected intellectual priorities in her life, and Greer, who turned forty, had decided to spend half the year in Tulsa, Oklahoma, starting the Center for the Study of Women's Literature. Her energy and drive were undiminished and now directed at the need to fertilize the field of feminist scholarship. Greer was still a formidable force of nature. David Plante describes her during this period at the farm she was restoring in Tuscany, showing him her garden and shouting, "Come on, you fucking flowers, come on! Bloom, bloom!"[28] Andrea Chambers, a reporter from *People* magazine, observed Greer in Tulsa in October 1979 and noted her adoption of local exclamations such as "Yip!" and "God damn!" and the bottle of Jack Daniel's under the front seat of her rented Mustang. Greer stayed at Tulsa for three years, training a dedicated group of students and launching a journal.

As the 1970s came to a close, Margaret Thatcher was elected prime minister. Greer had predicted it, but Thatcher's high-handed Tory regime alienated virtually all British feminists. Only Rebecca West would say a good word for Thatcher: "Men would rather be ruined by one of their own sex than saved by a woman."[29]

LIFE IN A TENURED POSITION

By the 1980s, feminist criticism had become normative and established in American universities, and feminist critics were getting tenure. But the feminist coalitions of the early 1970s were breaking down under the pressure of internal competition and differing racial, ethnic, and class agendas. Katha Pollitt writes that the media portrayed the 1980s as "one long funeral for feminism."[30] With the defeat of the Equal Rights Amendment, the rise of Reagan and the New Right, and a hostile political and economic climate, another feminist writer lamented, "The movement's diversity began to look alarmingly like balkanization. Programs like rape crisis centers and shelters for battered women are going under as they compete against each other for an increasingly smaller piece of what is fast becoming a nonexistent pie. . . . Women's centers too often have become havens for the already committed, rather than forums for educating and politicizing women. A younger generation of women has grown up taking for granted gains earlier feminists fought hard to win."[31]

As in the 1920s, feminists were once again discovering the gap between their principles and their daily lives. But this time there was also fragmentation, anger, and dissent within various branches of the women's movement. Marianne Hirsch and Evelyn Fox Keller called the eighties "a decade of intense mutual criticism and internal divisiveness: a decade in which the feminist illusion of 'sisterhood' and the 'dream of a common language' gave way to the realities of fractured discourse,"[32] in ethical splits over such emotionally charged topics as interracial rape, pornography, and surrogate motherhood.

Death in a Tenured Position (1981), a novel by Carolyn Heilbrun under her pseudonym, Amanda Cross, reflects this moment of change, although its tenured professor, Janet Mandelbaum, is not a feminist critic at all. Instead she is the first tenured woman professor in the Harvard English department, a scholar of seventeenth-century English literature outraged by the idea that she should "rally to some woman's cause." The old boys of the department have selected Professor Mandelbaum because she is an antifeminist, a "woman professor who was perfectly safe on the subject of feminism and women's studies." But suddenly terrible things begin to happen to Janet Mandelbaum. She is found one night "stewed to the gills" and passed out in the mahogany-sided bathtub in the ladies' room on the second floor of Warren House, the English department building. And shortly thereafter, she is found dead in the Warren House men's room. But although it appears that many of her openly misogynist colleagues might have had a motive to kill her, Mandelbaum turns out to have been a suicide. Disillusioned about the circumstances of her appointment, humiliated by the impossibility of her position, and defeated by the hostility and cynicism that surround her, she has taken cyanide. The mystery of her death is solved by Kate Fansler, Heilbrun's feminist detective, who deciphers the clue of the book Mandelbaum is reading before her death: a biography of Eleanor Marx. Like Marx, Mandelbaum kills herself "in despair at having no place to live her life, and no life to live."[33]

At the Modern Language Association (MLA) convention in

1981, Susan Kress, a newly tenured professor herself, read a paper on *Death in a Tenured Position*. "What fascinated me at that time about Heilbrun," she explains, "was the fact that, although she was certainly a feminist, she was grappling with conspicuous conflicts. She had developed a voice of assurance and authority, but issues did not necessarily have clear answers for her and she was struggling for clarity." To Kress, Heilbrun's life was a microcosm of the debates, contradictions and transformations of the modern academic women's movement, and Kress went on to write a study of Heilbrun as "the emergence of a public self, the making of a cultural critic, the formation of a public intellectual."[34]

The internal conflicts of the women's movement certainly made themselves felt at Rutgers, where I was still teaching. But when I was offered a job in the English department at Harvard in 1983, the thought of death in a tenured position hung over my head and I took a nervous peek at the bathroom where Mandelbaum had done herself in. What would have killed me was maintaining a commuting marriage and family. At the last minute, Princeton University offered jobs to both Sandra Gilbert and me, and I was able to transfer jobs without having to uproot my family. Sandra and I were not completely welcome at Princeton. One male faculty member attended the lectures in our team-taught course on women's writing to document our lack of scholarly credentials. He sat in the front row accompanied by his large woolly dog, but at the end of the semester, sent us bouquets of Hawaiian anthurium, that reddest, shiniest, and most unmistakably phallic of all flowers.

The right-wing campus magazine *Prospect* (now defunct) denounced us in a piece called "The Feminist Mistake." "Feminism," *Prospect* said, could "be found rearing its pock-marked face in the Women's Studies program," where its "main rationale" was that "thousands, if not millions, of great women poets, scientists, musicians, and philosophers" were waiting to be rediscovered. "For those taxing their minds coming up with names" of these "neglected nymphs," *Prospect* provided "The List" of "some outstanding women poets and philosophers 'discovered' by Women's

Studies: Mrs. Beulah Bunting. Sarah Slackjaw. Myra 'The Mad Woman' Jones. Taraki Taraki. Lotus Smith. 'The Lesbian Quartet.' Beverly Cousteau-Jackson-Weatherby-Jackson-Ramirez. Shanta Savage." The article was of course written by a woman, Laura Ingraham, who had previously been the editor at the notorious *Dartmouth Review,* in its heyday of smearing black, feminist, and gay students and faculty, and who went on to a brilliant career as a conservative attorney and media star.

By 1984, Greer had taken a radical change of direction, seemingly repudiating her own celebration of sexual freedom. Her book *Sex and Destiny* was a startling discussion of infertility as one of the prices of feminism that seemed to retreat into another kind of millenarian celebration of motherhood, and to attack medical and scientific interventions in the natural process of reproduction. Noticing that Greer took a sarcastic swipe in the book at "young, grinning couples" who have orgasms and consumer goods instead of children, the English journalist Linda Grant commented that "the author was no longer young, nor, by her own choice I assume, part of a couple. The loss of youth was one of the worst tricks that could be played on the Underground."[35] Gloria Steinem reflected that Greer had elevated her personal regret at not having a child to an ideological position. "So it came to seem as if the women's movements in various countries had advised women not to have children, which I don't think is the case—on the contrary, we were trying to talk about reproductive freedom. Or that all of us . . . that didn't have children regretted it, and that's not the case either. Certainly I don't feel that."[36]

But *Sex and Destiny* presaged a host of feminist complaints of the 1980s—involuntary singlehood, involuntary childlessness, loneliness. As Judith Stacey noted, "Few among us who deferred childbearing decisions until the biological limits considered the possibility that an affirmative decision might be impossible to implement."[37] Nancy Miller speculated about the meaning of the feminist as a childless daughter in a series of remarkable autobiographical essays. What did it mean that so many intellectual women of her generation had postponed or rejected childbirth? How did it affect their relationship to their own mother, and their reaction to their mother's death? "Choosing motherhood or refusing it," Miller wrote, "has proven to be more complex than we feminists had bravely imagined in our consciousness-raising groups of the early seventies."[38] For her part, Germaine Greer was still working out her long quarrel with, and alienation from, her mother. Her elevation of mothers collectively did not mean that she had been able to make her peace with her own.

DIVA TIME

Within the academic world, the generational conflicts in feminism emerged not only in divisiveness and competition, but also in the dramatic emergence of new models of the feminist intellectual. Some of the feminist academic icons of the late 1980s were coupled with powerful academic men; some were daringly self-referential (as the academic jargon called it) in their self-display and conference performance styles. But even those theorists as austere as the philosopher Judith Butler got the diva treatment from their fans.

In 1985, Toril Moi (1954–), a young Norwegian Ph.D. in French who for some years had been the partner of the Marxist critic Terry Eagleton, published *Sexual/Textual Politics,* a book that sternly chastised Anglo-American feminist literary critics for their humanistic and realistic bias, and credited the French feminist theorists Hélène Cixous, Luce Irigaray, and especially Julia Kristeva with defining a truly revolutionary feminist literary theory based on the work of Derrida and Lacan. Moi herself had never come up against sex discrimination or pressure. "When I was growing up," she says, "Norwegian schools were coeducational and egalitarian in all sorts of ways. There were no private schools or sexually segregated schools. . . . I never felt discriminated against in any sort of institutional sense. Yet Norway wasn't—and isn't—particularly feminist in the cultural and intellectual sphere." But she had nonetheless thought of herself as a feminist since adolescence: "I actually identified myself as a feminist, intellectually and politically, right from the age of fourteen or so. Perhaps it had to do with my generation: I was fourteen in 1968."[39] In the wake of *Sexual/Textual Politics,* and the lecture tours of the chic French, American feminists in the academy were made to feel dowdy and naive. Continental theory, even more than Parisian fashion, became the uniform of the feminist intellectual.

French professor Jane Gallop, however, combined French theory and a kind of Mae West flamboyance into another influential style. Gallop brought the roles of good girl and bad girl, cerebral theorist and voluptuous vamp, onto the conference circuit, where she delivered her erudite papers dressed in spike heels, fishnet stockings, Joan Crawford hats, and a skirt made out of men's ties. Gallop has also made her sexuality a recurrent motif in her writing; in her book *Thinking Through the Body* (1988), for example, she noted that in her twenties she had had "a series of affairs with thirty-six-year-old men," all married or unavailable.

Gloria Jean Watkins, an assistant professor of English and African-American studies at Yale who wrote under the name "bell hooks," was another prominent feminist who emerged in the 1980s. In her first book, *Ain't I a Woman: Black Women and Feminism* (1981), published while she was still a graduate student at Santa Cruz, hooks created a role as the iconic African-American feminist intellectual of the decade. Her use of her own life as a single, childless woman as exemplary, and her autobiographical writings about her family, won her many student followers, although other academics were critical of her work.

Eve Kosofsky Sedgwick was another feminist intellectual who defied the conventions and became an academic diva in the 1980s. A Ph.D. in English from Yale, Sedgwick had been married since the age of nineteen, although she did not share a home with her husband. But her brilliant first book, *Between Men: English Literature and Male Homosocial Desire,* became the bible of the new field of gender and gay studies. Although she described herself as shy, Sedgwick was bold in her thinking, writing, and choices of subject matter. Her lectures and conference papers got outraged national attention from right-wingers, especially when she titled a talk for the MLA convention "Jane Austen and the Masturbating Girl." But within the academy, Sedgwick was an inspiring example of courage and commitment, speaking out in behalf of "queer" studies, writing poetry along with literary criticism, and fearlessly using her own life and lifestyle to illustrate her ideas about sexual identity.

But by the end of the 1980s, as Germaine Greer reached her fiftieth birthday and started writing *The Change*—an important book about menopause—the glare of living as a feminist icon, and navigating the treacherous waters of hostility, rivalry, and competition, had become exhausting for many of those who had attempted to play a public role. There was a general retreat into the more personal and private. In 1989, Gloria Steinem was recovering from breast cancer and decorating her apartment for the first time: "It is filled with Indian fabrics, many drapes, shelves holding earrings, shoes, books, and so forth, a bed with a canopy from which flowing red cheesecloth draperies descend. Her former loft bed acquired floating white material resembling a baby's bassinet, and in Alice Walker's view it represents the much-cared-for baby Steinem believes she never was."[40]

At about this time, a number of feminist critics began to find other modes of writing—autobiography, literary journalism, cultural studies. It was partly a massive return of the repressed after a decade of mandatory high theory, partly, I think, resistance to being target practice for the latest gunslinger. Marianna Torgovnick, Alice Kaplan, Jane Tompkins, and Cathy Davidson formed a writing group at Duke. I myself stopped writing essays on feminist criticism in 1989; they had outlived their usefulness, like the cat we got for the children, who hung on, hungry, demanding, and querulous, long after the children had grown up and left home.

The stage was being cleared for the next act.

FOURTEEN

Feminist Personae

Camille Paglia—Woman Alone

Who is hotter than Mary McCarthy? Smarter than Susan Sontag? Funnier than Germaine Greer? Well, if you take her word for it, it's Camille Paglia, the head diva and feminist riot grrl of the 1990s. We last saw Paglia in the 1970s, at Bennington, campaigning against Gail Thain Parker. In her view, her staunch idealism and principled refusal to play by the rules led to her expulsion from the academic environment in which she had been trained: "I am just one of incalculable numbers of people of my generation whose fidelity to sixties principles led to their exclusion from the establishment."[1]

But in 1990, after having been rejected by seven New York publishers, Paglia's big book, *Sexual Personae: Art and Decadence from Nefertiti to Emily Dickinson,* was published by Yale University Press. To be neglected and forgotten, then lifted to fame, is a story with universal appeal, and Paglia has told it again and again. "In a sense," she has said, "*Sexual Personae* is my prison book. I felt like Cervantes, Genet. It took all the resources of being Catholic to cut myself off and sit in my cell."[2] Paglia has also presented herself as a scrappy Cinderella fighting against the ugly sisters of American academic feminism. Denouncing Ivy League feminist academics and women's studies, celebrating popular culture and sex symbols such as Madonna, she became a media celebrity, writing op-eds and gossip columns, appearing on TV, and telling her story to journalists everywhere.

In two collections of essays and book reviews, *Sex, Art, and American Culture* (1992) and *Vamps & Tramps* (1994), and in her on-line column at *Salon,* she has written about her life, passions, and beliefs. Ideologically, Paglia is a radical libertarian; she opposes state intervention in abortion, sodomy, prostitution, pornography, drug use, or suicide. Like a Wildean aesthete, Paglia argues that "nature's fascist scheme of menstruation and procreation *should* be defied, as a gross infringement of woman's free will."[3] A devotee of Wilde and Pater, Paglia cherishes performance, artifice, and play rather than earnestness. We recall how Olive Schreiner told Wilde that she had moved to the East End of London "because that is the only place where people do not wear masks upon their faces," but that Wilde replied, "I live in the West End because nothing interests me except the mask."[4] Similarly, Paglia rejects the earnestness of academic feminist identity and is interested only in the persona.

Paglia sees herself as the Amazonian champion of the feminist intellectual tradition in the 1990s and, perhaps more than any other feminist icon of this century, has explicitly allied herself with the icons of the past. Instead of Virginia Woolf's room of one's own, Paglia calls for "a car of one's own, the great equalizer . . . the mode of American Amazonism."[5] She frequently describes her wish to "reintroduce the scathing voices of Dorothy Parker and Mary McCarthy to American letters."[6] She lists herself as a great admirer of Simone de Beauvoir: "*The Second Sex* remains for me the supreme work of modern feminism. . . . Its deep learning and massive argument are unsurpassed."[7] She is a fan of Germaine Greer's: "When the history of modern women is written, Germaine Greer will be seen as one who . . . permanently redefined female intellect. Following her swift, swerving, sometimes reckless train of thought is like watching a champion slalom racer, jabbing the snow and hurtling past the trembling markers."[8]

But at the same time, Paglia is openly in competition with these other women, and unabashedly in love with her own brilliance. In Paglia's view, she herself is now the world's "greatest woman intellectual."[9] "Not since Simone de Beauvoir," she boasted to James Wolcott, "has there been a feminist with my frame of reference."[10] When "people look back at the twentieth century, at nonfiction books by women," she told another reporter, "it's going to be Jane Harrison, Simone de Beauvoir, and Paglia. . . . Susan Sontag will be a footnote."[11] In 1992, I heard Paglia tell an audience at Princeton, "You are in the presence of one of the great female scholars in the world. There is no one here in my intellectual league." "And you," retorted a faculty member in the audience, "are a sadly deluded woman."

Paglia herself admits that her own persona is comic, campy, and even cartoonish; and that she is an odd choice as a feminist icon, because she has few alliances with women, identifies primarily with gay men, and is a loner, individualist, and maverick, who cannot see herself as part of a movement. She calls her feminism "drag-queen feminism, because I identify with drag queens, who are more overtly sexual, they're aggressive, they have a mouth, they defend themselves, and they don't go running to committees and asking others to get them out of trouble."[12] But she also regards herself as "a wonderful role model for young women. I'm completely self-reliant. I don't look to anyone for approval. I've never lived with a man."[13] She offers "the New Sexism" as a movement for young women and believes that her "obligation as a woman is to develop my talents to the max."[14]

Many feminist icons of the past, including Olive Schreiner, sometimes saw themselves at odds with or indifferent to the women's movements of their day. But Paglia is unique in the hyperbole and virulence of her hostility to virtually all the prominent feminist activists, public figures, writers, and scholars of her generation. Feminist critics in universities, she charges, are "poor or narrowly trained scholars," "married women who never rocked a boat in their lives," "conventional fifties ladies who lived with men" and "had families," "third-rate minds running feminism, turning it into a closed shop."[15] To Paglia, Carolyn Heilbrun is

"Mrs. Fifties Tea Table";[16] French feminists "don't come to Simone de Beauvoir's anklebones";[17] Judith Butler is "very small potatoes," "derivative and unlearned." Carol Gilligan ("prim, solemn"), Marilyn French ("acridly cynical"), Zoe Baird and Kimba Wood ("spoiled, bland yuppies"), Susan Thomases ("grim, lantern-jawed"), and Hillary Clinton ("ice queen")[18] are among the many others on Paglia's ever-lengthening hit list. She regards academic feminists as losers in the one-woman battle she is waging against them. "They're gonna lose to me. My victory over them will come decade by decade by decade, okay? . . . Let them suck raw eggs and *eat my dust!*"[19]

Most of the women Paglia passionately admires are models, singers, or movie stars—Elizabeth Taylor, Madonna, Barbra Streisand—with the strong style and personality that makes them popular figures for drag queens. "Streisand has always been a kind of drag queen herself," she wrote in an essay. "That's true of Sandra Bernhard too, and it's true of me and of a lot of women who didn't feel particularly feminine when they were growing up. For women like that, by the time you've figured out what femininity is, you've become a female impersonator."[20] She revels in her celebrity image. "For my really grand appearances, for my theatrical persona, for La Paglia, as they call me in Italy, I put on Lancôme's Rouge Decor Creme. That's the perfect lipstick for her. Or should I say it."[21] She tells Andrew Billen of *The Observer,* "In Italy I exist as La Diva, while in Germany and Holland, I am the serious thinker, heir to Schopenhauer. In Brazil I am liked for my extremism: they love that picture of me showing my cleavage and flanked by two black bodyguards."[22]

AN ENTIRE LIFE

Paglia believes nonetheless that she avoided being corrupted by fame because it came so late. "Celebrity and success came too early to Germaine Greer and Susan Sontag," she explains, "very brilliant women whose development as thinkers and writers was terminated by the spotlight of the world. By the time it hit me four years ago I was forty-three years old. I had lived an entire life already."[23]

She has written and talked about that life in numerous articles and interviews. She was born in upstate Endicott, New York, in 1947, into an Italian-American Catholic family she credits for her success: "I got my intellectuality, studiousness, and severity from my father. And I got my energy, optimism, and practicality from my mother. And from both I got the Italian capacity for hard work and the ancient Roman genius for organization."[24] Even as a toddler, Paglia reports, she was an eccentric aesthete; when she was three, she saw Disney's *Snow White* and fell in love with the witch queen, as "a non-Christian, non-Catholic archetype or something."[25] She was also a tomboy. With her mother's help, she began early to play the heroic male roles that thrilled her, dressing up at Halloween as an Italian Renaissance soldier, Napoleon, or Hamlet. At summer camp, she called herself "Stacy" and "Stanley." Paglia says of her childhood, "My father taught me to put up my fists and defend myself like a man."[26]

When Camille was ten, her family moved from rural Oxford, New York, where her father had been a high school teacher, to Syracuse, where he got a Ph.D. in romance languages. They lived in graduate-student housing barracks until he became a professor at Le Moyne College. Soon after the move, she experienced a rebellious puberty. "Suddenly I went into open revolt, at eleven, because I didn't like this sexual thing, you know, a girl had to be a certain way, and it was like, I was very, I mean I was exploring, I was always like disappearing, they'd find me downtown, you know, at Woolworth's, looking at the fish or something like that. Teachers and women in the family, women expecting me to be . . . Teachers, teachers, Girl Scout leaders, nuns, you know, I mean, yeah."[27] It was 1957, and she was surrounded by the Sandra Dee, Debbie Reynolds, "sorority queen blondes" version of girlishness, "all that parochial pleasantness! So chirpy, peppy, and pink, so well-scrubbed, making the world safe for democracy."[28] Partly to escape this WASP dictatorship, she wanted to join the Jewish Community Center in junior high school, but was overruled by her parents.

In high school, in fact, Paglia "went through a rabid Streisand period, when I slept on giant rollers to get my hair like hers and had long nails with plum polish."[29] And from having been a child who thought of herself as a boy, she took on an unshakable but belligerent female persona, hunting in secondhand bookshops for the works of Dorothy Parker and Mary McCarthy. Since adolescence, Paglia has consistently thought of herself as a woman in competition—with men and with other women— rather than as a professional whose gender is secondary to her work. "I was an Amazon when I was very young . . . from my earliest years I had this burning desire to *do* something for women, to do something so massive for women, to demonstrate that women should be taken seriously."[30] "In high school, in the early sixties, I dreamed of intellectual work by women that would match the highest male standards and set men on their ear."[31]

When Paglia was fourteen, her only sister, Lenora, was born. On Paglia's sixteenth birthday, in 1963, a woman colleague of her father's gave her *The Second Sex*. "It made a tremendous impact on me and I date my intellectual independence from that moment. Beauvoir's imperious French voice, descending from cold, clear Enlightenment skepticism, is one source of the assertions and overassertions of *Sexual Personae*. *The Second Sex,* summing up my social complaints as a wild-eyed adolescent, released me from my passion of opposition to the fifties."[32]

Through most of high school, Paglia had been obsessed with Amelia Earhart and had gathered a huge archive about her. What fascinated her especially was Earhart's independence and self-sufficiency: "Amelia Earhart was to me an image of everything a woman should be. . . . She is woman alone. Not woman hand-holding in a group and whining about men. Woman *alone!*"[33] In July 1963, she wrote a letter to *Newsweek* pointing out that the Soviet cosmonaut Valentina Tereshkova had become the first woman to be launched into space exactly thirty-five years after Amelia Earhart's solo flight across the Atlantic,

and suggesting that Earhart's "lifelong fight for equal opportunity for American women apparently still needs to be won."[34]
But after reading *The Second Sex,* Paglia decided that "instead of
writing a book on Amelia Earhart, I will write a megabook that
will take *everything* in."[35]

In 1964, Paglia entered Harpur College in Binghamton, New
York. "Harpur, with its strong presence of avant-garde, intellectual Jewish students from New York City, was seething with raw
creative energy. People called it Berkeley East."[36] Among her
classmates was Deborah Tannen, who recalls, "The time we
were at Harpur was an amazing time. . . . It was the sixties, so it
was political ferment. Also, schools like Harvard and Yale are
very full of themselves. Harpur wasn't. We were all working-class
kids who were there because we were smart. It was at that time
the only small liberal arts college in the state system, and I think
most of us were in the same position. We had gotten a Regent's
Scholarship, our parents didn't have enough money to send us to
a big-name school, but they had just enough money that if we
could have our tuition paid, they could manage."[37]

Paglia was a brilliant undergraduate who became valedictorian
of her class. At the same time, her immersion in film, poetry,
Brahms symphonies, and art was experienced with men rather
than women—gay male friends, and a charismatic, bardic professor, Milton Kessler. Taking the Mods and Beats as her models,
she "affected men's ties, paisley Tom Jones shorts, Edwardian
pin-striped bell-bottoms, naval peacoats, and antique jodhpur
boots."[38] These were also years of shifting sexual identity. Paglia
comments, "I think that most powerful and talented women—I
mean, *really* powerful women like me—have had some sort of
difficulty with sexual adjustment in ways that very powerful
men don't necessarily have."[39] In Binghamton, she "struck one of
the first blows for contemporary feminism" when she beat up a
young drunk molesting a "tiny female acquaintance."[40]

By the time she arrived at Yale graduate school in the fall of
1968, Paglia had apparently declared herself to be lesbian,
although the label was somewhat abstract. "I was the only open

lesbian in Yale grad school, okay, and I didn't even have a girl-friend!" she laments.[41] Indeed, Yale did not even accept women undergraduates until 1969. Later, Paglia felt that she had "paid the career price for my pre-Stonewall candor."[42] At Yale, she was mentored by Harold Bloom and managed to bash a molester in Liggett's drugstore with her umbrella; but otherwise it was an unhappy time socially and personally. Her "hormones were at their height," and she had deliberately disguised her sexuality: "In the 1970s I vowed I would never wear a dress again because it was a badge of servitude. I was determined to sabotage my own sexual persona."[43]

BENNINGTON

In 1972, Paglia took a position teaching English at Bennington College, where she stayed until 1980. She has written nostalgically about her years at Bennington, among other "brash Young Turks [who] offered a serious challenge to the Bennington establish-ment, which was mired in a genteel liberalism, long on pater-nalistic sentimentality and short on political realism."[44] Here too her companions were primarily gay men, and she seems not to have had women friends. Indeed, despite some bonds with female students, Paglia's years at Bennington were filled with active and passive aggression toward successful women, many of whom she felt let her down. Gail Parker, Susan Sontag, and Germaine Greer were among them. "Arriving at my first teaching job at Ben-nington College in 1972," she writes, "I was still fully supportive of the women's movement and confident that it could correct its own errors and excesses. I was determined to be an uncompro-mising role model for young women and to put the radical new ideas about gender and sexual orientation into circulation on cam-pus."[45] Paglia organized a women's film festival, for which she chose the films and wrote the program. It included Bergman's *Persona,* about which Susan Sontag had written a memorable essay, and from which Paglia would take the title of her book.

At this point, Sontag was one of Paglia's greatest role models. The paperback of Sontag's first essay collection, *Against Interpretation,* which Paglia read at Harpur, "seemed to herald a dawning age of revolutionary achievement." In addition to its range, learning, and interest in popular culture, "the glamorous dust-jacket photo imprinted Sontag's sexual persona as a new kind of woman writer so indelibly on the mind that the image still lingers, wraithlike, and makes criticism of her very difficult." Moreover, Sontag was "an *au courant* woman intellectual," who "revived and modernized the woman of letters."[46] But whereas Sontag had dismissed the cult of the Dark Lady as "grotesque" and renounced its assumptions of tokenism and competition among women, Paglia accepted them fully. In the terms of her childhood belligerence, and her zero-sum game of feminist combat, there could be only one Dark Lady at a time. According to this model, she should have been next in line for the job.

As chair of the speakers committee of the languages and literatures division, Paglia "resolved to bring women of achievement to Bennington, despite the limited budget of an impoverished art school. Susan Sontag was my leading candidate, but it was a struggle to get the proposal accepted, because of her high fee." But Paglia persisted, driving to New Hampshire in a snowstorm to hear Sontag speak at Dartmouth and to persuade her to lower her fee, and winning the support of "the new college president, Gail Thain Parker," to offer Sontag twice as much as Bennington had ever paid any speaker.

On October 4, 1973, the great lecture day arrived, and Paglia blanketed the campus with posters and prepared to take Sontag to dinner before her talk. Disaster. The plane was late; Sontag arrived sleepy, puffy, "rumpled and haggard as a derelict." At dinner, moreover, Sontag "refused to be hurried" and ate her steak au poivre in "a maddeningly leisurely manner." By the time they arrived for the lecture, the audience was "tangibly simmering with hostility," and to top it off, Sontag read a short story that put everyone to sleep. At the reception afterward, she got into an argument with her host, Bernard Malamud.

When she managed a private meeting with Sontag, Paglia was bitterly disappointed by Sontag's refusal to see their encounter as a passing of the torch. Alone with Sontag after the talk, at Gail Parker's house, Paglia had talked about her work. "Finally, Sontag asked, 'What is it you *want* from me?' I stammered, 'Just to talk to you.' But that was wrong. I wanted to say, 'I'm your successor, dammit, and you don't have the wit to realize it.' It was *All About Eve,* and Sontag was Margo Channing stalked by the new girl." But Sontag did not play her part in this Hollywood cultural script, and Paglia never forgave her. Afterward, the Sontag visit "assumed legendary status as a low-water reference point," and the talk became "an inside joke at Bennington about any dreaded drudgery: 'Well, at least we don't have to listen to a Susan Sontag story!'" Paglia had to give up the lecture series.[47]

Anyone who has worked in a college or university will recognize this story as part of the folklore of the High-Priced Visiting Hotshot and knows that such visits are almost always disasters. At Princeton, we joke, an acceptable generic response to a question about any much-hyped lecture, whether you heard it or not, is "It was disappointing." But for Paglia this was public humiliation and private rejection, and she never forgot. Versions of the story crop up over and over in her interviews as a "very pivotal encounter."[48] "I realize now," she told the *Washington Post,* "I was looking for a female mentor. I was looking for someone, you know, who could have made a difference in my life. If she'd taken an interest in my mind I would have gotten published, you know. I mean, all the seventies I was rejected by everything."[49] Without Sontag's support, Paglia could not be a contender.

Germaine Greer was equally disappointing. On March 12, 1975, Paglia made another "pilgrimage to see the celebrated Germaine Greer, who was lecturing at the State University of New York at Albany, an hour's drive from where I was teaching in Vermont. . . . But the reserved, steely author who spoke to the packed hall in Albany was quite another person. All trace of humor or physicality was gone. Greer's tenacious subject was now the deplorable economic condition of women in Pakistan. During the question period, I nervously raised my hand from the crowd and asked if Greer would be writing on literary subjects again soon. Her reply was stern and swift: 'There are far more important things in the world than literature!' As a proponent of Wildean aestheticism who believed and still believes that art is the highest achievement of humanity, I was stunned by Greer's defection to the increasingly Stalinist ranks of feminist Utilitarians."[50] Indeed, far from being the glamorous groupie of 1971, Greer "looked like a harridan."[51]

Meanwhile, at Bennington, Paglia "got into one scrape after another."[52] The "scrapes and scandals" ranged from a "public ass-kicking to claims of clairvoyance to fisticuffs at a college dance, the latter of which led, after a clash of lawyers, to my departure."[53] Being fired from Bennington was, she has said, "a watershed in her life, a searing experience. For the next few years she was deeply in debt and on the unemployment line. But she scraped by, teaching factory workers in night classes, and came out the other end full of provocative ideas about the cushiness of academe."[54]

Paglia calls the 1980s her "Years in the Desert": "It must be understood, my complete isolation when I was writing *Sexual Personae,* my absolutely crushing isolation. . . . It was like ten years of arid desert in my life."[55] "During the seventies I was convinced of my future of fame, and then I said, 'It's not gonna happen.' . . . I could not get published. I got no jobs. I've been broke, okay."[56] She found a teaching position in the College of the Arts in Philadelphia, a long way from Bennington or the Ivy League. Over the years, her anger toward Sontag hardened, especially when Paglia was rejected by the *Partisan Review.* She "began to see Sontag as queen of the cliquish New York literary establishment," whose work, although still preferable to that of the "impostors and double-dealers who run women's studies," declined in seriousness and daring.[57] "When in a 1988 profile in *Time* magazine, she denied she had ever been that interested in pop ('It isn't as if I wrote an essay on the Supremes') and boasted that she did not own a television set, I was appalled and disgusted. Not having a TV is tantamount to saying, 'I know nothing of the time or country in which I live.' Television *is* America, and year by year it is becoming the world."[58]

By the time *Sexual Personae* appeared in 1990, Paglia "viewed Sontag and her coterie as fossilized petty tyrants." An interview in *New York* magazine had a photo of Paglia and Sontag at Bennington, with a caption reading: "I thought she was going to be this major intellectual."[59] Meanwhile, in another interview in *Vanity Fair,* Paglia chortled triumphantly, "I've been chasing that bitch for twenty-five years and I've finally passed her!" Sontag's maddening refusal to take any notice of Camille's presence at all was an additional insult. "She could scarcely retain her claim to intellectual preeminence," Paglia fumed, "while not having heard of a controversial woman thinker of my prominence."[60]

Much influenced by Beauvoir, *Sexual Personae* also credits de Sade as a major influence and argues that "sex is a far darker power than feminism has admitted." Whereas Ann Douglas singled out Margaret Fuller as the American feminist icon, Paglia chooses Emily Dickinson, "Amherst's Madame de Sade." Adapting Frazier, the Cambridge Ritualists, and Wildean aestheticism to literary history, Paglia finds an alternating cycle of Apollonian and Dionysian principles in Western art, driven by inevitable, Jungian archetypes of the male and female. Conflating the language and sexual imagery of 1890s High Aestheticism with the feminist anthropology of Jane Harrison and Jessie Weston, Paglia argues that male bonding and patriarchy were man's desperate response to his "terrible sense of woman's power, her imperviousness, her archetypal confederacy with chthonian nature. Woman's body is a labyrinth in which man is lost." She passionately admires the sexual persona of the femme fatale, the woman phallicized and frozen into an object of decadent art; but she deplores the flesh and blood of the female body in its natural form. "Menstruation and childbirth are an affront to beauty and form," she writes. "In aesthetic terms, they are spectacles of frightful squalor." Furthermore, "female genitals are lurid in color, vagrant in contour, and architecturally incoherent. Male genitals, on the other hand . . . have a rational mathematical design."[61]

Sensational passages like these delighted some critics, but offended feminist readers such as Marianna De Marco Torgovnick, who protested that she never "found it more tempting to defend menstruation, pregnancy, and birth than when reading Paglia." Torgovnick also questioned Paglia's persona as an Italian-American, "tough, working-class street kid," who "accuses other academics of hiding their ethnicity, of trying to please the WASP establishment." Paglia's father, Torgovnick points out, was a college professor and the family was central Italian; "there's a lot of willful downward mobility in Paglia."[62]

Overall, *Sexual Personae* is a massive, erudite, bold, and eccentric book of criticism, difficult to endure in full, but electrifying and renewing in small doses, like the paddles in an ER. In person, Paglia's frenetic, machine-gun delivery stunned and amused journalists who came to interview her, and the early interviews often make an effort to capture this outrageous, endearing stand-up quality of her voice, "talking so fast she smears away whole chunks of words, bites them off with the glottal stops of her Syracuse, New York, girlhood nasal accent—a frantic forty-four-year-old tomboy wearing a black sweater and stripes of blush on her cheekbones, utterly isolated and utterly visible at the same time, like an angry nun trapped in Snow White's glass coffin as she rails away at feminists, WASPs, Susan Sontag, deconstructionists, 'smug New York liberals,' Meryl Streep, academia, and French intellectuals." Henry Allen noted about Paglia that "there is no solitude like the solitude of an angry woman."[63] She told Carlin Romano that she would never marry and could not understand anyone's need for a mate. "When I look at other people, it puzzles me. What is that they're doing when they form dyads? Apparently, they need consolation, they need support, they need someone to tell them they're doing fine. They need nurturing. I don't need that."[64]

In the years immediately following the publication of *Sexual*

Personae, Paglia unleashed what seemed like decades of pent-up controversial opinions about academia, Elizabeth Taylor, Madonna, and feminist attitudes toward date rape and sexual harassment. Although she rapidly became a powerful media celebrity, Paglia maintained her anger, her solitude, and her adversarial stance toward those she felt had excluded her, and toward the women toadies, dowdies, dullards, and dimwits holding the Ivy League jobs she felt by intellectual right should have gone to her. In the traditional rhetoric of the feminist messiah, she compared herself to St. Teresa of Avila, "who wasn't famous until she was in her forties. She went against the whole establishment. She fought the bishops and the pope. She single-handedly started the reform of the Spanish convents. People said to me early on, 'Oh, what can you do. One person can't do anything.' And I said, 'Excuse me, one person can move mountains.' That's the example of the saints."[65]

RIOT GRRLS

In fact, Paglia was not single-handed, alone, isolated, or peculiar in her bad-girl, antiestablishment, antifeminist feminist role of the nineties; and to maintain her solo act, she had to fight off challenges from various young, streetwise, glamorous women writers outside of academia. One who particularly bothered her was Naomi Wolf (1962–), a Californian graduate of Yale, and Rhodes Scholar at New College, Oxford. Wolf's first book, *The Beauty Myth,* was also published in 1990 and created a sensation. In it, the author attacked the beauty industry and its impact on dieting, eating disorders, and cosmetic surgery as a new setback for women's liberation. Germaine Greer modestly praised the book (on the paperback cover) as "the most important feminist publication since *The Female Eunuch,*" but many longtime feminists found it wrongheaded and insisted with annoyance that Wolf, a young beauty with luxuriant brown hair, was hypocritical and hyperbolic.

In 1991, *Wall Street Journal* reporter Susan Faludi's devastating, often funny, and richly detailed exposé of antifeminism, *Backlash: The Undeclared War Against American Women,* became a bestseller.[66] Working as a journalist in Stockholm, Faludi had thought of Mary Wollstonecraft's Scandinavian journey: "She was in deep despair and came here with a broken heart, but she not only sorted out his business affairs, she compiled the letters she had written to him and turned it into a book, removing his name, removing any kind of evidence that she was writing to this creep, and it actually became a best-selling book at the time. Her passion and her ability to see everything in political terms and to believe in the importance of political change even after the French Revolution, I found very inspiring."[67]

Paglia heaped rhetorical scorn on both women; Naomi Wolf, she said, is "the Dan Quayle of feminism—a pretty airhead,"[68] who "has gotten any profile whatsoever . . . because of her hair."[69] Susan Faludi ("the Mary Tyler Moore of feminism") is "nice but easily flustered and cowed in public."[70] Paglia also argued against Anita Hill, whose testimony against Clarence Thomas galvanized black and white feminists in 1991.

But she was more sympathetic to Katie Roiphe, who published *The Morning After: Sex, Fear, and Feminism on Campus* (1993). Like Naomi Wolf, whose parents were sixties hippies and activists, Roiphe was a true daughter of the revolution. Her mother, novelist Anne Roiphe, had written the feminist bestseller *Up the Sandbox*. Like Paglia, Katie Roiphe had admired the feminist rebels: "One day," she wrote, "I was looking through my mother's bookshelves, and I found her old, battered copy of Germaine Greer's feminist classic, *The Female Eunuch*. The pages were dog-eared and whole passages were marked with penciled notes."[71] But when Katie Roiphe arrived at Harvard in 1986, she explained, everything had changed. "All of a sudden feminism meant being angry about men looking at you in the street and writing about 'the colonialist appropriation of the female discourse.'"

She was even more disturbed by the way things were by the

time she began graduate school in English at Princeton in 1990. Before her book, Katie had stood out among the graduate students primarily because of the large black hats she wore at all times and in all seasons. But after she published the *New York Times* op-ed about date rape that became the nucleus of *The Morning After,* she took off the hat and became a media celebrity at the age of twenty-three, speaking and writing about the puritanism and Victorianism of nineties feminist agendas. "Rape is a natural trump card for feminism," she wrote. "Arguments about rape can be used to sequester feminism in the teary province of trauma and crisis."[72]

Close behind Roiphe were a cluster of other young American women attacking feminist victimology—Rene Denfield, Karen Lehrman, Cathy Young. And at the same time that Courtney Love and the Spice Girls were defining a new kind of pop Girl Power, young women were writing about their own sexual exploits. Elizabeth Wurzel's *Prozac Nation* (1994) and *Bitch* (1998) defended misbehavior as a feminist prerogative: "I probably do need to learn to behave," she wrote. "But I don't like it. It seems like, all this, all these years of feminism, Mary Wollstonecraft, Charlotte Perkins Gilman, Simone de Beauvoir, Virginia Woolf, Gloria Steinem, Susan Faludi—all that smart writing so we could learn to behave?"[73] Naomi Wolf's memoir, *Promiscuities* (1997), explored the sexuality of teenage girls: "I want to explore the shadow 'slut' who walks alongside us as we grow up, sometimes jeopardizing us and sometimes presenting us with a new sense of authentic identity; sometimes doing both at once."[74] And Katie Roiphe's second book, *Last Night in Paradise* (1997), discussed the fear of sex and AIDS in the nineties.

By the end of the decade, Naomi Wolf and Susan Faludi had both moved on to different levels of feminist engagement, Faludi as the author of a study of men's discontent, *Stiffed* (1999); and Wolf making a controversial transition into politics as an adviser to Al Gore. In *Fire with Fire* (1993), Wolf had proposed a number of concrete suggestions that Third Wave power feminism might well consider: "Institute Power 101 courses in high schools so girls of all backgrounds know how to debate, fund-raise, call a press conference, run a campaign, read contracts, negotiate leases and salaries, and manage a portfolio." In November 1999, playing Power 101, she was coming up against the kind of opposition and ridicule she had believed were as obsolete as Second Wave feminism—attacks in the press and on Jay Leno's show about her alleged advice to Gore and her high salary. Meanwhile Paglia was having a field day, calling Wolf "a *Seventeen* magazine level of thinker," and calling Faludi "the product of a very bad Harvard education," while in her *Salon* column she praised Rush Limbaugh's "genuine intellectual service to American culture."[75]

By 1999, Paglia had found a partner, Alison Maddex, and was no longer militantly crusading as Woman Alone. But she had not softened or mellowed and seemed to be reliving past battles at ever greater length. Paglia's stance as Amazonian scourge of puritanism and hypocrisy makes lively reading, and I give her full credit for being a solo shock-trooper of popular culture and pizzazz in academia. Paglia is not without feeling and compassion, as her moving essay about the gay men she calls "my brothers in crime"—to me, her best essay—reveals. But she has not directed this compassion toward women's experience in a way that could connect her feminist persona to some of the fundamental contradictions in women's lives. Although she describes her academic exile in the eighties as a painful time of isolation and soul-searching, she emerged from it into the full glare of publicity breathing fire, seemingly untouched, unscarred, unscorched by suffering or self-doubt. Finally, Paglia's life seems narrow and ungenerous in contrast to the lives of feminist icons in the past. In these terms, she can spend the rest of her life chasing Sontag and never even get close enough to eat her dust.

EPILOGUE

First Ladies

The Way We Live Now

After the first London production of Ibsen's *Doll's House* in 1889, women lingered "breathless with excitement . . . this was either the end of the world or the beginning of a new world for women."[1] Where are our Saint Theresas and Noras of the 2000s, the women who leave us breathless with excitement? Where are the women who embody womanhood's radiant, sovereign self? Some cynics would say that the role models of the 2000s are only a shrunken simulacrum of the epic heroine. But in the age of mass communication and modern media, our feminist icons are more likely to be successful women raised to celebrity status by the power of publicity—real or representational First Ladies.

In many respects, the qualities of these iconic figures are similar to those of women in the past—ambition, consciousness, courage, willingness to adventure—but in the nineties, celebrity feminist heroines also need to fulfill a variety of new expectations, including beauty, compassion, and popular appeal. These expectations also reflect changing attitudes about womanhood. While many of the feminist icons of the past have been physically attractive, and some of them, such as Brittain, McCarthy, and Sontag, strikingly beautiful, officially, as Ellen Lambert writes in her book *The Face of Love: Feminism and the Beauty Question,* "in feminist thinking, from Mary Wollstonecraft in the late eigh-

teenth century, on down to Naomi Wolf in the late twentieth century, beauty has been associated with women's traditional pow-
erlessness."[2] To show concern for one's appearance seemed to
legitimate the definition of woman as frivolous and narcissistic
sex-object, and to collude with women's exploitation. Susan
Sontag looks at the problem of beauty in an essay in Annie Leibovitz's photo book of women: "In real life, it's still common to
begrudge a woman who has both beauty and intellectual brilliance . . . as if beauty, the ultimate enabler of feminine charm,
should by rights have barred other kinds of excellence." Moreover, Sontag argues, beauty is impersonal, constructed, a masquerade; while character is changing and authentic. The ideal
portrait of a beautiful woman turns her into a "mask on which
one can project whatever is desired."[3]

But Ellen Lambert defends the idea of beauty on feminist
terms and argues that women's full power and self-esteem
includes the need to feel attractive: "I believe in the very basic
need for an adult, as for a child, to be loved *in the body,* and as
feminists we are mistaken to deny the validity of that need."[4] If
beauty is one of the standards by which women are judged, why
should feminists deny themselves the means to achieve it? Beginning in the 1980s, writes Elizabeth Haiken, "popular conceptions
of feminism began to reflect the same emphasis on individual
achievement and fulfillment that swept the larger culture," and
cosmetic surgery began to be seen as self-realization, not self-
mutilation. "Cosmetic surgery may empower individual women
by curing their inferiority complexes, or, in less technical terms,
making them feel better about themselves. Overall, however, its
history offers a compelling reminder of just how limited has
been the range of options that women have perceived to be available to them—and of how provocative that angry and incisive
feminist critique of the tangled relationship between consumer
culture and sexism and beauty was."[5] In her book about "power
feminism," *Fire with Fire* (1993), Naomi Wolf pulled back from
her criticism of "the beauty myth" to insist that "what every
woman does with her body and in her bed is her own business."[6]

The alliance of feminism and plastic surgery suddenly became the subject of articles like "The New Plastic Feminism" and "Even Feminists Have Eye Jobs."[7] For ambitious women in the 1990s, a feminist role model not only had to be ambitious, caring, and inspiring, but also beautiful, fashionable, and thin. On one side, this change meant an acceptance of shopping, clothes, and makeup as a form of women's pleasure and play; but at the other extreme, the feminist power icons of the nineties sometimes seemed prouder and more admired for losing weight than for anything else they accomplished. Yet Hillary Clinton, Oprah Winfrey, and Diana, Princess of Wales, offered much more than beauty in their claims to prominence. They have been First Ladies of the mass media, figures to be looked at but also figures against whom we measure ourselves.

HILLARY CLINTON: FIRST WOMAN

When Victoria Woodhull ran for president in 1870, Harriet Beecher Stowe was horrified. "Who ever is set up to be President of the United States is just set up to have his character torn off from his back in shreds and to be mauled, pummeled, and covered with dirt by every filthy paper all over the country. And no woman that was not willing to be dragged through every kennel and slopped into every dirty pail of water like an old mop would ever consent to run as a candidate."[8]

Both the boiling resentment and the adoring worship directed at Hillary Rodham Clinton (1947–) seem to be symptoms of contemporary feelings about feminist intellectuals. Hillary Clinton is not the first First Lady to play a significant political role in government; Eleanor Roosevelt, Betty Ford, Rosalynn Carter, were all active in the role. Edith Mayo, the curator of the First Ladies collection at the Smithsonian Museum, says that "virtually every First Lady who has used her influence has been either ridiculed or vilified as deviating from women's proper role or has been feared as emasculating." But Clinton is the first professional woman and the first self-proclaimed feminist in the White House, as well as the first First Lady to run for political office. We shouldn't be surprised if even old mops get better treatment. Yet, according to Mayo, "the controversy is much less about Hillary Clinton than it is about America's continuing, deep-seated ambivalence, even hostility, toward power in the hands of women."[9] Martin Amis adds an English perspective, that "it should have been clear back in 1860 that First Ladydom was a terrible notion, reeking of fake precedence and popularity contests. Our baser instincts will always want to turn the First Lady into the Last Lady."[10]

Hillary Clinton herself remarked on her symbolic role during the 1992 presidential campaign: "I feel like there is this great national conversation going on of which I am but a part, but it is not so much about me personally but about all the changes going on in the country—about women and our roles, the choices we make in our lives."[11] Clinton suggested that American women wanted more than rights in their vision of feminist autonomy: "I think the nineties is a time when we're trying to reconcile a lot of the changes that we've lived through in the last twenty or thirty years, where we acknowledge that we have a right to have control over our own destinies, and to define ourselves as individuals; but where we also acknowledge that, whether it's biological or social, women want to be part of relationships as well, and to be connected to something bigger than themselves as part of the ongoing cycle of life."[12]

The national conversation about Hillary Clinton has turned out to be much more vicious than she or indeed any of us could have anticipated. In the *New York Times Magazine,* Michael Kelly went after Clinton's "politics of virtue," charging that she saw herself as a New Age feminist messiah, seeking a "unified-field theory of life." According to Kelly, Clinton was on a hubristic crusade for "national spiritual renewal."[13] By fall 1993, well before anyone had heard of Whitewater, Vince Foster, or Monica Lewinsky, Vietnam veterans' groups in Washington were selling bumper stickers that read, "Impeach Hillary, the Health-Care

Bitch," and giving a bimbo "Rodham" as a middle name was the movie joke of the year (see *Hot Shots! Part Deux*). The *Hillary Clinton Quarterly* published gossip, cartoons, poems, and song lyrics about the First Lady, along with requests for readers to send in their Hillary Clinton "daydreams and night dreams."[14] While reporters during the campaign had sniped at Hillary's dowdy style, they were equally nasty when she appeared in *Vogue* looking glamorous in a black velvet Donna Karan evening gown. Maureen Dowd also took a shot at Clinton's tastes in interior decor—"a swagging and swathing by Kaki Hockersmith of Little Rock, so ablaze in color, texture, and pattern that even Belle Watling might feel at home."[15]

Hillary Rodham Clinton's life was analyzed first in biographies of her husband and studies of his presidency, and then swiftly in books about her alone. Throughout the nineties, as Bill Clinton's infidelities brought her sympathetic, if prurient, attention, and as her own forays into the political arena made clear that she was not a silent partner, Clinton became an absorbing topic of analysis as a truly modern woman.

Her background suggests that she would have emerged as a leader even if she had not been married to a charismatic and controversial president. As the daughter of a self-made Republican businessman in Park Ridge, Illinois, Hillary grew up as a model student, Girl Scout, and patriot. Like Camille Paglia, she thought that American women should be part of the space program and wrote to NASA to apply as an astronaut long before they considered sending women into space.[16] She was also deeply influenced by religion, in her case the teaching of the Reverend Don Jones, the youth leader at her local Methodist church. Jones introduced the suburban teenagers in his "University of Life" to the ideas of Paul Tillich and Reinhold Niebuhr, took them to visit the Chicago ghetto and to hear Martin Luther King, and instilled in them a sense of social responsibility and service.

Hillary was already a leader when she arrived at Wellesley College in the class of 1969. As student government president, she spoke out on Class Day against Republican senator Edward

Brooke's warnings against protest. Discarding her prepared speech, she called upon her fellow students to emulate the French students of May 1968: "Demand the impossible. We will settle for nothing less."[17] The continued furor about this speech thirty years later, even from the docile, staid, and circumspect Camille Paglia, shows just how dramatic it must have been.

At Yale Law School, where she met Bill Clinton, she was an editor of the law review and a committed activist for children's rights. Working alongside Bill Clinton in Texas for the McGovern campaign, she made an enormous impression on veteran campaigner Betsy Wright, who later recalled, "I was less interested in Bill's political future than in Hillary's. I was obsessed with how far Hillary might go, with her mixture of brilliance, ambition, and self-assuredness."[18]

But already Hillary Rodham was facing demands for compromise, change, and self-subordination in the name of femininity and love. Rather than staying in the center of action in Washington, she moved to Arkansas to become the wife of a political wunderkind. The call for beauty makeovers started immediately. While journalists and biographers have quoted every Yale classmate, political hack, female love rival, and Arkansas socialite who ever objected to the way Hillary dressed, wore her hair, ignored makeup, and wore glasses, they have also noted with sarcasm every instance of cosmetic and fashion effort. When, as First Lady, she appeared before the House Ways and Means Committee to present the health reform bill she had helped to draft, it was noted that she was "sporting her seventh new hairstyle" in eight months.[19] A Web site went up to record Hillary's hairdos.

The elegance and high-class grooming Hillary Clinton now displays has obviously been cultivated and does not come from feminine vanity or narcissism. It is a professional style. But for prominent women who are not movie stars or models, beauty is a double-edged sword, which can cut because it must not appear to be the product of effort. In 1996, Camille Paglia was going after Clinton in an article called "Ice Queen, Drag Queen." Clinton, she wrote, was "the Great White Feminist Hope . . . a far more conflicted and self-destructive creature than either her admirers or revilers understand." With regard to Hillary Clinton, Paglia suddenly became an expert on natural femininity. The First Lady, she sneered, was a cold, androgynous person who "had to learn how to be a woman; it did not come easily or naturally. What we see in the present, superbly poised First Lady is a consummate theatrical artifact whose stages of self-development from butch to femme were motivated by unalloyed political ambition. She is the drag queen of modern politics, a bewitching symbol of professional women's sometimes confused search for identity in this era of unlimited options."[20]

In an interview called "The Intimate Hillary" in the premiere issue of Tina Brown's *Talk* magazine, Pulitzer Prize–winning journalist Lucinda Franks asked Clinton about her reactions to the president's infidelity, and Clinton described his philandering as "a weakness caused by psychological abuse when he was a small child."[21] Once again, Clinton became the focus and the catalyst of a national debate about women's roles and women's choices. Should she forgive her husband or should she forget him? Should nineties Woman be soft or hard, tender or tough? Is marriage to a president something bigger than all of us, requiring self-disciplined stoicism for the sake of the country and the party, or does the circle of life demand that women should put themselves first and dump the philandering creep as a model for their daughters?

Clinton's choices are further restricted by the burden of expectation she now carries as a potential candidate. Some pundits felt that she has the moral responsibility to punish her husband for what he did to the country. In the *Washington Post,* reporter Howard Kurtz pointed out acerbically that she never blames the president for "deceiving her or the country" and complained that "despite the yearlong national ordeal triggered by the president's lying, the first lady continues to blame his critics." Others, such as George Stephanopoulos, warned that she was making a huge political blunder by reopening the Lewinsky case at a point when Americans wanted to put it behind them, and making a

feminist blunder by reminding everyone that she is still the Little Woman.

Media-savvy feminists, on the other hand, have hinted that
Clinton isn't nearly little enough and would neutralize a lot of
jealousy by displaying some feminine pain, maybe a few cosmetic
tears. According to Katie Roiphe, Hillary "would be more effective if she showed a little weakness. There's something a little
steely and people are suspicious because she seems very political.
I think people would forgive her if she faltered for one minute."
This image of Hillary as tough and hard is not limited to the
United States either; when France's Antenne 2 started to broadcast the American TV series *My So-Called Life* in June 1999,
reviewers described it as a parable of the American family of the
nineties, with the tense blond mother as "a Hillary Clinton
clone."[22] Much of the resentment that has been directed at Hillary
Clinton is a measure of anxiety about feminist intellectuals and
professionals who do not seem to have paid the expected price for
their success in neurosis or misery.

But I like Clinton's gutsy refusal to shed tears, falter in public,
or show weakness. I like her feisty and tolerant admission that
Bill was always "a hard dog to keep on the porch." I support her
decision not to abandon a long-term marriage despite "enormous pain, enormous anger." This is the voice of a woman confident of being loved and able to balance the personal and the
political. As for her own motives in preserving her marriage,
Clinton recalled her mother's unhappy experience as the child
of divorce: "My mother never had any education. She had terrible obstacles but she vowed that she would break the pattern of
abandonment in her family and she did." The feminism of the
seventies said women should walk away from cheating guys and
never look back. The feminism of the nineties may look pious,
but I think it's really pragmatic.

In 1999, on the brink of her campaign for the Senate, Hillary
Clinton is fifty-two years old, at the point in her life where she
can begin to put her own values first and take the political consequences. With a political apprenticeship more rigorous than

that of most vice presidents, she has also suffered and survived as a woman and as the nation's image of the Wife. In the historical context of feminist icons, she is blazing a new path.

OPRAH WINFREY: CHANGING YOUR LIFE

In her recent writing on blues singers, Angela Davis has reminded readers not only that there are "multiple African-American feminist traditions," but also that these traditions are both written and oral.[23] Using the oral and vernacular traditions of black popular culture, and the power of the media, Oprah Winfrey (1954–) has become a feminist icon for millions of women of all races who would never read Angela Davis or learn about Mary Wollstonecraft, as well as for those who would never vote for Hillary Clinton.

Born in central Mississippi, Winfrey was raised by her grandparents until she was six. The next eight years of her life were severely troubled, as she joined her mother, who was working as a maid, in Milwaukee, where Oprah also had a half sister and a half brother. Her mother, Vernita Lee, punished Oprah's bookishness, even throwing her books away. Raped by a cousin when she was nine years old, Oprah endured further molestation by relatives between the ages of ten and fourteen. Although a teacher had noticed her intelligence and arranged for her to attend an Upward Bound Program in a good suburban school, she found the tension between the cultural worlds of her home and her school impossible to bear. This was a period of sexual promiscuity and delinquency.

At fourteen, Oprah ran away from home, and her mother threatened to put her in a home for wayward girls. Instead, she went to live in Nashville with her father, Vernon, by then a prosperous small-business owner and town councilman. He imposed academic values, a family structure, and a sense of high expectation that made the most of Oprah's intelligence and talent. "When my father took me in," Winfrey recalls, "it changed the course of my life. He saved me."[24] Upon her arrival in Nashville, Oprah had also revealed that she was pregnant; the baby was born prematurely and died soon after birth. She has called this sad experience the "most emotional, confusing, and traumatic" of her young life.[25]

Thus by the time she was a teenager, Winfrey had already had more firsthand experience of the economic and sexual oppression of women than most feminists would have in a lifetime. From adolescence on, her life would improve year by year to become what she has called "triumphal."[26] But this impoverished beginning would fuel her commitment to making a difference in people's lives, and to becoming a spokeswoman for African-Americans, for abused children, and for women. One of the richest women in America, she has created her wealth by her own efforts. Still conspicuously unmarried and childless, she has made these choices respectable and positive. As the most famous dieter in the world, she has made it acceptable for women to speak publicly about the pain of being fat in a society that adores the thin. She is surrounded by a community of women friends, to whom she is devoted. In all these respects, she is conveying feminist ideas to a wide general audience, the first African-American woman to become a national feminist icon.

Winfrey has used her TV celebrity and wealth in unprecedented ways and arguably has done more for literary culture than any intellectual of the century, through TV and movie dramatizations of the novels of Alice Walker, Gloria Naylor, and Toni Morrison, and through her remarkable Book Club, which has made overnight best-sellers of a range of contemporary novels. In 1998, she began an experiment in what she called Change Your Life TV—an effort to use her television exposure as a tool of spiritual teaching, to help viewers make use of their potential. In 1999, she is on the brink of another venture, partnership in the woman-oriented cable channel Oxygen, and publication of a lifestyle magazine focusing on women's spirituality and empowerment. It is a vision of feminist power that would have awed Charlotte Perkins Gilman or Margaret Mead, an adventure in womanhood geared for a new century.

DIANA: THE PEOPLE'S FEMINIST

"She was the People's Princess, and that is how she will stay, how she will remain in our hearts and our memories forever." Tony Blair's spontaneous tribute to Diana on the day of her death, August 31, 1997, captured and named an emotion that startled everyone by its intensity, and that, for some days that fall, threatened the British monarchy as no one had been able to do since the era of Cromwell. Within twenty-four hours, as the news spread, the British began to queue—at Buckingham Palace, at Kensington Palace—to light candles, to record their condolences, to leave flowers that became a kind of pyramid or royal tomb in themselves.

Around the world, friends, family, and total strangers came forward to testify, in print, to the shock and surprise not only of her sudden death, but also of their love for her. In England, where 570,000 people called London's Talk Radio, station manager Paul Robinson said that people "just wanted to talk to someone about how they felt; many were very confused about why they felt so upset about the death of someone they did not know personally."[27] In the *New York Times,* the feminist psychologist Carol Gilligan wrote in an op-ed, "I was surprised by my response to the death of Diana, Princess of Wales. I had not expected to feel such a raw edge of grief for this woman I did not know and whose life I had not particularly followed."[28] Therapists reported that their patients were talking about Diana, and recounting dreams about her; they were dreaming about her themselves. "Last night I mentioned to a group of female therapists that I was writing about Diana. For an hour and a half my colleagues talked nonstop about every detail of her life. . . . The group has met together monthly for years. This was the first time we had ever shared so many intimate perceptions about someone we each somehow thought we knew."[29]

Most of these witnesses were women. Joyce Carol Oates

explained that it was Diana's "significance for women that approaches the mystical. In Diana, the fairy-tale princess who was cruelly awakened to the world of hurt, betrayal, and humiliation, women of all ages found a mirror image of themselves, however magnified and glamorized. In her ordeals, in the courage, stubbornness, and idealism of her attempt to reinvent herself as an independent woman, women have found a model for themselves. It was this Diana, stronger for her own suffering, heroic for all that she was vulnerable, with whom women will continue to identify."[30]

Camille Paglia, who had written about Diana's sexual persona, identified with Diana as a mythological figure: "I personally have not recovered from Diana's death," she told a journalist a year later. "The shock was so profound it still feels unreal to me. As an Italian, I believe in rituals, the long mourning, and I'm still going through that. The highlight of my career was when I heard Earl Spencer quote from my work in his eulogy, talking about the hunter becoming the hunted. My ideas have never been so widely broadcast."[31] Typically, Paglia found a way to claim personal credit for Diana's apotheosis.

But alongside the requiems, the poems, the editorials, and the testimonials of friends, Diana's death was met as well by a kind of backlash, a sharp reaction to what some saw as emotionalism, hysteria, celebrity worship, and trash. "The academic career of Diana, Princess of Wales, was not very distinguished," wrote the novelist Julian Barnes with ponderous irony in *The New Yorker*, "but as a youngster she did win one key and proleptic prize: that for best-kept guinea pig."[32] He went on to suggest that she was a kind of prize guinea pig herself, a national pet. The British intelligentsia's condescension to Diana's education also extended to an aesthetic critique of the crowd of mourners outside Kensington Palace, and of the funeral. While some observers were struck by the heterogeneity of the crowd of mourners, others insisted they were all tourists, tabloid readers, or the British equivalent of trailer trash. "Nobody I knew bought flowers, wrote a condolence message, or joined the crowds in the streets," reported the historian Dorothy Thompson. "Few watched the televised funeral." Barnes noted the "truly dreadful poems" pinned to bouquets; a British poet told me at a dinner party that Elton John was "jumped-up trash." In *Granta,* dissenters sniped at "recreational grieving," "grief-lite," "floral fascism," "a feeding frenzy." Writer and broadcaster Isobel Hilton commented, "You felt that if a powerful demagogue had arisen from the crowd they would have stormed the palace gates. I suppose it was largely a tabloid crowd, and I was struck by the general kitsch of it—the cards, the teddy bears. . . . People seemed to be inventing religious ritual on the hoof." Brian Morton concluded that Diana "was a consumer item, and this was mass consumption postmortem, a feeding frenzy partly fueled by guilt."[33] In a kind of posthumous guilt by association, the manner in which Diana was mourned became evidence for her lowbrow tastes.

A major part of the controversy had to do with Diana's posthumous status as a feminist icon. The British journalist and novelist Joan Smith saw her as the lowest common denominator of a vulgarized, victimized feminist sensibility. Smith had written with dismissive scorn about Diana in her book *Different for Girls;* but the book appeared just as Diana died, and the essay was eerily prophetic. Smith began with a sarcastic account of Diana's reception in the United States at a ball to raise money for breast cancer: "There was a muted air of congratulation, as though the rich and famous had gathered to pay tribute to the survivor of some terrible ordeal—a train crash or massacre, say—who was only now venturing out in public after months of painful recuperation." Smith compared Diana to Miss Havisham in *Great Expectations,* the eternal jilted bride, "a woman wedded to her unhappy past." She criticized Diana for going to watch open-heart surgery: "Appropriating the language of such disparate discourses as traditional romance, psychotherapy, and even feminism, she had succeeded in reaching out to the broadest of all possible constituencies—so much so that the *Guardian* columnist Suzanne Moore rushed into print hailing the Princess, however improbably, as a heroine for the women's movement." Smith's idea of how Diana *should* behave reflected the new standards for the contemporary feminist: Diana should get a job, take back her maiden name, move to a smaller house in a less fashionable part of town. "This is the reality for most ex-wives in the 1990s: retrench, relocate, reorganize, and, once the initial shock is over, find new purpose and a less stressful existence." Instead, she concluded, Diana was emulating the victims of women's literature; but she "seemed to have forgotten . . . the traditional fate of the women with whom she had identified . . . they all wind up young, beautiful, and dead."[34]

Why was Princess Diana the last of the twentieth century's feminist icons and messiahs? Why was she able to stir women's emotions? Why did even her antagonists see her as doomed? Even before the terrible accident, anyone paying attention would have noticed the fascination women felt for Diana's life, and the emotion they had invested in seeing her become happy. In summer 1997, when Mario Testino's pictures of her were published in *Vanity Fair,* I walked into my London neighborhood hairdresser's on Marchmont Street to find all the stylists and customers minutely analyzing the pages. Her elegance, taste, and style were truly exceptional even in a beauty-conscious age; in years to come, museums like the Victoria & Albert will be staging exhibits of her clothes, with gowns donated by those who bought them for charity.

But she was anything but a fashion victim, and her clothes suited the active life she led as a woman of her time. She overcame her eating disorders, rather than allowing them to dictate her life, and glowed with energy and health. Diana was no hysteric, despite her highly publicized bouts with anorexia and bulimia; her much-mocked patronage of psychotherapists, psychics, alternative therapists, and New Age hygienes; and her easily trivialized devotion to fashion and beauty. She took the best from even the most eccentric therapies, living not as a querulous, self-protective neurotic, but as a courageous activist. In her remarkable Panorama interview on the BBC on November 20, 1995, she did not speak psychobabble, but rather gave an articulate and penetrating analysis of her own situation and that of the monarchy. Diana told the interviewer Martin Bashir that she had entered the marriage as an innocent: "At the age of nineteen, you always think you're prepared for everything and you think you have the knowledge of what's coming ahead. But although I was daunted by the prospect at the time, I felt I had the support of my husband-to-be." In her expectations too she was positive: "I think like any marriage, specially when you've had divorced parents like myself, you'd want to try even harder to make it work and you don't want to fall back into a pattern that you've seen happen in your own family. I desperately wanted it to work, I desperately loved my husband and I wanted to share everything together, and I thought that we were a very good team." Her conclusions were defiant: "I'll fight to the end, because I believe that I have a role to fulfill, and I've got two children to bring up." Judging by her strength, resilience, and determination to make her life count, Diana was one of the great success stories of contemporary psychotherapy. By the time of her death, she had achieved independence against enormous odds and seemed to be on the brink of realizing Freud's formula for adult psychological health: love and work.

Andrew Morton's biography, now revealed to be a sort of autobiography in Diana's own words, is an extraordinary document of her determination. Morton concludes that Diana's politics "revealed a developing feminism in her private and public life. Her view in essence was that so many issues and problems in a male-dominated world derive from the aggressive, secretive, and often insensitive male ego. Problems could be more effectively addressed, she felt, when female qualities of intuition, compassion, compromise, and harmony were added to the equation. Her thinking, influenced by New Age advisers, was also rooted in her jaded view of the monarchy as a male-dominated institution, her undoubted cynicism toward the opposite sex following the failure of her marriage, as well as frequent private visits to the Chiswick refuge for battered women." Morton concluded, "At heart she was a feminist who championed feminine values rather than simply craving acceptance in a male-dominated world."[35]

In the weeks, months, and years after the funeral, as the shock of Diana's death has worn off, the debate has continued and become in part a debate over women and feminism. Many believe that contemporary women had adopted Diana as their patron saint, "Die Heilige der Fraue," as the German newsmagazine *Der Spiegel* put it. By November 1997, academics had joined the business of placing Diana in context, through symposia, conferences, lecture series, and special issues of journals. The flood of books and tawdry revelations continues; but no details of her unhappy love affairs, superstitions, or turbulent emotions can truly tarnish her iconic status. Her flaws, her wounds, her scars, were part of what we saw in her, what we saw in ourselves.

SHRINES

Few of the great feminist icons have been commemorated in shrines. The church where Mary Wollstonecraft married, the house where she lived and died, are gone. Margaret Fuller's memorial was washed out to sea. Eleanor Marx's house doesn't even have a blue plaque; there's nowhere to go to honor Charlotte Perkins Gilman. In the absence of such tombs and memorials, those that do exist have become even more important as the symbolic shrines of all feminist aspiration.

In Francine Prose's short-story collection, *Guided Tours of Hell,* her heroine makes a pilgrimage to the grave of Simone de Beauvoir in Paris. "The tomb was covered with flowers, votive candles, marble eggs, handwritten notes pinned down by rocks, and a confetti-like sprinkle of punched metro tickets, faded and bloated by sun and rain. These were tokens pilgrims left as proof they'd completed their mission . . . 'thank you, dear Simone. . . . Thank you for being the first.'"[36]

Princess Diana is buried at her family home, Althorp. Visitors are reserved and decorous; as at any stately home, they keep to themselves, without the communal exchange that was so striking in the week before the funeral. The exhibit of her life, with its childhood memorabilia, home and professional videos, and gowns, is housed in the Italianate stables, described by Nicholas Pevsner as "the finest pieces of architecture at Althorp." Then the route goes on to Althorp House, where she grew up; and from there through an arboretum to the Round Oval, with a large urn marking the burial place on the tiny island. At the far end of the lake, a little temple, dating from 1901, has been transformed into a Diana shrine. On both sides are heaped the summer's floral offerings, in various stages of color and decay; and here too are notes and pictures. On a bench by the pond, a year after her death, I saw a woman crying. Meanwhile, in Paris, a shrine has been created by visitors to the place of the fatal crash on the Right Bank near Alma. In the summer of 1999, one could also take a "Diana Tour" of the Ritz, the Alma, the Salpêtrière.

The age of celebrity plays strange tricks on us all, but I believe that the impulse that sends pilgrims to these shrines deserves our understanding and respect. Women too need monuments to our fallen heroines, places of remembrance and thanks. In the conclusion to *Middlemarch,* George Eliot pays tribute to the millions of potential heroines and icons whose ardent spirit spends itself in uncharted acts that have "no great name on the earth." The world is better, Eliot decides, for these "later-born Theresas" who "lived faithfully a hidden life, and rest in unvisited tombs."

But those women who succeeded in an epic life of resonant action should not be consigned to the anonymity and obscurity that is the common destiny of womanhood. The lives of the unknown are redeemed and transfigured by the spirits and the shrines of the great. We need to pay them tribute.

NOTES

CHAPTER ONE
Adventures in Womanhood

1. Holly Brubach, "Heroine Worship: The Age of the Female Icon," *New York Times Magazine,* November 24, 1996, 55, in Brenda Silver, *Virginia Woolf Icon* (Chicago: University of Chicago Press, 1999), 7.
2. Wayne Koestenbaum, *Jackie Under My Skin: Interpreting an Icon* (New York: Farrar, Straus and Giroux, 1995), 4.
3. Ruth Benedict, *An Anthropologist at Work,* ed. Margaret Mead (Boston: Houghton Mifflin, 1959), 140.
4. Ibid., 491, 492, 494.
5. Lorna Sage, "The death of the author," *Granta* 41 (1992): 238.
6. Toril Moi, *Simone de Beauvoir: The Making of an Intellectual Woman* (Oxford: Blackwell, 1994), 3, 253–55.
7. Carolyn Heilbrun, *Writing a Woman's Life* (New York: Ballantine, 1988), 19, 130.
8. Simone de Beauvoir, *The Prime of Life,* trans. Peter Green (London: Penguin, 1965), 7.

CHAPTER TWO
Amazonian Beginnings: Mary Wollstonecraft

1. Mary Anne Radcliffe, preface to *The Female Advocate* (1799; reprint, Oxford and New York: Woodstock Books, 1994), xi.
2. Mary Wollstonecraft, *A Short Residence in Sweden,* ed. Richard Holmes (Harmondsworth: Penguin, 1987), 69.
3. Margaret Walters, "The Rights and Wrongs of Women," in *The Rights and Wrongs of Women,* eds. Juliet Mitchell and Ann Oakley (Harmondsworth: Penguin, 1976), 308.
4. William Godwin, *Memoir of Mary Wollstonecraft,* ed. Richard Holmes (Harmondsworth: Penguin, 1987), 207.
5. Ibid., 206.

6. Walters, "Rights and Wrongs," 310.

7. Ibid., 312.

8. Godwin, *Memoir,* 214.

9. Ibid., 218.

10. Ibid., 221.

11. Walters, "Rights and Wrongs," 312.

12. Claire Tomalin, *Hyenas in Petticoats: Mary Wollstonecraft & Mary Shelley* (London: The Wordsworth Trust, 1997), 2, 4.

13. C. Kegan Paul, *William Godwin* (Boston: Roberts Brothers, 1876), 191.

14. Claire Tomalin, *Mary Wollstonecraft* (London: Penguin, 1974), 131.

15. Ibid., 29.

16. Tomalin, *Hyenas in Petticoats,* 75.

17. Margaret Tims, *Mary Wollstonecraft: A Social Pioneer* (London: Millington, 1976), 152–53.

18. Tomalin, *Mary Wollstonecraft,* 85.

19. Ibid., 117.

20. Miriam Brody, "Introduction," in Mary Wollstonecraft, *A Vindication of the Rights of Woman* (Harmondsworth: Penguin, 1992), 1.

21. Ibid., 1, 2, 58.

22. Ibid., 70.

23. Ibid., 79, 82, 155–57.

24. Ibid., 267–68.

25. Richard Holmes, *Footsteps: Adventures of a Romantic Biographer* (London: Hodder and Stoughton, 1985), 90.

26. Ibid., 109.

27. Ibid., 96.

28. Ibid., 101.

29. Godwin, *Memoir,* 239, 242.

30. Holmes, *Footsteps,* 118.

31. Tims, *Mary Wollstonecraft,* 209.

32. Ibid., 209.

33. Wollstonecraft, *Vindication,* 139.

34. Richard Holmes, "Introduction," in Wollstonecraft, *Short Residence,* 25.

35. Ibid., 18.

36. Wollstonecraft, *Short Residence,* 68.

37. Ibid., 81.

38. Godwin, *Memoir,* 249.

39. Holmes, "Introduction," *Short Residence,* 15.

40. Tomalin, *Mary Wollstonecraft,* 257.

41. Miranda Seymour, "Tales from the Boxroom," *TLS,* January 1998.

42. Jennifer Lorche, *Mary Wollstonecraft: The Making of a Radical Feminist* (New York/Oxford: St. Martin's Press, 1990), 61.

43. Holmes, "Introduction," *Short Residence,* 43.

44. Joan Scott, "The Imagination of Olympe de Gouges," in *Mary Woll-*

stonecraft and 200 Years of Feminism, Eileen James Yeo, ed. (London/New York: Rivers Oram Press, 1997), 37.

45. George Eliot, "Margaret Fuller and Mary Wollstonecraft" (1855), in *Essays of George Eliot,* ed. Thomas Pinney (New York: Columbia University Press, 1963), 201.

46. Elizabeth Cady Stanton, quoted in Brody, "Introduction," *Vindication,* 61.

47. Tims, *Mary Wollstonecraft,* 356.

48. Alice Wexler, ed., "Emma Goldman on Mary Wollstonecraft," *Feminist Studies* 7 (spring 1981): 113–33.

CHAPTER THREE

Radiant Sovereign Self: Margaret Fuller

1. Quoted in Joan von Mehren, *Minerva and the Muse: A Life of Margaret Fuller* (Amherst: University of Massachusetts Press, 1994), 19.

2. Charles Capper, *Margaret Fuller: An American Romantic Life: The Private Years* (New York and Oxford: Oxford University Press, 1992), ix, 306.

3. Margaret Fuller, *Woman in the Nineteenth Century,* ed. Larry J. Reynolds (New York: W. W. Norton, 1998), 44.

4. Ibid., 43–44.

5. Bell Gale Chevigny, "To the Edges of Ideology: Margaret Fuller's Centrifugal Evolution," *American Quarterly* 38 (1986): 181.

6. Jeffrey Steele, *The Essential Margaret Fuller* (New Brunswick, N.J.: Rutgers University Press, 1992), xii.

7. Ibid., xxv.

8. Ibid., 24.

9. Ibid., 4.

10. Ibid., 5.

11. Ibid., 27.

12. Ibid., 5.

13. Capper, *Margaret Fuller,* 93.

14. Steele, *Essential Margaret Fuller,* 32.

15. Ibid., 23.

16. Capper, *Margaret Fuller,* 282.

17. Von Mehren, *Minerva and the Muse,* 113, 114.

18. Capper, *Margaret Fuller,* 288.

19. Ibid., 287.

20. Ibid., 288–89.

21. Quoted in Bell Gale Chevigny, *The Woman and the Myth: Margaret Fuller's Life and Writings* (New York: Feminist Press, 1976), 9.

22. Steele, *Essential Margaret Fuller,* 175.

23. Von Mehren, *Minerva and the Muse,* 133.

24. Elizabeth Palmer Peabody, "Boston Conversations: The 183940 Series," in Fuller, *Woman in the Nineteenth Century,* 177–80.

25. Nathaniel Hawthorne, *The Blithedale Romance* (1852), ed. Seymour Gross and Rosalie Murphy (New York: Norton, 1978), 232–33.

26. *The Journals and Miscellaneous Notebooks of Ralph Waldo Emerson,* ed. William H. Gilman, 16 vols. (Cambridge, Mass.: Harvard University Press, 1960–82), 8: 368–69.

27. Von Mehren, *Minerva and the Muse,* 186.

28. Ibid., 210.

29. Robert N. Hudspeth, *The Letters of Margaret Fuller,* vol. 4, 1845–47 (Ithaca and London: Cornell University Press, 1987), 177.

30. George Eliot, "Margaret Fuller and Mary Wollstonecraft," *Leader* 6 (October 13, 1985): 988.

31. Hudspeth, *Letters,* vol. 4, 239.

32. Von Mehren, *Minerva and the Muse,* 233.

33. Ibid., 248–49.

34. Ibid., 248.

35. Ibid., 264.

36. Ibid., 280.

37. Pauline Davis, *A History of the National Woman's Rights Movement* (New York: Journeymen Printers' Co-operative Association, 1871), 4.

38. Eliot, *The Letters of George Eliot,* vol. 2, ed. Gordon S. Haight (New Haven: Yale University Press, 1959), 15.

39. *The Una* (August 1854): 308–9.

40. Phyllis Cole, "Margaret Fuller in the Memory of Women's Rights Reformers, 1850–1870" (talk given at Modern Language Association convention, December 29, 1996). Quoted in "Memorial: Ednah Dow Littlehale Cheney, 1824–1904," New England Women's Club Papers, folder 40, p. 7, Schlesinger Library.

41. Hawthorne, *Blithedale Romance,* 15.

42. Ibid., 40.

43. Ibid., 218.

44. Von Mehren, *Minerva and the Muse,* 346–47.

45. Katherine Devereux Blake and Margaret Louise Wallace, *Champion of Women: The Life of Lillie Devereux Blake* (New York: Fleming H. Revell, 1943), 212–13.

46. Ann Douglas, *The Feminization of American Culture* (New York: Knopf, 1977), 261.

47. Review of the Hudspeth edition of Fuller's letters, "Growing Up Radical," quoted in *The Women's Review of Books* 1 (December 1983): 17–18.

CHAPTER FOUR

The New Women: The Feminine Predicament

1. Olive Schreiner, *Letters,* vol. 1, 1871–99, ed. Richard Rive (Oxford: Oxford University Press, 1988), 78.

2. Ibid., 111.

3. Ibid., 106.
4. Ibid., 137.
5. Ruth First and Ann Scott, *Olive Schreiner* (London: Virago, 1989), 28.
6. Ibid., 288, citing Cronwright-Schreiner's notes on the Schreiner MS., typescript, Albany Museum, 1820 Settlers Division.
7. E. P. Thompson, "Solitary Walker," *New Society,* September 19, 1974, quoted in First and Scott, *Olive Schreiner,* 18.
8. Sheila Rowbotham and Jeffrey Weeks, *Socialism and the New Life* (London: Pluto Press, 1977), 10.
9. Schreiner, *Letters,* 36–37.
10. Henrik Ibsen, *A Doll's House,* act 3.
11. Margaret Gullette, "Afterword," in Mona Caird, *The Daughters of Danaus* (New York: Feminist Press, 1989), 495.
12. Evelyn Sharp, *Unfinished Adventure* (London: John Lane, 1933), 56.
13. G. B. Shaw, preface to William Archer, *The Theatrical "World" of 1894* (London: Walter Scott, 1895).
14. "How to Court the 'Advanced Woman,'" *The Idler,* September 1894, 211.
15. Schreiner, *Letters,* 145.
16. See Lucy Bland, *Banishing the Beast: Sexuality and the Early Feminists* (New York: The New Press; London: Penguin, 1995), 84–85.
17. First and Scott, *Olive Schreiner,* 16.
18. Schreiner, *Letters,* 145.
19. Ibid., 39.
20. Ibid.
21. First and Scott, *Olive Schreiner,* 119.
22. Ibid., 136.
23. Ibid., 140.
24. Schreiner, *Letters,* 109.
25. Claudia Roth Pierpont, "A Woman's Place," *New Yorker,* January 27, 1992, 69–83.
26. Schreiner, *Letters,* 215.
27. Ibid., 223.
28. Ibid.
29. Ibid., 226.
30. Ibid., 233.
31. Ibid., 239.
32. First and Scott, *Olive Schreiner,* 257.
33. Ruth Brandon, *The New Women and the Old Men* (London: HarperCollins, 1991), 91.
34. Yvonne Kapp, *Eleanor Marx* (London: Virago, 1979), I:42.
35. Chushichi Tsuzuki, *The Life of Eleanor Marx: A Socialist Tragedy* (Oxford: Clarendon Press, 1967), 11.
36. Kapp, *Eleanor Marx,* I:101.
37. Brandon, *New Women,* 16.
38. Ibid., 18.

39. Tsuzuki, *Life of Eleanor Marx,* 107.

40. Annie Besant, quoted in Kapp, *Eleanor Marx,* II:115.

41. Tsuzuki, *Life of Eleanor Marx,* 107.

42. Ibid., 329.

43. Brandon, *New Women,* 23.

44. Kapp, *Eleanor Marx,* 15.

45. Tsuzuki, *Life of Eleanor Marx,* 105–6.

46. Kapp, *Eleanor Marx,* II:18.

47. Tsuzuki, *Life of Eleanor Marx,* 109.

48. Kapp, *Eleanor Marx,* II:31.

49. Tsuzuki, *Life of Eleanor Marx,* 126.

50. Brandon, *New Women,* 49.

51. Kapp, *Eleanor Marx,* I:267.

52. Edward and Eleanor Marx-Aveling, *The Woman Question* (London: Swan Sonneschein, Lowery, 1887).

53. Tsuzuki, *Life of Eleanor Marx,* 166.

54. Kapp, *Eleanor Marx,* II:204.

55. Ibid., II:361.

56. Ibid., II:521.

57. Tsuzuki, *Life of Eleanor Marx,* 176.

58. Kapp, *Eleanor Marx,* 76, 346.

59. Tsuzuki, *Life of Eleanor Marx,* 308.

60. Ellis, *The New Spirit* (London: George Bell, 1890), 9.

61. Liz Stanley, "Olive Schreiner," in *Feminist Theorists: Three Centuries of Women's Intellectual Traditions,* ed. Dale Spender (London: The Women's Press, 1983), 229.

62. First and Scott, *Olive Schreiner,* 339–40.

63. Nadine Gordimer, "The Prison-House of Colonialism," *TLS,* 1980, reprinted in *An Olive Schreiner Reader,* ed. Carol Barash (London: Pandora Press, 1987), 225.

64. Gordimer, "Foreword," in First and Scott, *Olive Schreiner,* 3.

65. Ibid., 3–4.

66. Ibid., 7.

67. Eric Hobsbawm, "Yvonne Kapp," *The Guardian,* June 29, 1999, 16.

68. Kapp, *Eleanor Marx,* II:708.

69. Faith Evans, "The Daughter of Modern Socialism," *The Independent,* April 1, 1998, 3.

70. W. B. Yeats, "Four Years, 1887–1891," *The Dial* 71 (August 1921): 179–83.

71. *More Letters of Oscar Wilde,* ed. Rupert Hart-Davis (New York: Vanguard Press, 1985), 95–96.

72. Elizabeth Stuart Phelps, *Chapters from a Life* (Boston: Houghton Mifflin, 1896), 263.

73. Unpublished letter to Mr. Goodman, August 7, 1891, in the private collection of Mark Samuels Lasner. Thanks to Mark Lasner for sharing this letter.

74. Cited in Kapp, *Eleanor Marx,* I:236.

75. Quoted in Sally Ledger, *The New Woman* (Manchester: Manchester University Press, 1997), 29.
76. Brandon, *New Women,* 54.
77. Ibid., 160, 249, 250.

CHAPTER FIVE

Transition Woman: Charlotte Perkins Gilman

1. Claudia Tate, "Introduction," in *Works of Katherine Davis Chapman Tillman* (New York: Oxford University Press, 1991), 6.
2. Clara Stillman, *Sunday Tribune,* quoted in Ann J. Lane, *To Herland and Beyond: The Life & Work of Charlotte Perkins Gilman* (New York: Pantheon, 1990), 362.
3. Mary A. Hill, ed., *A Journey from Within: The Love Letters of Charlotte Perkins Gilman, 1897–1900* (Lewisburg, Penn.: Bucknell University Press, 1995), 116.
4. Ibid., 17.
5. Lane, *To Herland,* 3.
6. Hill, *Journey from Within,* November 3, 1897, 114.
7. *The Living of Charlotte Perkins Gilman: An Autobiography* (1935; reprint, introduction by Ann J. Lane, Madison: University of Wisconsin Press, 1990), 5.
8. Lane, *To Herland,* 39.
9. *Living,* 17–18.
10. Ibid., 70–71.
11. Lane, *To Herland,* 55.
12. *Living,* 14; Lane, *To Herland,* 79.
13. Denise D. Knight, ed., *The Abridged Diaries of Charlotte Perkins Gilman* (Charlottesville: University of Virginia Press, 1998), 34.
14. Ibid., 241.
15. Charlotte Perkins Gilman, letter of January 31, 1882, in Knight, *Abridged Diaries,* 242–43.
16. Lane, *To Herland,* 82.
17. Ibid., 86.
18. Ibid., 85.
19. *Living,* 15.
20. Lane, *To Herland,* 94.
21. Knight, *Abridged Diaries,* 79.
22. Ibid., 81.
23. Ibid., 91.
24. *Living,* 91.
25. Knight, *Abridged Diaries,* 97.
26. *Living,* 96.
27. Ibid.
28. Lane, *To Herland,* 121.
29. Charlotte Perkins Gilman, *The Man-Made World; or, Our Androcentric Cul-*

ture (New York: Charlton Co., 1911; reprint, New York: Source Book Press, 1970), 105.

30. Lane, *To Herland,* 150.
31. Knight, *Abridged Diaries,* 124, 126.
32. Hill, *Journey from Within,* 44, 69, 341.
33. Mary Helen Washington, "Introduction," in Anna Julia Cooper, *A Voice from the South* (New York: Oxford University Press, 1988), xlv.
34. Lane, *To Herland,* 187–88.
35. Hill, *Journey from Within,* October 7, 1898, 187.
36. Ibid., on the possible reactions to their marriage: February 15, 1899, 239; December 18, 1898, 218.
37. Ibid., March 1899, 245.
38. Ibid., October 23, 1898, 193.
39. Ibid., May 29, 1898, 149.
40. Ibid., September 16, 1898, 175.
41. *The Charlotte Perkins Gilman Reader,* ed. Ann J. Lane (New York: Pantheon, 1980), xxxvii.
42. Larry Ceplair, "The Home: Its Work and Influence," in *Charlotte Perkins Gilman: A Non-Fiction Reader,* ed. Larry Ceplair (New York: Columbia University Press, 1991), 124.
43. Ibid., 164.
44. Henrietta Rodman, in June Sochen, *The New Woman in Greenwich Village, 1910–1920* (New York: Quadrangle, 1972), 49–50.
45. Ceplair, *Charlotte Perkins Gilman,* 245.
46. Ibid., 253.
47. Ibid., 288.
48. *Living,* 333.
49. Lane, *To Herland,* 359.
50. Mary A. Hill, *Charlotte Perkins Gilman: The Making of a Radical Feminist, 1860–1896* (Philadelphia: Temple University Press, 1980), 231, 234.
51. Ibid., 237.
52. Lane, *To Herland,* 323.
53. Ibid., 324.
54. Ibid., 326.
55. Hill, *Charlotte Perkins Gilman,* 3.
56. Ibid.

CHAPTER SIX

Heterodoxy in America: A Feminist Tribe

1. Florence Guy Woolston, "Marriage Customs and Taboo Among the Early Heterodites," in Judith Schwarz, *Radical Feminists of Heterodoxy* (Lebanon, N.H.: New Victoria Publishers, 1982), 95–96.
2. Mabel Dodge Luhan, *Intimate Memories* (New York: Harcourt, Brace & Co., 1936), III:143.

3. Schwarz, *Radical Feminists,* 96.

4. Ibid., 1.

5. Inez Haynes Irwin, "Adventures of Yesterday," unpublished autobiography, Inez Haynes Irwin papers, Schlesinger Library, quoted in Schwarz, *Radical Feminists,* 15.

6. Ibid.

7. Nancy Cott, *The Grounding of Modern Feminism* (New Haven: Yale University Press, 1987), 15, 17.

8. Ibid., 37.

9. Schwarz, *Radical Feminists,* 25; Marie Howe, *New Review,* August 1914, 441.

10. Cott, *Grounding,* 37–38; Marion Cox, *Forum,* May 1913, 548.

11. "Talk on Feminism Stirs Great Crowd," *New York Times,* February 18, 1914: 2.

12. "Emma Goldman on Mary Wollstonecraft," ed. and intro. by Alice Wexler, *Feminist Studies* 7 (spring 1981): 113–33.

13. Ibid., 121.

14. Ibid., 128.

15. Ellen C. DuBois, "Making Women's History: Activist Historians of Women's Rights, 1880–1940," in *Intellectuals and Public Life,* eds. Leon Fink, Stephen T. Leonard, Donald M. Reid (Ithaca, N.Y.: Cornell University Press, 1996), 222, 225.

16. Jane Howard, *Margaret Mead: A Life* (New York: Simon and Schuster, 1984), 69.

17. Margaret M. Caffrey, *Ruth Benedict: Stranger in This Land* (Austin: University of Texas Press, 1989), 118.

18. Margaret Mead, *Blackberry Winter* (New York: William Morrow, 1972), 112.

19. Margaret Mead, *An Anthropologist at Work: Writings by Ruth Benedict* (Boston: Houghton Mifflin, 1959), 9.

20. Ruth Behar, "Introduction," in *Women Writing Culture,* eds. Ruth Behar and Deborah A. Gordon (Berkeley: University of California Press, 1995), 17.

21. Desley Deacon, "Brave New Sociology? Elsie Clews Parsons and Me," in *Feminist Sociology: Life Histories of a Movement,* eds. Barbara Laslett and Barrie Thorne (New Brunswick, N.J.: Rutgers University Press, 1997), 171.

22. Desley Deacon, *Elsie Clews Parsons: Inventing Modern Life* (Chicago and London: University of Chicago Press, 1997), xiii.

23. Edith Wharton, *A Backward Glance* (New York: Charles Scribner's Sons, 1964), 5.

24. Deacon, *Elsie Clews Parsons,* 130–31.

25. Peter H. Hare, *A Woman's Quest for Science: Portrait of Anthropologist Elsie Clews Parsons* (Buffalo, N.Y.: Prometheus Books, 1985), 7.

26. Elsie Clews Parsons, *The Old-Fashioned Woman: Primitive Fancies About the Sex* (New York: G. Putnam's Sons, 1913), 91–92.

27. Deacon, *Elsie Clews Parsons,* 113.

28. Hare, *A Woman's Quest,* 89.

29. Deacon, *Elsie Clews Parsons,* 300.

30. Ibid.; and Elsie Clews Parsons, *The Journal of a Feminist* (England: Thoemmes Press, 1994), introduction by Margaret C. Jones.

31. Deacon, *Elsie Clews Parsons,* 384.

32. Barbara A. Babcock, " 'Not in the Absolute Singular': Rereading Ruth Benedict," in Behar and Gordon, *Women Writing Culture,* 108.

33. Caffrey, *Ruth Benedict,* vii.

34. Donald Fleming, "Ruth Benedict," in *Notable American Women* (Cambridge, Mass.: Harvard University Press, 1971), I:128.

35. Caffrey, *Ruth Benedict,* 7.

36. Mead, *Anthropologist at Work,* 119–20.

37. Caffrey, *Ruth Benedict,* 77.

38. Mead, *Anthropologist at Work,* 132.

39. Ibid., xxi–xxii.

40. Ibid., 491–519.

41. Judith Schacter Modell, *Ruth Benedict: Patterns of a Life* (Philadelphia: University of Pennsylvania Press, 1983), 107–8.

42. Caffrey, *Ruth Benedict,* 83.

43. Ibid., 84.

44. Mead, *Anthropologist at Work,* 8.

45. Margaret Mead, *Ruth Benedict* (New York: Columbia University Press, 1974), 3.

46. Mead, *Anthropologist at Work,* 5.

47. Mead, *Blackberry Winter,* 1.

48. Howard, *Margaret Mead,* 35–36.

49. Mead, *Blackberry Winter,* 85.

50. Ibid., 100.

51. Phyllis Grosskurth, *Margaret Mead* (London: Penguin, 1988), 20–21.

52. Mead, *Blackberry Winter,* 111.

53. Margaret Mead, *The Complete Bibliography,* ed. Joan Gordan (The Hague: Mouton, 1976), 2.

54. Mead, *Blackberry Winter,* 115.

55. Ibid., 117.

56. Howard, *Margaret Mead,* 63.

57. Grosskurth, *Margaret Mead,* 24.

58. Howard, *Margaret Mead,* 75.

59. Marianna Torgovnick makes this connection in *Gone Primitive: Savage Intellects, Modern Lives* (Chicago: University of Chicago Press, 1990), 293, n. 21.

60. Margaret Mead, *Coming of Age in Samoa* (New York: William Morrow, 1928), 157.

61. Babcock, "'Not in the Absolute Singular,'" 191.

62. Mead, *Blackberry Winter,* 245.

63. See Nancy C. Lutkehaus, "Margaret Mead and the 'Rustling-of-the-Wind-in-the-Palm-Trees School' of Ethnographic Writing," in Behar and Gordon, *Women Writing Culture,* 186.

64. Mary Catherine Bateson, *Composing a Life* (New York/London: Plume, 1990), 215.
65. Quoted in Lutkehaus, "Margaret Mead," 188, 196–97.
66. Grosskurth, *Margaret Mead,* 65, 76, 94.
67. Bateson, *Composing a Life,* 13, 114, 121–22.
68. Zora Neale Hurston, *Dust Tracks on a Road* (New York: HarperPerennial, 1996), 140.
69. Robert Hemenway, *Zora Neale Hurston* (Urbana: University of Illinois Press, 1977), 18: 93–94.
70. See Deborah A. Gordon, "The Politics of Ethnographic Authority: Race and Writing in the Ethnography of Margaret Mead and Zora Neale Hurston," in *Modernist Anthropology,* ed. Marc Manganaro (Princeton: Princeton University Press, 1990), 146–62.
71. Harry L. Hollingworth, *Leta Stetter Hollingworth: A Biography* (Lincoln: University of Nebraska Press, 1943), 98.
72. Quoted in June Sochen, *Movers and Shakers: American Women Thinkers and Activists, 1900–1973* (New York: Quadrangle, 1973), 51.
73. Ibid., 39, 126.
74. Sara Alpern, *Freda Kirchwey: A Woman of The Nation* (Cambridge, Mass.: Harvard University Press), 1987.
75. Eastman, *These Modern Women,* 141.
76. Ibid., 73.
77. Lorine Pruette, "Why Women Fail," in V. F. Calverton and Samuel Schmalhausen, eds., *Woman's Coming of Age* (New York: Horace Liveright, 1931), 255, 259.
78. I have drawn for this discussion on my introduction to *These Modern Women,* 3–27.

CHAPTER SEVEN

Heterodoxy in Britain

1. Marina Warner, "Rebecca West," in *Women Writers at Work: The Paris Review Interviews,* ed. George Plimpton (New York: Viking Penguin, 1989), 80.
2. Jill Benton, *Naomi Mitchison: A Biography* (London: Pandora, 1992), 50.
3. See Anthea Trodd, *Women's Writing in English: Britain, 1900–1945* (London and New York: Longman, 1998), 1–26.
4. Vera Brittain, "Semi-Detached Marriage," in *Testament of a Generation: The Journalism of Vera Brittain and Winifred Holtby,* eds. Paul Berry and Alan Bishop (London: Virago, 1985), 130.
5. Deborah Gorham, *Vera Brittain: A Feminist Life,* London: Blackwell, 1996, 200.
6. Ibid., 174.
7. Victoria Glendinning, *Rebecca West: A Life* (London: Weidenfeld and Nicolson, 1987), 1.

8. Gordon N. Ray, *H. G. Wells and Rebecca West* (New Haven: Yale University Press, 1974), 7.

9. "Marriage," in *The Young Rebecca: Writings of Rebecca West, 1911–1917,* ed. Jane Marcus (New York: Viking, 1982), 39, 71.

10. Ibid., 64.

11. Glendinning, *Rebecca West,* 84.

12. Carl Rollyson, *Rebecca West: A Saga of the Century* (London: Hodder & Stoughton, 1995), 28.

13. Ibid., 39.

14. Ibid., 47.

15. Ibid., 65.

16. Ibid., 77–78. The story is in the Beaverbrook papers at the House of Lords.

17. When the film was donated to the National Film Archives in London, the directors thought they should destroy it because it was so scurrilous; but it survived and had its first public showing at the National Film Theatre on June 30, 1999.

18. Rollyson, *Rebecca West,* 91.

19. Glendinning, *Rebecca West,* 113.

20. Ray, *Wells & West,* 204, n. 1.

21. Glendinning, *Rebecca West,* 86.

22. "Dame Rebecca West Talks to Anthony Curtis About Social Improvements and Literary Disasters," *The Listener,* February 15, 1973, 211.

23. Rebecca West, "And They All Lived Unhappily Ever After," *TLS,* July 26, 1974, 779.

24. Glendinning, *Rebecca West,* 3.

25. Rollyson, *Rebecca West,* 359.

26. Gorham, *Vera Brittain,* 4.

27. Ibid., 34.

28. Ibid., 35.

29. Ibid., 36–37.

30. Ibid., 38.

31. Ibid., 40.

32. Ibid., 59.

33. Ibid., 58.

34. Ibid., 59.

35. Ibid., 55, 56.

36. Ibid., 85, 89.

37. Ibid., 72.

38. Ibid., 88.

39. Ibid., 78.

40. Ibid., 80.

41. Ibid., 68.

42. Ibid., 72.

43. Ibid., 71.

44. Ibid., 83.

45. Ibid., 90.

46. Ibid., 107.

47. Ibid., 103.

48. Paul Berry and Mark Bostridge, *Vera Brittain: A Life* (London: Chatto & Windus, 1995), 523.

49. Gorham, *Vera Brittain,* 145.

50. Ibid., 163, 164.

51. Berry and Bostridge, *Vera Brittain,* 177.

52. Winifred Holtby, "Feminism Divided" (1926), in *Testament of a Generation: The Journalism of Vera Brittain and Winifred Holtby,* eds. Paul Berry and Alan Bishop (London: Virago, 1985), 48.

53. Brittain, "Semi-Detached Marriage," 130–31.

54. Gorham, *Vera Brittain,* 193.

55. Berry and Bostridge, *Vera Brittain,* 342.

56. Ibid., 282.

57. Ibid., 420.

58. Ibid., 271.

59. Vera Brittain, *Testament of Experience* (London: Virago, 1979), 257.

60. "Shirley Williams," in Sian Griffiths, ed., *Beyond the Glass Ceiling* (Manchester University Press, 1996), 274–80.

61. Berry and Bostridge, *Vera Brittain,* 1.

62. Rollyson, *Rebecca West,* 363.

63. Glendinning, *Rebecca West,* 36–37.

CHAPTER EIGHT

The Dark Ladies of New York: Zenobia on the Hudson

1. Philip Rahv, "The Dark Lady of Salem," *Partisan Review* 8 (1941): 362–81.

2. Richard Bernstein, "Susan Sontag, as Image and as Herself," *New York Times,* January 26, 1989.

3. Terry A. Cooney, *The Rise of the New York Intellectuals, Partisan Review and Its Circle, 1934–1945* (Madison: University of Wisconsin Press, 1986), 13.

4. Lionel Trilling, *The Beginning of the Journey* (New York: Harcourt Brace, 1993).

5. James Atlas, "The Changing World of New York Intellectuals," *New York Times Magazine,* August 25, 1985, 25.

6. Ibid., 71.

7. Cooney, *Rise of the New York Intellectuals,* 3, 4.

8. See Alan M. Wald, *The New York Intellectuals* (Chapel Hill: University of North Carolina Press, 1987).

9. Cooney, *Rise of the New York Intellectuals,* 5.

10. See Harvey Teres, *Renewing the Left: Politics, Imagination, and the New York Intellectuals* (New York: Oxford University Press, 1996), chapter 8.

11. William Barrett, *The Truants* (New York: Anchor Press, 1982), 67, 48.

12. Carol Brightman, *Writing Dangerously: Mary McCarthy and Her World* (New York: Harcourt Brace, 1992), xiv–xv.

13. Mary McCarthy, *Intellectual Memoirs: New York, 1936–1938* (Harcourt Brace Jovanovich, 1992), 94.

14. Mary McCarthy, *The Groves of Academe* (London: Weidenfeld & Nicolson, 1951), 37–39.

15. Quoted in Michiko Kakutani, "Mary McCarthy, 77, Is Dead; Novelist, Memoirist, and Critic," *New York Times,* October 26, 1989, 1, B10.

16. Mary McCarthy, "The Vassar Girl," *On the Contrary: Articles of Belief, 1946–1961* (New York: Noonday Press, 1963), 197, 198.

17. Carol Brightman, *Writing Dangerously: Mary McCarthy and Her World* (New York: Clarkson Potter, 1993), 67.

18. Ibid., 90.

19. Frances Kiernan, "Group Encounter," *New Yorker,* June 7, 1993, 57.

20. Ibid.

21. McCarthy, *On the Contrary,* 84.

22. McCarthy, *Intellectual Memoirs,* 52.

23. Ibid., 26–27.

24. Interview by Elisabeth Sifton in *Women Writers at Work: The Paris Review Interviews* (New York: Viking Penguin, 1989), 183.

25. McCarthy, *Intellectual Memoirs,* 65.

26. Joseph Epstein, "Mary McCarthy in Retrospect," *Commentary,* May 1993, 44.

27. Eve Stwertka, quoted in Brightman, *Writing Dangerously,* 148.

28. Epstein, "Mary McCarthy," 41.

29. Brightman, *Writing Dangerously,* 146–47.

30. McCarthy, *Intellectual Memoirs,* 62.

31. Ibid., 11, 67–68.

32. Brightman, *Writing Dangerously,* 159.

33. Quoted in Alix Kates Shulman, *A Good Enough Daughter* (New York: Schocken, 1999), 91.

34. Carol Brightman, ed., *Between Friends: The Correspondence of Hannah Arendt and Mary McCarthy, 1949–1975* (New York: Harcourt Brace, 1995), xxviii–xxix.

35. Brightman, *Writing Dangerously,* 299.

36. Arendt on Margaret Mead, June 20, 1960, in Brightman, *Between Friends,* 80.

37. Ibid., 200.

38. Norman Podhoretz, *Ex-Friends* (New York: The Free Press, 1999), 146.

39. Bonnie Honig, "Introduction," *Feminist Interpretations of Hannah Arendt,* ed. Bonnie Honig (University Park: Pennsylvania State University Press, 1995), 1–2.

40. Adelbert Reif, ed., *Gespräche mit Hannah Arendt* (Munich: Piper, 1976), 15–16.

41. Hannah Arendt, *Rahel Varnhagen: The Life of a Jewess,* trans. Richard and

Clara Winston, ed. Lilian Weissberg (Baltimore and London: Johns Hopkins University Press, 1997), 87.

42. Elizabeth Young-Bruehl, *Hannah Arendt: For Love of the World* (New Haven: Yale University Press, 1982), 49.

43. Karl Loewith, *Mein Leben in Deutschland vor und nach 1939* (Stuttgart: Metzler, 1986), 42–43, quoted in Elzbieta Ettinger, *Hannah Arendt and Martin Heidegger* (New Haven: Yale University Press, 1995), 11.

44. Ettinger, *Arendt and Heidegger,* 16.

45. Ibid., 3.

46. Ibid., 21

47. Ibid., 19.

48. Young-Bruehl, *Hannah Arendt,* 99.

49. Ettinger, *Arendt and Heidegger,* 39, 75.

50. Ibid., 35.

51. Young-Bruehl, *Hannah Arendt,* 108.

52. Ibid., 109.

53. Ibid., 153–57, 268.

54. Elizabeth Hardwick, "Foreword," in McCarthy, *Intellectual Memoirs,* xviii.

55. Young-Bruehl, *Hannah Arendt,* lx, 268.

56. Ibid., 272.

57. Ettinger, *Arendt and Heidegger,* 116.

58. Elisabeth Sifton, "Mary McCarthy," in *Women Writers at Work: The Paris Review Interviews,* 173–74.

59. Brightman, *Writing Dangerously,* 484.

60. Carolyn Heilbrun, *Reinventing Womanhood* (New York: Norton, 1979), 87.

61. Brightman, *Writing Dangerously,* xviii.

62. Richard Bernstein, "Obsession Transcends 'The Banality of Evil,'" *New York Times,* September 11, 1995, C16.

63. Julia Kristeva, *Le génie féminin* (Paris: Fayard, 1999), I:59–60.

64. Ibid., I:47.

65. Linda M. G. Zerilli, "The Arendtian Body," in Honig, *Feminist Interpretations of Hannah Arendt,* 169.

CHAPTER NINE

The Lost Sex and the Second Sex: Simone de Beauvoir

1. Mary McCarthy, "Mlle. Gulliver en Amérique," *On the Contrary: Articles of Belief, 1946–1961* (New York: Noonday Press, 1963), 24.

2. William Phillips, *A Partisan View: Five Decades of the Literary Life* (New York: Stein and Day, 1983), 128–29.

3. Deirdre Bair, *Simone de Beauvoir: A Biography* (New York: Summit Books, 1990), 339.

4. Simone de Beauvoir, *America Day by Day,* trans. Carol Cosman (London: Gollancz, 1998), 323.

5. Bair, *Simone de Beauvoir,* 632 n. 5.

6. Mary McCarthy, *Intellectual Memoirs: New York, 1936–1938* (Harcourt Brace Jovanovich, 1992), 88.

7. Ibid., vi–xxii.

8. Ferdinand Lundberg and Marynia F. Farnham, *Modern Woman: The Lost Sex* (New York: Harper & Brothers, 1947), 145.

9. Ibid., 149.

10. See Deirdre Bair, "Introduction," in Simone de Beauvoir, *The Second Sex* (New York: Vintage, 1989), xx, xxi.

11. Bair, *Simone de Beauvoir,* x.

12. Toril Moi, *Simone de Beauvoir: The Making of an Intellectual Woman* (Oxford: Blackwell, 1994), 5.

13. Judith Okeley, *Simone de Beauvoir* (London: Virago, 1986), 1.

14. Simone de Beauvoir, *Memoirs of a Dutiful Daughter,* trans. James Kerkup (New York: HarperCollins, 1974), 160.

15. Ibid., 104.

16. Bair, *Simone de Beauvoir,* 624 n. 5.

17. Beauvoir, *Dutiful Daughter,* 101.

18. Bair, *Simone de Beauvoir,* 86. Deirdre Bair comments that Beauvoir was seventy-six when she made this remark about her parents and still believed that "people in their forties were too old for sex" (625 n. 16).

19. Beauvoir, *Dutiful Daughter,* 90.

20. Ibid., 145, 218.

21. Ibid., 97.

22. Ibid., 160.

23. Moi, *Simone de Beauvoir,* 57.

24. Albert Thibaudet, *La république des professeurs* (Paris: B. Grasset, 1927), 139.

25. This passage from Leontine Zanta's 1921 novel, *La science and et l'amour,* is quoted by Moi, *Simone de Beauvoir,* 58.

26. Gérard Lefort, "La Dame au turban," *Libération,* April 15, 1986, 11. Translation by English Showalter.

27. Simone de Beauvoir, *The Prime of Life,* trans. Peter Green (London: Penguin, 1965), 11.

28. Ibid., 12.

29. Beauvoir, *Dutiful Daughter,* 345.

30. Bair, *Simone de Beauvoir,* 623 n. 5.

31. Ibid., 628 n. 34.

32. Beauvoir, *Prime of Life,* 13.

33. Ibid., 19–20, 22.

34. Bair, *Simone de Beauvoir,* 678 n. 4.

35. Beauvoir, *Prime of Life,* 77–78.

36. Bair, *Simone de Beauvoir,* 397.

37. Beauvoir, *Prime of Life,* 503.

38. Ibid.

39. Moi, *Simone de Beauvoir,* 201.

40 . Bair, *Simone de Beauvoir,* 211, 302.

41. Simone de Beauvoir, *The Force of Circumstance,* trans. Richard Howard (London: Penguin, 1987), 103.

42. Bair, *Simone de Beauvoir,* 335.

43. Ibid., 33.

44. Beauvoir, *Second Sex,* 217.

45. Bair, *Simone de Beauvoir,* 340.

46. Ibid., 368–69.

47. Simone de Beauvoir, *Beloved Chicago Man: Letters to Nelson Algren, 1947–1962,* ed. Sylvie Le Bon de Beauvoir (London: Victor Gollancz, 1997), 43.

48. Bair, *Simone de Beauvoir,* 364.

49. Bair, introduction to Beauvoir, *Second Sex,* x.

50. Bair, *Simone de Beauvoir,* 371.

51. Ibid., 373.

52. Ibid., 405.

53. See Bair, introduction to Beauvoir, *Second Sex,* vii.

54. Bair, *Simone de Beauvoir,* 419.

55. Margaret Mead, *Male and Female* (New York: William Morrow, 1949), 300.

56. Beauvoir, *Second Sex,* 698.

57. Ibid., 708.

58. Ibid., 575.

59. Bair, *Simone de Beauvoir,* 431.

60. Ibid., 409.

61. Ibid., 44–45.

62. Ibid., 462–63.

63. Simone de Beauvoir, *A Very Easy Death* (London: Penguin, 1969), 89.

64. Bair, *Simone de Beauvoir,* 554.

65. Ibid., 509, 602.

CHAPTER TEN

Writing Well Is the Best Revenge: Susan Sontag

1. Jean-Louis Servan-Schreiber, "An Emigrant of Thought," in *Conversations with Susan Sontag,* ed. Leland Pogue (Jackson: University Press of Mississippi, 1995), 155.

2. Victoria Schultz, "Susan Sontag on Film," in Pogue, *Conversations,* 31.

3. Susan Sontag, "The Third World of Women," *Partisan Review* 40 (1973): 205.

4. Ibid., 181.

5. Charles Ruas, "Susan Sontag: Past, Present, and Future," *New York Times Book Review,* October 24, 1982, 11, 39.

6. Susan Sontag, *The Volcano Lover* (New York: Farrar, Straus & Giroux, 1992), 417.

7. Sohnya Sayres, *Susan Sontag: The Elegiac Modernist* (New York: Routledge, 1990), 16.

8. Burton Feldman, "Evangelist of the New," *Denver Quarterly* (spring 1966): 152.

9. Norman Podhoretz, *Making It* (New York: Random House, 1967), 154–55.

10. Richard Bernstein, "Susan Sontag, as Image and as Herself," *New York Times,* January 26, 1989, C17.

11. Joseph Epstein, "Mary McCarthy in Retrospect," *Commentary,* May 1993, 45–46, 47.

12. Helen Benedict, "The Passionate Mind," *New York Woman,* November 1988, 75.

13. Bernstein, "Susan Sontag," C17.

14. Joe David Bellamy, "Susan Sontag," in Pogue, *Conversations,* 46.

15. Lesley Garis, "Susan Sontag Finds Romance," *New York Times Magazine,* August 2, 1992, 31.

16. Richard Lacayo, "Stand Aside, Sisyphus," *Time,* October 24, 1988, 88.

17. Susan Sontag, "Project for a Trip to China" (1972), in *A Susan Sontag Reader* (London: Penguin, 1982), 269.

18. Ibid., 274.

19. Ibid., 282.

20. Ruas, "Susan Sontag," 40.

21. Jonathan Cott, "Susan Sontag: The *Rolling Stone* Interview," in Pogue, *Conversations,* 121.

22. Susan Sontag, "Pilgrimage," *New Yorker,* December 21, 1987, 38.

23. Garis, "Susan Sontag," 31.

24. Ibid.

25. Sontag, "Pilgrimage," 39.

26. Cott, "Susan Sontag," 121.

27. Garis, "Susan Sontag," 131.

28. Sontag, "Pilgrimage," 38.

29. Guy Scarpetta, "Dissidence as Seen from the USA," in Pogue, *Conversations,* 99.

30. Sontag, "Pilgrimage," 38.

31. Ibid., 42.

32. Ibid., 38–54.

33. Elizabeth Hardwick, "Introduction," *Susan Sontag Reader,* x–xi.

34. Ibid., xii.

35. Molly McQuade, "A Gluttonous Reader: Susan Sontag," in Pogue, *Conversations,* 271, 272.

36. Ibid., 273–74, 275, 278.

37. Ibid., 276.

38. B. Rowes, "Bio," *People,* March 20, 1978, 79.

39. Garis, "Susan Sontag," 131.

40. Sayre, "Susan Sontag," 27.

41. McQuade, "Gluttonous Reader," 277.

42. Judith Grossman, *Her Own Terms* (New York: Soho, 1988), 231–32.

43. Cott, "Susan Sontag," 115.

44. Rowes, "Bio," 80.
45. Cott, "Susan Sontag," 129.
46. Garis, "Susan Sontag," 31.
47. Sontag, "Third World of Women," 205.
48. Monika Beyer, "A Life Style Is Not Yet a Life," in Pogue, *Conversations,* 172.
49. Ruas, "Susan Sontag," 39.
50. *Journal of Sylvia Plath* (New York: Dial Press, 1982), 332.
51. William Phillips, *A Partisan View: Five Decades of the Literary Life* (New York: Stein & Day, 1983), 255–56.
52. Carole Brightman, *Writing Dangerously: Mary McCarthy and Her World* (New York: Harcourt Brace, 1992), 491.
53. Pogue, *Conversations,* 70.
54. Michele Wallace, "To Hell and Back: On the Road with Black Feminism," in *The Feminist Memoir Project,* eds. Rachel Blau DuPlessis and Ann Snitow (New York: Three Rivers Press, 1998), 428, 429.
55. Benedict, "Passionate Mind," 78.
56. Schultz, "Susan Sontag," in Pogue, *Conversations,* 23.
57. Charles Ruas, in Pogue, *Conversations,* 175.
58. Schultz, "Susan Sontag," 33.
59. Eileen Manion and Sherry Simon, "Interview with Susan Sontag," in Pogue, *Conversations,* 210.
60. Sontag, "Third World of Women," 206.
61. Sayres, *Susan Sontag,* 20.
62. Ruas, "Susan Sontag," 40.
63. Benedict, "Passionate Mind," 79.
64. Cott, "Susan Sontag," 108–9.
65. Elizabeth Hardwick, *Paris Review* interview, 1985.
66. Ruas, "Susan Sontag," 11.
67. Edwin McDowell, "Women at PEN Caucus Demand a Greater Role," *New York Times,* January 17, 1986.
68. Paula Span, "Susan Sontag, Hot at Last," in Pogue, *Conversations,* 262.
69. Manion and Simon, "Interview with Susan Sontag," 208.
70. Kenny Fries, "AIDS and Its Metaphors," in Pogue, *Conversations,* 256–57.
71. Garis, "Susan Sontag," 23.
72. Susan Sontag, *Alice in Bed* (New York: Farrar, Straus and Giroux, 1993).
73. Susan Sontag, "Introduction," in Annie Liebovitz, *Women* (New York: Random House, 1999), 20–23.

CHAPTER ELEVEN

The Inner Revolution of the 1960s: Before the Revolution

1. Helene V. Wenzel, "Introduction," *Yale French Studies: Simone de Beauvoir: Witness to a Century* (New Haven: Yale University Press, 1986), vi.
2. Juliet Mitchell, *Women: The Longest Revolution* (New York: Pantheon, 1984), 17.

3. Rachel Brownstein, *Becoming a Heroine* (New York: Viking, 1984), 18.

4. Eleanor Flexner, *Century of Struggle: The Woman's Rights Movement in the United States* (Cambridge, Mass.: Harvard University Press, 1959), 235.

5. Judith Okeley, *Simone de Beauvoir* (London: Virago, 1986), 19.

6. Ibid., 146.

7. Angela Davis, *The Angela Y. Davis Reader,* ed. Joy James (London: Blackwell, 1998), 284, 289.

8. Wendy Martin, letter to ES, October 14, 1995.

9. Quoted in Lorna Sage, "Death of the Author," *Granta* 41 (1992): 235.

10. Richard Holmes, *Footsteps: Adventures of a Romantic Biographer* (London: Hodder & Stoughton, 1985), 75.

11. Ibid., 75.

12. Antoinette Fouque, *Women in Movements: Yesterday, Today, Tomorrow* (Paris: des femmes, 1992), trans. Anne Berger and Arthur Denner, 35.

13. Ibid., 15.

14. Ibid., 25.

15. Nancy K. Miller, "Decades," in *Changing Subjects: The Making of Feminist Literary Criticism,* ed. Gayle Greene and Coppelia Kahn (London and New York: Routledge, 1993), 41.

16. Toril Moi, "Psychoanalysis, Feminism, and Politics: A Conversation with Juliet Mitchell," *South Atlantic Quarterly* 93, no. 4 (fall 1994): 969.

17. Ibid., 932.

18. Ibid., 926–27.

19. Ibid., 935, 945.

CHAPTER TWELVE
Talkin' 'Bout My Generation: The 1970s

1. Lois W. Banner, *Finding Fran* (New York: Columbia University Press, 1998), 153.

2. Adrienne Rich, *Of Woman Born* (New York: Norton, 1976), 246.

3. Nancy K. Miller, "Decades," *South Atlantic Quarterly* (winter 1992): 70.

4. Ginny Foster, "Women as Liberators," in *Female Studies VI, Closer to the Ground: Women's Classes, Criticism, Programs,* eds. Nancy Hoffman, Cynthia Secor, and Adrian Tinsley (Old Westbury, N.Y.: Feminist Press, 1972), 8, 118.

5. Carolyn Heilbrun, *Reinventing Womanhood* (New York: Norton, 1979), 121.

6. Norman Podhoretz, "An *Annual* Seminar?" *Commentary,* December 1974, 38.

7. Miller, "Decades," 74, 75.

8. Ann Douglas, "House of Spirits," *Vogue,* August 1999, 72.

9. Ann Douglas, "Crashing the Top," *Salon,* October 1999.

10. Ibid.

11. Ann Douglas, *The Feminization of American Culture* (New York: Knopf, 1977), 3.

12. Julie Salamon, "At Lunch with Ann Douglas: Feeling Safest in New York," *New York Times,* May 17, 1995, C8.
13. Douglas, "House of Spirits," 76.
14. "No Time Like the Past," *New York Times Magazine,* April 18, 1999, 48, 50.
15. Douglas, "House of Spirits," 79.
16. Gail Parker, *The Oven Birds* (New York: Anchor, 1972), 1, 3, 5, 12, 16, 17.
17. Nora Ephron, "The Bennington Affair," *Esquire,* September 1976, 52–53.
18. Ibid., 145, 146.
19. Ibid., 148.
20. Ibid., 142.
21. Ibid., 143.
22. Frank Gannon, "Letters," *Esquire,* December 1976, 46.
23. Ephron, "Bennington Affair," 144.
24. Ibid., 145.
25. Ibid., 148.
26. Ibid., 148.
27. Miller, "Decades," 77–78.
28. Heilbrun, *Reinventing Womanhood,* 17.
29. Ibid., 18, 20.

CHAPTER THIRTEEN
Divas: Germaine Greer and the Female Eunuch

1. Carol Brightman, ed., *Between Friends: The Correspondence of Hannah Arendt and Mary McCarthy, 1949–1975* (New York: Harcourt Brace, 1995), 275.
2. Christine Wallace, *Germaine Greer: Untamed Shrew* (New York: Faber & Faber, 1998), 176.
3. Ibid., 158.
4. Germaine Greer, *The Female Eunuch* (New York: McGraw-Hill, 1971), 11.
5. Sheila Rowbotham, *Women* (New York: Viking, 1997), 401.
6. Quoted in Linda Grant, *Sexing the Millennium* (London: HarperCollins, 1994), 207.
7. Caroline Coon, "Look Back in Anger," *The Guardian,* August 9, 1999, 6.
8. Arianna Stassinopoulos, *The Female Woman* (London: Davis-Poynter, 1973), 11–12, 21.
9. Camille Paglia, "Back to the Barricades," *New York Times Book Review,* May 9, 1999, 19.
10. Wallace, *Germaine Greer,* 182, 206.
11. Ibid., 203.
12. Victoria Schultz, "Susan Sontag on Film," in *Conversations with Susan Sontag,* ed. Leland Poague (Jackson: University Press of Mississippi, 1995), 32.
13. Claudia Dreifus, "The Selling of a Feminist," in *Radical Feminism,* eds. Anne Koedt, Ellen Levine, and Anita Rappone (New York: Quadrangle Books, 1973), 360–61.

14. Wallace, *Germaine Greer,* 227.
15. Ibid., 249.
16. Ibid., 49.
17. Ibid., 393.
18. Ibid., 75.
19. Ibid., 77.
20. Ibid., 80.
21. Ibid., 122.
22. Susan Brownmiller, *In Our Time: Memoir of a Revolution* (New York: The Dial Press, 1999), 160.
23. See Carolyn G. Heilbrun, *The Education of a Woman: The Life of Gloria Steinem* (New York: The Dial Press, 1995).
24. Theodore H. White, *The Making of the President 1972* (New York: Athenaeum, 1973), 168.
25. Wallace, *Germaine Greer,* 212.
26. *The Observer,* June 13, 1999.
27. Wallace, *Germaine Greer,* 221.
28. David Plante, *Difficult Women* (New York: Athenaeum, 1983), 113.
29. Linda Charlton, "Dame Rebecca West Dies in London," *New York Times,* March 16, 1983, B7.
30. Katha Pollitt, *Reasonable Creatures: Essays on Women and Feminism* (New York: Knopf, 1994), xii.
31. Sarah Stage, "Feminism in the 1980s," in *Major Problems in American Women's History,* ed. Mary Beth Norton (Lexington, Mass.: D. C. Heath, 1989), 460.
32. Marianne Hirsch and Evelyn Fox Keller, *Conflicts in Feminism* (New York and London: Routledge, 1990), 1.
33. Amanda Cross, *Death in a Tenured Position* (New York: Ballantine, 1981), 154.
34. Susan Kress, *Carolyn G. Heilbrun: Feminist in a Tenured Position* (Charlottesville: University Press of Virginia, 1997), 3, 7.
35. Grant, *Sexing the Millennium,* 211.
36. Wallace, *Germaine Greer,* 240.
37. Judith Stacey, "Are Feminists Afraid to Leave Home? The Challenge of the Conservative Pro-Family Feminism," in *What Is Feminism? A Re-Examination,* eds. Juliet Mitchell and Ann Oakley (New York: Pantheon, 1986), 228.
38. Nancy K. Miller, *Bequest and Betrayal* (New York: Oxford University Press, 1996), 64.
39. Toril Moi, "Psychoanalysis, Feminism, and Politics: A Conversation with Juliet Mitchell," *South Atlantic Quarterly* 93, no. 4 (fall 1994): 929.
40. Heilbrun, *Education of a Woman,* 388–89.

CHAPTER FOURTEEN
Feminist Personae: Camille Paglia—Woman Alone

1. Camille Paglia, *Vamps & Tramps* (New York: Vintage, 1994), 119.
2. James Wolcott, "Paglia's Power Trip," *Vanity Fair,* September 1992, 300.
3. Paglia, *Vamps & Tramps,* 40.
4. W. B. Yeats, "Four Years, 1887–1891," *The Dial* 71 (August 1921): 179–83.
5. Paglia, *Vamps & Tramps,* xi.
6. Camille Paglia, *Sex, Art, and American Culture* (New York: Vintage, 1992), xi.
7. Ibid., 112.
8. Camille Paglia, "Loose Canons," *The Observer,* October 8, 1995, 14.
9. Henry Allen, "Paglia's Mad, Mad Worldwide," *Washington Post,* April 15, 1991, B01.
10. Wolcott, "Paglia's Power Trip," 302.
11. Carlin Romano, "Philadelphia's Academic Bombshell," *Philadelphia Inquirer,* November 13, 1990, C01.
12. Kara Hailey, "Acid Tongue," *Princeton Nassau Weekly,* December 3, 1992, 12.
13. Wolcott, "Paglia's Power Trip," 303.
14. Romano, "Philadelphia's Academic Bombshell," C01.
15. Hailey, "Acid Tongue," 12, 13; Wolcott, "Paglia's Power Trip," 301.
16. Paglia, *Sex, Art, and American Culture,* 244.
17. Ibid., 243.
18. Camille Paglia, "Ice Queen, Drag Queen," *The New Republic,* March 4, 1996, 24–26.
19. Paglia, *Vamps & Tramps,* 249.
20. Ibid., 143.
21. James Servin, "Can Lipstick Change Your Life?" *Harper's Bazaar,* February 1994.
22. Andrew Billen, "The Billen Interview," *The Observer,* March 12, 1995, 6.
23. Ibid.
24. Francesca Stanfill, "Woman Warrior," *New York,* March 4, 1991, 26.
25. Allen, "Paglia's Mad," B01.
26. Ita O'Kelly Browne, "The Passion of Paglia," *The Irish Independent,* January 12, 1994. Also Billen, "Billen Interview," 6: "I have always been slugging and punching. My father taught me to fight when young."
27. Allen, "Paglia's Mad," B01.
28. Paglia, *Sex, Art, and American Culture,* 14–15.
29. Paglia, *Vamps & Tramps,* 142.
30. Paglia, *Sex, Art, and American Culture,* 256.
31. Ibid., 206.
32. Ibid., 112.
33. Ibid., 258.
34. "Cosmonautka and Aviatrix," *Newsweek,* July 8, 1963, 2.
35. Paglia, *Sex, Art, and American Culture,* 259.

36. Ibid., 125.
37. Lucy Hodges, interview with Deborah Tannen, *Beyond the Glass Ceiling* (Manchester and New York: Manchester University Press, 1996), 247.
38. Paglia, *Vamps & Tramps,* 219.
39. Ibid., 245.
40. Ibid., 214.
41. Hailey, "Acid Tongue," 12.
42. Paglia, *Vamps & Tramps,* 119.
43. Ibid., 234, 178.
44. Ibid., 222.
45. Ibid., 348.
46. Ibid., 344–45, 347.
47. Ibid., 344–60.
48. Wolcott, "Paglia's Power Trip," 300.
49. Allen, "Paglia's Mad," B01.
50. Paglia, "Loose Canons," 14.
51. Wolcott, "Paglia's Power Trip," 300.
52. Hodges, interview with Camille Paglia, *Beyond the Glass Ceiling,* 188.
53. Paglia, *Vamps & Tramps,* 231.
54. Hodges, *Beyond the Glass Ceiling,* 188.
55. Billen, "Billen Interview," 6.
56. Allen, "Paglia's Mad," B01.
57. Paglia, *Vamps & Tramps,* 354.
58. Ibid., 347.
59. Ibid., 354.
60. Ibid., 355.
61. Camille Paglia, *Sexual Personae* (New York: Vintage, 1991), 3, 12, 17.
62. Marianna De Marco Torgovnick, *Crossing Ocean Parkway: Readings by an Italian-American Daughter* (Chicago: University of Chicago Press, 1994), 97–98.
63. Allen, "Paglia's Mad," B01.
64. Romano, "Philadelphia's Academic Bombshell," C01.
65. Thomas J. Ferraro, "An Interview with Camille Paglia," *South Atlantic Quarterly,* summer 1994, 742–43.
66. Camille Paglia, *Salon,* February 24, 1999; Camille Paglia, "Academic Feminists Must Begin to Fulfill Their Noble, Animating Ideal," *Chronicle of Higher Education,* July 25, 1997, B4.
67. Susan Mitchell, *Icons, Saints and Divas: Intimate Conversations with Women Who Changed the World* (London: HarperCollins, 1997), 260.
68. Wolcott, "Paglia's Power Trip," 302.
69. Hailey, "Acid Tongue," 12.
70. Paglia, *Vamps & Tramps,* 55.
71. Katie Roiphe, *The Morning After* (Boston and London: Little, Brown, 1993), 84.
72. Ibid., 5, 56.

73. Elizabeth Wurtzel, *Bitch: In Praise of Difficult Women* (London: Quarter, 1998), 28.

74. Naomi Wolf, *Promiscuities: A Secret History of Female Desire* (London: Chatto & Windus, 1997), 14.

75. Camille Paglia, "Hillary, Naomi, Susan, and Rush, Sheesh!" *Salon,* November 7, 1999.

EPILOGUE

First Ladies: The Way We Live Now

1. Edith Lees, "Olive Schreiner and Her Relation to the Woman Movement," *Book News Monthly* (New York): 33 (February 1915).

2. Ellen Zetzel Lambert, *The Face of Love: Feminism and the Beauty Question* (Boston: Beacon Press, 1995), 14–15.

3. Susan Sontag, "Essay," in Annie Liebovitz, *Women* (New York: Random House, 1999), 30–31.

4. Lambert, *Face of Love,* 13–14.

5. Elizabeth Haiken, *Venus Envy: A History of Cosmetic Surgery* (Baltimore and London: The Johns Hopkins University Press, 1997), 275–76.

6. Naomi Wolf, *Fire with Fire: The New Female Power and How It Will Change the 21st Century* (New York: Random House, 1993), 137.

7. Katherine Viner, *The Guardian,* July 21, 1997, 4.

8. Barbara Goldsmith, *Other Powers* (New York: Knopf, 1998).

9. Edith P. Mayo, "The Influence and Power of First Ladies," *Chronicle of Higher Education,* September 15, 1993, A52.

10. Martin Amis, *Sunday Times Books,* March 17, 1996, 7/1.

11. "Lessons of a Lightning Rod," *Newsweek,* November/December 1992, 11.

12. Eleanor Clift and Mark Miller, "Hillary: Behind the Scenes," *Newsweek,* December 28, 1992, 25.

13. Michael Kelly, "Saint Hillary," *New York Times Magazine,* May 23, 1992, 24, 25.

14. "Detritus," *Hillary Clinton Quarterly,* fall 1993, 10.

15. Maureen Dowd, "Hillary Rodham Clinton Strikes a New Pose and Multiplies Her Images," *New York Times,* December 12, 1993, E3.

16. Martin Walker, *Clinton: The President They Deserve* (London: Vintage, 1997), 73.

17. Miriam Horn, *Rebels in White Gloves: Coming of Age with Hillary's Class— Wellesley '69* (New York: Times Books, 1999), 46.

18. Joyce Milton, *The First Partner: Hillary Rodham Clinton* (New York: William Morrow, 1999), 54.

19. Walker, *Clinton,* 214.

20. Camille Paglia, "Ice Queen, Drag Queen," *The New Republic,* March 2, 1996, 24.

21. Lucinda Franks, "The Intimate Hillary," *Talk,* summer 1999.

22. J.S., "Les chemins de la réussite," *Le Figaro,* June 14, 1999, 33.

23. Angela Y. Davis, *Blues Legacies and Black Feminism* (New York: Pantheon, 1998), xix.

24. Merell Noden, *People Profiles: Oprah Winfrey* (New York: Bishop Books, 1999), 33.

25. Ibid., 34.

26. George Mair, *Oprah Winfrey: The Real Story* (Secaucus, N.J.: Birch Lane Press, 1994), 155.

27. Paul Donovan, "Royal Seal of Approval," *Sunday Times Culture,* September 14, 1997, 11/30.

28. Carol Gilligan, "For Many Women, Gazing at Diana Was Gazing Within," *New York Times,* September 9, 1997.

29. Janna Malamud Smith, "Our Celebrities, Ourselves," *New York Times,* September 8, 1997, A19.

30. Joyce Carol Oates, "The Love She Searched For," *Time,* September 15, 1997, 58.

31. Rex Fontaine, "Getting the Bird from Camille," *Independent on Sunday,* June 28, 1998, 28.

32. Julian Barnes, "Kitty Zipper," *New Yorker,* September 29, 1997, 78.

33. *Granta* (1998), 60: 30, 32.

34. Joan Smith, *Different for Girls* (London: Chatto & Windus, 1998), 4, 5, 7.

35. Andrew Morton, *Diana: Her True Story,* rev ed. (New York: Simon and Schuster, 1997), 256–57, 283.

36. Francine Prose, *Guided Tours of Hell* (New York: Henry Holt, 1997), 196.